THE POLITICS OF

TWENTIETH-CENTURY

NOVELISTS

By George A. Panichas

Adventure in Consciousness:
The Meaning of D. H. Lawrence's Religious Quest

Epicurus

Mansions of the Spirit:
Essays in Literature and Religion
(editor)

The Politics of Twentieth-Century Novelists
(editor)

Promise of Greatness:
The War of 1914–1918
(editor)

THE POLITICS OF TWENTIETH-CENTURY NOVELISTS

EDITED BY

George A. Panichas

FOREWORD BY JOHN W. ALDRIDGE

Thomas Y. Crowell Company
New York   Established 1834

Apollo Edition 1974

The editor gratefully acknowledges permission to quote:

From *The Complete Poems of D. H. Lawrence*, Volume II, edited by Vivian de Sola Pinto and F. Warren Roberts. Copyright © 1964 by Angelo Ravagli and C. Montague Weekley, Executors of the Estate of Frieda Lawrence Ravagli. Reprinted by permission of The Viking Press, Inc.

From the works of George Orwell. Reprinted by permission of Sonia Brownell Orwell.

From *The Complete Poetical Works of James Russell Lowell*. Reprinted by permission of Houghton Mifflin Company.

From *Selected Poems*, by Günter Grass. Reprinted by permission of Harcourt Brace Jovanovich, Inc.

From *Howl and Other Poems*, by Allen Ginsberg. Copyright © 1956, 1959, by Allen Ginsberg. Reprinted by permission of City Lights Books.

From *Poems*, by W. H. Auden. Reprinted by permission of Random House, Inc.

PREFATORY NOTE

THE PRESENT VOLUME, a sequel to the book that I edited under the title *Mansions of the Spirit: Essays in Literature and Religion* (1967), seeks to develop further what I wrote in the Preface to the latter: "Any cessation of interdisciplinary dialogue in the world of letters would inevitably signalize the triumph of the mechanical mind, belonging to the spirit of time, over the creative mind, belonging to the spirit of eternity." The essays here, all original and expressly written for this volume, seek to implement and to extend this dialogue. Given the political situation in the world today, the relations between the writer and society, between art and life, suggest a definite need for careful exploration and appraisal. This collection of essays is presented, then, with the hope that a better understanding of literary-political problems will be attained. It is hardly necessary to add that it would be affectation of the worst kind to claim any final solution to these problems.

My Introduction deals with the broader subject of the writer and society, rather than exclusively with "the politics of twentieth-century novelists," as do all the other essays. It seemed to me that it would be more worthwhile, from an introductory standpoint, to preface a collection such as this with a detailed (but by no means definitive) and overall view of the subject in its different aesthetic and theoretical dimensions. Obviously, the Introduction contains my own thoughts, which are not necessarily endorsed by the essayists. It should also be noted that the British, continental, and American novelists examined in this volume are major and representative rather than comprehensive in coverage, insofar as the choice of novelists was dictated by the particular interests and the availability of the essayists themselves.

I am happy and privileged to record my debt to Martha Seabrook, of the University of Maryland Library, for scrutinizing the Introduction and for making valuable editorial and stylistic changes in it; and to Mary E.

Slayton, of the Library of Congress, for unstintingly assisting me in the endless details involving both the planning and the preparation of the manuscript. To Hedy Bergida, finally, I want to express my thanks for her support and to wish her deserving success in the publishing world.

G. A. P.

FOREWORD

by John W. Aldridge

I

I HAVE GIVEN some thought to the question of the appropriateness of the following remarks to the book they are intended to introduce. The writing of a foreword is obviously an occasion for having one's say about the subject discussed or, in some cases, the author or authors represented in the work. There are various ways of going about this, and I am conscious of having chosen an approach that is, to say the least, unconventional. Since George Panichas in his Introduction has presented a most informative general discussion of the problem of the writer, politics, and society, however, I felt that my own comments should be, could only be, in the nature of a personal speculation on one aspect of this very broad subject which he does not explore in close detail: the place of social and political ideas in a context of abiding interest to me—the literary and cultural situation prevailing in the United States at this time.

I have made, therefore, no explicit comment on the questions raised by the essays in this book but am offering instead a kind of correlative or contiguous statement that may have value to the extent that it emphasizes the contemporary problem posed by the dramatic and often abrasive confrontations occurring between political and literary interests throughout our society today, particularly in the intellectual and academic communities. I have learned so much from the statements of the various critics here represented, and am in substantial agreement with such a large part of what they have to say, that I could not possibly offer my views as a challenge to theirs. Let us assume that I am another contributor to this volume rather than in any sense its host or sponsor. My contribution happens to be placed at the beginning in the form of a foreword, and I take pleasure in that because there is intelligence and critical discernment to be found everywhere in the pages that follow after it.

II

Twenty years ago a collection of essays having to do with the politics of novelists would almost certainly have been dismissed in critical circles as fatuous or philistine. At that time and for a considerable time thereafter, the controlling interest of our most serious criticism was aesthetic and formalist. The supreme question to be asked about a work of art was emphatically not, as James Joyce's A.E. said, "out of how deep a life does it spring." Modern criticism cared little, perhaps nothing at all, about life except as it found its apotheosis in the perfection of the work. Life, in fact, was something critics would have been much better off without, since it distracted them, like an obscene shout in the street, from the real matter at hand, the detached contemplation of the work in and for itself. The supreme question, finally the only question, was whether the work represented a meaningful and harmonious ordering of language and form, an effective employment of materials that had somehow mysteriously sprung into being at the moment of composition. The origin and nature of these materials were problems deemed extraneous to the critical pursuit, as were most considerations of artistic intent and effect, whether upon the reader or the world at large. Hence, sociopolitical concerns, all efforts to discern a connection between literature and the life of men in society, were regarded as impure, the crass preoccupations of historical, psychological, and journalistic critics who, undoubtedly because of some defect of sensibility, cared more for experience than they did for art. In short, the aesthetic bias in criticism was enforced with an evangelical fastidiousness that was extremely hard to resist, particularly when any attempt to do so was made to seem so patently a failure of intelligence and not in the least a triumph of vitality or morals.

But then who, in those years, would have had the impulse to resist? There seemed to be simply no other direction for modern criticism to take except toward a further expansion and deepening of the formalist mode. By the end of the forties that *was* the official mode and had been for a good many years, but it was also evident by that time that the great pioneering work of the New Criticism had been completed, the basic aesthetic principles laid down, and the textual analysis of poetry brought to a peak of methodological perfection beyond which it seemed that continued investigation of poetry at that level and in those terms would soon end in a sterile repetitiveness. There remained, however, two objectives still to be attained, both of which seemed essential to the future health of the formalist approach. The first was the establishment of a language and a set of critical principles which would make it possible to examine fiction with the same care and attentiveness to textual detail as had formerly been directed upon poetry, the aim being to achieve for fiction comparably high status as a literary art. The second objective, closely interlocking with the first, was to rescue fiction once and for all from the kinds of critical approach which emphasized social, historical, and political considerations over those of structure and language and thus threatened to debase fiction to the level of mere realistic documentation and propaganda—as if the social and political views of the writer might be said to have some meaning or value apart from the aesthetic properties of the work.

Obviously, there were hazards here that the early proponents of a New Criticism of fiction could hardly be expected to have foreseen, if only because the works that most challenged their critical powers tended to be precisely those that lent themselves most readily to formalist analysis. The novels, for example, of Gustave Flaubert, Henry James, Joseph Conrad, James Joyce, William Faulkner, and Ernest Hemingway were beautiful and obliging receptors of the kind of investigation their New Critical education had taught them to make. It was not immediately evident at the time that there were other novelists of perhaps a different but not necessarily a lower order of distinction—one thinks of Stephen Crane, Sherwood Anderson, D. H. Lawrence, Aldous Huxley, Theodore Dreiser, Frank Norris, and James Farrell—whose works would prove to be incompatible with this approach, and might be so not because of their inferior aesthetic qualities but because the critical standards applied to them were the improper ones for measuring those qualities beyond the aesthetic which they did possess. Even though, as early as 1949, the warning had been issued by Mark Schorer that the novel, because of its intrinsic nature as an art form, necessarily opens itself to "first questions about philosophy ... politics and conduct," the central thrust of the New Criticism of fiction was concentrated largely in the aesthetic appraisal and reappraisal of writers whose novels least opened themselves to these embarrassing questions.

R. P. Blackmur had observed at about the same time that we may one day find we can no longer be "so verbal, nor so imagistic, nor so 'symbolic' (in the logical senses) in our analyses" of fiction. He had also predicted somewhat earlier that we would shortly be "in for" a little New Criticism of the novel, and he was shortly proved correct. It became evident, however, that he had counted too soon on a radical departure from methods that had demonstrated not only their value but also their infectiousness in the analysis of poetry, for the fiction criticism that came to be written was everything he said it would no longer be. It was verbal, imagistic, and symbolic with a vengeance—partly because it had behind it a missionary determination to treat fiction as an art form but also because the effort was made against the strong countertendency of the form to open itself to those questions that could not be easily or satisfactorily answered by means of the aesthetic approach alone.

The truth was, of course, that a New Criticism of the novel had been in the process of development long before Blackmur made his prediction that we would shortly have one. As early as 1921, Percy Lubbock, working from the prefaces of Henry James, had set down in *The Craft of Fiction* the first principles on which such a criticism could begin to be written. Blackmur was right, however, in the sense that by the late forties there was still no fully defined or codified aesthetic, no distinctive mode or strategy, which specifically characterized the formalist approach to fiction.

As this criticism evolved through the fifties and sixties and took on the institutional structure, if not the flexibility, Blackmur had prophesied, it nevertheless found expression in analytical studies as vigorous and exacting as any produced during the great period of the poetic New Criticism. The best achievements of both movements now belong to the Age of the Anthology, and they constitute the basic materials of our understanding of critical possibility in our time. Critics like Schorer and Blackmur, Allen Tate, Cleanth Brooks, Robert Penn Warren, Joseph Frank, Morton Dauwen Zabel, Lionel Trilling, Philip Rahv, and Richard Chase all helped to make it possible for fiction at last to catch up with poetry as a respectable object of aesthetic analysis and to gain wide acceptance for the point that Mr. Schorer in 1949 advanced—and at the time still felt the need to advance—with a certain defiance: "Criticism [of fiction] ... must begin with the base of language, with the word, with figurative structures, with rhetoric as skeleton and style as body of meaning."

Inevitably, of course, a reaction set in. A second (or was it a third?) generation of fiction critics began to rebel against the puritan rigidity and narrowness of the formalist approach, and we had the liberating heresies of those who, following the example of Northrop Frye and Wayne Booth, sought to establish a critical perspective broad enough to include not only considerations of form and language but also others relating to reader response, auctorial intention, the function of rhetoric, and ultimately the areas of philosophy, politics, and conduct which earlier critics had been unable or unwilling to explore.

Partly as a result of this development, the suddenly old-style formalist approach to fiction lost authority and came to be practiced more and more timidly and unimaginatively. It became in the end the enterprise largely of professors who, in another age, would have devoted themselves to turning out little squibs for *Notes and Queries* but who now turned out little squibs for *Modern Fiction Studies* about such subjects as the architectonics of Conrad's *Victory* and the symbolism of the caraway seed in *The Great Gatsby*. Meanwhile, literary journalism operating in the mass media opened the discussion of fiction to a large literate and semiliterate audience. The merely impressionistic brief review began to be superseded by the long analytical essay-review, in which it was not at all unusual to find the principles of Brooks and Warren applied to the close examination of novels that at one time would simply have been gushed over by literary ladies with three names. The result was that not only the exclusiveness but also the pioneering force of the New Criticism of fiction diminished as its methods were appropriated by and adulterated in the marketplace, as the movement as a whole became an adjunct of sophisticated Pop Culture on the one hand and a source of academic busy-work on the other.

It now appears—if the essays in this book may be taken as symptomatic—that we are entering a second phase of reaction. We even seem, in our approach to the novel, to have come full circle. Where the principal effort of modern criticism has been to substitute an aesthetic reading for the older view of fiction as realistic documentation or propaganda, where we were once comfortable with the idea that form and language were the central and only really proper critical concerns, where we subsequently witnessed a shift toward a greater catholicity of approach but with due allowance still for aesthetic considerations, we now seem to have moved on, or turned back, to the position against which the formalist movement was originally a reaction: the idea that fiction should be read with some primary regard for the social and political views of the author.

If this is not a wholly retrograde development, if we have not simply canceled out the critical gains of the last fifty years in order to conform to certain pietistic demands for topicality at any price, then we must assume that these new or resurrected sociopolitical interests are not antithetical to the aesthetic approach but represent rather a further liberalization of it. Surely, if this were not the case, we would be trading one authoritarianism for another and would be in as much danger from the militant self-righteousness of the New Left as we used to be from the militant self-consciousness of the Old Right—these positions being in this context wholly literary, but in the current social context rabidly political. Surely also, it does not seem possible that the novel can ever again be read as though its form were one thing and its content another, or as though its content had some special meaning or virtue apart from its form. It may be that the novel from now on will be seen in some more healthily realistic relationship to the life that provides its raw materials, but the artful representation of that life would still appear to be an ines-

capable first consideration for any criticism alive to the best teachings of
the modern literary past.

At least one hopes that this is so. Yet there are signs to indicate that it
may not be, for we live at the moment in a political climate in which all
of us are under the greatest pressure to prove the "relevance" of our
interests to issues deemed crucial by those who insist that practical applicability to social problems is the only criterion of "relevance." We are
also oppressed by the reductivist hysteria that equates any concern for
standards, any effort to discriminate among qualities, whether in life or
literature, with a reactionary elitism—the act of critical judgment becoming, by elaborate extension, an offense against democratic principles,
against the God-given right of all things, even good and bad books, to be
considered equal. It would be a pity if these undoubtedly well-intentioned
attempts to humanize our intellectual morals should become dictatorial
to the point where we had a repetition of what occurred during World
War II, when American writers—and some of the best of them—were
charged with "irresponsibility" for not presenting a more flattering and
patriotic view of our society in that dark time of national peril. Certain
quite serious and sincere intellectuals felt then—as clearly their less intellectual counterparts feel today—that we cannot successfully fight the
battle for democratic freedom unless we deprive our writers of their
democratic freedom to tell the truth as they see it, or unless we pressure
them into telling only certain acceptable truths in only certain acceptable
ways. Obviously, there is a difference between the panic engendered by
world war and the panic engendered by social and political revolution.
We can only hope that that difference will save us yet.

Although we may take it for granted that writers do not function well
under conditions of enforced orthodoxy—whether an orthodoxy imposed
by the Right or by the Left—it may also be true that there is something
incompatible, some natural enmity, between the values of literature and
those of politics. When writers are embarrassed or provoked by existing
social conditions and pressures into making a political case or arranging
their work to conform to the requirements of some programmatic vision
of society, the result can often be disastrous in the extreme. In witness of
this we have—as George Panichas reminds us in his Introduction—the
thoroughly depressing experience of the thirties. Then we elevated quan-
tities of third-rate tractarian work to prominence simply because the
right social and political attitudes were articulated, whereas writers of
first-rate novels having to do with subjects other than the sufferings of
the proletariat and the corruption of the capitalistic system tended to be
either ignored or dismissed as "irrelevant" and "irresponsible."

The problem, however, is not merely that the felt obligation to deal
explicitly with social or political issues may result in a distortion and

cheapening of a novelist's work. It may also conflict with something very
basic to the philosophical orientation that causes a novelist to be a novelist rather than a sociologist or a political pamphleteer. Katherine Anne
Porter seems to have had this in mind when she said in reference to
Eudora Welty:

> She has not expressed, except implicitly, any attitude at all on
> the state of politics or the condition of society. But there is an
> ancient system of ethics, an unanswerable, indispensable moral
> law, on which she is grounded firmly, and this, it would seem
> to me, is ample domain enough. These laws have never been the
> peculiar property of any party, creed, or nation. They relate to
> that true and human world of which the artist is a living part;
> and when he dissociates himself from it in favor of a set of po-
> litical, which is to say, inhuman, rules, he cuts himself away
> from his proper society—living men. . . . All working, practical
> political systems, even those professing to originate in moral
> grandeur, are based upon and operate by contempt of human
> life and the individual fate; in accepting any one of them and
> shaping his mind and work to that mold, the artist dehumanizes
> himself, unfits himself for the practice of any art.

How diabolically subversive such a statement must seem when set
against the current belief that political and social concerns are the only
human and humanizing concerns, that those political systems to which so
many of us attribute moral grandeur are, above all, based upon *love* of
human life and the individual fate, not contempt for them. Yet Miss
Porter is clearly not writing here as an antiliberal heretic. She is simply
proposing that Eudora Welty—and, by implication, fiction writers in general—necessarily function in accordance with a different view of life, one
that must finally be described as apolitical or prepolitical, and one that is
imposed by the particular demands of the fictional medium. Although it
may be perfectly true that the novel finally opens itself to first questions
about politics, society, conduct, philosophy, perhaps even religion, the
writer, insofar as he is an artist and something more than a social historian, is compelled in his intimate, practical relationship with his materials
to work with specifics, with the single dramatic instances and concrete
particulars of the experience he wishes to represent. This is to say that he
must begin with an event before he can proceed to develop an abstract
idea. He must begin with a portrait of a man or a community of interacting men before he can create a portrait of an entire society, a political
system, or mankind as a whole. He must write about the agony of one
man dying before he can write about death. There can be no such thing
as a novel about romantic love unless it presents the experience of two

people *in* love. The writer, in other words, is committed to a belief in the individual person and in the primacy of individual experience over collective experience, living human fact over social doctrine.

III

That seems to me one of the serious problems facing the contemporary writer today, particularly the writer in America. In some peculiar way and without our being more than sporadically conscious of the fact, we have ceased in recent years to believe in the reality and authority, the concrete *factualness*, of individual experience—and it may even be that we have lost our ability to respond as we once did to the reality of a specific social situation. It is not merely that we have been conditioned by the mass media to the stereotypical rather than the personally felt, to the cliché formulations of life rather than the originally perceived realities of life. Yet there is no doubt that we have. The mass media have increasingly usurped the place once occupied in our lives by events. This is to say that the media are becoming more and more our substitutes for experience, that television is doing more and more of our living for us and persuading us that what it is doing for us really *is* living. Most of us now seem to accept it as a matter of course that we will participate far less vigorously in personal relationships, in direct confrontations between the self and the environment, than we do in filmed versions of somebody's imaginary experience—and these filmed versions need not relate any longer to events in the actual world, need not be *like life* but only like themselves.

It is also undoubtedly true that the conditions of life in a mass society force us to do more and more of our living at second hand, to relate to experience tangentially and voyeuristically, and that because of the sheer density of population and our lack of access to population units of engageable size, we feel deprived of the traditional means of relating to others as private persons and of valuing our relationship with others just because it is an intimate and precious ingredient of our total relationship to life. It is an old story today that, to use Conrad's wonderful phrase, we are "camped like bewildered travelers in a garish unrestful hotel," but the trouble is that we no longer enjoy the luxury of camping in anything so compact and potentially sociable as a hotel. We exist now, with our accelerating bewilderment, in some sort of vast unfurnished territory of open social space, through which travelers move and move on continuously, and our grasp of their reality and humanity is diminished because there are so very many of them, and we know that soon, very soon, they will be replaced by other travelers whose faces we will also not remember for much longer than the moment. In short, we all suffer from a dissociation of social sensibility, an abstractedness created by life lived among perpetual strangers, because the terms of our existence in a mass society are what they are.

Whatever the reasons, when we think of society today, we seem most aware of some vague and generalized entity, a vast impersonal macrocosm rather than an engageable microcosm, a symbolic representation or a sociological abstraction which, for want of other language, we call society, but which we seem able only to label, never reach. Perhaps most often today we perceive society as a condition, an issue, or a set of problems rather than an experience, as something we obsessively analyze, compile statistics about, conduct surveys in, publish reports on—the very magnitude and diversity of the statistics and reports being an exact indication of just how mysterious and seemingly inaccessible society now seems to us.

When we try to visualize American society at the present time, to perceive it imaginatively, I believe that most of us find it extremely difficult to visualize it in terms of specific human situations, to think of it, for example, in relation to places we have lived, things that have happened to us in those places, the emotions we felt there, the people who caused us to feel them. All that seems to belong to some order of perception, some primal world of experience, we left behind in childhood, that lost world of specific locales, palpable details, and enclosed psychic spaces. Yet that is the kind of world a writer needs to have available if he is to find the dramatic materials necessary to the creation of a vital literature— and one more vital than merely a literature about childhood.

All this may simply explain why it is that this has been primarily an age of sociology rather than a literary age. If we cannot engage our society specifically and personally, if we do not feel that its reality has some meaningful relation to our individual reality, if it seems to us only a phenomenon or a statistical construct, then of course we will be moved to try to analyze it scientifically—if only so that we can explain away its strangeness. Just as obviously, we are not likely to be moved to treat it imaginatively or to try to capture its essential reality in a novel, play, or narrative poem, for its essential reality is just its unreality and inaccessibility. In this regard, such a work as John Dos Passos's U.S.A. or Hart Crane's *The Bridge* would be unthinkable today because we have lost the sense of an encompassable and knowable society, just as we seem to have lost our capacity for generalizing social statement in literature—that capacity depending presumably upon some perception of underlying social coherence, the possibility of discovering the defining metaphor of our condition.

It is perfectly true that a sense of estrangement from society is nothing new for Americans, and surely it is nothing new for American writers.

Traditionally, the American writer has been an isolated, often a provincial, observer devoting himself to taking social notes and moral readings on a culture to which he felt no particular bond of loyalty or connection. As a rule, he has been powerfully and incurably afflicted with what Henry James called "the perspective of otherness"—the otherness of other people, the otherness of himself in relation to other people. He has also been, or felt secretly at heart, rather like the young boy in Joyce's "Araby," "bearing his chalice safely through a throng of foes"—bearing, that is, the fragile vessel of his art through a society that did not, and does not, value very highly either art or the artist. At certain times in history this sense of estrangement, coupled with a feeling of working within and against a predominantly hostile environment, has led the American writer to assume the somewhat belligerent but still spectatorial stance of a Sinclair Lewis satirizing the George F. Babbitts of the Middle West or an H. L. Mencken huffing in delighted outrage over the hypocritical manners and morals of what he called *Boobus Americanus.*

It is becoming evident, however, that some kinds of estrangement serve writers better than other kinds. So long as a writer believes that he himself is the chief custodian of sanity and civilization, he will be able to criticize his society for failing to be civilized and sane, and he will be able to do this even better just because he feels estranged from his society. But if a writer feels *so* estranged that he can perceive his society only as an abstraction or an impenetrable mass of undifferentiated humanoids who can no longer be held to standards of sanity and civilization, then clearly he will not be able to engage it creatively with very much vigor. The connection will have been broken that once made it possible for him to assume a critical stance, and the perspective will be lost that once made satire possible. I believe this is a very real, although largely unacknowledged, part of the American writer's dilemma at the present time, and there is added to it another debilitating element: He does not feel free to assume a satirical or critical stance toward society—even if he found it possible for other reasons to do so—because he can no longer be certain that enlightened opinion is on his side, that not only he but also others like him, the members of the literary and intellectual community, are still the chief custodians of sanity and civilization or would be in agreement with him or with one another as to what those standards are.

Such men as Lewis and Mencken were the spokesmen in their day for a minority of enlightened people who did generally share such agreement and who also shared certain common attitudes toward American society. Theirs was, like ours, an age of social revolution and social criticism, but the principal target of criticism was the way of life and thinking of the unenlightened majority, the vast population we now call Middle America. The issues in dispute must seem to us very simple and even rather naïve.

The conflict was largely between truth and hypocrisy, freedom against repression, liberalism against prejudice, cosmopolitanism against provincialism. The intellectuals who were crusading for truth and freedom clearly had *right* on their side. Civilization was waging and finally winning the war against barbarism.

The interesting fact about the present time, however, is that the most powerfully evident cultural influence is no longer that of provincial and small-town America. We know that that America still exists, but it no longer creates the prevailing ideological climate of the country. Today we live in a climate of political activism and moral idealism generated in large part by the youth movement, with the encouragement of significant elements of the adult intellectual community. It would seem, on the face of it, that the youth movement may be, and ought to be, as vulnerable to criticism and satire as the provincial culture of Lewis's and Mencken's day. In fact, there is more than a little justice in the charge that the youth culture has become the influential and conformist society at this time, that it constitutes a sort of new Babbittry or *Booboisie* of the Left, and that it is characterized by as much self-righteousness, smugness, humorlessness, and generalized sentimentality and vapidity as could ever have been encountered fifty years ago on the streets of Gopher Prairie. Furthermore, many of the social attitudes and life-styles of the youth culture are just as dictatorial and repressive of individuality as the most authoritarian codes of the old middle-class Establishment.

The very great difference is that whereas Mencken and Lewis knew that they represented, and were speaking for, enlightened opinion, the youth culture seems to have very nearly all the weight of enlightened opinion on its side. Many intellectuals and others who would normally be champions of civilized values have closed down their critical faculties with regard to much that the young stand for, because they are so impressed by the idealism of the young and by the indisputable moral rightness of many of their social aims. Hence, the writer who would attempt to criticize or satirize some of the reprehensible or just plain ridiculous features of the youth culture would almost inevitably find himself categorized as a reactionary or even a fascist, an apologist for the Establishment, and relegated to the company of many people whose social and political philosophy he would undoubtedly find abhorrent in the extreme. In other words, he would not be able to write honestly about many vulnerable characteristics of the young without seeming to provide ammunition to the enemy, and to *his* enemy, without violating some of his own liberal-humanitarian convictions. By a nicely ironic turning of the tables, the subversive critical opinion is now the unenlightened reactionary opinion, and the enlightened opinion is the liberal conformist opinion.

There is also the difficulty that satire is most effectively written about hypocrisy and the effort of an entrenched society to preserve appearances by lying about its behavior and its real motives. Usually, satire exposes the disparity between appearances and reality, between humanitarian or libertarian professions and self-seeking actions, between snobbery about material values and pretensions about moral or spiritual values. Now, clearly there are elements in the youth movement which are open to satire on these grounds. There is snobbery. There is pretentiousness. There may even be hypocrisy about the real self-seeking motives behind the movement.

Again the difference is that the young have right and righteousness, at least in principle, on their side. They are not calling for the preservation of outmoded institutions, but just the opposite. They are not calling for repression—even if they are themselves sometimes repressive. They are calling for freedom. It would at least appear that they are not materialistic but militantly antimaterialistic. There may be much insufferable pietism connected with their position, but so much of it is morally unimpeachable that to satirize it would be to impugn the good principles on which it is based. Hence, the impulse to satire must inevitably be short-circuited, and the writer loses one of his most important freedoms: the freedom to pronounce upon the condition of his society according to the honesty of his vision.

IV

It is perfectly true, as Mr. Panichas has observed, that criticism, particularly in our day, "cannot be political, cannot subscribe to a theory of politics." It would also seem, however, that novelists, unless they have the breadth of vision of a Stendhal, not only cannot be political but also cannot *afford* to be. We have lived through an age in which certain highly gifted novelists such as H. G. Wells, Huxley, and others herein discussed were often able, perhaps because of their favored position in history, to deal directly and profoundly with political ideas without adulterating the dramatic values of their work or distorting it to conform to a particular theory of politics. It would appear that such a possibility is beyond the grasp of most novelists at the present time. This collection of essays may, therefore, in a sense be as much a memorial as a critical examination, for it commemorates an age that may have ended years ago or may now be gradually coming to an end.

The intimate relationship between politics, the individual life, and the creative life has evidently broken down in our day, and for some of the reasons I have suggested. Clearly in our day to be political as a creative writer—to be *acceptably* political—would be to lend support to causes that, if they are successful, could easily lead to the debasement, if not destruction, of everything a writer is committed to value. In an anti-intellectual and vigorously egalitarian political climate such as ours, the writer, like all intellectuals, must by definition be considered the enemy. The practice of literature at the highest imaginative level is, in the currently fashionable view, an aristocratic practice, just as the old ideal of creative self-development is an undemocratic ideal. Both presume to delegate powers of absolute personal authority to the writer, and by implication they make a virtue of powers of taste and comprehension which only a few exceptional people have ever possessed. Hence, the serious writer may come to be viewed more and more as a partisan of the Establishment. He is a symbol not only of elitist privilege and reactionary individualism but also of a subversive psychic arrangement: that of the intransigent and undoubtedly neurotic person who does not confront experience directly, who does not share—or even particularly wish to share—a sense of identity with the mass of mankind, but who rather relates to experience privately and imaginatively, preferring perhaps to create experience rather than to have it, finding the experience of creation perhaps more challenging and rewarding than the experience of collective identity and mass action.

Such presumptuousness seems intolerable now and will probably seem even more intolerable in the years ahead. Yet it has behind it values that are absolutely essential to all writers who function now or ever will function as creative artists. How, then, will such writers continue to survive in a world that finds everything they stand for increasingly intolerable? The answer of course is that, by whatever means, the best of them will survive as they always have. To the extent that they are committed to literature and ideas, they will retain their identity as custodians of literary standards and intellectual distinctions. One hopes that they will also retain their traditional right to work against the grain of the official culture, even if, *particularly* if, the official culture professes to have all moral grandeur on its side. Such smugness, whether liberal or reactionary, egalitarian or elitist, must sooner or later stimulate any serious writer to recover the courage of his dissent and, with it, his historic role as critic and satirist of human pretentiousness.

Lionel Trilling once said that the characteristic function of the novel is "to record the illusion that snobbery generates and to try to penetrate to the truth which ... lies hidden beneath all the false appearances." It would seem that this is a function that novelists and critics alike need now, with particular urgency, to resume, for in spite of all efforts to pretend it does not exist or to see it as a halo of virtue, the illusion generated by snobbery has never been more in evidence or more oppressive than it is at the present time.

CONTENTS

PART III: AMERICAN

INTRODUCTION

The Writer and Society: Some Reflections

by George A. Panichas

I

ANY DISCUSSION OF the relationship between literature and society leads to inevitable and thorny problems. The nature of some of these problems can perhaps best be compared by way of warning, as found in René Wellek and Austin Warren's *The Theory of Literature*: "... literature is no substitute for sociology or politics. It has its own justification and aim."[1] Such a warning is not without precedent, nor without celebrated proponents and antagonists. From an early time in the history of aesthetics, works of literary art have prompted varying, often opposing, aesthetic responses. Plato, it will be remembered, equated the study of art with the study of moral values, and Aristotle equated art with poetic values and the study of aesthetics.

Proponents of what can be called the purist, or formalist, point of view judge a work of art according to criteria of craftsmanship. What matters is the purity of the imagination as it is communicated by its "structure of words," by form, by technique ("technique as discovery," as the phrase goes), set forth in transcendent detachment. A work of art is an expression and ordering of vision, its style achieved through the "organization of originality," to use Paul Valéry's phrase. The creator, hence, must be judged not as a "thinker," an ideologue, a dialectician, or a didactician, but rather as an artist. His is "the struggle—which alone constitutes life for a poet—" as T. S. Eliot predicates (he is talking about Shakespeare), "to transmute his personal and private agonies into something rich and strange, something universal and impersonal."[2] And the artist must be judged according to how far he has managed to separate himself from the subjective world and thus, through the "continual extinction of personality," to purify himself in relation to his art. In a well-known passage in *A Portrait of the Artist as a Young Man* (1916) James Joyce suggests some of the formulary principles of this aesthetic approach: "The artist, like the God of the creation, remains within or behind or beyond or above his handiwork, invisible, refined out of existence, indifferent, paring his fingernails."

Those who dissent from this view see the artist and his work in less exclusive and autonomous dimensions. For the social critic, as opposed to the critic as purist, the functions and the frontiers of art are much deeper and much wider. For him literature is a never-ending process and not some autotelic end in itself. He finds the values of art interacting with and even blending with other values: economic, religious, moral, philosophical, historical, political. He agrees with Charles Augustin Sainte-Beuve that "no aspect of human life is alien to literature." Literature, as such, is not merely the narrative of an age but "an invitation to action." Ultimately what and how the artist writes interweaves with the world in which he lives, the people whom he observes, and the civilization and conduct that he comprehends and reflects in his vision and to which he constantly returns for his inspiration. In this respect the artist is a poet in the ancient Hellenic sense of a maker, a creator, one who conveys a certain esoteric wisdom and who, as a result, helps to form what is sometimes described as "the normative consciousness" of the human race. Leo Tolstoy crystallized these views about art when he wrote: "Art, like speech, is a means of communication, and therefore of progress, i.e., of the movement of humanity forward toward perfection."[3]

Twentieth-century critics have often echoed the Tolstoyan view of art by emphasizing "a sociological criticism of literature" and a "historical interpretation of literature"—"literature as equipment for living," in Kenneth Burke's phraseology. Since man is in the highest degree a historical being, social critics tell us, all his creative efforts must be seen in their historical and cultural facets, for, as Matthew Arnold would have it, these creative efforts are "a criticism of life." The creative imagination, like its proper critical evaluation, must, under the circumstances, address itself to the overarching question of how man lives. The great artist is he who speaks about life and the possibilities of life. If his vision, in its rendered power, is achieved by intrinsic values, his view of life—the statement about life that will ensue—has extrinsic cognitive values. In turn, literary criticism ought to be "a history of man's ideas and imaginings in the setting of the conditions which have shaped them," as Edmund Wilson, echoing some of the ideas of nineteenth-century critics like Hippolyte Taine and Sainte-Beuve, writes in *Axel's Castle*.[4]

The metaphysic of the artist and how it is incorporated into his vision are controlling factors in the creative imagination and in its "powerful and profound applications of ideas to life," again to quote Arnold. The artist, if he speaks to life and for life, can rarely avoid responding to the world around him. This does not mean that he must be subservient to a metaphysic. Rather, he reveals the power of his creative imagination in direct relationship to his ability to transcend a metaphysic without consciously ignoring or dispensing with its integral substances as these affect human experience. In a large sense, perhaps in the final sense, his art is a mediation between his metaphysic—his cognitive view of life: the life of man and the meaning of the world—and his vision, his revelation, which, in its artifices—that is, through the organic processes of craftsmanship—helps us to understand the infinite variety of existence. In an early essay on Ivan Turgenev, Henry James, who for too long has been identified with the exponents of what goes under the (misleading) rubric of "pure art," addresses himself to the relation between art and metaphysic, between—in a broader, more germane context—literature and society:

> The great question as to a poet or a novelist is, How does he feel about life? what, in the last analysis, is his philosophy? When vigorous writers have reached maturity, we are at liberty to gather from their works some expression of a total view of the world they have been so actively observing. This is the most interesting thing their works offer us. Details are interesting in proportion as they contribute to make it clear.[5]

Clearly, the distempers of the twentieth century have sharpened some of the attitudes toward what exactly the relationship is between literature and society, or, as James would have it, what some of the ways are in which an artist expresses in his writings "a total view of the world." Modern history has strengthened the position of the social critic, while that of the critic as purist has steadily weakened. Today we need only think of the immensely diminished status of the New Critics to gauge the truth of this fact. Even the currently widespread use of the words "relevance" and "meaning" should underline, with respect to both the study and the criticism of literature, the direction of things. More than at any other time in history, literature today is seen against and appraised in the light of major historical events, forces, and ideas. The historical situation, in effect, is always there, even central to the literary imagination. The vision of the artist is not able to distance the reality of history—not even, it seems, the "dialectical vision of history" which constitutes the major concern of Marxist critics like Georg Lukács and Ernst Fischer. This is by no means to claim that literature has become dialectic and ideology (except, of course, for Soviet literature). It does mean that twentieth-century literature reflects historical developments and that it is impelled and colored by social and political developments. And it means, necessarily, that we must be able, as Lionel Trilling writes, "to see literary situations as cultural situations."[6]

To a large degree, history, not literary aesthetic, dictates sensibility and belief in twentieth-century literature. Any consideration of the major works of the imagination during this century corroborates this generalization. When Joseph Conrad, in his novel *Victory* (1915), saw this age as one "in which we are camped like bewildered travellers in a garish, unrestful hotel," he was prophetically evoking the condition of twentieth-century life. Immediately behind Conrad's insight were the radical transformations, the drift, of culture being occasioned by Marxism and Darwinism and Freudianism. Before him lay the successions to a pervasive disequilibrium characterizing the history of the crises of civilization in the twentieth century: war and "the growing murderousness of the world"; the erosion of the "ancient edifices" and the breakdown of traditional schemata of civilized life and values; the ascendancy and often the total domination of life by science and technology; the heightened tensions between man's "inner life" and his "outer life"; the unchecked spread of loneliness, anxiety, depersonalization, alienation, and uprootedness, as well as the growing enforcement of the laws of uniformity, of standardization, and of collectivization, particularly as disclosed in concrete political movements like Stalinism, fascism, and Nazism and in any other form of modern tyranny, totalitarian or "democratic," enforcing "the collectivist discipline." As Simone Weil observes: "The powerful means are oppressive, the non-powerful remain inoperative."

This brief summary of the human condition in the twentieth century is given here not only to emphasize the broken world which a modern writer cannot escape and which helps to mold his vision but also to instance the despiritualizing scope of twentieth-century life. In *Man in the Modern World* Karl Jaspers suggests some of the deeper ideological significances of "epochal" changes gradually destroying the life of man and his acceptance of transcendent values:

> There were periods in which man felt his world to be durable, an unchanging intermediate between the vanished Golden Age and the End that would come in due course when the Almighty's purposes were fulfilled. Man accommodated himself to life as he found it, without wishing to change it. His activities were limited to an endeavour to better his own position amid environ-

ing circumstances deemed to be substantially unalterable. Within these circumstances he had safe harbourage, linked as he was both with heaven and with earth. The world was his own world, even though it was of no account, because for him true being existed only in a transcendental realm.[7]

Jaspers published his book in 1931; in his Foreword to the 1951 edition he writes: "The facts remain unaltered." Now, two decades later, there are no reasons to emend this later remark. Man remains passive before the mechanized nature of mass order and technical life-order.

The social and religious implications of Jaspers's *Man in the Modern World* are given their literary and critical relevance in Edwin Muir's *Essays on Literature and Society,* chiefly in such chapters as "The Political View of Literature," "The Decline of the Novel," and "The Natural Man and the Political Man." As these titles indicate, Muir concerns himself with some of the ideological problems one encounters in modern literature, especially in prose fiction. The world in cultural transformation that Jaspers examines is the world that Muir identifies as the novelist's. It is a world in upheaval. And the upheaval is explained by, is the result of, ideological change—that change in attitude toward life that Jaspers traces and that, in the historical limit-situation, is reflected in active, actualized historical movements and conflicts. Above all, Muir shows how the writer responds to ideology, how his vision, as it is ordered by his craft and by his use of language, re-creates the impact of this response. In this connection the aesthetic question itself is not a matter of literature *versus* ideology but of literature *and* ideology, or better, as Muir points out, it is a question of defining "the difference between the position of the novelist fifty or a hundred years ago and his position today."

Inevitably this difference of position is a difference of ideology resulting from the writer's (changed and changing) "total view of the world." Like critics preoccupied with aesthetic experience, Muir admits his concern with a novelist's "story," his "grammatical construction," and his "skill in insinuating explanatory and qualifying clauses and all sorts of parentheses." But he is also preoccupied with some of the ideological changes peculiar to the modern age and to the modern novelist, who all along has been listening to and recording the "voices of a new world." (These are the voices that Jaspers hears in all their far-ranging ideological tones.) The difference, however, is that Muir recognizes in modern works of art a difference of tone and accent and meaning: a difference of orientation and approach, a difference of sensibility. This difference is ideological, Muir insists, and he associates it with a story that has no ending because the modern novelist's "sentence remains hanging in the air." The reasons for this suspension are dependent on the force and thrust of ideology. As Muir explains it:

> This is another way of saying that the contemporary novelist has an imaginative grasp of origins but not of ends. There was a time when the novelist (and the poet and everybody) had a grasp of both. To have this is a mark of that order of thought and imagination which is generally called classical. Our own order is not a classical order; we have a grasp of origins but not of ends; our existence, like our works, is an unfinished sentence. And the novel describing the life we live is a symptom of the order in which we live; its incompleteness is a reflection of the incompleteness of a whole region of thought and belief.[8]

Basically, then, literature in the twentieth century has reflected an unimpeded secularization of history. This secularization has been accompanied by great changes in the view of man and his universe and by the proliferation of new and revolutionary ideas affecting one's conception of life. The traditional novel, Muir notes, was a story of time against a pattern of permanence, whereas the modern novel has become a story of time against a background of time. Even in the works of Henry Fielding and Jane Austen a concern with eternal truths still prevailed. New and unsettling ideas, whether about evil or about God or about moral values, had not yet overwhelmed, secularized, the concept of life. A certain sense of permanence, human and superhuman, still prevailed, even as the ideas of the Enlightenment gathered momentum. Muir goes on to say:

> But they [Fielding and Jane Austen] lived in an order in which everybody possessed without thinking about it much the feeling for a permanence above the permanence of one human existence, and believed that the ceaseless flux of life passed against an unchangeable background. Men still felt this whether they were Christians or not. They felt also that there was a relation between the brief story of man and that unchangeable order; and this sentiment, in whatever terms it was held, was the final earnest of the completeness of their conception of life.[9]

The history of the modern novel is in essence the history of the mutation of this concept; it is the history of ideological change, of a fervent interplay of ideas. This interplay of ideas has revolved around the total rearrangement of society. The portrayal of man in the modern novel gives an index to the process of this rearrangement and evinces the spirit and the direction of changing ideological forces. There has emerged,

Muir believes, "a new species of the natural man dovetailed into a biological sequence and a social structure." Natural man "is simply a human
model capable of indefinite improvement on the natural plane; the
improvement depending ultimately on the progress of society, and of
things in general."[10]

Muir's observations point to the great power wielded by ideas, which
are inevitable to the creative process. The writer, and particularly the
novelist, cannot avoid contact with these ideas as they touch and shape
his attitudes toward life. Increasingly the writer has been compelled to
speak out on major issues. "Today everything is changed," Camus writes,
"and even silence has dangerous implications." And increasingly the
writer has viewed himself as an "architect of history," to borrow John
Dos Passos's apt description. Unable to escape history, the writer in his
art becomes its conscience as well as its consciousness. Henry Miller has
gone so far as to claim that the man who is to be called a poet must be
"capable of profoundly altering the world." At no other time in the history of literature have writers responded so intensely to the problems of
man in society as they have in the twentieth century. How man is ruled
and what his place is in society; how life and culture will survive; how
man's freedom will be saved; how the economic questions will be solved:
these are some of the problems that modern writers have had to deal
with precisely because they have been some of the most stubborn and
painful problems that have confronted man during this century. Indeed,
the traditional role of the writer as storyteller has merged with what can
be termed the prophetic role, whereby the writer in his art combines
craft with moral and ultimately apocalyptic meaning—becoming a
"spokesman of tragic times" of whom much is expected. "It may well be
that at this point in history," according to one critic, "we all need the aid
of the novelist's imagination simply to help us imagine what seems to be
more and more unimaginable. . . ."[11]

During the twentieth century we have come to rely a great deal on the
writer to help us understand a world in the midst of ideological turmoil
and cultural fragmentation. We have come to identify him with concern,
candor, courage. To him we have turned for the help that we seem
unable to get from the traditional sources of state and school and church.
Often, too, we have heeded the voice of the writer when other voices
have been silenced or corrupted. It is the writer in his "meditation on history" who can achieve "metapolitical objectivity" and can even be (in the
extreme Marxist view) an "engineer of human souls" who can be of use
in bringing about "a decent ordering of human affairs." When Simone
Weil, that most passionate Platonist of modern philosophers, asserts, "I
believe in the responsibility of the writers of recent years for the disaster
of our times," she helps to define, despite the perverseness of her conten-

tion, the magnified power of the writer in the modern world. As standards and values have collapsed, the need for them has become more manifestly urgent. To turn to literature in order to better understand social and political matters can equip one with those advantages of discrimination and discipline that are all too often missing or neglected in other areas of culture. "Art-speech is the only truth," we hear D. H. Lawrence saying to us.

II

Increasingly unable to separate himself from the moral and political events of his time, the modern writer, like Jean-Paul Sartre in his celebrated manifesto, has had to address himself to the question, "What is literature?" This question, especially in the years following World War I, became more pronounced as writers became more aware of their place in the historical process and its concomitant "tragic sense of life." In the years since World War II, this question has become for the writer a central question—as central, in fact, as What is "the future of mankind"? Indeed, the shaping—the demanding—spirit of literature in the twentieth century can be said to be precisely this question. ("The past," as Irving Howe notes, "was devoted to answers; the modern period confines itself to questions."[12]) The writer, Sartre believes, "establishes a historical contact among men who are steeped in the same history and who likewise contribute to its making." His literary work is an appeal, and its value is commensurate with this appeal. One of the main results of this concept of art and its function and responsibility in the twentieth century has been the writer's conscious (or unconscious) sense of commitment: an awareness of one's literary contribution as in itself an involvement in the problems and disasters of the age, as well as an awareness that, in Sartre's words, "the written work can be an essential condition of action, that is, the moment of reflective consciousness."

The historic and essentially aristocratic case against a "committed literature" has been argued by Eliot, who insisted that "the meddling of men of letters in practical affairs ... is only one phenomenon of a general confusion." Yet even Eliot did not rule out the presence, or the passion, of ideological elements in matters of art. "If there is a right relation of emotion to thought in practical affairs," he stipulates, "so there is in speculation and art too." What Eliot and others sharing his view have feared is that writers, misled by their own social-political illusions, may become theorists who impose a form of political ideology on their writings. By no one has the condemnation of a "committed literature" been stated better than by Julien Benda in his famous work *The Betrayal of the Intellectuals (La Trahison des clercs)*. First appearing in 1927, this book was in

many ways what sparked the antipodal position taken by Sartre in his
Qu'est-ce que la littérature? (1947). No other two books better define
some of the problems that have beset both the theory and the criticism of
literature in the modern age. Benda, it is clear, looks back to the past;
Sartre is the voice of the present, if not the future. The sharpness of the
debate between the two is illustrated in Sartre's pointed attack on Benda:

> If the writer has chosen, as Benda has it, to talk drivel, he can
> speak in fine, rolling periods of that eternal freedom which
> National Socialism, Stalinist communism, and the capitalist
> democracies all lay claim to. He won't disturb anybody; he
> won't address anybody. Everything he asks for is granted him in
> advance. But it is an abstract dream. Whether he wants to or
> not, and even if he has his eyes on eternal laurels, the writer is
> speaking to his contemporaries and brothers of his class and
> race.[13]

Sartre's, not Benda's, voice rings louder. Modern literature reflects not
only the writer's awareness of his social responsibility but also his involvement in what Benda derided as "the realism of the multitude." Indeed,
some believe the state of literature today is characterized by what Benda
especially feared: the man of letters exercising "political passions with all
the characteristics of passion—the tendency to action, the thirst for
immediate results, the exclusive preoccupation with the desired end, the
scorn for argument, the excess, the hatred, the fixed ideas."[14] Is not Sartre's concept of the writer's social responsibility, it is asked, precisely that
ideology, so suspect to men like Eliot and Benda, that has led to a mutation of literature? And is not the steady collapse of standards, of delicacy
and restraint, evident in the whole of literature as it all too easily
becomes, say, physiology on the one hand and politics on the other?
When ideology invades literature, it is claimed, it produces an extreme
individualism of views and no clear rules regarding the limitations of a
literary work. Ideology personalizes art; and the artist, as Eliot once
wrote about Lawrence, becomes a propagandist, a "promoter of personality," a "seeker for myths." As such, the ideological element as a standard
of *engagement* is an intrusion into literature which introduces problems
alien to "the pursuit of criticism" and the judgment of an artist's achievement, which, Eliot declared, is not required to serve or be aware of certain ends or beliefs, "and indeed performs its function, whatever that
may be, according to various theories of value, much better by indifference to them." "The poet makes poetry," Eliot states, "the metaphysician
makes metaphysics, the bee makes honey, the spider secretes a filament;
you can hardly say that any of these agents believes: he merely does."[15]
Whatever the problems of criticism or the pronouncements of critics

may be, it is certain that creative artists in the modern age are increasingly preoccupied with social problems as a whole and with political problems in particular. For the modern writer politics in all its forms, as theory, as commitment, as action, has become a matter of consciousness and of conscience. Aesthetic considerations are invariably colored by social-political demands. In effect, the writer as seen in his art and in his actions has—sometimes reluctantly, at other times fearlessly and confidently—ventured into the public realm. He has, to use Robert Lowell's image, gone into "the bullring." If he has rendered the experience of this "bullring," it can also be said that the political situation, especially since 1918, that comprises this experience has affected the theory and the execution of his art. The essentially patrician attitude that "a creator is one who makes others create" has been steadily transformed into the populist belief, as it were, that a creator is one who makes others act, that man's destiny is primarily one of action: It is the recognition of this fact that the modern writer has disclosed with his creative powers.

To preserve, as Joseph Conrad advised, "an attitude of perfect indifference ... because directly the 'Fiat!' has issued from his lips, there are the creatures made in his image that'll try to drag him down from his eminence—and belittle him by their worship—"[16] to preserve this aesthetic attitude has become an increasingly difficult goal for the creative artist in the twentieth century. For as political situations have changed and polarized, as national interests have given way to international problems, as the emphasis on theological and ontological issues has been transferred to ethical and political formulations—in short, as social-political dialectic has replaced metaphysical concepts, with the unpolitical and even the antipolitical attitude toward culture definitely waning and, in some ways, extinct—modern literature has witnessed the invasion of its aesthetic sanctuary. Writers have become protesters and partisans. Their writings have as themes "resistance, rebellion, and death." As Lionel Trilling reminds us in *Beyond Culture*: "Modern literature ... is directed toward moral and spiritual renovation; its subject is damnation and salvation. It is a literature of doctrine which, although often concealed, is very aggressive."[17] Ever present is the secular world and secular man; and ever present, too, is an intensifying concern with the salvation of man in an existential cultural situation. "A man's—and how much more an artist's—[political] opinions are today bound up with the salvation of his soul," writes Thomas Mann, who fled from Nazi Germany in 1936.

Just how aggressive, even belligerent, the writer has become was illustrated at the Chicago conspiracy trial when the poet Allen Ginsberg took the stand and recited from his poem "Howl." Wheeling in his chair and pointing an accusing finger at the seventy-four-year-old judge, Ginsberg intoned: "Moloch the vast stone of war! Moloch the stunned govern-ments!/ Moloch whose ear is a smoking tomb! Moloch whose blood is running money!" Such passionate and frightening words remind us that not infrequently the poet combines the rage of his inspiration with action, whether in the "guerrilla theater" at Chicago or in ancient Judah, to which the "weeping poet"—that first great pacifist, *the* prophet Jere-miah—addressed his words of terror and doom from the day he was first divinely "set . . . over the nations and over the kingdoms, to root out, and to pull down, and to destroy, and to throw down, to build, and to plant."[18] Artists in the twentieth century, it could be said, have been lavish in the renderings of their vision that they have addressed to modern man. Undoubtedly, their visions have not always been rendered with striking artistic success. Not all writers have become acceptable members of a "priesthood of craftsmanship." Perhaps there have been too many words and too much anger to permit unqualified achievement. But modern history has been a history of men who live in "dark times," so that the artist, so much more sensitive to the darkness of his world, has not been immune to making propaganda an impelling determinant of his art. "I have always maintained," George Orwell asserts, "that every artist is a propagandist . . . in the sense that he is trying, directly or indirectly, to impose a vision of life that seems to him desirable."[19]

The interrelations of radical politics and radical literature were most apparent in the 1930's, a period that, as William Phillips points out, despite contradictions, illusions, and duplicities, was a time "when re-sponsibility meant responsibility to ideas and convictions, justice seemed more important than expediency, the greater good meant more than the lesser evil, dreams seemed more cogent than reality."[20] In the United States, where the Great Depression had as profound an impact on Ameri-can cultural life and thought as the Great War had had on the European consciousness (if any analogy can capture the distresses of the situation of this period), radical fiction—or "proletarian literature," as it is referred to—was induced by a Marxist view of society. In the forefront of "American literary communism" were writers like James T. Farrell and Waldo Frank. Preceding them, in the early part of the 1900's, were writ-ers like Jack London and Upton Sinclair, who were responsive to the principles of socialism. The phenomenon of this literary responsiveness to, this quarrel with, society was peculiarly American. It was, Daniel Aaron has told us, as empirical as it was evangelical, as intense as it was uneasy and ambivalent, as didactic as it was angry and impatient. "The history of American literary communism," Aaron goes on to say, "is the story of one more turn in the cycle of revolt. Like the earlier experiments in rebellion, it has its ancestors and founders, its foreign prophets, its manifestoes, its saints and renegades. It also begins in joy and ends in disenchantment. And growing amidst its monuments and ruins are the shoots of the rebellions to come."[21]

Moods of social protest in the thirties were not limited to the American scene and to writing. In the "English thirties poetry" the relationships of literature and society were evident in the belief that public poetry, as opposed to private poetry, in the form of "heightened conversation," was what was demanded if the experience of literature was to be made accessible to all people. In contradistinction to Eliot's feeling that "all great poetry gives the illusion of a view of life," poets like Stephen Spender, W. H. Auden, Louis MacNeice, and C. Day Lewis saw their proper functions as being not merely the mouthpiece of a community but also its critical faculty and its conscience. More than contemplation and sensitive perception were demanded of the poet. "I would have a poet," MacNeice writes in *Modern Poetry: A Personal Essay*, "able-bodied, fond of talking, a reader of the newspapers, capable of pity and laughter, informed in economics, appreciative of women, involved in personal relationships, actively interested in politics, susceptible to physical impressions." And poetry itself, either as entertainment or as criticism, MacNeice declares, "is only valuable if it can add something to the experience of its public, this addition often consisting merely in the illumination of that public's own experience."[22] It is undoubtedly the "illumination" of precisely this experience that is found in these lines from Auden's poem on the England of the Great Slump:

> Get there if you can and see the land you once were proud to own
> Though the roads have almost vanished and the expresses never run:
> Smokeless chimneys, damaged bridges, rotting wharves and choked canals,
> Tramlines buckled, smashed trucks lying on their sides across the rails;
> Power-stations locked, deserted, since they drew the boiler fires;
> Pylons falling or subsiding, trailing dead high-tension wires.

On the European continent, throughout the 1930's and the 1940's, the political plays of the German Marxist Bertolt Brecht illustrated brilliantly the connections between "the didactic play" and social purposes. Brecht sought to represent human conditions in a world of economic rapaciousness, war, prejudice, brutality, political evil. As such, for Brecht the theater was necessarily an "epic theater": externalizing, argumentative, didactic, one in which the spectator becomes an active observer and arouses his will to action, calling for decisions and a world outlook. This theater, by "making gestures quotable," demands a struggle of social convictions. For Brecht the social-political situation served to catalyze both his view and his practice of dramatic art. He too showed how political consciousness inspires art—how social background and dialectic can inhere in the artist's imagination and give rise to art. In the long run what writers like Brecht do in their works (whatever the genre) is to remind us that the social-political element plays its appropriate role in the artist's vision and technique, activates this vision, and in times of intense ideological turmoil assumes a prominence in and even a technical and at times innovative direction of works of art. Certainly, when considering the literature of the 1930's, one cannot ignore some of the implicit and explicit political elements at work in the writer's imagination. One cannot, that is to say, disregard the truth of the contention that "the essential life of a period is best understood through its literature; not because of what the literature describes, but because of what it embodies."[23]

Here we can well be reminded of the difficulties that arise in the twentieth century concerning the purpose of the artist and the task of the critic. A classic illustration of these difficulties was the awarding of the first Bollingen Prize for Poetry to Ezra Pound for *The Pisan Cantos* as "the highest achievement of American poetry in 1948." Judges were the Fellows in American Letters of the Library of Congress, consisting of Conrad Aiken, W. H. Auden, Louise Bogan, Katherine Garrison Chapin, T. S. Eliot, Paul Green, Robert Lowell, Katherine Anne Porter, Karl Shapiro, Theodore Spencer, Willard Thorp, Robert Penn Warren, and Léonie Adams. Aware of the controversy that would surround their choice, in the light of Pound's career as a fascist and an anti-Semite, the judges were careful to issue this statement: "To permit other considerations than that of poetic achievement to sway the decision would destroy the significance of the award and would in principle deny the validity of that objective perception of value on which civilized society must rest." (Goethe's belief that more is permitted to poets than to ordinary mortals—*"Dichter sündgen nicht schwer"*—can be adduced at this point.) Both the choice of Pound and the judges' Eliotic statement were unsettling, to say the least. No other literary event could better focus on the debate that goes on between those who see literature in its social and cultural implications and those who see it in its purist callings: between, as it were, the judgment of imagination as dialectic and of imagination as art.

William Barrett, an editor of the *Partisan Review*, reflected the acerbity of this debate when, writing in the April 1949 issue, he questioned the merits of the choice of *The Pisan Cantos* and specifically "the validity of aesthetic principles" employed by the judges. Barrett accented the fact that we could not easily "forget all about the humanly ugly attitudes" of which Pound was a spokesman—attitudes that recur in some of the poems comprising *The Pisan Cantos*. And with evident dissatisfaction, he also used the Pound case to confront the aestheticians, who formulated the criteria for the award—"the validity of that objective perception of value," to recall the most important of their critical standards—with the question, "How far is it possible, in a lyric poem, for technical embellishment to transform vicious and ugly matter into beautiful poetry?"

Reaction to Barrett was heated. Of the Bollingen jurors who replied in the May 1949 issue of the *Partisan Review* Tate was the most outraged. Barrett, he felt, had in essence charged the Bollingen jurors with anti-Semitism. "I hope that persons who wish to accuse me of cowardice and dishonor will do so henceforth personally, in my presence, so that I may dispose of the charge at some other level than the public discussion. Courage and honor are not subjects of literary controversy, but occasions for action." Barrett was not to be intimidated. Tate's "challenge to a personal duel," he noted, "is strictly extra-curricular sport—having nothing to do with the public issue." Thus Karl Shapiro, who had voted against Pound, said in his "statement of principle" that "the poet's political and moral philosophy ultimately vitiates his poetry and lowers its standards as a literary work." Artists everywhere "should stand against this poet for his greater crime against civilization." In Pound's *Cantos*, Shapiro concluded, fascism is undeniably "one of the 'myths.'" The question that remains to be answered is: Through his experience with vicious and ugly ideas, what poetic insights into our world has this poet given us? These ungracious facts in the "Case of Ezra Pound" are given here not to rekindle old feuds but rather to show the acrimony that surrounds a discussion of literature and society generally and of literature and politics specifically. Barrett and Shapiro, in the questions they raised, underline a position taken by critics concerned with the mythopoeic and moral functions of art, with what Sartre speaks of as the writer's social responsibility, especially in an age of acute historical awareness.

III

A more recent example of the trend this questioning has led to is John R. Harrison's *The Reactionaries: A Study of the Anti-Democratic Intelligentsia*, in which W. B. Yeats, Wyndham Lewis, Ezra Pound, T. S. Eliot, and D. H. Lawrence are selected as the literary-ideological exemplars of the "anti-democratic intelligentsia" in the twentieth century. Harrison summarizes the purpose of his work and the overall direction of his arguments and conclusions in these words:

> What Yeats, Pound, Lewis and Eliot wanted in literature was bareness, a hard intellectual approach ruled by the authority of

strict literary principles. They rejected the humanist tradition in literature, and in society, the democratic, humanitarian tradition. The same principles governed their social criticism as their literary criticism, and led them to support the fascist cause, either directly, as Pound and Lewis did, or indirectly, as Yeats and Eliot did.[24]

This book was much discussed by the literary establishment. It was often applauded. In England Anthony Burgess, writing in the *Spectator*, observed: "Mr. Harrison is really very good and very fair. . . . He states where the reactionaries went wrong, and—if we regard the politics of men of letters as of any interest at all—we shall not be unhappy to find him right."[25] In the United States Philip Rahv, writing in *The New York Review of Books*, largely endorsed Harrison's findings, though he quibbled with the "gummy use of the label 'fascist.'" What the five writers discussed by Harrison, Rahv said, "can be truly accused of is presumption in undertaking to speak portentously about matters they knew little about. This presumption by quite a few men of letters is a cultural phenomenon—a symptom of certain antinomian qualities intrinsic to the literature of the modern age. . . ."[26]

Yet the weakness inherent in these critical views becomes as apparent and disputable as, in its peculiar ways, the Marxist view of literature as an "ideological superstructure," the values of which stem from determinations of its "objective reality." The problem with Harrison's study is perhaps also a problem of the social and cultural approach to literature as a whole: excessive reliance on empirical presuppositions, which become in the end an oversimplified aesthetic, no less harmful and limited than the Marxist conclusion. As an example of how the "beliefs" of a writer affecting his work are appraised in what Rahv proclaims as an "important" book, *The Reactionaries* also instances the nature of the weakness in an approach to a subject which requires some subtle considerations. Harrison fails in his work because unlike, say, Irving Howe in *Politics and the Novel* (1957), he is not concerned, as he should be, with "perspectives of observation" but rather with "categories of classification." Implicit in this latter concern is the danger of the disparity that one writer, not surprisingly, detects in *The Reactionaries* when he writes: "The book's chief limitation is that Mr. Harrison never faces the central question raised by the awkward social attitudes of his subjects. If it is accepted that some or all of them were among the finest artists of their time, how was it that their art found so much nourishment in authoritarian ideas?"[27]

The "perspective of observation" that Harrison lacks is afforded by Stephen Spender in an essay, "Writers and Politics," in which he discusses *The Reactionaries*, Conor Cruise O'Brien's *Writers and Politics*, and Peter

Stansky and William Abraham's *Journey to the Frontier*, a study dealing with the participation of two promising young writers, John Cornford and Julian Bell, in the Spanish Civil War, 1936–1938.[28] Spender discusses precisely those problematic aspects of the relationship between a writer and society that are too often ignored or oversimplified. A writer's politics, he shows, cannot be discarded from an imaginative work of art. The "appeal of politics in the guise of metaphor," as seen in Pound's case, was tempting to writers united in "their condemnation of a society which they saw as the disintegration of civilization." "The temptation for the poet," Spender goes on to observe, "is to take over the rhetoric of political will and action and translate it into the rhetoric of poetry without confronting the public rhetoric of politics with the private values of poetry." In a country like France, where "there is a tradition of intellectually respect-worthy opinion about politics to which the writer can relate his own views" (views as various as those of André Gide, Paul Claudel, Georges Bernanos, and André Malraux), he emphasizes, it is not difficult to judge seriously and even accurately a writer's expressed opinions. But because no such tradition exists in England and America, the ways in which the writer intervenes in politics "tend to be sporadic and occasional and perhaps not consistent with his truest, that is his most imaginative insights."

Spender's observations comprise a basic corrective attitude that can hardly be stressed enough in "the pursuit of criticism" relating to the writer and society. Writers between 1910 and 1930 were sensitive to a society that they saw as representing the decay of civilization and as constituting a real and a potential destroyer of the imagination. Indeed, Spender feels, the politics, even the excrescences of the political beliefs, of writers like Yeats, Eliot, Pound, Lewis, and Lawrence showed only that "they cared less for politics than for literature." The upshot of all this is, he insists, that a writer's political gestures and attitudes are often largely rhetorical; that, in the case of the five writers in question, the political elements "are secondary effects of their thoughts about the tragedy of culture in modern industrial societies." Spender's insistence on the necessity to keep in mind the infinitely subtle facets of the artistic imagination in relation to social-political ideas and movements, and thus to maintain the balance that is demanded of a critic in terms of "standards of discrimination," becomes all the more necessary if "categories of classification" are to be avoided.

What, then, can make the writer different (and at the same time insist on that difference in any judgment of his vision as it is consummated in his art) from a political activist? What, in a word, can distinguish the subtlety of art, even in its politics, from the politics of ideology? Certainly, as Spender asserts, with Yeats, Eliot, Pound, Lewis, and Lawrence, the difference in all its nuances remains inescapable precisely because it is wrought in paradox, which no critical efforts can explain away. The explanation lies in the vision that the imagination finally renders. What Spender achieves in the following passage is precisely that "perspective of observation" that makes criticism legitimate and shows how the subject of literature and society can be of value if the criteria of interpretation do not in themselves become politicalized:

> There was, then, the paradox that the reactionaries who were on the side of the past, the dead, had to live for the sake of literature, whereas circumstances drove the most sincere anti-Fascists—men like Cornford, Bell, [Ralph] Fox and [Christopher] Caudwell—to death as absolution in a cause which they had made absolute. The reactionaries wrote out their tragic sense of modern life. The Cornfords and Bells lived and died the tragedy.

Spender's observations trenchantly demonstrate that the subject of the writer and society demands responsible inquiry. Harrison's *The Reactionaries* (even the choice of title conveys dangerous implications) is an example of what can go wrong, particularly of what can go wrong when one's view of his role as a critic discloses both general confusion and, worse, a failure, or an inability, to define or apply the standards of criticism which are necessary in examining a writer's social and political beliefs and expressions. Only when Spender's essay is read as a corrective to Harrison's work are we able to grasp the complexities that determine a writer's relationship to society. Hence, the assessment of such a relationship involves at once larger and more intricate considerations: the need to be aware of the full power of the ideological forces that constitute the social-political structure and of the way in which dialectical elements affect a writer's vision. The dangers, the disparities, of such critical assessment can polarize into positions impervious, on the one hand, to the complexity of a social-literary integration and, on the other hand, to the miracle of imaginative vision, the creative process, as it transcends social doctrine and programs to become art. One can never disregard the mysterious hidden patterns of the creative process and the creative paradoxes that defy rigid aesthetic classification. Ernst Cassirer in his magisterial *An Essay on Man* reminds us of the nonempirical, aesthetic "forms" of the imagination when he writes:

> It is not the same thing to live in the realm of forms as to live in that of things, of the empirical objects of our surroundings. The forms of art, on the other hand, are not empty forms. They perform a definite task in the construction and organization of

human experience. To live in the realm of forms does not signify an evasion of the issues of life; it represents, on the contrary, the realization of one of the highest energies of life itself. We cannot speak of art as "extrahuman" or "superhuman" without overlooking one of its fundamental features, its constructive power in the framing of our human universe.[29]

Intrinsic literary and cultural values to be realized in the examination of the relationships between literature and society are possible only if certain cautions are kept in mind—if, that is, any critical attempt in this direction is not to be muted in its effectiveness because of the need to correct it, as Spender's essay on Harrison's *The Reactionaries* demonstrates. This is not to say that such an examination of the problem can ever be final. It is to insist that the examination of literary and cultural interrelationships, if there are present in it relevant principles of commentation and exposition of works of art, can be both (aesthetically) elucidation, or illumination, and (culturally) "correction of taste." By relevant, one means, as a start, the critic's "sense of the past," a recognition that "the literary work is ineluctably a historical fact, and, what is more important . . . its historicity is a fact in our aesthetic experience."[30] This historical sense—central to the aesthetic faculty, as Trilling shows—reconciles the experience of literature with a sense of the age, with the question of cultural continuity, with the meaning of life and the destiny of man. Ultimately—and this point always needs stressing—this historical sense complements the discipline of literary studies and criticism, and thus enables one to see literature in its living relationships with the whole of society, as Lionel C. Knights sees these relationships in his *Explorations* (and earlier in his pioneering *Drama and Society in the Age of Jonson*), in which he writes:

> In an attempt to understand the quality of living in a past period—to understand, that is, all those intangible modes of being which are only hinted at in the documents on which economic and political history is based—the study of that period's literature is central, and some degree of *critical* ability is indispensable to the historian of culture.[31]

A "disciplined exploration" of literature, Knights contends, remains indispensable to an understanding of society, that is, to an understanding of the organization of life, the ordered human community—that "system or mode of life adopted by a body of individuals for the purpose of harmonious co-existence or for mutual benefit, defense, etc.," to cite one working definition. Criticism and history, as Knights discloses, have their interacting roles to play in their cultural contexts insofar as both relate to the larger questions of life, thought, and literature: "What, in the given age, were the main lines of force as expressed in human thought and action? What were the underlying, conscious or unconscious motives and energies which shaped its art and philosophy, its social, moral and legal codes, no less than its scientific, industrial and political achievements?"[32] Answers to these questions, Knights asserts, can be realized through a proper correlation between criticism and history, "with a view to that wider and deeper understanding of the sources of cultural health."

The critical study of the literature of a period in relation to its sense of the social realities, its cultural artifacts, its civilization, is conducive to "the first-hand apprehension of realized values"—values that in themselves arise from the fact that literature provides important evidence of the prevailing culture precisely because "it is itself a large part *of* that culture in its intellectual aspects, and it can only be used as 'evidence' when it has been assessed critically as literature." To work back through literature to the life of the time can provide, according to Knights, three essential advantages: first, that of giving evidence of style and language, which in their viable differences are "conditioned by social factors which they can be made, in part, to reveal"; second, that of revealing the tastes and intellectual ability of the audience for which the literature was intended, and, more specifically, "how the interests reflected in literature of different degrees of popularity were formed"; and third, that of determining what constitutes the highly subtle (and problematical) relationship between the standards a writer adopts and "current social codes," the determination of which "demands a cultivated literary sense as well as historical knowledge."[33]

Knights's observations acutely remind us of the constant need for critics to exert special cautions, as noted earlier, in investigating the relationships between literature and society. A principal caution is that of avoiding the extreme of an aesthetic purism of those who prefer to view an imaginative artist as one (borrowing here words that Eliot applied to Henry James) whose mind is too fine to be violated by ideas. This totalitarian attitude reduces literature either to the dead ends of formalism, which rejects viewing literature in terms of cultural concerns, or to obscurantism. Likewise, there is the need of avoiding another form of totalitarian literary theory, the Marxizing, which examines art in canonical terms of the dialectical method and historical structuralism—in terms, that is to say, of the canon laid down by Marx himself when he wrote in his preface to the *Critique of Political Economy*: "The methods of production in material life determine the general character of the social, political, and spiritual processes of life. It is not the consciousness of men that determines their being, but, on the contrary, their social being determines their consciousness." (In various ways it is this Marxist principle that Knights tests, and then corrects, in his work, as, more recently, English social critics of the New Left like Richard Hoggart, in *The Uses of Literacy*, and Raymond Williams in *Culture and Society, 1780-1950*, have also done.)

Of the two extremes, the Marxist sensibility has played a more important role in sharpening, as George Steiner calls to our attention, the critic's sense of time and place and in contributing "a sociological awareness to the best of modern criticism." "A vital tradition [like the Marxist], vital even in its polemics, is not a luxury but a rigorous need," Steiner observes.[34] But criticism, if it is not to be made imperfect by what is restrictive and doctrinaire, and if it is to transcend a tolerant eclecticism, which in time is reduced to what has been labeled a "pluralistic ambiguity," needs to adhere to the caution of balance. And this balance can be achieved only by recognizing the primacy of the creative process, which, as one social scientist notes, "transcends the horizon of society, only when integrating the hell and paradise of human life into the symbols of the whole, a task which the sociologist [for example] is incapable of realizing."[35] Dr. F. R. Leavis, whose writings are paradigms of how literary and cultural elements can be vigorously balanced and sustained in works of criticism (for example, in his treatment of writers like John Bunyan, Charles Dickens, D. H. Lawrence, and E. M. Forster in works like *The Great Tradition* [1948], *The Common Pursuit* [1952], and *Anna Karenina and Other Essays* [1967]), alludes, in the following remarks, to some of the cautions emphasized above:

> Without the sensitizing familiarity with the subtleties of language, and the insight into the relations between abstract or generalizing thought and the concrete of human experience, that the trained frequentation of literature alone can bring, the thinking that attends social and political studies will not have the edge and force it should.[36]

Some of the critical writings of George Orwell can serve as additional (and, for the purposes of this essay, final) examples of how disciplined criticism and keen historical and social awareness can work together—of how, in fact, each is indispensable to the other—illustrating, in the end, how responsible criticism is established on the principle that "the judgments the literary critic is concerned with are judgments about life," to use Leavis's phraseology. A glance at any part of the four-volume edition of *The Collected Essays, Journalism and Letters of George Orwell* should remind one of the clarity and the honesty of Orwell's work as a critic and thinker. That he was no more than an "apologist for cynicism," "a reactionary rebel," "a peculiarly complex and ambiguous man," "a writer of brilliant perception, but also of ridiculous quirks and oddities," or that the effect of his entire thought "is an effect of paradox," or that he was a "nagger ... who extended discomfort into agony"—these are the recurrent and at present fashionable charges which diminish in their substance as one examines Orwell's writings on the relationships between the writer and society. In the early forties Orwell defined his approach to this subject in a concluding statement to his essay on Yeats: "... a writer's political and religious beliefs are not excrescences to be laughed away, but something that will leave their mark even on the smallest detail of his work."[37] Modern critics—particularly the generalists, rather than the purely literary specialists—have in fact come to be concerned precisely with the problems that Orwell underlines here.

Perhaps the best example of Orwell's social criticism is his essay on Rudyard Kipling (though his essays on Charles Dickens, Jonathan Swift, or P. G. Wodehouse, as well as his "Politics and the English Language," could as easily serve the purpose).[38] The occasion for this essay was the publication of *A Choice of Kipling's Verse* (1941), containing a long introduction by T. S. Eliot. In Kipling Orwell saw a writer who could stand toward H. G. Wells as a corrective: a writer, in other words, "who was not deaf to the evil forces of power and military 'glory.'" Unlike a Wells who is "too sane to understand the modern world," Orwell contends, "Kipling would have understood the appeal of Hitler, or for that matter of Stalin, whatever his attitude towards them might be."[39] Orwell made these observations in an earlier essay, "Wells, Hitler and the World State." The essay on Kipling, as a kind of follow-up, contains Orwell's evaluation of Kipling's work and of his reputation as a poet. In contrast to Eliot's "defensive" position on Kipling ("answering the shallow and familiar charge that Kipling is a 'Fascist'") Orwell begins by admitting that Kipling "*is* a jingo imperialist, he *is* morally insensitive and aesthetically disgusting." He nevertheless believes that one must go on to try to find out why Kipling "survives while the refined people who have sniggered at him seem to wear badly." The first clue to any understanding of Kipling, he shows, is that morally or politically Kipling "was *not* a Fascist." Rather, his outlook was pre-Fascist, the nineteenth-century imperialist outlook as opposed to the modern gangster outlook. Kipling, Orwell goes on to state, belonged to the period 1885–1902; and though the Great War and its aftermath embittered him, "he shows little sign of having learned anything from any event later than the Boer War." As a result, "all his confidence, his bouncing vulgar vitality, sprang out of limitations which no Fascist or near-Fascist shares."

By identifying himself with the official class, Kipling possessed "a sense of responsibility," or as Eliot writes: "... he was aiming to communicate the awareness of something in existence of which he felt that most people were very imperfectly aware. It was an awareness of grandeur, certainly, but it was much more an awareness of responsibility."[40] Orwell particularly singles out "the middle-class Left" for their aversion to Kipling:

> All left-wing parties in the highly industrialised countries are at bottom a sham, because they make it their business to fight against something which they do not really wish to destroy. They have internationalist aims, and at the same time they struggle to keep up a standard of life with which those aims are incompatible. We all live by robbing Asiatic coolies, and those of us who are "enlightened" all maintain that those coolies ought to be set free; but our standard of living, and hence our "enlightenment," demands that the robbery shall continue. A humanitarian is always a hypocrite, and Kipling's understanding of this is perhaps the central secret of his power to create telling phrases. It would be difficult to hit off the one-eyed pacifism of the English in fewer words than in the phrase, "making mock of uniforms that guard you while you sleep."

The indictment is both tough and jarring. No wonder E. M. Forster says that "no one can embrace Orwell's works who hopes for ease. Just as one is nestling against them, they prickle." Yet feelings and political implications notwithstanding, Orwell's words point to the essential nature of the task in judging Kipling's work and reputation from the standpoint of a poet's special "grasp of function" to convey, as Eliot felt, "a simple forceful statement rather than a musical pattern of emotional overtones." The middle-class Left, Orwell insists, sniggered at Kipling because they hated him for his sense of responsibility quite as much as for his cruelty and vulgarity. And an aesthetic judgment on Kipling's work must always return to "his sense of responsibility, which made it possible for him to have a world-view, even though it happened to be a false one."

Although one may disagree with, even snigger at, some of the social-political attitudes in Kipling's work, one cannot, Orwell argues, say that they are frivolous attitudes: "The fact is that Kipling, apart from his snack-bar wisdom and his gift for packing much cheap picturesqueness into a few words . . . is generally talking about things that are of urgent interest." His thought, if vulgar, is permanent, so that much of his poetry gives "pleasure to people who know what poetry means." Thus, Kipling can best be described "simply as a good bad poet": "He is as a poet what Harriet Beecher Stowe was as a novelist. And the mere existence of this kind, which is perceived by generation after generation to be vulgar and yet goes on being read, tells something about the age we live in." Orwell defines a good bad poem as "a graceful monument to the obvious," recording in memorable form "some emotion which very nearly every human being can share." As a good bad poet who was a Conservative identifying himself with the ruling power and not the opposition, Kipling, Orwell maintains, enjoyed the advantage of having "a certain grip of reality."

Of course, "Kipling sold out to the British governing class, not financially but emotionally," a fact that helped to warp his political judgment, "for the British ruling class were not what he imagined, and it led him into abysses of folly and snobbery." On the other hand, and most important of all considerations, Kipling "gained a corresponding advantage from having at least tried to imagine what action and responsibility are like." The business of the critic is to save the writer from misunderstanding and, in the case of Kipling, from the misrepresentation that can arise from the conscious or unconscious surrender to political theory or notion. The critic must rise above such a weakness if he is to be capable of judging the value of a writer, in the way that Orwell judges Kipling throughout his essay and, exemplarily, in this final judgment:

> It is a great thing in his favour that he is not witty, not "daring," has no wish to *épater les bourgeois*. He dealt largely in platitudes, and since we live in a world of platitudes, much of what he said sticks. Even his worst follies seem less shallow and less irritating than the "enlightened" utterances of the same period, such as Wilde's epigrams or the collection of cracker-mottoes at the end of *Man and Superman*.

IV

As the modern world has increasingly come to mean alienation-situation-history, to cite Sartre's triad, the aesthetic function of art has reflected change. Literature has become much more than mere "aesthetic experience," an "intransitive apprehension" of aesthetic object. To stay inside a self-contained work of art is deemed neither feasible nor desirable. The modern artist has come to see his role as one not of entertainment but rather of the expression of meaning, the communication of insight into some aspect of reality and human experience, the questioning and the redefining of life values. Indeed, Sartre has gone so far as to claim that the empire of meaning is prose. Leavis has gone on to claim that "it is the great novelists above all who give us our social history; compared with what is done in *their* work—their creative work—the histories of the professional social historian seem empty and unenlightening."[41] Such claims, coming from two writers profoundly dissimilar in critical temperament and approach, point to the extension of aesthetic boundaries in the twentieth century and to the recognition of art as a force for life.

Modern artists have more and more affirmed their place in the world in all its predicament and paradox. The kind of remoteness from the human spectacle that Ezra Pound admires in the following passage from a letter to James Joyce concerning *A Portrait of the Artist as a Young Man* is what has become less acceptable: "I think the book hard, perfect stuff. I doubt if you could have done it in the 'lap of luxury' or in the whirl of a metropolis with the attrition of endless small amusements and endless calls on one's time, and endless trivialities of enjoyment (or the reverse)."[42] Rather it is the artist's sense of responsibility and his commitment that inform his role in the world and in the creative process: "For me," asserts the Italian novelist and politician Ignazio Silone, "writing has not been, and never could be, except in a few favored moments of grace, a serene aesthetic enjoyment, but rather the painful and lonely continuation of a struggle."[43] That art must reveal this struggle and, in the end, help change the world instead of just reflecting it instances the kind of aesthetic transformation that has ripened in the twentieth century. (In some ways this transformation has accompanied the socialist view of life as an instrument of social influence in dynamic relation to the "meaning of life" and in terms of what Ernst Fischer speaks of as "a large vision of the future, a hopeful historical perspective."[44])

Not unexpectedly, academic literary study has also been undergoing sharp changes, with old, established, and essentially conservative attitudes being rejected or at least challenged. (Tate's contention that Pound's verbal sensibility is at the mercy of "Icarian self-indulgences of prejudice which are not checked by a total view to which they could be subordinated," but that, regardless, "Pound's language remains our particular concern," exemplifies a conservative literary attitude that is being challenged.[45]) Particularly in the United States the rise of "the dissenting academy," to borrow the title of a volume of essays edited by Theodore Roszak, is in fact everywhere apparent among scholars in the various humanistic disciplines; and everywhere in the "multiversity" protests are being heard against "mindless" specialization and irrelevant pedantry," against the "tradition of official conformity," against the "condition of entrenched social irrelevance" that has characterized American academics—to the extent that this condition, as Roszak suggests, can be "condemned as an act of criminal delinquency."[46] More than ever, protesting scholars and teachers and students are angry, their tempers radical. Genuine "humanist" social responsibility, "critical social relevance," it is claimed, has been sacrificed or betrayed. Thus, Louis Kampf in his essay "The Scandal of Literary Scholarship," which significantly (symptomatically?) is the first essay in *The Dissenting Academy*, bitterly attacks the proliferation of "criticism without real social relevance." The academic bureaucracy, commercial values (or the lack of any values), careerism ("making it"?), the pervasive absence of any sense of commitment in literary criticism are what have led to "this sellout," Kampf charges. "The study of literature must begin with an exploration of our social needs," he insists.[47]

Dissenting literary scholars, even if they constitute a small but militant minority, "a phalanx from the left," as it has been described, are asking questions that demand answers. ("Dangerous as it is," Kampf notes, "we may have to accept some student's honest feeling that, for example, Milton's use of pastoral in 'Lycidas' is a foolish irrelevance."[48]) Behind this dissatisfaction is a growing belief that the critical discipline itself must be "liberated," to apply here the widely used terminology of Herbert Marcuse, plenipotentiary theoretician of intellectuals of the New Left; that the critical faculty, as an energizing form of moral discrimination, must not be surrendered to "the forces of domination" in an advanced industrial society "organized as things and instrumentalities." Criticism, like the art it mediates, must contain "the rationality of negation" and be part of "the Great Refusal," to borrow Marcuse's terms once more.[49] What activist critics are often decrying is the habit of both scholar and teacher of dissociating literature from life and thought, or as Diana Trilling has well expressed the crux of the problem: "The teaching of modern subjects in our universities, especially literature, proceeds of course on some unadmitted (because inadmissible) assumption of a drastic discontinuity between art and life."[50]

Not to be overlooked, too, is the anti-Arnoldian thesis advanced elsewhere by one young critic. "The mainstream of modern critical interpretation of literature," this radical energumen states, "though it would claim for itself an objective, scientific basis, can be reasonably seen as the development of what is only implied in Arnold, the administration of literature." Arnold's politics and his culture, in effect, are not unrelated but are connected by ideas of centralization, control, and administration, precisely the elements that have made "literature seem unusable in fighting those tendencies in society."[51] Another critic asserts that there must be not only a complete repudiation of "reactionary formalism" but also a fearless radicalization of the teaching and criticism of literature by teachers and scholars who "are bringing some politics into the classrooms . . . [and] have even removed their ties."[52] And if one is to judge by the continuing protests, there appears to be little letup in the offing. Literary orthodoxy, in any event, is under pressure, even as literary philistinism is in retreat. Compartmentalization and departmentalization of literature is surely coming to an end. Thus, if some of the outcries and gestures of the radical critics often seem intemperate, or if some of their solutions (for example, the "radicalized curriculum") are shockingly simplistic, their pleas for a revaluation of both the teaching and the criticism of literature, freed at last from "administrative" control by academy and by academic coterie alike, is not without that desired quality of integrity that both dignifies the creative act and validates the critical function.

For some, no doubt, it is tempting to seek to discredit the views of the radical critics; and no doubt there are good reasons for opposing these critics. After all, removing one's tie does not exactly give to a critic any credentials or, more importantly, any critical insights into literature. Neither the radicalization nor the politicalization of literature and of literary studies is the answer. We need merely consider the happenings in the thirties to see some of the consequences of a radicalized literature: to see, that is, some of the aberrations that emerged in those years in the course of "literary class war." There were, to be sure, some valuable contributions to the study of literature in terms of its relevance to man and society, especially in a time of economic deprivation. Not a few men of letters dared to make what Arthur Koestler calls "the journey into communism." Granville Hicks illustrated what he called "the clarifying effect of revolutionary allegiance," and his book *The Great Tradition* (1933) was an outgrowth of the American experience. Although Hicks's interpretation of American literature was characterized, as it was charged, by a "mechanical Marxism," its thesis that revolutionary writing since the Civil War was at the heart of the American tradition could not be discounted.

But for Hicks and for other "comrades of the Pink decade" (the names of Koestler, André Gide, and Richard Wright come immediately to mind) the journey into communism was followed by a return from it. Communism became the "god that failed." In 1940, in a retrospective mood, as he looked back to the form and results of his "allegiance," Hicks concluded: "Politics is no game for a person whose attention is mostly directed elsewhere."[53] These are more than words of repudiation, as they again bring to the forefront the problem of the radicalization of literature as well as the subject of the relationship of the writer, both artist and critic, to the human condition in its social-political ramifications. And again questions of legitimacy and of function arise, as consequently do words of caution. For, above all, what literature must be saved from is the narrow critical and mechanical strictures that limit the value of Hicks's *The Great Tradition*. The "closed myth of concern" that Northrop Frye sees as shackling Marxist writing is one way of describing something that writers must avoid. The insistence on making literature relevant in terms of social needs or action can easily lead to a form of this closed myth. "Not only is there always a pressure within society to close its mythology," Frye reflects, "but the efforts to keep it open have to be strenuous, constant, delicate, unpopular, and above all largely negative."[54] (Frye here makes more meaningful Edwin Muir's fear that "when the natural man becomes political, there seem to be only two directions in which he can advance: towards Communism or towards Fascism."[55])

Thus we are returned inevitably to the cautionary note struck earlier and to the critical ambivalence that any discussion of literature and society arouses. And we are returned particularly to the fact that though the so-called administration of literature often leads to what is pedantic, the element of discipline in the forms of discrimination and resistance—resistance to the expedient and imperfect, to the quantitative as opposed to the qualitative (the closed myth of concern as opposed to the open myth)—cannot be ignored in the study of literature. The disciplinary element is a mainstay of civilization itself, as Yeats reminds us:

> A civilization is a struggle to keep self-control, and in this it is like some great tragic person, some Niobe who must display an almost superhuman will or the cry will not touch our sympathy. The loss of control over thought comes towards the end; first a sinking in upon the moral being, then the last surrender, the irrational cry, revelation—the scream of Juno's peacock.[56]

In this struggle for the survival of civilization the critical process remains fundamental. To be vigorous in the best cultural sense, this process must at the same time transcend categorizations of conservative versus modern, reactionary versus liberal. Indeed, perhaps what most harmed the proletarian critics of the thirties and, earlier, the critics of "the conservative mind" (Irving Babbitt and Paul Elmer More, for instance) was an inability to transcend the limitations of their social or classical presuppositions.

As modern writers have steadily disclosed their concern with social and political issues, the result of this concern has been the emergence of what is called a radical literature. Yet what critics must remember is that radical literature is not to be evaluated in terms of radical politics. "Maybe the lesson of the 30's," William Phillips points out, "is that radical politics has not been able to escape the dilemma of being distorted by power or left hanging without power, while literature to be radical need not—perhaps cannot—be tied to radical politics."[57] These words help to bring attention to problems that today require careful thought. For the critic the differences between radicalization and politicalization are always in need of being identified. One important service a critic can do today is to assess some of the radical—radical in the sense of the socially aware, relevant, exigent, and radical in terms of the modern temper—techniques and tendencies, such as language and meaning in literature. But this critical task has to be free from any imposition of a blatantly political attitude. The critic best fulfills his function by discerning the radical and the political without surrendering to either one or both elements. Criticism, at its best and most helpful, is an exercise in freedom; and though it can be radical, it cannot be political, cannot subscribe to a theory of politics.

By no means should these remarks imply that the responsible critic must be "scientific," "objective," or "scholarly." With respect to the function and the pursuit of criticism, these adjectives of criteria have long been misapplied, to the point of the irrelevance that activist writers are now castigating. "Criticism can never be a science: it is, in the first place, much too personal," D. H. Lawrence avers, "and in the second, it is concerned with values that science ignores."[58] Lawrence helps to define the limits of criticism even as he suggests its responsibilities and challenges. Modern literary studies—or, in a more technical sense, "English studies"—have not always been alert to Lawrence's words. In fact, though it is getting rather late in the century, English studies are just beginning to explore what literature has to say about man in his social and political lives. It has been taking a long time, it seems, to unload some of the old and stifling attitudes toward the relations between literature and society—attitudes that, in the grip of parochial specialisms, have been hostile to probing and dynamic relations between a writer and society.

Hence, the impatience shown in recent years by activist critics is not unwarranted, despite some of their shock tactics and rhetoric (the title of an essay by one such critic, "The Teaching of Literature in the Highest Academies of the Empire," instances just how self-deceiving the rhetoric becomes). It *is* unwarranted when it begins to tie criticism exclusively to the "desperate need of social change," at which point the critical task becomes as distorted as it has all along been constricted by administrators of literature. (Any glance at the essays found in *Publications of the Modern Language Association* will confirm this constriction.) It is probably with such facts in mind that one scholar and teacher, Richard Poirier, warns:

> English studies cannot be the body of English literature but it can be at one with its spirit: of struggling, of wrestling with words and meaning. Otherwise English studies may go one of two ways: it can shrink, hopefully in a manner as distinguished and health-giving as that which accompanied the retrenchment of Classics departments; or it can become distended by claims to a relevance merely topical.[59]

The spirit of "literary revolutionism" is powerful, and for the critic it poses special problems. More and more demands are being made that literary scholarship should be allied with political activism; that the critic play his appropriate political role in opposing some of the wrongs in society—"social mechanisms," "industrial capitalism," the "system of acculturation"; that the critic who judges literature should judge it in accordance with the ways in which literature is, or is not, attuned to pressing social issues and promulgates political action and social change; that, in short, the act of criticism, given the revolutionism of the age, must be seen within "social contexts" if it is in any way to be deemed useful. The critic is being asked to be more than what he is: to be, at the same time, political scientist, economist, religious thinker, philosopher, social historian, and theorist. Yet it is too easily forgotten that "the basic experience of everyone is the experience of human limitation."[60] Criticism, then, finds itself in something of a condition of crisis requiring redefinition of tasks, concepts, approaches. Obviously, the activist critics do not have a solution, their preoccupation with immediate and often local and temporary social needs (in literary contexts) being in itself symptomatic of party spirit and provincialism. In one major respect, nevertheless, this crisis has had the fortunate consequence of forcing critics and teachers of literature to review the nature of their work, their function, and to reappraise their ends and values. "Criticism," as William Hazlitt writes in his famous essay, "is an art that undergoes a great variety of changes, and aims at different objects at different times."

Today, when one thinks of the way in which the world is "turning and turning in the widening gyre," the need for critical perspective and for an understanding of man and of his society is itself critical. Imaginative literature as the book of life contains countless clues to this understanding. It can provide for us not only an understanding of what life is but also a vision of the world in which human experience achieves its quintessence, its concreteness and meaning as a whole. Toward the achievement of this understanding the critic can be of considerable service, service that reaches beyond mere literary code and that is both relevant and responsible. "The central problem of literary criticism," Theodore Spencer wrote back in the early and uncertain years of World War II, "is not only a problem of form, not only a problem of literary value—it is the problem of what it means to be a conscious being in a world that may darken to annihilation."[61] It is in the process of his criticism that the critic registers this greater consciousness, and he can—he must—do so above party feelings and ideologies. "His job, as the trustee of tradition," to quote Spencer again, "is to know as fully, as quantitatively, as possible what is included in human experience, and on the basis of that knowledge to be as dispassionate as he is aware."[62]

Admittedly a critic cannot always be a "trustee of tradition." But if he is in any way to begin to fulfill his function as a critic, he should be aware, supremely aware. For the modern critic this desideratum connotes, more than anything else and more than at any other time in history, an awareness of relationships that connect (and "connect," not "exist between," is the better term to use here) literature and other areas of human effort. It is true enough, as Richard Hoggart has warily said, that "if we forget the 'celebratory' or 'playful' element in literature we will sooner or later stop talking about literature and find ourselves talking about history or sociology or philosophy—and probably about bad history and bad sociology and bad philosophy." But just as importantly and even more relevantly, Hoggart does not fail to add that literature "has to do with language exploring human experience, in all its flux and complexity. It is therefore always in an active relation with its age; and some students of literature—many more students of literature than at present—ought to try to understand these relationships better."[63] This statement, it becomes indisputably evident in our world, affirms the positive, the legitimate, as well as the living and central connection that is there in the very words "the writer and society."

NOTES

1. New York, 1942, p. 106.
2. *Selected Essays* (New York, 1964), p. 117.
3. *What Is Art?*, trans. from the Russian by Aylmer Maude (New York, 1960), p. 142.
4. See Dedication to Christian Gauss, *Axel's Castle: A Study of the Imaginative Literature of 1870–1930* (New York, 1931).
5. "Ivan Turgéniew," *The North American Review*, April 1874, p. 350.
6. *Beyond Culture: Essays on Literature and Learning* (New York, 1968), p. 13.
7. Trans. from the German by Eden and Cedar Paul (Garden City, New York, 1957), pp. 1–2.
8. *Essays on Literature and Society* (Cambridge, Massachusetts, 1965), pp. 143–144.
9. *Ibid.*, p. 147.
10. *Ibid.*, p. 150.
11. See Robert Alter's essay on Norman Mailer in this book.
12. "The Idea of the Modern," *Literary Modernism*, Irving Howe, ed. (New York, 1967), p. 18.
13. *What Is Literature?*, trans. from the French by Bernard Frechtman (New York, 1965), pp. 61–62.
14. *The Betrayal of the Intellectuals*, trans. from the French by Richard Aldington (Boston, 1955), p. 32.

15. *Selected Essays*, pp. 13, 118.
16. G. Jean-Aubry, *Joseph Conrad: Life and Letters* (New York, 1927), pp. 301–302. Letter to John Galsworthy, dated 11 November 1901.
17. P. 231.
18. Jeremiah 1:10.
19. *The Collected Essays, Journalism and Letters of George Orwell*, Sonia Orwell and Ian Angus, eds. (New York, 1968), II, 41.
20. "What Happened in the 30's," *Commentary*, September 1962, p. 204.
21. *Writers on the Left: Episodes in American Literary Communism* (New York, 1961), p. 4. See also Walter B. Rideout, *The Radical Novel in the United States, 1900–1954: Some Interrelations of Literature and Society* (Cambridge, Massachusetts, 1956).
22. Oxford, England, 1968 [1938], pp. 198, 200.
23. Lionel C. Knights, *Drama and Society in the Age of Jonson* (New York, 1968 [1937]), p. 177.
24. New York, 1967, p. 33.
25. September 9, 1966, p. 326.
26. June 1, 1967, p. 21.
27. *The Times Literary Supplement*, September 15, 1966, p. 855.
28. See *Partisan Review*, Summer 1967, pp. 359–381.
29. Garden City, New York, 1953 [1944], pp. 212–213.
30. Lionel Trilling, *The Liberal Imagination* (Garden City, New York, 1953 [1950]), p. 179.
31. New York, 1947, p. 214.
32. *Ibid.*, p. 218.
33. *Ibid.*, pp. 216–217.
34. *Language and Silence: Essays on Language, Literature, and the Inhuman* (New York, 1967), pp. 322–323.
35. Albert Salomon, "Sociology and the Literary Artist," *Spiritual Problems in Contemporary Literature*, Stanley Romaine Hopper, ed. (New York, 1952), p. 24.
36. *The Common Pursuit* (London, 1952), p. 194.
37. *The Collected Essays, Journalism and Letters of George Orwell*, II, 276.
38. See *Ibid.*, II, 184–197.
39. *Ibid.*, II, 144–145.
40. "Rudyard Kipling," *On Poetry and Poets* (New York, 1961 [1957]), p. 284.
41. *Lectures in America* (New York, 1969), p. 7.
42. *Letters of James Joyce*, Richard Ellmann, ed. (New York, 1966), II, 364.
43. *The God That Failed*, Richard Crossman, ed. (New York, 1949), p. 81.
44. *The Necessity of Art: A Marxist Approach* (Baltimore, Maryland, 1963), p. 214.
45. *Ezra Pound: Perspectives. Essays in Honor of His Eightieth Birthday*, Noel Stock, ed. (Chicago, 1965), pp. 87, 89.
46. See Theodore Roszak's Introduction, "On Academic Delinquency," in *The Dissenting Academy* (New York, 1968), pp. 36, 12, 13.
47. *Ibid.*, p. 59.
48. *Ibid.*, p. 58.
49. See Herbert Marcuse, *One-Dimensional Man: Studies in the Ideology of Advanced Industrial Society* (Boston, 1966 [1964]).
50. "On the Steps of Low Library. Liberalism and the Revolution of the Young," *Commentary* (November 1968), p. 36.

51. James F. Goldberg, " 'Culture' and 'Anarchy' and the Present Time," *The Kenyon Review*, XXXI (1969), 607.

52. Bruce Franklin, "The Teaching of Literature in the Highest Academies of the Empire," *College English* (March 1970), p. 557.

53. "The Failure of Left Criticism," *The New Republic*, September 9, 1940, p. 346.

54. "The Critical Path: An Essay on the Social Context of Literary Criticism," *Daedalus*, Spring 1970, p. 342.

55. *Essays on Literature and Society*, p. 158.

56. Book V of *A Vision*, dated February 1925.

57. "What Happened in the 30's," *Commentary*, September 1962, p. 212.

58. *Phoenix: The Posthumous Papers of D. H. Lawrence*, Edward D. McDonald, ed. (London, 1936), p. 539.

59. "What Is English Studies, and If You Know What That Is, What Is English Literature?" *Partisan Review*, XXXVII (1970), 58.

60. *Flannery O'Connor. Mystery and Manners*, Sally and Robert Fitzgerald, eds. (New York, 1969), p. 131.

61. "The Central Problem in Literary Criticism," *College English*, IV (1942), 163.

62. *Theodore Spencer: Selected Essays*, Alan C. Purves, ed. (New Brunswick, New Jersey, 1966), pp. 8–9.

63. *Speaking to Each Other*, Vol. II: *About Literature* (New York, 1970), p. 259.

The opinion that art should have nothing to do with politics is itself a political attitude.

GEORGE ORWELL

PART I

BRITISH

H. G. WELLS
(1866-1946)

by Bernard Bergonzi

As AN EAGER and impoverished science student in the 1880's, H. G. Wells had declared himself a socialist, even though he was not at all sure what being a socialist meant. Nor, indeed, were most other English socialists, beyond a general agreement on the undesirability of the profit motive. In his semiautobiographical novel *Love and Mr. Lewisham* Wells conveyed the hopeful atmosphere of those days, which he referred to again in his *Experiment in Autobiography*:

> Wearing our red ties to give zest to our frayed and shabby cos-
> tumes we went great distances through the gas-lit winter streets
> of London and by the sulphurous Underground Railway, to
> hear and criticize and cheer and believe in William Morris, the
> Webbs, Bernard Shaw, Hubert Bland, Graham Wallas and all
> the rest of them, who were to lead us to that millennial world.

Yet though the young Wells responded enthusiastically to the ideas that he heard expounded on these occasions, his iconoclastic and critical intelligence was never able to swallow them whole. But it was at such meetings that Wells first became interested in the possibility of a "millennial world," a topic that was to dominate his later literary career. "World" was a favorite word of Wells's—it occurs in the titles of many of his books—and it was part of his achievement that he was able from the beginning to think in the all-embracing, global terms that have only lately become a common part of our intellectual intercourse.

3

In his early days as a creative writer Wells entertained global visions that were apocalyptic rather than millennial. He established his reputation in the 1890's as a writer of scientific romances, which were both brilliantly entertaining narratives and oblique, mythic reflections of the dilemmas and perturbations of the time. In the first of them, *The Time Machine* (1895), Wells looks far into the future, to the year 802701, when the elements of the late-nineteenth-century class struggle have become incorporated into the evolutionary development of mankind. Humanity has divided itself into the Eloi, who are frail, aesthetic, childlike creatures, and the Morlocks, who are stunted and brutish, living in underground machine shops, and who feed upon the Eloi, whom they breed like cattle. The vivid but repulsive presentation of the Morlocks is the first appearance in Wells's writing of a recurring element: the conviction that the proletariat was inherently barbarous and hateful. Toward the end of *The Time Machine* the time-traveler moves forward many millions of years to witness the extinction of all life upon a dying planet. In *The War of the Worlds* (1898) Wells showed, with great imaginative relish, the destruction of late-Victorian bourgeois society by Martian invaders. There is a similarly apocalyptic note in the short stories that Wells published in the nineties; in one of the finest of them, "The Star," he describes the global havoc that ensues when a star passes close to the earth and plunges into the sun. On a smaller scale, *When the Sleeper Wakes* (1899) is a projection into the future of the urban brutality and chaos, the accumulative monopoly of capitalism, and the violent class struggles of late-Victorian England or America. It also reflects Wells's interest in the Nietzschean concept of the *Übermensch* that was becoming fashionable in England in the nineties, and which he had already touched on in the most horrifying of all his scientific romances, *The Island of Dr. Moreau* (1896). A version of the Superman, though sociologically cut down to size and dedicated to useful work as a member of a ruling elite, occurs throughout Wells's fiction and speculative writings in the twentieth century.

In the scientific romances, which I have discussed in detail in *The Early H. G. Wells* (Manchester and Toronto, 1961), we see some of the major facets of Wells's imagination: in particular, his ability to think and feel in large-scale spatial and temporal terms, and his intense curiosity about the future state of the world. There is also a fascination with images of destruction and particularly of fire (V. S. Pritchett has remarked on the way in which fires occur in practically all Wells's novels). In these novels and stories we see Wells contemplating his environment, speculating on the possibilities that could descend upon it, and imaginatively transforming it. But the author's will is not exercised upon his material: Wells is content to reflect on the world as it is and might become, without attempting to make projections about what it should become. The tone throughout is cool and detached, and this detachment was an important element in the early development of Wells's literary persona. In the opening paragraph of *The War of the Worlds* the Martians observe the futile and pretentious activity of late-Victorian society with the cool gaze of a scientific observer looking at a specimen under a microscope. It was rather in this spirit that Wells himself dwelt on the future discomfort—or even disappearance—of humanity. In his early fiction Wells is admittedly concerned with humanity in the mass rather than with individuals, although Griffin, the Invisible Man, is presented as an interestingly realized character.

In Wells's first serious attempt at a realistic novel, *Love and Mr. Lewisham* (1900), the detachment is preserved in a way that partly adheres to the canons of "scientific" naturalism but which is also combined, a little uneasily, with an affectionate and even sentimental regard for the hero, who so clearly represents the genteel failure that Wells himself, minus his particular genius and drive, might so easily have become. Wells's own social origins provide further reasons for his stance of observant detachment: Springing from the insecure lowest stratum of English middle-class life, he hated and feared the workers—his socialism was always elitist rather than populist—but at the same time he did not have the advantages of a conventional upper-middle-class background and education like most English men of letters. There was no class he could readily identify with, though after 1900 his striking literary success meant that he could enter the English establishment on his own terms. In fact, Wells's need to discover a class or group that he could identify with seems to have expressed itself in the frequently updated versions of a ruling elite that recur throughout his writings. They are variously described as scientists, teachers, trained administrators, practical idealists, and clearheaded idea-men with the ability to make decisions. They first occur as the samurai of *A Modern Utopia* (1905), and in later versions they appear as the progressive businessmen of *The World of William Clissold* and the airmen of *The Shape of Things to Come*. But in all versions they possess essentially the same attributes: They are highly intelligent men and women who have risen by their own abilities (meritocrats, to use a later terminology); they are courageous, energetic, and far-sighted. In short, they are idealized versions of what Wells was himself, being free from the inherited privileges and mental limitations of the upper and upper-middle classes and equally removed from what Wells regarded as the mental poverty and bloody-mindedness of the working class. In his later life Wells was constantly trying to detect the possible elements of such an elite in the world around him, and he claimed to have discovered it variously in the Russian Communist party and Franklin Roosevelt's Brain Trust.

During the opening phase of his literary career he remained in an ill-defined way a socialist, but there is little trace of direct political conviction in his writings of the 1890's. If anything, the combination of a keen but detached interest in disaster and a vigorous stylistic energy would suggest a conservative rather than a radical cast of mind. Even where Wells writes realistically about the common lot of suffering humanity, as in *Love and Mr. Lewisham,* he is more concerned with the pathetic or dramatic possibilities of his material than with protesting against the intolerable. With a writer of more ordinary gifts or less expansive temperament this limited but effective literary approach might have continued indefinitely. But although Wells was a fiction writer of genius, he was, in his own estimation of himself, a great many other things, too. By about 1900 other aspects of his personality had begun to emerge: notably those of the journalist and the sociological speculator and even the preacher.

During the next ten years the artist in Wells existed in uneasy tension with these other personas and in the end was defeated; in a famous letter to Henry James, written in 1915, Wells remarked, "I had rather be called a journalist than an artist—that is the essence of it." With these new aspects of his literary personality a sense of direction appears in Wells's writing: He projects images of the future which are not merely exciting or terrifying but which contain hopefully constructive suggestions about improving the human condition. Wells, who began as a bold and inventive drafter of antiutopias, now turned to positive utopias. The cool pessimism of the nineties was displaced by a reasoned faith in the possibility (and in some moods, the certainty) of human betterment. The reasons for this shift of attitude on Wells's part at the end of the 1890's are not at all clear, but it seems likely that his restless speculative intellect did not find enough outlet in the production of "pure" fiction and was increasingly impelled to take over from the contemplative imagination. Again, the attainment of an increasing degree of personal success and even prosperity from his writing might have given Wells a greater sense of security and correspondingly less motive to subject the existing social order to ingenious forms of symbolic destruction.

For whatever reason, Wells became more systematic and discursive in his descriptions of the future, and the first result of this new approach was *Anticipations,* published in 1901, which Samuel Hynes has described in *The Edwardian Turn of Mind* (Princeton, 1968) in these words:

> Coming as it did just after the turn of a new century, it appealed to a natural popular curiosity about what this twentieth century was going to be like. Wells offered a vivid, simplified, credible image of the future, based apparently on the firm

authority of scientific principles, but thoughtfully sparing readers the dull details of science—the evidence, the logic, and the proofs. The tone of the book is the confident, categorical tone of a classroom lecturer, enlivened with imagined scenes of future wars in the style of Wells's romances.

The confident tone is very persuasive, but the book is essentially a compilation of bold guesses about the future. Wells was more right about technological than political developments. He foresaw trench warfare and tanks but was remarkably cautious about flying; he said no more than that a successful airplane might well have flown by 1950! However, Wells shrewdly foresaw that the improvement of methods of transportation would mean that the future city would consist of widely scattered low-density dwellings (like present-day Los Angeles) rather than the dense, roofed-in metropolis that he had described in *When the Sleeper Wakes*.

Beatrice Webb was very impressed with *Anticipations* while regretting Wells's lack of detailed knowledge of social organization and invited him to join the Fabians. Wells accepted; he was very willing to regard the Fabian Society as an elite dedicated to the socialist reconstruction of society. But the mutual admiration did not last long; Wells found himself temperamentally at odds with the Webbs, however much he might have agreed in a purely intellectual way with their approach. The Webbs were diligent and conscientious and essentially bureaucratic; they had no sympathy with Wells's speculative, high-flying, imaginative cast of mind. Relations soon deteriorated, although Wells remained in the Fabian Society for several years and tried to reshape it in accordance with his own ideas. When faced with a dedicated practitioner of "pure" literature like Henry James, Wells impatiently preferred to regard himself as a journalist; but, on the other hand, when faced with a statistically minded sociologist like Beatrice Webb, he could not disguise the fact that he was, in essence, an imaginative writer of idiosyncratic temperament, however much he, too, tried to be a sociologist. In the end, Wells broke with the Webbs, and in 1911 he pilloried them in *The New Machiavelli* as Altiora and Oscar Bailey: There is a long and absorbing account of the whole tragicomic episode in Mr. Hynes's book.

In 1905 Wells published *A Modern Utopia*, his first attempt to combine speculation about the future with a fairly coherent fictional framework. The book was immensely popular and influential: Henry James was delighted by it, and Beatrice Webb at least approved to the extent of assuming that the samurai showed how far Wells had absorbed her ideas. Wells took a good deal of trouble over the form of *A Modern Utopia*, saying that he aimed at a "sort of shot-silk texture between philosophical discussion on the one hand and imaginative narration on the other." At the beginning of the book the narrator and his companion, a rather gloomy and difficult person who is referred to as the "botanist," are on a walking tour in the Alps: As a result of some cosmic conjuring trick, they are transported to the corresponding spot on another planet, which is physically identical with our own, but where life and its environment have been utterly changed for the better by advanced technology and improved social organization. An English critic, David Lodge, has summed up the limitations of A Modern Utopia as they appear to the present-day reader:

> Time has been cruel to A Modern Utopia. It would be difficult to arouse any enthusiasm for this vision of the good life today. Most of the things against which the current wave of youthful protest is directed in the Western world are to be found hopefully foreshadowed in Wells' Utopia: an examination-selected meritocracy, mixed economy, paternalistic state welfare, bureaucratic control over personal freedom, privilege based on productivity but controlled by fiscal means, minority participation in government, academic monopoly over culture, and a generally low-keyed, rather conformist contentment regarded as the desirable norm in behaviour. Wells' Utopia is a class society in which the classes are distinguished not by breeding or by cash, but by intelligence and vocational aptitude, with a decent middle-class standard of living available to all. In a sense it was a generous attempt on Wells' part to imagine a social structure which would make available to everyone the kind of success and happiness he had personally achieved in the teeth of great disadvantages ["Utopia and Criticism," Encounter, April 1969].

There are, perhaps, elements of Fabian thinking in A Modern Utopia, but as Samuel Hynes has remarked, "the Webbs worked for precise and particular reforms within the existing social fabric, whereas A Modern Utopia abandons the present for a spacious, self-indulgent daydream." All utopias are, in one sense, daydreams; but to say as much is not to dismiss their utility. As Karl Mannheim has shown in Ideology and Utopia, one function of "utopian" thinking is to present the less fortunate members of a society with images of transcendence, with goals which can be politically striven for. Yet Mr. Hynes is right in underlining the hierarchical and undemocratic nature of Wells's ideal society: Below the "voluntary nobility" of the samurai—the dedicated, ascetic elite who actually run the country—there exist four fixed classes. Mr. Hynes describes them in these words:

> The Poetic, based on creative imagination; the Kinetic, based on unimaginative intelligence; the Dull, based on lack of intelli-

gence; and the Base, a class containing all those who lack moral sense. Wells' profoundly anti-democratic turn of mind reveals itself here not only in the *fact* of this class division, but also in the very language he used—the Dull and the Base classes.

A *Modern Utopia* sets out most of the elements that were to become an abiding part of Wells's political thinking. As well as the elitist conception of administration, it demonstrates his conviction that the application of really rational, and particularly scientific, thinking to social problems would inevitably cause them to disappear. For Wells the scientific spirit was always the embodiment of true wisdom: Only at the end of his life, after Hiroshima, did he have any doubts about this axiom, and by then the only alternative was flat despair. Wells was more interested in organization than in ideology, and his lifelong quarrel with Marxism arose from the Marxists' refusal to plan actively for the utopian society and to project what Wells called a "competent receiver" for the new social forms (the Marxist reliance on the working class as the prime agent of revolutionary change was an even more fundamental reason for his opposition).

Wells had little real interest in how the necessary changes in society would come about. Sometimes, in his more imaginatively excited moods, he would envisage a traditional form of violent insurrection; occasionally, as in his novel *In the Days of the Comet* (1906), social change would follow on an accidental transformation of the physical environment, but usually it would come with the inevitable onward march of evolution. In the twenties Wells imagined a new society being established by what he called the Open Conspiracy, in which the social forms of the new order would be established alongside those of the old, gradually making the latter obsolete. All of this was very removed from the meticulous, middle-range planning that the Fabians favored. At the same time, Wells had no grasp of the Marxist contention that the forms of consciousness are dependent on the patterns of ownership of the forces of production—and still less of the later and subtler applications of this approach in terms of the sociology of knowledge. Wells was happy to remain the quintessential bourgeois that Lenin described him as being. For Wells, the ideal society was some form of managerial capitalism, with a sizable degree of state intervention, large-scale planning, and a strong emphasis on science and technology. This is precisely the state of affairs that exists in most of the western world at the present time, and although it has made the lot of the populace physically easier than ever before, it has not radically diminished discontent. The long-term response to *A Modern Utopia* is Marcuse's *One-Dimensional Man*.

The truth is that Wells was not genuinely interested in politics in the strict sense, which is concerned with the reconcilement of legitimate but opposed claims, with balancing the needs of society with those of the individual and coping with all the obstacles to progress that arise from material shortages or human perversity. Wells's utopia is apolitical or postpolitical: It assumes that all opposed claims have been brought into harmony and concentrates on describing the technologically efficient and mildly hedonistic society that has come into being. (There is, admittedly, an aesthetic rebel against the utopian order in *A Modern Utopia*, but he is treated as an amiable fool.) To some extent, this partial vision is inherent in the literary form Wells adopted. In his realistic fiction he understood very well the gritty recalcitrance and unpredictability of human beings. There is a significant passage in the opening chapter of *A Modern Utopia* in which the narrator reflects on the artistic limitations of the utopian mode; it shows Wells's awareness of the tension between the artist and the prophet and indicates the way in which a literary form can have political implications:

> There must always be a certain effect of hardness and thinness about Utopian speculations. Their common fault is to be comprehensively jejune. That which is the blood and warmth and reality of life is largely absent; there are no individualities, but only generalised people. In almost every Utopia—except, perhaps, Morris's *News from Nowhere*—one sees handsome but characterless buildings, symmetrical and perfect cultivations, and a multitude of people, healthy, happy, beautifully dressed, but without any personal distinction whatever. . . . It is a disadvantage that has to be accepted. Whatever institution has existed or exists, however irrational, however preposterous, has by virtue of its contact with individualities, an effect of realness and rightness no untried thing may share. It has ripened, it has been christened with blood, it has been stained and mellowed by handling, it has been rounded and dented to the softened contours that we associate with life; it has been salted, maybe, in a brine of tears. But the thing that is merely proposed, the thing that is merely suggested, however rational, however necessary, seems strange and inhuman in its clear, hard, uncompromising lines, its unqualified angles and surfaces.

This is an eloquent statement of the way in which traditional literature, and particularly the novel as opposed to the utopian blueprint, speaks to the conservative rather than to the innovating aspects of the human imagination. One recalls Hyacinth Robinson's shattering realization, in Henry James's *The Princess Casamassima*, that the bloody history of civilization is interwoven with much magnificence. For some years after *A Modern Utopia* Wells continued to write novels that would embody both the confusions and the "blood and warmth and reality" of

life itself. The characteristically Wellsian persona of the little man who is
a victim of external circumstance in the conventional naturalistic manner,
but who ebulliently and comically refuses to surrender to fate, is splendidly visible in *Kipps* (1905) and *The History of Mr. Polly* (1910): In
both books, the hero, after many vicissitudes and humiliations, ends up in
semipastoral seclusion from the cruel demands of an unjust and inefficient social order, which is left to continue its progress undeflected. *Mr.
Polly* is a pure gem of Dickensian comedy and Wells's finest achievement
in the realistic mode, just as *The Time Machine* is his finest achievement
in the field of fantasy. But it is a small-scale creation and rather less
interesting than Wells's major attempt at a substantial panoramic novel
in the Victorian manner, *Tono-Bungay* (1909). This is an imperfect but
immensely vital book, which combines the existing strands of Wells's literary interests: science fiction, social comedy, the "discussion" of human
problems. Among other things, it is an incisive anatomy of late-Victorian
and Edwardian society, with a remarkable degree of imaginative unity.

The difficulty of combining the collective vision of utopian fiction with
the interest in individual character of the true novel continued to preoc-
cupy Wells, and in one of his later utopian books, *Men Like Gods*
(1923), he made a vigorous attempt to provide interesting characters.
But in *A Modern Utopia* the stress, as Wells was uncomfortably aware,
was very much on the collective, and the problems of the individual are
rather airily dismissed. This, at least, is the impression one gets in the
treatment of the "botanist," whom the narrator chides for complaining
bitterly about the unhappy love affair he is involved in back on earth
instead of appreciating the marvels that surround him. Love, as Wells
was well aware, is not easily reconciled with dreams of a tidy utopian
order. Wells's imagination was deeply divided on this point, and the
other side of the picture is seen in his realistic novels of the next few
years. To point the contrast, I should like to refer not to the relatively
successful and well-known novels I have just mentioned but to *The New
Machiavelli* (1911), which was a systematic attempt to write a political
novel in the narrow sense—that is to say, in the manner of Anthony Trollope's Palliser sequence—and which shows quite clearly the vulnerability
of large schemes for collective improvement when faced with the irrational desires of the individual.

Considered in purely literary terms, *The New Machiavelli* is not a particularly good novel, and the comparison with Trollope's political novels
can only be damaging to Wells. But it has some merits, both as a story
and as a source of insights into the embittered political climate of England at the end of Edward's reign. For Wells, it marked the close of his
Fabian phase, and it has an interesting antithetical relationship with *A
Modern Utopia*. Samuel Hynes, as I have remarked, described the earlier

book as "a spacious, self-indulgent daydream," and he uses a similar phrase about *The New Machiavelli* in his succinct summary of that novel:

> The novel is in fact a fictionalized account of Wells' Edwardian political life, improved and elevated, as one improves an unsat-isfactory conversation after the fact; it is, as so many of Wells' topical novels are, a kind of daydream version of actuality. It has for its hero one of Wells' alter egos, a poor boy called Rich-ard Remington, out of a Kentish town, who enters Parliament as a Liberal, revolutionizes British politics with a campaign for the Endowment of Motherhood (the slogan that sweeps the nation is "Love and Fine Thinking"!), switches parties, and finally throws his career away to go off with the woman he loves.

All Wells's novels, one should add, contain elements of fantasy or day-dream, and their heroes are recognizable projections of their author at different stages of his life. Nevertheless, in the best of his realistic fiction the fantasy is subjected to a genuine imaginative transformation. This is not so in *The New Machiavelli*, and for that reason Wells's dominant preoccupations loom much more palpably through the narrative. The book has some effective moments. The waspish caricature of the Webbs, with which Wells closed his account with the Fabians, is entertainingly done. And there is a vivid episode at a dinner party, where a fire breaks out in an upper part of the house, while the conversation round the table imperturbably continues, reflecting on the crimes committed by the rep-resentatives of the so-called civilized western nations during the Boxer Rising in Peking. While efforts are going on upstairs to put out the fire, one of the diners remarks on the flimsiness of civilization: "a mere thin net of habits and associations." Here Wells momentarily anticipates the symbolic insight of George Bernard Shaw's *Heartbreak House*.

In most of the book, though, Wells—or his hero—is not concerned with apocalyptic possibilities but with the perennial problem of the large-scale ordering and transformation of society. Remington, having asso-ciated first with the socialists, in both their working-class and their Fabian variety, and then with the Liberals, finds both groups insufferably small-minded and lacking in vision. Although a Liberal M.P., he turns to the Conservatives and the upholders of the imperialist ideal in the hope that here, at last, he might find the largeness of thought that he had always desired. Remington describes the attraction for him of the imperi-alist movement while admitting the evils that have so far been associated with it:

> But a big child is permitted big mischief, and my mind was now continually returning to the persuasion that after all in some

development of the idea of Imperial patriotism might be found that wide, rough, politically acceptable expression of a constructive dream capable of sustaining a great educational and philosophical movement such as no formula of Liberalism supplied. The fact that it readily took vulgar forms only witnessed to its strong popular appeal. Mixed in with the noisiness and humbug of the movement there appeared a real regard for social efficiency, a real spirit of animation and enterprise.

This is Remington talking and not Wells, but the emphases are very familiar: Ideology is far less important than largeness of vision and energy and efficiency. After this passage, Remington refers approvingly to the Boy Scout movement, which he seems to see as something like a Samurai League of Youth. But in the end, all Remington's vision and attempts at a large-scale transformation of society come to nothing. His love for Isabel Rivers proves too strong: He leaves his wife and parliamentary career and settles with his mistress in Italy, where he devotes himself to writing his autobiography, like Machiavelli in an earlier exile. In *The New Machiavelli* the intractable realities of individual human life triumph over utopian aspirations: It is as though the unhappy botanist of *A Modern Utopia*, having been scoldingly hushed up by the narrator of that book, is finally permitted to show that he, too, has a case, and an embarrassingly strong one.

During the Edwardian decade Wells was active both as a straightforward novelist and as a would-be sociological analyst and speculator. Although he was aware of the opposition between the two roles, he contrived with some success to keep them in balance. During those years his involvement with the Fabians took him closer to practical politics than ever again (except for a brief and unfruitful flirtation with the Labour party in the early twenties). Mr. Hynes is undoubtedly right to regret the waste of an imaginative writer's time and effort that this activity meant for Wells. Nevertheless, it is a tribute to Wells's energy and powers of concentration that he was still able to produce works of high literary merit, like *Kipps, The War in the Air, Tono-Bungay,* and *The History of Mr. Polly.* From the beginning Wells had taken the art of fiction with a good deal of seriousness, and in these novels the creative imagination was allowed to go on its autonomous way. But after 1910 the impulse to discuss and explain took over from the desire to contemplate and explore. In 1915 came the symbolic rift with his old friend Henry James and his rejection of the title of "artist."

For thirty more years Wells continued to write works which read more or less like novels but are essentially arguments or tracts. Not all of them are devoid of interest: It would be surprising if they were, coming from such a mind, and occasionally there are flickers of the old Wellsian imagination. For most of this time, Wells had nothing really new to say, and although he wrote copiously, he was doing no more than enlarge on and refurbish the arguments that had taken possession of his mind during the first decade of this century. As George Orwell showed in his sharp but just essay "Wells, Hitler and the World State," written during World War II, Wells was quite unable to grasp the true meaning of modern totalitarianism. Orwell remarked that many of Wells's ideas had been embodied in Nazi Germany: "The order, the planning, the State encouragement of science, the steel, the concrete, the aeroplanes, are all there, but in the service of ideas appropriate to the Stone Age." In his later redraftings of the ordered future Wells became increasingly willful and mechanical and less and less inclined to heed the warning that the artist in him had inserted in the first chapter of A Modern Utopia: that all such projections are liable to founder on a basic sense of unreality. Only in the Experiment in Autobiography (1934), the most impressive work of Wells's later years, does he rise again to his full stature as a writer, in a remarkable book that combines the novelist's narrative gifts and interest in people with the teacher-prophet's large-scale, expository interest in ideas.

E. M. FORSTER
(1879-1970)

by J. K. Johnstone

In *Howards End* (1910), E. M. Forster's fourth novel, Margaret Schlegel, starting from the house in Hertfordshire from which the novel takes its name, attempts intuitively to "realize" England. "She failed—visions do not come when we try, though they may come through trying. But an unexpected love of the island awoke in her, connecting on this side with the joys of the flesh, on that with the inconceivable."[1] This passage, with its realization of the likelihood of failure, its religious overtones, and its emphasis upon both the spiritual and the physical experience of the individual, on moments of intense perception, and on a love of England, especially the countryside of England, is a convenient place from which to begin an exploration of Forster's politics.

During most of his childhood, Forster lived with his widowed mother in the house near Stevenage, Hertfordshire, that is the original of Howards End. It gave him, he says in his biography of his great-aunt, Marianne Thornton, "a slant upon society and history . . . a middle-class slant, atavistic, derived from the Thorntons . . . corrected by contact with friends who have never had a home in the Thornton sense, and do not want one."[2] The Thorntons were wealthy bankers, evangelical in religion, close friends of Hannah More, the Macaulays, the Wilberforces, and other members of the "Clapham Sect." Their Clapham home, Battersea Rise, built early in the eighteenth century, was bought by Forster's great-grandfather in 1792 and enlarged. It remained at the center of the affections of his children and grandchildren throughout the nineteenth century. From the eldest child, Marianne, Forster received a legacy of eight thousand pounds, which enabled him to go to Cambridge University, to travel, and to write. From his Thornton ancestors generally, he received a more complex heritage. Part of it, as he has told us, was love of a home, of "the precious distillation of the years," as he puts it in *Howards End*,[3] in a place which has known a family's experience; but this feeling, if inherited from the Thorntons, was derived chiefly from Forster's childhood home and from his later home at Abinger Hammer, Surrey. Other aspects of Forster's Thornton inheritance may be represented by Battersea Rise itself, built during the Enlightenment, extended during the French Revolution, occupied by sound businessmen, a center of serious Protestant religion and of effective paternalistic philanthropy; or by Hannah More, the much respected older friend, confidante, and adviser of Marianne Thornton. Hannah More, whose name is possibly memorialized in the similar name of Mrs. Moore of Forster's *A Passage to India*, had known and been admired by Dr. Johnson, David Garrick, and Sir Joshua Reynolds, and later, Zachary Macaulay and William Wilberforce. After writing plays that were influenced by pastoral and operatic traditions of the eighteenth century, she produced works of moral and religious instruction, including the poem *Slavery* (1788). Her philanthropy was directed toward the education of the children of Somerset laborers.

Business sense, a respect for money and property, and a serious conception of personal responsibility, wit, skepticism, and sensibility characterize Forster's moral and social outlook and, of course, his novels. The creator of the Wilcoxes of *Howards End* could himself have been a successful businessman had he so chosen. He did not so choose, partly because he found more interesting and difficult things to do (it is easier, he asserts in *Howards End*, to see segments of life steadily, as he thinks the businessman does, than to see life whole), partly because his eight thousand pounds made choice easier for him. Like Margaret Schlegel, he is uneasily aware of his debt to businessmen both for his capital and for the interest it earns him. He fair-mindedly admits that communism "might mean a new order where younger people could be happy and the head and the heart have a chance to grow," though he fears that it would "destroy all I care for and could only be reached through violence."[4] When he visits the Soviet Pavilion at the Paris Exhibition of 1937, he finds "a realm which is earnest, cheerful, instructive, constructive and consistent, but which has had to blunt some of the vagrant sensibilities of mankind and is consequently not wholly alive."[5] It was characteristic of his love of the countryside and of property that when he received a good check from the American sale of *A Passage to India*, he bought a wood. Then he criticizes, whimsically but pointedly, the instincts that its possession awakens in him.[6]

Forster's affection for the English countryside grew from his childhood home at Stevenage, where he lived from the age of four to fourteen, and was developed by his attachment to the neighborhood of his next home, at Abinger Hammer; by his years at the university, county, and market town of Cambridge, with its river and Backs that bring the countryside to the town and the colleges; and by his vacations in England. It is associated particularly with Hertfordshire, Cambridgeshire, Wiltshire, and the Downs.

Myths of the Golden Age may have a close association with poignant memories of a happy childhood. In this, as in other respects, Forster has a good deal in common with William Wordsworth. At Stevenage he played with the farmer's boy who lived through the hedge, with Ansell, a garden boy who was given Wednesday afternoons off by Forster's mother to play with her son, and with Emma, a rather simple maid, who was dismissed because she hit Forster after he hit her.

Spontaneity, in spite of this instance of its repression, was apparently not absent at Stevenage, and Forster associates it particularly with his mother's family, the Whichelos. In some respects, in the relative poverty and confusion of their affairs, they were a sorry contrast to the Thorntons, but they were evidently preeminent in Forster's affections in his childhood: "How I adored my grandmother!—we played for hours together. In later life I became high-minded and critical, but we remained friends, and it is with her—with them [the Whichelos]—that my heart lies."[7] His sympathy for the impulsive widow Lilia Herriton, of *Where Angels Fear to Tread*, as her husband's family tries to control her may owe something to his understanding of some of his mother's differences with the Thorntons or, more particularly, to the experience, when she wished to remarry against the Thorntons' wishes, of his mother's friend Maimie Synnot, the widow of Marianne Thornton's favorite nephew. In her youth Maimie, like Lilia, was "vague and immature, and a hanger-on of her husband's relatives, to be loved, but to be laughed at, and ordered about."[8]

Forster looks back upon his childhood at Stevenage with an attachment intensified, one suspects, by the death of his father when Forster was nine months old, by the contrast between the fortunes of his mother and the Thorntons, and by his dislike of Tonbridge, the public school he attended from the age of fourteen to seventeen. "The truth is that she and I had fallen in love with our Hertfordshire home and did not want to leave it. . . . From the time I entered the house at the age of four . . . I took it to my heart and hoped, as Marianne had of Battersea Rise, that I should live and die there. We were out of it in ten years."[9] These lines, from *Marianne Thornton*, were written when Forster was in his seventies. The world of Ansell and Emma seemed to him better than the great

world. Ansell's name is given to the wisest and most trustworthy character in *The Longest Journey*. The house at Stevenage, with its sheltering
wych elm, becomes the central setting and the most significant image of
Howards End, imbued by Forster with the recollected emotions of those
childhood years. A romantic vision of innocent happiness haunts several
of Forster's essays and stories: The essays "Happiness!" and "A Letter to
Madan Blanchard" fancifully praise those who have chosen to live in
remote places to escape civilization; in the story "Other Kingdom" a girl
turns into a tree to escape a fiancé who is a bully; the narrator of "The
Other Side of the Hedge" finds that progress is an illusion and Eden is
through the hedge at the side of a road that appears to be straight but in
fact doubles on itself. The theme of dispossession appears frequently in
Forster's fiction, most notably in *Howards End*, in which Ruth Wilcox,
whose first name, with its biblical associations, suggests the theme,
removed by her husband from her home of Howards End to London,
withers and dies there; her wish that Margaret Schlegel inherit Howards
End is ignored by her family; the Schlegels have to move from their
London home when their lease expires; and when Margaret is
established at Howards End as the second Mrs. Wilcox, the approaching
London suburbs threaten the existence of the house.

Liberalism and conservatism are entwined in the complexities of
romanticism and of Forster's outlook. Like Wordsworth, Forster gains
from his childhood in the country a love of rural areas, a democratic
affection for rural folk, trust in spontaneous and apparently simple and
natural responses, the belief that external nature, in a rural setting, nur-
tures and sustains the individual, a respect for rural traditions, and a distrust of industrialization, of cities, and of the growth of cities.

Howards End is written from the point of view of the Edwardian
upper middle class, but it distrusts both the city and the stuffier
middle-class conventions. Margaret Schlegel is "not beautiful, not
supremely brilliant, but filled with something that took the place of both
qualities—something best described as a profound vivacity, a continual
and sincere response to all that she encountered in her path through
life."[10] She jumps from a moving car to try to comfort a girl whose cat
has been run over; when she had been rude to Ruth Wilcox, "she flung
on a hat and shawl, just like a poor woman, and plunged into the fog"[11]
to go to Ruth to make amends. The feeling for her fellows that Margaret
expresses is directed particularly toward the inarticulate: to the girl at the
side of the road, to Leonard Bast, and to Henry Wilcox, whose suspicion
of his own emotions has made him, in this respect, a eunuch. Margaret
herself becomes quieter after she marries Henry, not because she is inarticulate but because she is "passing from words to things"[12] and filling
the role of Ruth Wilcox, who had the ability of Wordsworth's Michael to

express emotion stoically. In the essays "Me, Them and You" and "Our Graves in Gallipoli" Forster expresses sympathy similar to Margaret's for the common soldiers of World War I and indignation for their "betters" (particularly for John Singer Sargent, who painted some of them), who did not see them as they were.

Forster's respect for honest emotion and individuality included both ebullient expression and silent feeling. He criticizes the middle-class, public-school Englishman for his "undeveloped heart" and admires the quick, unaffected expression of emotion that he finds in Italy. "It is this undeveloped heart that is largely responsible for the difficulties of Englishmen abroad,"[13] and even for Britain's imperial difficulties, he believes. Ronny Heaslop, of *A Passage to India* (1924), is a notable example of a character who suffers from this shortcoming. "One touch of regret —not the canny substitute but the true regret from the heart—would have made him a different man, and the British Empire a different institution."[14] Forster expresses a similar view in articles about India in *The Nation and Athenaeum* in 1922, a view that, while useful as a reminder that the character of an institution depends partly upon the personal relationships of its members, is surely a large oversimplification. It looks forward, or back, to a state that is pictured in the frescoes of the Ajanta caves in India, as Forster describes them: "All who have visited Ajanta have noted the easiness and happiness in its atmosphere. Men and animals seem to meet on equal terms, as do the various races of men."[15] It is a state that Forster perhaps experienced occasionally in childhood and that he kept as an ideal, though he found it in adult life only in art and imagination. In India it seemed to him to have once been within reach but now to be irretrievably lost:

> The decent Anglo-Indian of today realizes that the great blunder of the past is neither political nor economic nor educational, but social; that he was associated with a system that supported rudeness in railway carriages, and is paying the penalty.
> The penalty is inevitable. The mischief has been done, and though friendships between individuals will continue and courtesies between high officials increase, there is little hope now of spontaneous intercourse between the two races.[16]

The sense of an achievement once possible, now out of reach, that this statement conveys is familiar in Forster's work. The major fault, as far as western civilization is concerned, he believes to be the rapid development of technology with its attendant industrialization and commercialism. In this process man is removed more and more from his natural environment, and the unformulated knowledge which has developed

through generations is, Forster fears, lost. The following quotations from
his essays may make his thought and feeling on this subject clearer:

> There is a huge economic movement which has been taking
> the whole world, Great Britain included, from agriculture
> towards industrialism. . . . It has meant the destruction of feu-
> dalism and relationship based on the land, it has meant the
> transference of power from the aristocrat to the bureaucrat and
> the manager and the technician. Perhaps it will mean democ-
> racy, but it has not meant it yet, and personally I hate it.[17]

> We cannot reach social and political stability for the reason that
> we continue to make scientific discoveries and to apply them,
> and thus to destroy the arrangements which were based on
> more elementary discoveries. If Science would discover rather
> than apply—if, in other words, men were more interested in
> knowledge than in power—mankind would be in a far safer posi-
> tion, the stability statesmen talk about would be a possibility,
> there could be a new order based on vital harmony, and the
> earthly millennium might approach. . . . How can man get into
> harmony with his surroundings when he is constantly altering
> them? The future of our race is, in this direction, more unpleas-
> ant than we care to admit, and it has sometimes seemed to me
> that its best chance lies through apathy, uninventiveness, and
> inertia.[18]

> If you drop tradition and culture you lose your chance of con-
> necting work and play and creating a life which is all of a piece.
> The past did not succeed in doing that, but it can help us to do
> it, and that is why it is so useful.[19]

The threat of the technological revolution to things Forster values is
best represented in his fiction by the approach of the "red rust" of subur-
bia toward Howards End. Of Ruth Wilcox, the descendant of the original
owners of Howards End, Forster observes that "one knew that she wor-
shipped the past, and that the instinctive wisdom the past can alone
bestow had descended upon her. . . . Assuredly she cared about her ancestors, and let them help her."[20] He remarks that "under cosmopolitanism,
if it comes, we shall receive no help from the earth. Trees and meadows
and mountains will only be a spectacle, and the binding force that they
once exercised on character must be entrusted to Love alone. May Love
be equal to the task!"[21] In the short story "The Road from Colonus" old
Mr. Lucas, traveling in Greece, has a sense of rejuvenation, insight, and
peace at a roadside shrine, from which he is wrested by his daughter and
her companions. "The moment was so tremendous that he abandoned
words and arguments as useless, and rested on the strength of his mighty

unrevealed allies: silent men, murmuring water, and whispering trees." In the story "The Eternal Moment" Miss Raby returns after twenty years to an alpine village she had used as a setting for a novel, to find that it has been transformed by tourism encouraged by her book.

> A village must have some trade; and this village had always been full of virility and power. Obscure and happy, its splendid energies had found employment in wresting a livelihood out of the earth, whence had come a certain dignity, and kindliness, and love for other men. Civilisation did not relax these energies, but it had diverted them; and all the precious qualities, which might have helped to heal the world, had been destroyed. The family affection, the affection for the commune, the sane pastoral virtues—all had perished while the campanile which was to embody them was being built.

In his own life Forster has supported the preservation of the English countryside in numerous articles and letters to editors, in parish pageants, and in membership in the National Trust and the Commons, Open Spaces and Footpaths Preservation Society. "It is not now as it hath been of yore." Wordsworth's lament in the "Ode on the Intimations of Immortality" is Forster's also, in a somewhat broader, more social context than Wordsworth intended in the ode, though Forster's lament, too, is intimately associated with his youth. The lines

> There was a time when meadow, grove, and stream,
> The earth, and every common sight,
> > To me did seem
> > Apparelled in celestial light,
> The glory and the freshness of a dream

might have been written by Rickie Elliot of *The Longest Journey* about his years at Cambridge, or by Mr. Lucas, or by Forster himself, although Forster would likely not have used the past tense. If "the visionary gleam" did not desert Forster, his power as an artist did, as did Wordsworth's, in middle age.

Yet if there is sentimentality in the account of the alpine village quoted above that is not only Miss Raby's, it was not possible in a post-Darwinian, post-Freudian age for Forster to view nature in quite the same way as Wordsworth did. This fact accounts for part of the complexity critics have noted in Forster's work, for he is deeply aware of evil as well as of innocence. Frequently, like Rousseau, he attributes innocence to the individual and evil to society and its institutions, as he does in "What I Believe" when he asserts, "The more highly public life is organised the lower does its morality sink."[22] But in "The Menace to Freedom" he inverts a famous pronouncement of Rousseau's: "Our freedom is really menaced to-day because a million years ago Man was born in chains. . . . He has been a coward for centuries, afraid of the universe outside him and of the herd wherein he took refuge."[23] The eighteenth and nineteenth centuries, Forster says in this essay, believed that freedom had only to be recovered; the twentieth century, if it hopes for freedom at all, knows that it must be discovered. Yet, in the same essay, in spite of the foregoing statements, he says that "only Heaven knows" what men might accomplish if they acted as individuals and succeeded in combining the wish to be free and the wish to love. The menace to freedom might then disappear.

Similarly, while he usually trusts spontaneous feelings and actions of individuals, he recognizes primitive cunning and calculated cruelty in a character such as Giuseppe, of "The Story of the Siren," sudden violence in Stephen Wonham, of *The Longest Journey*, and spontaneous cruelty in Gino Carella, who twists Philip Herriton's broken arm when Philip tells him of the death of his son in *Where Angels Fear to Tread*. The actions of these characters are forgivable; the meddlesome behavior, distorted by convention, of such characters as Mrs. Herriton, Cecil Vyse and Mr. Beebe, of *A Room with a View*, and Agnes and Herbert Pembroke or Mrs. Failing, of *The Longest Journey*, are not so easily forgiven, but there are few villains in Forster's fiction: His most harmful characters usually mean well.

Forster's psychology, if one may speak of broad classifications and generalize unprofessionally about a subject concerning which Forster himself is unprofessional, is Jungian rather than Freudian and owes something to Goldsworthy Lowes Dickinson and to Samuel Butler. As Forster's essay "Anonymity" makes clear, he believes, as did Butler and Dickinson,[24] in an unconscious mind closely akin to Jung's collective unconscious, and he holds that promptings from this source should be heeded. Old Mr. Emerson, who in *A Room with a View* quotes Samuel Butler as "a friend of mine,"[25] advises Lucy Honeychurch: "You are inclined to get muddled. . . . Let yourself go. Pull out from the depths those thoughts that you do not understand, and spread them out in the sunlight and know the meaning of them."[26] Experiences that the mystic might ascribe to divine enlightenment, Forster attributes to the unconscious, a place where, for him, no monster lurks.

As far as nature external to man is concerned, we have seen that, like "England's pleasant land," a term that Forster uses for the title of a pageant, it is, in Forster's view, usually benign. Occasionally, however, he is aware of the need for that primeval alertness that is depicted for the twentieth century by some of Henry Moore's figures. At Blind Oak Gate, near Abinger, he has "a sense of something vaguely sinister, which would do harm if it could, but which cannot, this being Surrey; of something muffled up and recalcitrant; of something which rises upon its elbow when no one is present and looks down the converging paths."[27] Infrequently, he expresses a point of view similar to Hardy's. "Failure or success seem to have been allotted to men by their stars. But they retain the power of wriggling," he says in the essay "The Game of Life." After the death of Rickie Elliot's deformed daughter, Rickie "perceived more clearly the cruelty of Nature, to whom our refinement and piety are but as bubbles, hurrying downwards on the turbid waters. They break, and the stream continues."[28] Forster's strongest intuition of evil, or rather, of the nothingness that is more terrifying than evil, is expressed in *A Passage to India* in the echo of the Marabar caves that is reiterated in the minds of some of the characters of the novel. It is born in a barren tract of alien landscape from the realization of the inability of European experience and belief to cope with the confusion and variety of India:

> Coming at a moment when [Mrs. Moore] chanced to be fatigued, it had managed to murmur, "Pathos, piety, courage— they exist, but are identical, and so is filth. Everything exists, nothing has value." If one had spoken vileness in that place, or quoted lofty poetry, the comment would have been the same— "ou-boum." If one had spoken with the tongues of angels and pleaded for all the unhappiness and misunderstanding in the world, past, present, and to come, for all the misery men must undergo whatever their opinion and position, and however much they dodge or bluff—it would amount to the same, the serpent would descend and return to the ceiling. Devils are of the North, and poems can be written about them, but no one could romanticize the Marabar because it robbed infinity and eternity of their vastness, the only quality that accommodates them to mankind. . . .
>
> Suddenly, at the edge of her mind, Religion appeared, poor little talkative Christianity, and she knew that all its divine words from "Let there be Light" to "It is finished" only amounted to "boum." Then she was terrified over an area larger than usual; the universe, never comprehensible to her intellect, offered no repose to her soul . . . and she realised that she . . . didn't want to communicate with anyone, not even with God.[29]

The Sea of Faith which Matthew Arnold heard retreating has ebbed completely here. Yet the echo is banished and its malign effects are checked by Mrs. Moore's unconscious influence.

It is significant that the nadir of hope and apogee of art that this passage displays should come in Forster's fifth and last novel, published in

1924, a novel in which not only is western thought questioned but even
the possibility of a continuing friendship between Englishman and
Indian is seen to be doubtful as long as Britain remained India's ruler.
What happened between the 1920's and Forster's departure in 1893 from
the house at Stevenage to make this passage possible? The obvious
answer is that he matured and remained open to the experiences of the
twentieth century, while retaining his own heritage, as the style of the
passage itself, with its allusions to St. Paul and the Pentateuch, combined
with phrases that manage both to belittle and to suggest a wistful respect
for those ancient sources, makes clear. But it is worth looking more
closely to attempt to see how Forster reached this maturity.

The years at school at Tonbridge seem to have done little more than
confirm his attachment to the memory of his childhood home, cause him
to criticize the institution of the public school and the middle-class conventions that supported it (a criticism that is the basis for his portraits of
Sawston, town and school, respectively, in *Where Angels Fear to Tread*
and *The Longest Journey*), and to prepare him to welcome Cambridge,
when he went up to the university in 1897, with the enthusiasm that is
reflected in his biography of Goldsworthy Lowes Dickinson and in Rickie
Elliot's experience at Cambridge in *The Longest Journey*.

Forster's years at Cambridge, while they of course gave him new ideas
and experiences, also confirmed some of his older beliefs, so that they
were for him years of growth rather than of change. The countryside
remained as important as it had been, and his concern for the harmful
effects of industrialization was reinforced, if not articulated, by Dickinson, a don who became Forster's close friend and who regarded life in
ancient Greece as nearly ideal, admired the East, and criticized the governments and industrialists of the modern West. Dickinson was a founder
in 1903 of *The Independent Review*, a journal that Forster, who was a
contributor, describes as "not so much a Liberal review as an appeal to
Liberalism from the Left to be its better self."[30] In 1915 Dickinson was a
founder of the League of Nations Society, and through it, of the League
of Nations itself.

Forster was an undergraduate at a time when Victorian beliefs were
being questioned, and although in some respects he may have been as
naïve as Rickie Elliot and have questioned older values less than some of
those undergraduates, most of them a few years younger than he, who
were later to be his friends in the Bloomsbury group, he was at one with
them at least in his questioning of prudery and censorship. He brought
with him to Cambridge, as did his friends, the educated Victorian's habit
of asking awkward questions, a habit that was part of both his Thornton
and his Whichelo heritage. The Thorntons, with notable success, had
joined societies to effect change. Forster sometimes found himself joining

societies, such as the two that have already been mentioned and the National Council for Civil Liberties, to protect things he valued. The Whichelos, less wealthy and less committed to religion and good deeds than the Thorntons, had been "averse to piety and quick to detect the falsity sometimes accompanying it."[31] Forster's mother disapproved of the celebration of Queen Victoria's Golden Jubilee in 1887, and Forster, then eight, was "violently anti-Jubilee. . . . my grandmother [Whichelo] and I planned to spend the day together in strict seclusion"—an attitude that his Great-aunt Marianne did not admire. She sent Forster a geography book and information that, however it read to Forster and his mother when they received it, now reads deliciously: "The sun they say always is shining on some bit of the globe that belongs to *us* meaning by us all English people—and that reminds me that I heard you did not like the Queen—but I think that must be because you do not know her, neither do I as an acquaintance, but I do know she is the best Queen or King we have ever had."[32] Years later, in letters and articles in *The Spectator* and *The New Statesman and Nation*, Forster criticized both the excessive national mourning and the extravagant preparations for joy, as he found them, after the death of George V and before the coronation of George VI.

Forster inherited from his Victorian forebears a strong sense both of the worth of the individual and of the individual's responsibility to his conscience and to society, a hatred of coercion, and especially from his mother's side, a healthy skepticism. These characteristics, which are the essential and effective equipment of a democrat, were strengthened at Cambridge. There, particularly, perhaps, in the Society of Apostles, which had been founded in the 1820's, Forster learned more fully to value the disinterested pursuit of truth and to distrust the "muddle," self-interest, and dogmatism which he was to portray in his Sawston. Years later, writing of another Apostle, Desmond MacCarthy, Forster praised MacCarthy's "disinterested ardour for the truth" and his combination of "the candour that was Cambridge with knowledge of the world,"[33] as he praises, elsewhere, "ruthless analysis" and "cultured tradition," which he calls "essentials of democracy."[34] Forster also found at Cambridge, as he had in a different way at Stevenage, a completeness that he was not to find again and that no doubt contributed to his conception of the ideal that is suggested by the motto of *Howards End*, "Only connect." "As Cambridge filled up with friends it acquired a magic quality," he says in his biography of Dickinson. "Body and spirit, reason and emotion, work and play, architecture and scenery, laughter and seriousness, life and art—these pairs which are elsewhere contrasted were there fused into one. People and books reinforced one another, intelligence joined hands with affection, speculation became a passion, and discussion was made profound by love."[35] Forster's undergraduate years at Cambridge enabled him to create Margaret and Helen Schlegel—"who cared deeply about politics, though not as politicians would have us care; they desired that public life should mirror whatever is good in the life within"[36]—and to admire the *Antigone* of Sophocles: "Of all the great tragic utterances that comes closest to my heart, that is my central faith," he says.[37] His Antigone, one may safely surmise, remembers fine days with her brother in the fields where his body now lies unburied, and in her resistance to the arbitrary use of power she is motivated by a Protestant conscience. At the side of Antigone, in Forster's mind, is an unexpected figure, Samuel Butler, who is admired particularly for his lack of dogmatism and whose *Erewhon* is the book referred to in the title of the essay "A Book That Influenced Me," which contains the praise of Sophocles' play.

This juxtaposition indicates something of the eclecticism and complexity of Forster. In the eighteenth or nineteenth centuries he might, just possibly, have been consistently liberal and optimistic. In the twentieth century, having discovered that "the Primal Curse . . . is not—as the Authorized Version suggests—the knowledge of good and evil, but the knowledge of good-and-evil,"[38] he is a pessimistic optimist and a conservative liberal. Now he protests and asserts the need for protest, now he persuades us of the need for tolerance. These are not, of course, weathercock swings, but reactions to a world that is far from simple; they are illustrated in his fiction in such instances as the relationship between the Schlegels and the Wilcoxes or between Fielding and Aziz.

If the relatively crude didacticism of his early fiction is a reliable indication, Forster left Cambridge with considerable confidence. As he became more experienced and as the twentieth century advanced and enabled him to see more clearly the threat that it posed to the older values, he became less confident and his outlook and his fiction became more complex. Moreover, he saw more clearly flaws in the older world, particularly in imperialism and capitalism. "In came the nice fat dividends, up rose the lofty thoughts," he says as he looks back on his youth, "and we did not realise that all the time we were exploiting the poor of our own country and the backward races abroad, and getting bigger profits from our investments than we should."[39] Yet he was convinced that the quality of civilization depended upon the creativity of individuals which could not be regimented or directed by the community. He decided that "the doctrine of *laisser-faire* will not work in the material world" but that it is "the only one that seems to work in the world of the spirit."[40] He remained depressed by the monotony that bureaucracy, industrialization, and urbanization were bringing about.

At least five or six years before the outbreak of World War I Forster foresaw the probability of the disaster that destroyed the stable Europe of the Victorians. *Howards End* is in part an attempt to show how that disaster might be prevented by a synthesis of the values of the man of affairs and of the cultured intellectual. In this respect it is a failure, not only historically, but also aesthetically in the unconvincing marriage of Margaret Schlegel and Henry Wilcox and morally in the uncharacteristic and un-Forsterian insincerity that Margaret displays at times in her relationship with Henry. In other respects, some of which have been glanced at in this essay, it is successful, most interestingly, perhaps, in the way in which aspects of its structure, based upon the antithesis between Howards End and London and an antithesis that Helen Schlegel finds in the last two movements of Beethoven's Fifth Symphony between empty panic and heroism, forecast danger in spite of more superficial expressions of hope.

By this time Forster had arrived at the idea, stated implicitly in the structure of *Howards End* and explicitly in an essay published in 1938,[41] that periods of civilization, when freedom and creativity prevail, alternate with periods of violence, when force is dominant. It is a rhythm that happens to coincide with the movement in his own life from Stevenage to Tonbridge to Cambridge. A similar idea is expressed in *A Passage to India*: Irrationality and force rule when the echo is heard and Aziz is accused of attempted rape; freedom, creativeness, and friendship are dominant in the last part of the book, set at Mau, but it is clear that they will not last, and the possibility of the triumph of the echo has been considered.

That Forster wrote no fiction after *A Passage to India* is perhaps not surprising, since that novel expresses his profoundest intuition and raises questions that have not yet been answered and may never be answered—since the twentieth century, though it believes in the possibility of a universal cataclysm, does not believe in a day of judgment when the truth shall be known. Of course, the British have withdrawn from India, but whether eastern and western modes of thought, feeling, and action can meet without disaster, or whether panic will prevail and civilization will be replaced by nothingness, is not yet known.

What makes Forster an especially valuable novelist is this ability to grasp major social, political, and psychological problems and, at his best, to grasp them not as a technologist who applies the ideas of others but, to use a term he has applied to other novelists, as a prophet, who has seen, before most men, some of the major dilemmas of our century and has expressed them, in spite of their multiplicity, in the complexity and order of art.

NOTES

1. *Howards End*, p. 216. All references to Forster's novels are to the pocket edition, London, Edward Arnold, 1947.
2. *Marianne Thornton 1797–1887* (London, 1956), p. 270.
3. P. 158.
4. "Notes on the Way," *Time and Tide*, XV, No. 24 (June 16, 1934), 766.
5. "The Last Parade," *Two Cheers for Democracy* (London, 1951), p. 18.
6. "My Wood," *Abinger Harvest* (London, 1936), pp. 23–26.
7. *Marianne Thornton*, p. 250.
8. *Ibid.*, p. 258.
9. *Ibid.*, p. 269.
10. P. 10.
11. P. 71.
12. P. 277.
13. "Notes on the English Character," *Abinger Harvest*, p. 5.
14. P. 54.
15. Unsigned review of *India: Paintings from Ajanta Caves, The Listener*, LII, No. 1328 (August 12, 1954), 253.
16. "Reflections in India," *The Nation and Athenaeum*, XXX, No. 17 (January 21, 1922), 614.
17. "English Prose Between 1918 and 1939," *Two Cheers for Democracy*. p. 281.
18. "Art for Art's Sake," *Two Cheers for Democracy*, p. 100.
19. "Does Culture Matter?" *Two Cheers for Democracy*, p. 112.
20. *Howards End*, p. 23.
21. *Ibid.*, p. 275.
22. *Two Cheers for Democracy*, pp. 83–84.
23. *Ibid.*, p. 21.
24. See, for example, Butler's *God the Known and God the Unknown* (London, 1909), first published in 1879 as a series of articles, and *Unconscious Memory* (London, 1890); and Dickinson's *After Two Thousand Years* (London, 1930), pp. 205–206.
25. P. 246.
26. P. 37.
27. "The Last of Abinger," *Two Cheers for Democracy*, p. 368.
28. *The Longest Journey*, p. 217.
29. Pp. 156–157.
30. *Goldsworthy Lowes Dickinson* (London, 1934), p. 115.

31. *Marianne Thornton*, p. 250.
32. *Ibid.*, p. 286.
33. "Affable Hawk," *The Spectator*, No. 5430 (July 23, 1932), p. 125.
34. Letter to the editor, *The New Statesman and Nation*, n.s., XV, No. 360 (January 15, 1938), 78–79.
35. *Goldsworthy Lowes Dickinson*, p. 35.
36. *Howards End*, p. 29.
37. *Two Cheers for Democracy*, p. 227.
38. *The Longest Journey*, p. 194.
39. *Two Cheers for Democracy*, p. 68.
40. *Ibid.*
41. Reprinted in *Two Cheers for Democracy* as "What I Believe."

D. H. LAWRENCE
(1885-1930)

by Vivian de Sola Pinto

I am a democrat in so far as I love the free sun in men and an aristocrat in so far as I detest narrow-gutted possessive persons.
D. H. Lawrence, "Democracy" in *Pansies*

I must insist that he wrote about these things as a poet, and not as a philosopher with a system to expound.
Richard Aldington, Introduction to *Apocalypse*

I

BERTRAND RUSSELL IN his autobiography describes his brief cooperation with D. H. Lawrence and his subsequent realization that there could be no real agreement between them: "It was only gradually that I came to feel him a positive force for evil and that he came to have the same feeling about me. . . . I was a firm believer in democracy, whereas he developed the whole philosophy of Fascism before the politicians had thought of it." He goes on to ascribe to Lawrence "a mystical philosophy of 'blood.' " "This," he adds, "seemed to me frankly rubbish, and I rejected it vehemently, though I did not then know that it led straight to Auschwitz. . . . His thought was a mass of self-deception masquerading as stark realism. His descriptive powers were remarkable, but his ideas cannot be too soon forgotten . . . I do not think in retrospect that they have any merit whatever."[1]

The short-lived collaboration between Russell and Lawrence is surely one of the strangest episodes in English literary history. A parallel might be an imaginary collaboration between Jeremy Bentham and William Blake. Russell and Lawrence represent two different and opposing strands in English civilization. Russell, by birth and education a Whig aristocrat, is a scientific and rationalist philosopher in the English empirical tradition of Thomas Hobbes, John Locke, and David Hume. He was brought up in a wealthy household and educated privately till he went to Cambridge. Lawrence, the son of a miner, was educated at a national primary school and a provincial high school and university college. He belongs to a tradition of working-class culture which goes back to the mystical, heterodox Puritans and "mechanick preachers" of the seventeenth century.

Russell's sweeping adverse judgment is certainly colored by dislike of the man, doubtless sharpened by Lawrence's caricature of him in *Women in Love* as Sir Joshua, the "learned, dry baronet of fifty" who was "always making witticisms and laughing at them heartily, in a harsh horse-laugh."[2] Lawrence, on his side, reacted strongly against the intellectual society of pre-1914 Cambridge, where Russell was a leading figure. J. M. Keynes, another great Cambridge pundit, who met Lawrence at this time, judges him much more fairly. Commenting on Lawrence's disgust with the Cambridge intellectuals ("rotten and rotting others"), Keynes writes:

> It is impossible to imagine moods more antagonistic than those of Lawrence and pre-war Cambridge. But when all that has been said, was there something true and right in what Lawrence felt? There generally was. His reactions were incomplete and unfair but they were not usually baseless. . . . If I imagine us coming under the observation of Lawrence's ignorant, jealous, hostile eyes, what a combination of qualities we offered to arouse his passionate distaste: this thin rationalism skipping on the crust of the lava . . . joined to libertinism and comprehensive irreverence. . . . All this was very unfair to poor, silly, well-meaning us. But that is why I say there may have been just a grain of truth when Lawrence said . . . that we were "done for."[3]

Russell's indictment of Lawrence is repeated in a milder form with some qualifications in John R. Harrison's interesting and provocative study called *The Reactionaries*, where Lawrence is classed with Yeats, Wyndham Lewis, Ezra Pound, and T. S. Eliot as authors representing a "swerve to the right" of English intellectuals in the period between the two wars. While admitting that Lawrence was "obviously right" in his contention that "there is something radically wrong" with our civilization and that "there is much to be said for his criticism of the sexual relations between individuals," Harrison stresses his "violent rejection of the democratic politics of modern industrial society" and his (alleged) "latent pro-Germanism" and "dislike of Jews and Celts." His "concern with blood, blood sacrifice and human sacrifice" is described as "near lunatic" and his "views on social leadership" as "inherently close to the fascist conception of society." He quotes with approval the opinion of Bertrand Russell "who knew him well," though he does not completely endorse Russell's wholesale condemnation. His conclusion is that Lawrence "deserves sympathy when he struggles to describe entirely new and much better personal and social relationships, but a certain viciousness of temperament, together with the evasiveness of his style, do[es] much to counteract the sympathy."[4]

Bertrand Russell certainly knew Lawrence well for a short time in the early part of his life, but his wife Frieda Lawrence knew him a great deal better for a much longer period and her testimony deserves attention. In a short reply to Bertrand Russell's strictures she writes: "As for calling Lawrence an exponent of Nazism, that is pure nonsense. You might as well call St. Augustine a Nazi. Many of the young instinctively know that Lawrence's *raison d'être* was love. . . ."[5] To some the comparison with St. Augustine may appear grotesque, but Frieda is really trying to say something profoundly true. Like Augustine, in this respect, if in no other, Lawrence was a religious genius, and a religious genius was exactly what the positivist, "scientific" mind of Russell was incapable of understanding.

Russell's sweeping condemnation and Harrison's more moderate assessment are both based on an excessive simplification. Lawrence, like all great artists, had a highly complex character. We can distinguish at least four Lawrences. There is, first of all, and by far the most important, Lawrence the inspired prophetic poet and creative artist. Secondly, there is Lawrence the preacher and would-be Messiah and leader of a renovated social order. Thirdly, there is Lawrence the "near lunatic" or manic. To admit the presence of this element in his character is no derogation of his genius. "Great wits to madness sure are near allied," and there is a "mad" or at least irrational strain, often sadomasochistic, in most men of genius. The "near lunatic" or manic Lawrence often mingles with and distorts Lawrence the prophetic poet and Lawrence the preacher and would-be Messiah. His opposite or antidote is the Lawrence who might be called the Sancho Panza of Lawrence the inspired prophet-poet and Lawrence the preacher and Messiah. He is the down-to-earth, bloody-minded, humorous, irreverent little Midlander ("cockney," as Lawrence himself wrote[6]) who crops up in all sorts of places in the novels and stories and finds, perhaps, his most typical expression in some of the satiric

Pansies and *Nettles*. Lawrence the preacher and Messiah is the spiritual descendant of the Puritan preachers of the seventeenth century; it must be remembered that Lawrence was brought up in the Congregational Church and received part of his early education from a Congregational minister. The Congregationalists are the direct inheritors of the tradition of Oliver Cromwell's Independents. Lawrence's preaching is often eloquent and provocative, but it is seen at its weakest when he attempts to deal with the problems of practical politics. Max Beerbohm's judgment of this aspect of Lawrence is too summary, but it contains a grain of truth: "Poor D. H. Lawrence. . . . Although his prose style was slovenly, he was a man of unquestionable genius. But then he became afflicted with Messiahdom. Now what equipment had poor D. H. Lawrence for Messiahdom? . . . He had a real feeling for nature and in this he was at his best. But through his landscapes cantered hallucinations."[7] Perhaps Max was incapable of distinguishing "hallucinations" from true poetic vision, but I believe that, up to a point, he was right in questioning Lawrence's equipment for Messiahdom.

As to the manic Lawrence it must be remembered that Lawrence, like Jonathan Swift and Friedrich Nietzsche, was a sick man for most of his life and a "psychological case." This is the Lawrence of the "disrupted soul," about whom John Middleton Murry has written with such perception in *Love, Freedom and Society*. The origins of this psychopathic condition of Lawrence can only be guessed at. He was tubercular and probably, like Swift, suffered from sexual frustration. He ascribed this condition to the deep psychological trauma due to excessive love for his mother and outward hostility masking an inner attachment to his father. As Murry writes, "We are in the presence of what the doctors call a syndrome: mother fixation, phthisis, intensity of genius. That psychosomatic syndrome does not, of course, account for the genius itself. . . . But it does account for the most disturbing manifestations of that genius."[8] It is important to notice, however, that unlike Swift and Nietzsche, Lawrence did not go mad. He was a greater poet and a saner and more intelligent man than either of them. What critics like Russell and Harrison overlook is that he made an almost miraculous recovery in the last few years of his life, passing, as Murry writes, "into a new dimension,"[9] a condition of religious vision, very hard to describe in abstract terms, which irradiates his wonderful last writings in verse and prose.

II

An essential preliminary to any account of an imaginative writer's relation to politics and society is to ask what we must expect to find when he deals with such subjects. We must not expect to find the practical sagac-

ity of a statesman or the ingenious solutions to social problems pro-
pounded by political philosophers. What we find when the great poets
deal with politics and society is the quality of wisdom arising out of what
Keats called the "negative capability," the power of looking at the world
from a vantage point outside the rational and moral values of contemporary civilization, "without any irritable reaching after fact and reason."[10]
Of course the poet is also a man of his age, and when he is not using his
imaginative gift, he will speak like a man of his age and then what he
says will simply be of historical interest. This is the meaning of Lawrence's two famous comments on the meaning of works of art: "two
blankly opposing morals, the artist's and the tale's. Never trust the artist.
Trust the tale";[11] and "Let me hear what the novel says. As for the novelist he is usually a dribbling liar."[12] These sayings show that Lawrence recognized clearly that there was often a conflict between what I
have called Lawrence the prophet-poet and Lawrence the preacher and
would-be Messiah.

Let us, then, hear what Lawrence the prophet-poet tells us about politics and society in his major novels and tales. A good starting point is
the early story "The Prussian Officer" (originally "Honour and Arms"),
first published in 1913, when Lawrence had seen something of German
military life. This astonishing tale is a vivid and intense vision of the
horror of militarism embodied in the cold, sadistic cruelty of the captain and the violation of the innocence of the gentle young orderly, leading with swift and terrible inevitability to the climax of the murder and
the pity and terror of the conclusion, heightened by the exquisite evocation of the beauty of the natural surroundings. In this story (written, it
must be remembered, before World War I) we hear the voice of Lawrence the prophetic poet, speaking with the deep insight and compassion
of a great artist, who does not allow a single word of moralizing comment to come between the tragic vision and the reader. A reading of this
story alone should be sufficient to refute the charges of "latent pro-
Germanism" and incipient Nazism. The immediate reaction of the leaders
of the Third Reich, if they had cast their eyes through this story, would
surely have been to order the burning of all Lawrence's works.

It may be said that "The Prussian Officer" is early work and does not
represent the mature Lawrence. Let us see how far a "whole philosophy
of fascism" can be found in his major novels and tales. I doubt if the
most hostile critic would find it in the three great novels of his early
maturity, Sons and Lovers (1913), The Rainbow (1915), and Women in
Love (1920). These works are all concerned with the sexual life of individuals and especially with the poisoning of that life by the growth of a
mechanized industrial society. This is what wrecks the marriage of the
naturally generous and warmhearted Walter Morel by turning him into a

drunken brute, with the result that his sensitive, cultivated wife turns from him to seek satisfaction in the possessive love which has a disastrous effect on the sexual life of their son Paul. In *Sons and Lovers* the ugliness and brutality of the life of the miners is contrasted with the wholesome decency of the family at Willey Farm, who have managed to preserve a fragment of the old agricultural England outside the industrial system. In *The Rainbow*, working on an epic scale, Lawrence shows the traditional culture of the farming Brangwens, based on the rhythm of the seasons and the old hierarchy of the English village, disintegrating in the later generations under the influence of the modern industrialism which produces such horrors as the mining village of Wiggiston:

> The streets were like visions of pure ugliness; a grey-black macadamized road, asphalt causeways, held in between a flat succession of wall, window and door, a new-brick channel that began nowhere and ended nowhere. Everything was amorphous, yet everything repeated itself endlessly. . . . In the middle of the town was a large, open, shapeless space or market-place, of black trodden earth, surrounded by the same flat material of dwellings, new red-brick becoming grimy . . . with just, at one corner, a great and gaudy public-house . . . The place had the strange desolation of a ruin. Colliers hanging about in gangs or groups, or passing along the asphalt pavements heavily to work, seemed not like living people but like spectres. The rigidity of the blank streets, the homogeneous amorphous sterility of the whole suggested death rather than life.[13]

This is a description worthy to be placed by the Coketown of *Hard Times*. Like Dickens, Lawrence is at his best when he is making us feel the dreariness and ugliness of the modern industrial world rather than when he is suggesting remedies.

Women in Love contains the tragic figure of Gerald Crich, a new type of industrialist, determined to destroy the old patriarchal type of capitalism represented by his father, who had tried to conduct his business on Christian principles. The elder Crich can be compared with such figures in Dickens's novels as the Cheeryble brothers. Dickens was still able to believe that a kindly paternalism could solve the problems of industrial England. Lawrence a half century later saw that this was a delusion. Gerald remodels his father's collieries with a terrible, ruthless efficiency, entirely oblivious of human values. We may notice that Gudrun, when she is thinking of marrying Gerald, envisages a political future for him: "He would go into Parliament in the Conservative interest, he would clear up the great muddle of labour and industry. He was so superbly fearless, masterful. . . . And he would care nothing for himself, nor about anything but the pure working out of the problem. ... He would be a Napoleon of peace, or a Bismarck. ...[14] This is surely something very like what we would now call a fascist dictator. When Lawrence wrote *Women in Love*, the words "fascism" and "fascist" had not yet been heard, but Gerald Crich, the soldier-explorer and business administrator, is a prophetic picture of the mentality out of which fascism was to grow in the next decade. What he is seeking is a new "radicalism of the right" that would destroy the values of democracy in the interest not of the traditional upper-class hierarchy but of mechanical efficiency. It was Lawrence the prophet who created Gerald and who saw with the insight of a prophetic poet that his devotion to a purely mechanical ideal would lead to spiritual, and ultimately to physical, annihilation. The destruction of Gerald is a forecast of the destruction of Mussolini and Hitler.

There is a good deal of Lawrence the preacher and Messiah in the character of Rupert Birkin, obviously an idealization of the author, an idealization which is, nevertheless, severely criticized by the down-to-earth Lawrence, whose voice is heard in the reflections of Ursula when she has been listening to Birkin's philosophizing and sees in him "a certain priggish Sunday School stiffness . . . priggish and detestable. . . . There was his wonderful life-rapidity . . . and there was at the same time this ridiculous mean effacement into a Salvator Mundi and a Sunday School teacher."[15] The same note is heard when Gudrun and Ursula are discussing Birkin: "In a way he is not clever enough, he is too intense in spots. . . . Yes . . . too much of a preacher, he is really a priest. . . . He cannot allow that there is any other mind but his own. And then the real clumsiness of his mind is its lack of self criticism."[16] Birkin's mind may have lacked self-criticism, but Lawrence's certainly did not. The down-to-earth Lawrence, the voice of sanity, is always at hand to criticize, even to mock at, Lawrence the preacher, the would-be Salvator Mundi, and Lawrence the "near lunatic."

There are significant passages in *Touch and Go* (1920), the play that is closely connected with *Women in Love* and which contains some of the same characters as the novel. The subject of this play is what Gudrun called "the great muddle of Labour and industry" and the failure of both Capital and Labour to provide adequate leadership. Gerald Barlow (the Gerald Crich of the novel) is certainly voicing Lawrence's own view when he calls the "Labour" of his day "a great swarm of hopelessly little men ... just mechanical little motions and then they're done."[17] On the other hand, Job Arthur Freer, the Labour leader, is also undoubtedly speaking with Lawrence's voice when (anticipating Aneurin Bevan) he describes the rich as "vermin ... that live on the sweat and blood of the people—live on it and get rich on it—get rich through living on other people's lives, the lives of the working men—living on the bodies of the working men."[18] There seemed to be no way out of the impasse except the rather vague remedy prescribed at the end of the play by Oliver Turton (the Rupert Birkin of the novel), who rejects both the capitalist and socialist solutions as equally materialistic and "bullying" in favor of "'a better way' in which every man will be able to live and be free. But we shall never manage it by fighting for money." A great deal of Lawrence's subsequent work consists of an imaginative exploration of the possible nature of this "better way."

It is well known that the great crisis in Lawrence's life was his estrangement from his fellow countrymen at the time of World War I, when, as he wrote to Lady Cynthia Asquith, he felt himself to be "torn off from the body of mankind."[19] In the lives of great artists a certain pattern can be discerned. After the creation of a tragic masterpiece or master-pieces comes a "time of troubles," of bitter disillusion and disgust. At the end of Shakespeare's great series of tragedies comes the terrible "disrup-tion in the soul" of *King Lear*, reaching a climax in *Timon of Athens*. Only some of the greatest artists, a Sophocles, a Dante, a Shakespeare, or a Blake, have passed beyond this phase to a final moment of transcendent vision, the vision of *Oedipus at Colonus, The Paradiso, The Tempest*, or *Jerusalem*. I believe Lawrence is one of the few European writers of the present century who have succeeded in passing through to this final phase. The title of the early sequence of poems on his married life, *Look! We Have Come Through!* might be taken as an appropriate description of his whole literary career. His tragic masterpieces were the two linked novels *The Rainbow* and *Women in Love*. The suppression of *The Rain-bow* by a stupid puritanical officialdom, the senseless harrying which he received from the British authorities during World War I because of his marriage to Frieda von Richthofen, the daughter of a Prussian general, together with his horror and disgust at the betrayal of human values in World War I, helped to produce the bitter, traumatic experience which is reflected in his writings of the early 1920's.

Already before the war, after passing through the usual adolescent stages of a revolt from the Christian teaching of his youth and the adop-tion of the fashionable agnosticism of the early twentieth century, he had adumbrated his philosophy of "blood consciousness," which Bertrand Russell quite wrongly identifies with the "blood and soil" nonsense of the Nazis and their apologists. In a famous passage in a letter to Ernest Col-lings written as early as January 1913, Lawrence describes his "great reli-gion" as "a belief in the blood, the flesh, as being wiser than the intellect."[20] Here, as in many other places where he writes in a similar vein, he is protesting against the modern limitation of consciousness to the brain and the nerves. "The brain," he writes in *Psychoanalysis and the Unconscious*, "is the seat of the ideal consciousness. And ideal consciousness is only the dead end of consciousness, the spun silk. The vast bulk of consciousness is non-cerebral."[21] This noncerebral consciousness, according to Lawrence, so strong in primitive peoples, had to be recovered if modern man was to achieve spiritual health. This, I believe, was a true and valuable insight and it bears no resemblance whatever to the racist theories of Houston Stewart Chamberlain and Alfred Rosenberg. Lawrence had no admiration for the blond, fair-skinned Aryans; on the contrary, he was drawn rather to the dark-skinned Mediterranean races and the Amerindians. Nor, as commonly supposed, did he make a cult of irrationality. In his essay "On Human Destiny" he wrote, "Man *can't* live by instinct because he has a mind. ... Man has a mind, and ideas, so it is just puerile to sigh for innocence and naïve spontaneity. ... Emotions by themselves become just a nuisance. The mind by itself becomes just a sterile thing, making everything sterile. So what's to be done? You've got to marry the pair of them."[22] And in his *Studies in Classic American Literature* he declared that "we can't go back. We can't go back to the savages: not a stride. We can be in sympathy with them. We can take a great curve in their direction, onwards. But we cannot turn the current of our lives backwards, back to their soft, warm twilight and uncreate mud."[23]

Lawrence believed that Christianity with its doctrine of "faked love" and its neglect of the body had produced the unhealthy growth of the cerebral or ideal consciousness which was responsible for the spiritual sickness of modern industrial democracy. Whatever truth there may be in this doctrine, it certainly had an element of danger and encouraged the manic Lawrence to indulge in fantasies of power-worship and the cult of "strong" leadership which appealed to many minds in Europe directly after World War I. His admirably written and stimulating little schoolbook *Movements in European History*, published under the name of Lawrence Davison in 1921, contains significant passages in this connection. It ends with descriptions of the unifications of Italy and Germany. Lawrence describes the "freedom fighters" of the Risorgimento, Giuseppe Mazzini and Giuseppe Garibaldi, with sympathy, but he notes that their efforts have only led to disillusion: "fretfulness, irritation, and nothing in life except money. ... No wonder liberty so often turns to ashes in the mouth, after being so fair a fruit to contemplate. Man needs more than liberty."[24] These words express admirably the feelings of thousands of sensitive spirits in the years immediately following World War I when it seemed that all the hopes of nineteenth-century liberals had been disappointed and that "democracy" only led to drabness, mediocrity, money-grubbing, and social injustice.

The conclusion of the final chapter strikes a new ominous note. After forecasting a new integration of Europe based on "the unity of the labouring classes," Lawrence prophesies that "a great united Europe of productive working people all materially equal will never be able to continue or stand firm unless it unites also round some great, chosen figure who can lead a great war as well as administer a wide peace. .... He must be chosen but at the same time responsible to God alone."[25] This prophecy was in some measure fulfilled by the rise of such figures as Mussolini, Hitler, and Stalin, but it must be remembered that when it was written, Nazism with its concentration camps and Stalinism with its purges were still in the future. In it we can hear the combination of Lawrence the messianic preacher and Lawrence the "near lunatic" psychopath obsessed by the concept of power, which characterizes much of his writing in the early 1920's. It is this aspect of his work which has provided some of the ammunition for those who have seen in him a forerunner of fascism or Nazism. What they overlook, however, as I hope to show, is that the Lawrence of prophetic wisdom and the Lawrence of down-to-earth sanity were never extinguished.

III

Italy made a deep impression on Lawrence when he first went there in 1913, and, as soon as it was possible for him to leave England after the war, he returned to Italy and was there till 1922. On his first visit he had been attracted by the Italian Futuristi writers and painters who were, in some measure, forerunners of the fascists. He was in Italy at the time of the fascist revolution and, like many English observers, was interested in the new movement, though, to judge from his letters,[26] he regarded it in a detached way and certainly never "fell for fascism" like Ezra Pound. The three novels which are the products of Lawrence's "time of troubles" between 1920 and 1925, *Aaron's Rod, Kangaroo*, and *The Plumed Serpent*, are all in some measure concerned with fascism, and they provide plenty of quotations for the superficial reader who classes Lawrence as a power-worshiping reactionary. In all these books, however, even in *The Plumed Serpent*, where the manic Lawrence is most prominent, his attitude to fascism is ambivalent and very far from that of an enthusiastic supporter. In fact these books, to use a favorite expression of Lawrence's, can be described as "thought-adventures," in which his mind is playing round the problems of leadership and a reordering of society, problems for which fascism supplied a crude and unsuccessful solution.

Aaron's Rod was written when Lawrence had his first glimpse of Italian fascism in 1920–1921, and the violence that he saw in the streets of Milan and Florence finds a place in his story. The hero, Aaron Sisson, is Lawrence as he might have been if he had been a musician instead of a writer and if he had married someone like Louie Burrows, had two children by her, and then in a fit of disgust at bourgeois domesticity had deserted his wife and children, fallen in with a bohemian set of intellectuals in London, and then wandered off to Italy. Sisson is Lawrence the prophetic artist, combined with Lawrence the down-to-earth Midlander. Rawdon Lilly, the writer whom Sisson meets in London, though resembling John Middleton Murry in some ways, is essentially Lawrence the preacher with touches of the manic Lawrence. It is Lilly who argues with the Jewish intellectual Levison that the whole of the Christian-democratic ideal has "gone dead and putrid" and "the logical sequence is only stink." He goes further and says that you "have to have a sort of slavery again. People are not men, they are insects and instruments and their destiny is slavery. . . . Ultimately they will be brought to agree—after sufficient extermination and then they will elect for themselves a proper and healthy and energetic slavery." This is certainly the voice of the manic Lawrence, but it is important to notice that having let the "near lunatic" have his say, Lawrence the prophetic artist pulls back from the abyss and Lilly is made to declare that he would "say the blank opposite with just as much fervour." He proceeds to tell what he calls the real truth, and here the prophetic voice of Lawrence is heard in a memorable passage: "I think every man is a sacred and holy individual, never to be violated. I think there is only one thing I hate to the verge of madness and that is bullying. To see any living creature *bullied* in *any* way almost makes a murderer of me."[27]

This extraordinary *volte-face* represents very well Lawrence's dilemma in his "time of troubles." He saw clearly that modern pseudodemocracy had failed and that a new principle of order was needed. The psychopathic side of him was tempted by the idea of a forcible imposition of this order. On the other hand, he was always aware that such an imposition would almost certainly involve the crime of violating the "sacred and holy individual." In the rather unsatisfactory final chapter of *Aaron's Rod* (entitled, significantly, "Words") he makes Lilly orate about the necessity of submission by woman to man and by men "to a greater soul in man," "the positive power soul in man." It can be noticed that Lilly is now made to describe this submission as voluntary and to reject his former advocacy of "slavery": "No slavery, a deep unfathomable free submission . . . never bully, never force the conscious will. That's where Nietzsche was wrong." Lawrence the down-to-earth Midlander, in the person of Aaron Sisson, remarks drily: "You'll never get it."[28]

The unsatisfactory nature of the two novels that followed *Aaron's Rod*—*Kangaroo* and *The Plumed Serpent*—in spite of the brilliance of many passages in them, is due largely to the fact that they are attempts to combine three literary forms which do not easily blend: the realistic novel, the travel book, and the philosophic-poetic utopia. Both novels

owe something to Lawrence's impressions of Italian fascism, but it would
be misleading to regard them as fascist utopias. Lawrence understood the
causes of fascism, and, to some extent, sympathized with the motives of
some of the people who were attracted by it, but he had no sympathy
whatever with the militarism and chauvinism of the fascists. *Kangaroo*
and *The Plumed Serpent* can be regarded as experiments in imagining a
reordering of society carried out in a more humane way than either Italian fascism or Russian bolshevism, but the artistic and down-to-earth part
of him remained skeptical of even such an ideal revolution.

The Diggers' movement described in *Kangaroo* is obviously based on
what Lawrence had seen of the Italian fascists, and the imaginary Digger
groups of ex-soldiers are simply Mussolini's *fascios* imported into Australia. But Ben Cooley, the Kangaroo, is a very different figure from Mussolini. He is a humane, liberal-minded, intellectual Jew! This, surely,
would have been enough to make the Nazis repudiate with horror the
notion that Lawrence was one of their forerunners. Whatever he was, he
was certainly never a racist. It is true that he has occasional snorts at
Jewish financiers and Celtic politicians, but from many passages in his
writings, it is clear that he found much to admire in both the Celtic and
the Jewish traditions. He liked the Cornish people with whom he lived
in Zennor in 1915–1916, and he owed much to two Jewish friends, Solo-
mon Koteliansky, the writer and translator, and Dr. David Eder, the
psychologist and Zionist. He gave the Hebrew name *Rananim* to his
projected ideal colony, and to judge from one of his letters to Eder written
early in 1919, he even thought at one time of joining the Zionists! "Oh,
do take me to Palestine, and I will love you for ever. Let me come and
spy out the land with you—it would rejoice my heart into the heavens.
And I will write you such a beautiful little book, 'The Entry of the
Blessed into Palestine.' "29

Kangaroo is a strange book; it is like a series of explosions, and of
course, the big explosion is to be found in the two chapters "Nightmare"
and "Revenge Timotheus Cries," where the voice of the manic Lawrence
rises to a scream of frenzy. The travel-book element, with its wonderfully
sensitive evocation of the Australian scene, is in the best Lawrentian
manner, but the realistic-novel element is extremely slight and scarcely
more than thinly disguised autobiography. The political myth, however, is
the essence of the book. Lovat Somers, the little English author of working-class origin, has a great deal of the Sancho Panza in him. He is both
attracted and repelled by Kangaroo and his plan for a sort of idealized
fascism based on "love": "the rule of a quiet gentle father who uses his
authority in the name of the living life and who is absolutely stern
against anti-life."30 He is also attracted to a certain extent by the program of Willie Struthers, the Labour leader, though he complains that

Struthers's socialism has "no spunk in it."[31] In the end he refuses to cooperate either with Kangaroo or with Struthers, and his criticism of fascism and bolshevism is a notable piece of political wisdom:

> Kangaroo . . . is in a false position. He wants to save property for the property-owners, and he wants to save Labour from the capitalist and the politician and all. In fact he wants to save everything as we have it and it can't be done. You can't eat your cake and have it, and I prefer Willie Struthers. Bolshevism is at least not sentimental. It's a last step towards an end, a hopeless end, but better disaster than an equivocal nothingness, like the present. Kangaroo wants to be God Himself and save everybody, which is just as irritating, at last. Kangaroo as God Himself . . . is worse than Struthers's absolute of the People. Though it's a choice of evils, and I choose neither. I choose the Lord Almighty.[32]

Those who accuse Lawrence of being a fascist should ponder this passage carefully. It is clear from it that if there had to be a choice between fascism and communism he would choose communism, but that he regarded both as evils and refused to surrender to either of the "absolute" ideologies.

The manic Lawrence, as many critics have pointed out, appears in the incident of the riotous socialist meeting broken up by the Diggers, where, for a moment, Somers shares the frenzy of Jack Callcott and his fellow thugs. But afterward, when Jack exults in his brutality ("Killing's natural to a man. . . . It is just as natural as lying with a woman."), Somers finds him "weird" and "gruesome" and refuses to answer when Jack asks if he agrees with these murderous sentiments.[33]

Kangaroo might be described as an incomplete "thought-adventure"; it was followed by *The Plumed Serpent*, which grew out of Lawrence's Mexican experience as *Kangaroo* grew out of his visit to Australia. The starting point of *The Plumed Serpent* is really Somers's declaration in *Kangaroo* that he chooses "the Lord Almighty" in preference to both fascism and bolshevism; in other words he had now come to believe that the only satisfactory basis for a renovation of society must be religious. "The Lord Almighty" in this context is certainly not the Nobodaddy of conventional Christianity but "the deep God Who is the source of all passion and life . . . the great dark God, the ithyphallic of the first dark religions."[34] *The Plumed Serpent* is a thought-adventure or experiment in imagining what a revolution with such a religious basis might be like in a country like Mexico.

It is a less explosive, more sensuous and "poetic" book than *Kangaroo*. It is remarkable that it is the only novel of Lawrence's which contains long passages in verse or near-verse. Perhaps it would have been better if Lawrence had written two books: a realistic novel cum travel book about Mexico and a Blakean poem or prophetic book embodying Don Ramón's new mythology. There are three important characters in the story: Kate Forrester, the attractive and intelligent Irish widow; Don Ramón Carrasco, the Spanish-Mexican aristocrat; and Don Cipriano Viedma, the Mexican-Indian general with the veneer of an Oxford education. It is significant that, for the first time in a major work of Lawrence's, the central figure in *The Plumed Serpent* is a woman. This can be taken as a sign that he was entering the last, posttragic phase of his art. In this phase the female figure is always important: Antigone and Ismene in the *Oedipus at Colonus* of Sophocles; Perdita, Imogen, and Miranda in Shakespeare's last plays; and Jerusalem, the bride of Albion, in Blake's final epic. In Jung's terminology these figures represent the *anima*, or the imaginative part of the soul. Kate Forrester is a mixture of Lawrence the prophet-poet and Lawrence the down-to-earth Midlander, the imaginative self and the voice of sanity and good sense. Don Ramón, the leader and philosopher of the new religion of Quetzalcoatl, is partly Lawrence the poet and partly Lawrence the messianic preacher, while Don Cipriano is the demonic, "dark" Lawrence with fantasies of sexual potency and sadistic tendencies.

It is wrong to call Don Ramón's revolution a fascist movement. Actually the reactionary Mexican *fascistas* are shown to be his bitter opponents. The revolution of Quetzalcoatl is religious rather than political, though it is backed by Cipriano and his soldiers. Don Ramón's main object is to replace the decadent Roman Catholicism of Mexico by a new religion based on a purified version of the old Mexican mythology without the bloodstained sacrifices of the Aztecs. In a significant conversation with Kate he speaks with the voice of Lawrence the prophet: " 'When Man has nothing but his will to assert—even his good-will—it is always bullying. Bolshevism is one sort of bullying, capitalism is another: and liberty is a change of chains.' 'Then what's to be done?,' said Kate. 'Just nothing?' ... 'One is driven at last, back to the far distance, to look for God,' said Ramón, uneasily."[35] This word, "uneasily," is, perhaps, the keynote of the book. The revolution of Quetzalcoatl with the Indian dances, the drummings, the hymns, the burning of the Christian images, and the ritual execution of the assassins is a kind of grandiose Wagnerian drama with a flavor of what we now call "science fiction" (without, of course, the "science"). But, as Dr. Leavis has pointed out, one has the feeling throughout that Lawrence has failed "to convince himself."[36] It is as though the messianic Lawrence and the manic Lawrence are constantly surging forward (or, perhaps, downward), and Lawrence the prophet-poet and Lawrence the down-to-earth Midlander are periodically pulling them back. In a letter to Martin Secker, Lawrence wrote that he meant "everything that Ramon says,"[37] but, following his own precept, we must believe the tale rather than the novelist and regard these words as an utterance of the "dribbling liar."

The voice of sanity is constantly heard when Kate expresses her distrust and weariness: " 'Oh,' she cried to herself, stifling. 'For heaven's sake let me get out of this, and back to simple, human people. I loathe the very sound of Quetzalcoatl and Huitzilopochtli. I would die rather than be mixed up with it any more. Horrible, really, both Ramón and Cipriano. And they want to put it over me with their high-flown bunk and their Malintzi.' "[38] It is true that Kate finally gives way and consents to become first the bride of Huitzilopochtli and then the legal wife of Cipriano, but, right up to the end, she is uneasy and is preparing to return to Europe. In the Harvard typescript, apparently, she does not even become a goddess and a wife; the story breaks off as she is packing to return to Europe.[39] It is clear, too, that Lawrence regards the outcome of Don Ramón's revolution with some misgiving. It succeeds insofar as President Montes adopts the new creed and it becomes the official religion of Mexico, but there is a note of foreboding at the end: "The whole country was thrilling with a new thing, with a release of new energy. But there was a sense of violence and crudity in it all, a touch of horror."[40] These last words, surely, are prophetic of the Nazi movement. We feel that the noble and humane Don Ramón will be swept aside by Don Cipriano and that the revolution, like all violent revolutions, will end in a military tyranny and perhaps a reversion to the blood sacrifices of Cipriano's Aztec ancestors. L. D. Clark has rightly noted that "as an imaginative adventure of the human psyche, The Plumed Serpent is a dangerous undertaking."[41] It is important, however, to recognize that Lawrence was always aware of the danger.

IV

The Plumed Serpent marks the end of Lawrence's traumatic phase, his "time of troubles." In this phase of his career he was obsessed by the sickness of western society and the attempt to find a way out by means of a new order based on leadership and the cult of power. He tried in this period, in John Middleton Murry's words, to "de-Christianize himself,"[42] or rather, perhaps we should say, the manic Lawrence tried to de-Christianize him but never quite succeeded. His own words in his "Study of Thomas Hardy" provide the best criticism of his work during this period: "Because a novel is a microcosm and because man in viewing the universe must view it in the light of a theory, therefore every novel must have the background or structural skeleton of some theory of being,

some metaphysic. But the metaphysic must always serve the artistic purpose. Otherwise the novel becomes a treatise."[43] *Aaron's Rod, Kangaroo,*
and *The Plumed Serpent,* in spite of much brilliant writing and observation of people and places, are all full of theory that "fails to subserve the
artistic purpose." Lawrence's deeper artistic self is always uneasy about
the theory and Lawrence the down-to-earth Midlander mocks it as
"high-flown bunk."

Lawrence's true greatness is seen in his success in "coming through" his
time of troubles to a final phase of imaginative vision in the last years of
his short life. It is this phase which is neglected by the superficial critics
who have tried to tie the label "fascist" onto him. In these years he explicitly rejected the concept of leadership which had haunted him for so
long. Commenting on *The Plumed Serpent* and "the hero" in a letter to
Witter Bynner, dated March 13, 1928, he wrote:

> On the whole, I think you're right. The hero is obsolete, and the
> leader of men is a back number. After all, at the back of the
> hero is the militant ideal, or the militant ideal seems to me also
> a cold egg. We're sort of sick of all forms of militarism and mili-
> tantism. . . . On the whole I agree with you, the leader-
> cum-follower relationship is a bore. And the new relationship
> will be some sort of tenderness, sensitive, between men and men
> and men and women, and not the one up one down, lead on I
> follow, *ich dien* ... but still in a *way,* one has to fight ... for the
> phallic reality, against the non-phallic cerebration unrealities.[44]

"Tenderness" is the key word to Lawrence's last works. It was the title
that he originally intended to give to *Lady Chatterley's Lover.* This
brings us back to Frieda's statement that "Lawrence's *raison d'être* was
love." I believe she was right, but Lawrence would not use the word
"love," because for him it was hopelessly defiled by the "faked love" of
conventional Christianity.

His "tenderness" was the Christian love (not the faked sort) united
with "love" of the sensuous, or, as he called it, the "phallic" kind. It was to
be a combination of the *agapē* of the New Testament and the *erōs* of the
Greeks. In the wonderful series of works written in the last years of his
life, *St. Mawr, The Virgin and the Gipsy, Lady Chatterley's Lover,* with
its superb epilogue, *A Propos of Lady Chatterley's Lover, Etruscan
Places, The Man Who Died, Apocalypse,* and the *Last Poems,* the
"mechanical willed" quality of *Aaron's Rod, Kangaroo,* and *The Plumed
Serpent* disappears and with it the voice of the manic Lawrence. Like
Shakespeare in his last plays, Lawrence in these works has reached the
rare condition of imaginative consciousness which enables the artist to do
consciously what primitive, myth-making man did unconsciously: to

think in concrete images.[45] Any summarizing of this thinking of Lawrence in his last works must be abstract and inadequate, but it may briefly
be described as a rejection of all political nostrums for the sickness of
western society and an insistence that the only cure must be the regeneration of the individual, the regaining of what Christians call a state of
grace. Such regeneration must take place before any political action can
be meaningful, and it will be a slow process, as he writes in the Preface
to the 1925 edition of *The Crown*:

> There was nothing to be "done" in Murry's sense of the words.
> There is still nothing to be "done." Probably not for many, many
> years will men start to "do" something. And even then only after
> they have changed gradually and deeply. It is no use trying to
> modify present forms. The whole great form of our era will have
> to go. And nothing will send it down but the new shoots of life
> springing up and slowly bursting the foundations. And one can
> do nothing but fight tooth and nail to defend the new shoots of
> life from being crushed out and let them grow.[46]

All Lawrence's last works are parables, pictorial thinking about this
process of regeneration. At its simplest such thinking is seen in *The
Virgin and the Gipsy*, where the destruction of "the great form of our
era" is symbolized by the flood that sweeps away the stuffy old rectory
and the dreadful old mater, the "new shoots of life" by the girl Yvette,
and the regeneration of the body by her healing embrace with the gipsy.
St. Mawr, certainly one of Lawrence's greatest works, is far more complex. Here, like Swift in Gulliver's fourth voyage, Lawrence seems to
have despaired of finding a human symbol for his idea of perfection and
has used instead the image of a magnificent stallion. The revolt of St.
Mawr against the domination of the pseudoartist Rico is a memorable
image of the revolt of the life of the body against the arrogant domination of the superficial intellect. But the philosophic core of the tale is
Lou's terrible vision of the rottenness of "civilization" with its significant
denunciation of both bolshevism and fascism:

> The evil! the mysterious potency of evil. She could see it all the
> time in individuals, in society, in the press. There it was in
> socialism and bolshevism: the same end. But bolshevism made a
> mess of the outside of life. So turn it down. Try fascism. *Fas-
> cism would keep the surface of life intact, and carry on the
> undermining business all the better*. Never draw blood. Keep
> the hemorrhage internal, invisible. And as soon as fascism makes
> a break—which it is bound to—*because all evil works up to a
> break*—then turn it down.[47]

The voice of Lawrence the prophetic poet is heard in Lou's conclusion, which echoes the words of the Preface to *The Crown:*

> What's to be done. Generally speaking, nothing. The dead will have to bury their dead, while the earth stinks of corpses. The individual can but depart from the mass, and try to cleanse himself. Try to hold fast to the living thing, which destroys as it goes, but remains sweet. And in his soul fight, fight, fight to preserve that which is life in himself from the ghastly kisses ... but in itself, is strong and at peace.[48]

In *Lady Chatterley's Lover* and in the even more important *A Propos of Lady Chatterley's Lover* there is added the demand for that renewal and cleansing of marriage and the relationship of the sexes, which Lawrence always saw as the essential foundation for a regenerated humanity. Mellors's diagnosis of the sickness of industrial society is as valid today as it was in the 1920's:

> Their whole life depends on spending money.... That's our civilization and our education: bring up the masses to depend entirely on spending money, and then the money gives out.... If you could only tell them that living and spending isn't the same thing! But it's no good. If only they were educated to *live* instead of earn and spend ... if they could dance and hop and skip, and sing and swagger and be handsome, they could do with very little cash.... They ought to learn to be naked and handsome, and to sing in a mass and dance the old group dances, and carve the stools they sit on, and embroider their own emblems. Then they wouldn't need money. And that's the only way to solve the industrial problem: train the people to be able to live, and live in handsomeness, without the need to spend![49]

But Mellors-Lawrence has no illusion that this William Morris–like paradise can be achieved in the foreseeable future: "I feel the devil in the air, and he'll try to get us. Or not the devil, Mammon, which I think, after all, is only the mass-will of people wanting money and hating life." But he maintains his faith in the "little flame" of true married love: "The higher mystery, that doesn't even let the crocus be blown out."[50]

Lawrence's final and most mature pictorial thinking is seen in *The Man Who Died,* where the teacher who came to life again after being crucified renounces Messiahdom and rediscovers "the immortality of being alive," the wonder of the phenomenal world. His union with the priestess of Isis prefigures a religion which will unite the *agapē* of Christianity with the *erōs* or purified sensuality of the best kind of paganism. It might be said that, in this last phase, Lawrence neither accepts nor rejects Christianity but demands that it be reborn. His "message" is that of Blake: "If the doors of perception were cleansed, every thing would appear to man, as it is, infinite."[51] This is the doctrine of *Etruscan Places*, with its vision of "the natural flowering of life ... a religion of life ... even a science of life, a conception of the universe and man's place in it which made men live to the depth of their capacity,"[52] and of the *Last Poems*:

> Know thyself, and that thou art mortal.
> But know thyself, denying that thou art mortal:
> a thing of kisses and strife
> a lit-up shaft of rain
> a calling column of blood
> a rose tree bronzey with thorns
> a mixture of yea and nay
> a rainbow of love and hate
> a wind that blows back and forth
> a creature of beautiful peace, like a river
> and a creature of conflict, like a cataract. ...[53]

It is a vision that is all the more compelling because it is combined with a clear-eyed understanding of and a deep compassion for the condition of the industrial masses:

> Ah the people, the people!
> surely they are flesh of my flesh!
>
> When, in the streets of the working quarters
> they stream past, stream past, going to work;
>
> then, when I see the iron hooked in their faces,
> their poor, their fearful faces
>
> then I scream in my soul, for I know I cannot
> cut the iron hook out of their faces, that makes them so drawn,
> nor cut the invisible wires of steel that pull them. ...[54]

Lawrence was not a trained philosopher, and his thinking about politics and society is not systematic but full of contradictions and paradoxes. What we find in his works when he deals with these subjects is the penetrating criticisms and probings of a powerful and free intelligence illuminated by the richness and vitality of a poet's vision. To speak of the thought of such a writer as "leading to Auschwitz" is sheer nonsense, and it is equally beside the point to class him with Pound and Yeats as part of a reactionary "swerve to the right." He was a freer and saner spirit than either Pound or Yeats. Unlike Pound, he never surrendered to fascism, and, unlike Yeats, he was never misled by an obsolete aristocratic ideal. He was a prophetic poet like Blake, whose wisdom and vision were beyond the reach of his contemporaries and are now only beginning to be understood as he recedes in time.

NOTES

1. Bertrand Russell, *Autobiography*, II (London, 1968), 21–23.
2. *Women in Love*, Chap. 8.
3. J. M. Keynes, *Two Memoirs*, quoted in E. Nehls, *D. H. Lawrence: A Composite Biography*, I (Madison, Wisconsin, 1957), 287, 288.
4. John R. Harrison, *The Reactionaries* (London, 1967), pp. 178–189.
5. Frieda Lawrence, "Bertrand Russell's Article on Lawrence," in E. W. Tedlock, ed., *Frieda Lawrence: Memoirs and Correspondence* (London, 1961), p. 137.
6. *Letters*, A. Huxley, ed. (London, 1934), p. 190.
7. Max Beerbohm, quoted in David Cecil, *Max: A Biography* (London, 1964), p. 483.
8. John Middleton Murry, *Love, Freedom and Society* (London, 1957), p. 65.
9. *Ibid.*, p. 72.
10. Letter to George and Thomas Keats, December 28, 1817.
11. *Studies in Classic American Literature* (London, 1923), p. 13.
12. "The Novel," *Phoenix II* (London, 1968), p. 426.
13. *The Rainbow*, Chap. 12.
14. *Women in Love*, Chap. 24.
15. *Ibid.*, Chap. 11.
16. *Ibid.*, Chap. 19.
17. *The Complete Plays of D. H. Lawrence* (London, 1965), p. 361.
18. *Ibid.*, p. 375.
19. *Letters*, p. 379.
20. *Ibid.*, p. 94.
21. London, 1923, p. 47.
22. *Assorted Articles* (London, 1930), p. 205.
23. P. 148.
24. *Movements in European History* (Oxford, 1925), p. 328.
25. *Ibid.*, p. 344.
26. *Letters*, p. 531.
27. *Aaron's Rod*, Chap. 20.
28. *Ibid.*, Chap. 21.

29. J. B. Hobman, ed., *David Eder: Memoirs of a Modern Pioneer* (London, 1945) p. 121.
30. *Kangaroo* (London, 1923), Chap. 6.
31. *Ibid.*, Chap. 11.
32. *Ibid.*, Chap. 16.
33. *Ibid.*
34. *Ibid.*, Chap. 11.
35. *The Plumed Serpent*, Chap. 4.
36. F. R. Leavis, *D. H. Lawrence, Novelist* (London, 1955), p. 69.
37. *Letters*, p. 640.
38. *The Plumed Serpent*, Chap. 22.
39. L. D. Clark, *The Dark Night of the Body: D. H. Lawrence's The Plumed Serpent* (Austin, Texas, 1964), p. 101.
40. *The Plumed Serpent*, Chap. 26.
41. Clark, p. 98.
42. Murry, p. 78.
43. "A Study of Thomas Hardy," *Phoenix* (London, 1936), p. 479.
44. *Letters*, p. 711.
45. See A. C. Harwood, *Shakespeare's Prophetic Mind* (London, 1964), pp. 48–50.
46. "Introductory Note to *The Crown*" (London, 1925), quoted in K. Sagar, *The Art of D. H. Lawrence* (London, 1966), p. 178.
47. *St. Mawr*, in *Collected Tales of D. H. Lawrence* (London, 1934), p. 613. Italics mine.
48. *Ibid.*, p. 614.
49. *Lady Chatterley's Lover* (New York, 1957), pp. 362–363.
50. *Ibid.*, p. 365.
51. William Blake, *The Marriage of Heaven and Hell*, in Geoffrey Keynes, ed., *Complete Writings* (London, 1966), p. 154.
52. *Etruscan Places* (London, 1932), pp. 88–89.
53. *Complete Poems* (London, 1967), p. 714.
54. *Ibid.*, p. 585.

WYNDHAM LEWIS
(1886-1957)

by Geoffrey Wagner

"IF," WROTE ERNEST HEMINGWAY in 1934, "you want to abandon your trade and get into politics, go ahead, but it is a sign that you are afraid to go on and do the other, because it is getting hard and you have to do it alone and so you want to do something where you can have friends and well-wishers. . . ." The British author-artist Percy Wyndham Lewis, Hemingway's enemy as well as his own, presents an extreme case of the contemporary aesthetic infatuation with politics, one that has ended for more than one on the gallows. He was a draftsman and (some say) portraitist of the first rank. T. S. Eliot considered him one of the few great prose stylists of the twentieth century, yet of the forty books he published in his lifetime at least sixteen must be considered as explicitly and almost entirely political; and this does not take into account volumes of autobiography and quasi-political art criticism. We note too that, never a rich man, Lewis made little money by these repeated political forays. What, then, was their motive and their nature?

To begin with, Lewis is a rigorously self-contradictory figure and no serious reader can take at face value his repeated expressions of political impartiality; the most charitable summary of these evasive statements about his own politics might be to regard them as techniques for concealment, similar to the "masks" of Yeats or Pound. It is well known, however, that he reversed himself in the practice of fact, two volumes of 1939, *The Jews, Are They Human?* and *The Hitler Cult*, quite definitely attempting not only to correct, but also to fudge over by ellipsis, earlier opinions made in particular in Lewis's celebrated book on the German dictator, which originally appeared as a series of articles in *Time and Tide*. The fictional satires Lewis wrote immediately subsequent to these corrective volumes, such as *America, I Presume* and *The Vulgar Streak*, clearly reinforce the feeling that he was urgently rewriting himself; finally, at the end of *Rotting Hill* (1951) his narrator makes peace with these demons of his past by shooting down effigies of both Hitler and Mussolini in a fair booth and dropping a threepenny bit in the mug of a figure of Britannia, whom the author had abandoned (for Canada) in World War II. In short, we cannot accept Lewis's own estimate of Lewis: his word, for instance, in *The Hitler Cult*, that he "saw through" Hitler from the start, or his disarming assurance, made in 1950, that *Count Your Dead: They Are Alive!* of 1937, a work that indicted England as a Russophile tyranny, supporting "Red" atrocities in Spain (while Franco fought gallantly against the minions of Moses Rosenberg), was "a first-rate peace pamphlet."

If in April 1929 T. S. Eliot grouped Wyndham Lewis as one of those writers who "incline in the direction of some kind of fascism," Lewis could in the same year describe his own politics as "partly communist and partly fascist, with a distinct streak of monarchism in my marxism, but at bottom anarchist with a healthy passion for order." As he addresses the British Fascist party, he throws off the statement that "at no time, however, have I been in the least danger of falling in love with a political state or becoming excited about a party."

Despite these obfuscations, a consistent attitude can be sorted out, and, in fact, one charts a strangely fascinating trail in so doing, since these very visions and revisions have provided the context of aesthetic life in the past century. Thomas Mann has well explained the lure of politics for the contemporary artist and was able, with Joyce, to rise superior to it or at least to formulate his genius in terms not subject to the tugs of over-topical pressures. Lewis remained mesmerized by them, and finally they crippled his fiction and all but put an end to his painting (in an unusually touching article for *The Listener* he himself saw his final blindness as symbolic). The man who could once write "I am not a politician but an artist" found himself compelled to declare a decade later, "With candour, and an almost criminal indifference to my personal interests, I have given myself up to the study of the State."

It would be tempting to align Lewis's Zarathustrian political pronouncements under the heading of a new, and English, Nietzsche. There is no doubt at all of the spell which the German thinker held over Lewis, evinced by a tell-tale exposition in the fiction and accompanying excoriation in the polemic. Tarr, the hero of Lewis's first and, some think, greatest novel, is a true Nietzschean individual, a successor to Turgenev's Bazarov, Fëdor Dostoevski's Raskolnikov, Knut Hamsun's Glahn—with the exception that Tarr was conscious of the ancestry himself. What, then, was the result of Lewis's study of the state?

The most useful way to consider this subject is with the tools of Lewis's own vocabulary, idiosyncratic as this at times may be, since his purely political books are already forgotten and readers will need clues to the consciousness at work behind the satirical fiction that will endure. It would, for instance, be possible to make a kind of digest of modern European neoclassical thought—out of Charles Maurras, Henri Massis, Benda (whom Lewis so admired), Ernest Seillière, and the German anti-Bergsonists—and to compound such with the political thought of Eliot, Thomas Hulme, and Pound; but even so, the terms would not be true to Lewis (his admiration for Oriental art could only be squeezed in, unrepresentatively, under Pound). No, Lewis's semantic is his own and that it is frequently tortuous and unamenable to consistency is part of the pattern of his mind.[1] It was Camus who declared that contemporary philosophy is sometimes the hardest of all to understand, since we cannot recognize our own complexities.

The key work in Lewis's political canon was *The Art of Being Ruled* (1926), a far more impressive and coherent book than the better known, because more sensational, *Time and Western Man* of the following year. Here is Lewis's first full outline of human society and his division of it into two components, the *person* (Nietzsche's master) and the *thing* (Nietzsche's herd). Of these two elements Lewis almost boringly insists that the latter is today predominant, in the form of idiotic units that have no desire to feel deeply or think clearly, "hallucinatory automata," or, as he also calls them, larvae, performing mice. A quick summary might run as follows: "In the mass people wish to be automata." "The mass of men ask nothing better than to be *Puppets*." "Men find their greatest happiness in type-life."[2]

This view of the masses would surely be relatively uninteresting unless it helped categorize the perils of what Lionel Trilling has defined as the "liberal imagination," with its irony that those British writers with the acutest ear for words this century—Yeats, Lawrence, Lewis, Eliot—have often held the most outlawed political opinions. For Pound's "Student," in *An Anachronism at Chinon*, "Humanity is a herd, eaten by perpetual follies." Eliot was no more sanguine: "The majority is capable neither of strong emotion nor of strong resistance"; and again, "At the moment when the public's interest is aroused, the public is never well enough informed to have the right to an opinion."[3]

The paradox remains, as Trilling suggests, that these heretical opinions occasionally lend strength to the creative sense, rather than refuting it. Céline comes to mind. He would be little without his bigotry. But my own feeling is that this applies particularly to British fiction (and perhaps American), whereas in France the neoclassicists never turned up a satirist of Lewis's stature. For certainly Céline was not among their ranks. Until Sartre at least, the French debate was conducted in the arena, and on the level, of philosophical polemic. The fact that so many of France's best writers since the last war have been philosophers demonstrates a basic questioning of national values largely unknown to England.

Yet it is possible to say that Lewis's essentially repellent view of ordinary humanity gave impetus to his best satire under the aegis of the Bergsonian *pantin*, or dummy. Lewis had attended Bergson's lectures on laughter in Paris and there undoubtedly found, as any reader will readily concede, an outlet for his own sympathies in the idea of the human being reduced to a robot or machine as the core of satirical humor. The fine collection of early short stories given the title *The Wild Body* (1927) gains its power from this vision of men as machines—one which has overtaken us today. A "wild body," for Lewis, is a creature of such primitivity that it is no more than an animal machine and includes those subject to their particular state or view of life. Any reader will soon see that this is the source of nearly all Wyndham Lewis's unheroic characters. They are not really living at all; they are thus novices, tyros, or, as he described a tyro in his own short-lived periodical of that name—and the description might have been taken verbatim out of Bergson's *Le Rire*—"a puppet worked with deft fingers with a screaming voice underneath."

This comic rigidity, or clownlike mechanism, which Bergson had postulated as the representative marionette of today's various absurdities, was Lewis's "thing." The idea acted like a tonic on his satiric gift. Here the philosopher will infer that Lewis's satire is basically Cartesian, in the sense that the more primitive a man is, the more mechanical. Lewis uses "mechanical" to mean "thing"-like, that is, coerced by the environment or culture group and driven into animality by lack of awareness. He thus calls the American Negro "mechanical" and criticizes Lawrence for adulating "mechanical" Mexicans. In his travel book *Filibusters in Barbary* he will similarly call the North Moroccan a "machine." Science today is everywhere on the side of the "thing."

This must at once be recognized as the formal basis of much of his characterization. The man-machine of this nature is borrowed from René Descartes, as also from the eighteenth-century French materialist Julien Offroy de La Mettrie, author of *L'Homme-machine* (1748). La Mettrie supposed just those mechanical puppets who parade in clockwork packs through Lewis's later fiction. Unless one concedes his terminology here, one cannot understand him. Of the emotional, romantic Bertha in *Tarr* we read, "The machine, the sentimental, the indiscriminate side of her awoke." A statement like this—equating mechanical and indiscriminate as cognates, say—contrives to say a great deal about contemporary civilization, but it must be confessed that Bergson's conception of the comic is of a generous function restoring man to society, while Lewis was content to disrupt and distort.

In *Paleface: The Philosophy of the "Melting-Pot"* (1929) Lewis elaborated rather fully on the Roman or Goethean *persona*, whom he opposed to his *res*, or "thing." For the "person" is the genuine individual, opposed to the social stereotype or group "rhythm."[4] The form or abstract of the human, the "person" alone, is fully free and is referred to, in a Hegelian borrowing, as the "Not-Self." Clearly the "Not-Self" is associated with the neoclassical "anti-self" of Yeats, with Irving Babbitt's "distinguished person," and with the ideal individual of Jacques Maritain. But for Lewis a "person" is born, not made, and a "thing" can never become a "person." This effectively jettisons any program of social melioration whereby material improvement will lead to moral betterment, and in fact his "Not-Self" is envied and hated by the majority—"It is an enemy principle." Or again, it shows "the human mind in its traditional role of the enemy of life, as an oddity outside the machine."[5] Lewis edited a famous periodical of the twenties called *The Enemy* and frequently referred to himself as such.

Thus, in essence, the only politics Lewis would logically espouse would be one that safeguarded the "person" (or, as he liked to pun, the "person"-ality); discontinuity, or flux, worked against the preservation of the true individual. In the ideal state the artist's duty was to maintain our continuity, since "continuity, in the individual as in the race, is the diagnostic of a civilized condition."[6] So we find Major "Corkers" Corcoran, in *America, I Presume*, noting with distaste the "discontinuity of the American people." This continuity of culture, we know, was equated with true wisdom by Eliot and found by him to be, in a borrowing from Babbitt, the essence of a truly contemporary mind. Consequently, Lewis excoriated in particular the individual who gave in to a "group-rhythm," surrendered his sense of continuity, and became prey to the fluxes of his time.

This type Lewis predicated as the "Split-Man," or person divided against himself, exemplifying such as Jamesjulius (that is, James Joyce) Ratner in *The Apes of God*, where there is to be found a fictional follow-up to the long and celebrated attack on Joyce in *Time and Western Man* (though part of the satire, "Mr. Zagreus and the Split-Man," antedated the criticism, having appeared in Eliot's *The Criterion* in 1924). Horace Zagreus explains the nature of the split in *The Apes of God*, insisting that it is a form of philosophical self-crippling. The longitudinal cleft in the figure drawn by Lewis at the start of Part V of *The Apes*,

called "The Split-Man" and characterizing Joyce-Ratner (also alias Rod-
ker), carries this out graphically and reminds us that it is not a Jekyll-
and-Hyde affair; the split is rather a kind of constant, subsuming, and
intrinsic self-treachery. Some of us might prefer to call it the ability to
see both sides at once. But Lewis's mind militated against tolerance. The
more absurd appellants at the Bailiff's Court in *The Childermass* are
synonymously "split-men or half-men." There is a useful summary in *Paleface:* "In Rome what constituted 'abnormality' was the being either a
slave, a stranger or a minor (of whatever age) within the potestas of
some head of a family. A slave and, originally, a stranger, a 'peregrinus,'
was legally a 'thing.'"[7]

Given such general principles (or lack of them), it would seem logical
for Lewis, seeing himself as a satirist, to expose symptoms of political
instability and discontinuity. The body of his written work is exactly this,
and it led him into not only some ridiculously rococo social history but
also a series of more intellectually unpopular opinions than have been
expressed by any other British writer of his consequence in this century.
The contemporary folly he chiefly flays in his satire is the "group-
rhythm," the coagulation of individuals into mass units, whether on
behalf of class or color or age or sex. We are reminded of Ernst
Toller's mass-man. *Paleface*, through attacks on D. H. Lawrence and
Sherwood Anderson, derided the white man's alleged inferiority complex
vis-à-vis the black—"negro-worship." *The Doom of Youth* (1932) attacked
the encouragement of intense consciousness of youth, in an endeavor to
reverse the values of experience, though in *Hitler* (1931) Lewis praises
Hitler's "youth-politics," since here youth is presumed to be made more
rational and, one supposes, tolerant of authority. In nearly all his satire
Lewis exhibits a male chauvinism (characteristic, too, of the early Benda)
that can be summarized by his admission that the extension of the fran-
chise to women has dreadfully decreased the common political sagacity.
There but remains the so-called class "rhythm," and it is significant that,
though he ridiculed British upper-class philistinism in a number of characters, Lewis failed to engage his mind with this topic.

It must be conceded that there lies considerable intelligence, and
prescience, too, in his identification of the political utilization of youth as
some sort of unique value, even if the acrobatic reversal in *Hitler* must
cast doubt on his sincerity. But it is in his arraignment of woman as a
vehicle of romance, revolutionary humanitarianism, and antiauthoritar-
ianism in general that Lewis's biases surpass the van of even contemporary neoclassical writings or ravings. For this suspicion of woman is
paralleled in the French antiromanticists, like Seillière, Maurras, and Lasserre, but Lewis lets it have its head in a body of fictive literature. The
Zarathustra-like advice to his early character, The Herdsman, is simply,

"As to women: wherever you can, substitute the society of men." In fact, Lewis cites more than once Nietzsche's indirect advice to take a whip when you go to make love to a woman. Tarr's treatment of Bertha is clearly in this context: "Surrender to a woman was a sort of suicide for an artist," Tarr reflects at one point and, at another, "God was man: the woman was a lower form of life."

What is parenthetically interesting here is that Lewis has evidently organized this vehicle of visceral sensation to be German, in the form of a character like Bertha (note the Big Bertha German trench-gun). Yet if the shade of Mme. de Staël stands behind such a characterization, it was actually a German, Karl Joël, who largely anticipated this "pro-French" criticism of the emasculating influence of women.[8] Here Lewis chooses for his purposes to stand squarely beside the French neoclassicists and "thinkers."

Alas, a bias bores. Lewis's work is limited and hurt by his inability to do more than caricature women of this type. His belief that contact with the female kind is a capitulation to the animal has to be reasserted in book after book, in none of which is any single example of happy, fruitful love. Perhaps this would not matter—and in his drawing it does not matter—but his reiteration of the fat, sleepy, indolent, and subjectively sensual woman must rob the reader of any feeling of perspective. One can have little confidence in this procession of female dummies through his pages, from the obese Anastasya and Bertha, of *Tarr*, from Hotshepsot, of *The Enemy of the Stars* ("a big girl with a big roll in the hips"), to Lily, of *Snooty Baronet* ("sultry about the joints," etc.), to Maddie, of *The Vulgar Streak*, to Gillian, of *The Revenge for Love*, and to a dozen more. Emile Faguet, among others, has pointed out the weaknesses of this inclusive charge of women as chaotically emotional, ignoring, as it does, the Renaissance or Parnassian poetess, with her clarity of definition and adoration of the classics.

Lewis liked to push the charge further, however. His dislike of woman in this sense provided him with the pabulum of satire in more than one form. For woman was responsible also for a general effeminization of our culture. The increase of war in our society, he proposed, negated the reproductory function and caricatured the institution of manhood. So the wake of world wars brought us "sex-transformation" or "shamanization," which once more played into the hands of womanish values, as the disenchanted male yielded more and more of his norms to the irresponsible female. More than once Lewis fulminated, "The 'homo' is the legitimate child of the 'suffragette,'" meaning that both share in an "instinctive capitulation of the will on the part of the ruling male sex." We find this echoed from book to book, from *The Art of Being Ruled* to *Rude Assignment*, from *The Doom of Youth* to *Snooty Baronet*, and to that declaration at the close of the first part of *The Childermass* when a character called Alectryon (meaning cock—he is a member of Maurras's *L'Action française*) shouts out, "Homosexuality is a branch of the Feminist Revolution. The pathic is the political twin of the suffragette." The "sex-war" was for Lewis an obsessive group-rhythm and he was not able, or willing, to organize his thought to accommodate it within a novel.

The mind that sees all about it symptoms of decay (the "rot" of *Rotting Hill*) can scarcely be expected to view contemporary democratic politics with pleasure. We know that neither Lewis nor Eliot, Pound nor Hulme, did so. In *After Strange Gods* T. S. Eliot found our democracies "wormeaten with Liberalism" (the metaphor is significant). Similarly for Lewis, at roughly the same time, "It is the 'democratic' conceit that is at fault, is it not?" Democratic freedom was license, a cloak for totalitarianism; of England of the thirties we find him writing, "No Party-state could be more autocratic." This conception of "dictatorial" democracy, of "proletarian imperialism" (*Paleface*), is essentially familiar by now, with its concomitant criticism of an orthodoxy of liberalism (Lewis's "rebel 'fixation'"); the latter is the basis of satire in *The Revenge for Love* (1937). Lewis lends little to these worn debates, so many borrowed from stricter critics of liberalism a century ago, and his long poem *One-Way Song* (1933) contains a passage of very shrill invective against unreflecting, standardized revolutionaries of our times, puppetlike busybodies playing at social change, mere dolts who "strut and pant in insect packs." No, Lewis's criticism of contemporary democracy reads as disappointingly unoriginal, and is only interesting as a stepping-stone to one of the most alarming political positions, with its attendant abrogation of intelligence, taken by any British writer of this century. This was Lewis's flirtation with fascism, already mentioned.

The reader of *The Art of Being Ruled* had been warned in 1926, of course: "The disciplined *fascist* party in Italy can be taken as representing the new and healthy type of 'freedom.'" It is equally true that in this work Lewis praised certain aspects of early Russian communism. But here again his opposites, or contraries, reconcile themselves, for he was always searching for—and overready to find—a society that seemed to protect the "person"; he was understandably interested in early Soviet art. Yet it is undeniable that Lewis's analysis of the state led him prematurely and dangerously to espouse the Nazi creed. In 1930 he went to Germany, met Hitler, and returned to England to write a series of articles, later collected into a book, on the new German regime. Despite his efforts to do so, Lewis was never able to rewrite this ideological error, and it haunted him to his death.

Naturally it must be seen within a certain reportorial context. Lewis liked to travel and was ready to accept commissions. To some extent he was reporting modern Germany as he would report "Barbary." This was the attitude he was himself to adopt when, soon after its publication, he saw how *Hitler* had hurt him; in *Blasting and Bombardiering* (1937) he protests that the book was simply a series of impressions given "as a spectator, not as a partisan." We could add in his defense, too, that he showed less enthusiasm for Mosley than did Eliot, though there is praise for the British fascist leader in an article curiously tucked away in Germany, in German, in 1937.

But any reading of *Hitler* must show that this is not enough. In 1936 the British *Fascist Quarterly* was listing *Hitler* as "still about the best study of the man and the movement," while in the same year Lewis was writing in *Left Wings over Europe*, "it is an undeniable fact that *democracy* is being practised in Germany at present, with surprising success." (We had thought that he despised democracy.) In any event, Lewis was at this time being financially supported by my uncle, the realist painter Edward Wadsworth, who had also met and liked Hitler and whose house in Sussex was searched from top to bottom by the C.I.D. on outbreak of hostilities in 1938. If Lewis wanted, in Hemingway's words, "to do something where you can have friends and well-wishers," his bile had led him badly, and sadly, astray. Indeed, his mind was never to recover from the treachery he played it at this time. He never wrote another *Tarr*, nor even another *The Revenge for Love*—though the latter makes an interesting point, in connection with literature and politics, to which I will return later.

Read alongside *Left Wings* and *Count Your Dead*, Lewis's *Hitler* is a committed defense of both German and Italian fascist politics, an attack on the League of Nations, and an analysis of representative government as occult, usurious, and despotic (though Hitler himself is conceived, as above, as having been democratically elected). British parliamentary politics is an egregious sham. Germany should be allowed to rearm. Even the Abyssinian war was one of "liberation," we read, forced on Mussolini by Great Britain. Here, at least, in the fascist states, is a chance for the "person" or "Not-Self" to emerge, above ethics, beyond morality—*jenseits*, as Nietzsche phrased it, on the other side of inhibiting and vulgarized concepts of ordinary good and evil. There remains, then, the racial question.

In *Hitler* itself the Jewish question in Germany is called a "racial red-herring." Was Lewis anti-Semitic? A recent work addressed to such vexed discriminations marks the distinction for a creative writer when he crosses the border line between inherited stereotypes of Jewry, the importing of archetypal villains (as in Shakespeare), and consciously evaluated attitudes with resultantly contrived characters of unpleasant Jews (as in T. S. Eliot). Lewis certainly peopled his fiction with many

unlikable Jews: In *The Revenge for Love* Isaac Wohl is one of the principal forgers, while in *The Apes* Archie Margolin is described as a "militant
slum-Jew" or "Sham Yid" with a "mass-production grin." In *The Red
Priest* Father Card is in danger of becoming "the victim of the Jews."
And so on. These stereotypes are, however, common to a large number of
contemporary British writers, and more detestable examples could be
found in the fiction of Graham Greene and Evelyn Waugh. Moreover, in
The Jews, Are They Human? (1939), a "revisionist" work, Lewis pays
tribute to Jewish ability in criticizing current German racial theories.
Unfortunately, by this point in Lewis's career one is legitimately on one's
guard against the cant in such recantations.

There is no doubt that with Nietzsche Lewis saw the Jewish psychology as an intrinsic "group-rhythm," one that threatened the "person"—see
his atrabilious attack on Gertrude Stein ("the dark stammering voice of a
social dissolution"). In an article contributed to *The New Statesman* in
1924 the Jew is characterized by "an almost morbid sociability, clinging
gregariousness, and satisfaction in crowds." He repeats this criticism in
Paleface and elsewhere—"Jewish success is a triumph of organization, the
subordination of the individual to the race." There is a passage, placed
below in brackets, which Lewis can be seen to have deleted from the
second edition of *Tarr*: "Rembrandt paints decrepit old Jews [the most
decayed specimens of the lowest race on earth that is]." (In the margin
of the manuscript of an article on art, to go into *The Dial* in 1921, he
cancelled a passage on the emotional nature of the Jew.)[9]

At least these evasions cannot be said to have actively contributed to
the wholesale massacre of Jews in Europe, as surely did those of another
antiromanticist, Charles Maurras. Moreover, Lewis does not proceed
much further in this connection than a mid-nineteenth-century writer like
Alphonse Toussenel, who indicted Jerusalem as the seat of revolution and
the Jews as sponsoring Protestantism.[10] If Lewis guarded himself against
such paroxysms, he nonetheless found, in *Hitler* at any rate, the racial
homogeneity of the Nazis a healthy counter to American "negro-
worship," and Hitler's Aryanism (as then formulated) wholly desirable.

We are, in short, dealing at this point with an intelligent mind *in
extremis*, and to any student of literature, to any psychologist, surely, the
degree of artistic conscience still operating in Lewis alongside these distortions and contortions must be most interesting. *The Revenge for Love*
was Lewis's one satire almost entirely concerned with politics, and it was
written at the same time as *Left Wings* and *Count Your Dead*, his most
violent political diatribes. The latter book, composed of the supposed
notebooks of one Launcelot Nidwit, everywhere advances the contention
that British democracy is a total sham ("The Death of John Bull" was
erased from the title page of the manuscript). British democracy is here,

in fact, no less than a Russophile tyranny: "All you have to say to Britannia is 'Hitler' and she sees Red! She clenches her fist, links arms with Blum and Litvinov, and is ready for anything."[11] The B.B.C. is on the side of the "Reds," while in the United States the Hearst Press alone approximates the truth. Baldwin has stifled public opinion and made England a tool in the hands of the Soviet, with the result that "we are about to go to war to make the world safe for Communism." Not even Pound's *Jefferson and/or Mussolini* made more denunciatory accusations. Yet in the midst of their maelstrom Lewis could write a controlled, and often moving, fiction. It was as if his fact had become such fantasy that the rhetoric of a fiction demanded its own truth. There is something of the same occurring in Eliot, who satirized Mosley in *The Rock* while praising him at the same moment in *The Criterion.* In a lesser way Eliot showed the same ambivalence when treating Maurras, his "Coriolan."

Lewis himself set *The Revenge for Love* higher than *Tarr.* The book was originally called *False Bottoms*, since this is the sham that pervades the book from the false bottom in the peasant girl's basket at the start (food-hiding sedition) to Victor Stamp's discovery of bricks instead of guns in the false bottom of his car at the end. In this, Lewis's nearest approach to direct tragedy, sham is the human norm; earlier in the same year, in an article addressed to the British Fascist party, he had called Marxism "an enormous sham," and he was to accuse Great Britain, in *Left Wings*, of being no more than a "sham-bulldog." "We are only free once in our lives," says an almost existentialist Lewis through a character here. "That is when at last we gaze into the bottom of the heart of our beloved and find that it is false." Set in a tormented contemporary Spain, the novel studies the betrayals of love—which presumes attachment, inimical to Lewis—and is one of the firmest and finest right-wing fictions of our time.

It is so because Hardcaster, the one man of honor whose love for a creed, that of communism, is intellectual, represents that aspect of himself which Lewis had betrayed. He is taken prisoner in an act of unselfishness designed to protect one of the "salon pinks" who are the puppets, or "things," of the satire. It is quite true that the rigidity of Marxism is ridiculed in Hardcaster, as that of nihilism had been in Kreisler, of *Tarr.* But we note that Hardcaster is called, with his creator, Percy and that his surname suggests a "hard cast" only. There is a human being within, struggling to emerge through the dogma. The act of belief is pitifully human. Spurned by the other political prisoners, spat on by a beggar crone, this "man of truth" with his "incorruptible intellect" at last lets a tear fall down his poker face.[12] No physical suffering has brought this reaction from him, but only the thought of those like Margot, the vulnerable and tender, to whose kind his politics has played Judas. The irony comes full circle. The satirist is satirized as England's right-wing masterpiece in fact expresses compassion for a communist!

Reciprocally, in tracing this power of artistic conscience, we find that in the purely political writings Lewis did not parallel his enthusiasm for Hitler with the same for Mussolini. Why not? Two answers are possible. In one place he differentiates Mussolini from Hitler by calling the Duce more communist. But, second, Lewis had seen Italian fascism express itself, and, for him, expose itself, on the level of art—in the Futurism of Emilio Marinetti and others, including I Rondisti (the group around the magazine *La Ronda*). Lewis repeatedly criticized Italian fascism as so much political Futurism, charging both Marinetti (whom he had met) and Mussolini with being unthinking apostles of "action." He was eventually to see Hitler in the same light, but the distinction remains that Italian fascism was ushered in with a metaphoric movement in which Lewis could identify reprehensible traits in a way that German fascism was not. Moreover, Mussolini's lengthy article on "Fascismo" for the *Enciclopedia italiana*, with its stress on youth (*"Giovinezza, impeto, fede"*), openly advocated principles with which Lewis would, and did, disagree.

This examination of a modern writer's politics may have seemed over-familiar to some. "Politics are 'below' morals, below the reason," we read in *Rude Assignment*, and "Politics is a melodrama for teen-aged minds," in *America and Cosmic Man*; yet *Rotting Hill*, of approximately the same era, tells us that contemporary fiction must be steeped in politics to be an adequate reflection of reality. By its inherent nature the metaphoric mind cannot divorce itself from morality in the manner Lewis and Machiavelli proposed for the ideal ruler. In the lion and fox episode of *Il principe* (taken as a text for Lewis's book on Shakespeare), and again in Chapter 3 of the first book of the *Discorsi*, Machiavelli—in a distinction that has escaped more than one critic desiring to present him as impartial—assumed that men were normally evil.

Such was Lewis's paradox, and it is surely one that has shadowed our times. As an instrument of power, politics is required to dictate morals, and this, for the artist, is an abrogation of the metaphoric role. I. A. Richards calls language "dramatic"; it has its intrinsic morality. Let us assume that it was for this reason that writers like Lewis and Pound became involved in fascism, in which for a moment there were aesthetic temptations. Such, at least, is the rosiest interpretation to put on these misunderstandings. In "The Old Gang and the New Gang," a pamphlet of 1933, Lewis assumes that politicians are on a par with policemen or soldiers—what we today call law-enforcers—going on to suggest that intellectual equipment may actually be a handicap to them.

However, even the most tyrannical of law-enforcers enforce a certain law, and Lewis never prescribed how governments should discipline themselves if not by the so-despised democratic vote. Extraordinary power carries with it the assumption that it should be used, and *quis custodiet custodies?* It is a melancholy task to examine human disease in any form, but we can only learn by doing so. The terms of Lewis's excesses are extremely uncongenial to the academic mind, and there is something unpleasantly unworthy of the man in the craven nature of his rapid rewritings. Wyndham Lewis called his "the politics of the intellect," but it was, for many, a strangely emotional elite he championed in his lifetime as his "ideal giant" for society.

NOTES

1. For instance: Anyone who completes a reading of all Lewis's work cannot escape being baffled by his views on nationhood. Throughout his career, from the second issue of *Blast*, where we read, "All Nationality is a congealing and conventionalizing," to his reviews of London exhibitions at the end, he preached an internationalism on behalf of art. Nationalism was everywhere antipathetic to true creative endeavor.

How, then, could Lewis support Hitler?

Here one meets an interesting case in aesthetic emotion. Lewis's views on painting were strongly and confidently held, and he sacrificed them with obvious reluctance. They were far from politically reprehensible and, by themselves, might today rather be classed as "liberal." In this case he evolved the paradox, chiefly expressed in *Left Wings*, that the new fascist nation-state was in reality facing a "collectivism" represented by the League of Nations and was thus equivalent to the pluralistic individual resisting the dictatorial "monism" of a group society (here the United States, the U.S.S.R., Great Britain, and France). Almost needless to say, Lewis achieved a very rapid and spectacular *volte-face* of this view in *America and Cosmic Man* (1948).

2. Wyndham Lewis, *The Art of Being Ruled* (New York, 1926), p. 173; *The Doom of Youth* (New York, 1932), p. 93; *Rude Assignment* (London, 1950), p. 178, respectively.

3. T. S. Eliot, *After Strange Gods* (New York, 1934), p. 60; *The Idea of a Christian Society* (New York, 1940), p. 8.

4. Those readers who sense something of Sartre's terminology behind these coinings might be interested to inspect Lewis's essay on that thinker in *The Writer and the Absolute* (1952).

5. Wyndham Lewis, *The Enemy of the Stars* (London, 1932), p. 51. See also Lewis's "The Physics of the Not-Self" in *The Chapbook*, Harold Monro, ed., No. 40 (London, 1925), p. 68.

6. *The Art of Being Ruled*, p. 235.

7. *Paleface: The Philosophy of the "Melting-Pot"* (London, 1929), p. 70.

8. Karl Joël, *Die Frauen in der Philosophie* (Hamburg, 1896).

9. Lockwood Memorial Library, University of Buffalo. And is it deliberately that when quoting a passage concerning world capitalism from the *Völkische Beobachter*, Lewis mistranslates the Nazi epithet for it, *"wucherischen,"* as "accursed"?

10. Alphonse Toussenel, *Les Juifs, rois de l'époque: histoire de la féodalité financière* (Paris, 1847). Toussenel enjoyed a resurrection in occupied France: See Louis Thomas's *Alphonse Toussenel, socialiste national antisémite* (Paris, 1941).

11. Wyndham Lewis, *Count Your Dead: They Are Alive! or A New War in the Making* (London, 1937), p. 199.

12. I am aware that Hardcaster feels "self-pity" at this point but do not feel this qualifies my analysis. It is a misreading to claim, as does Marvin Mudrick, that Hardcaster "cleverly betrayed" Victor and Margot at the end; he did the reverse.

ALDOUS HUXLEY
(1894-1963)

by Milton Birnbaum

IRVING HOWE DEFINES a political novel as one "in which political ideas play a dominant role or in which the political milieu is the dominant setting."[1] To this extent, Aldous Huxley cannot be considered a political novelist. It is even questionable whether he can be considered a novelist at all. He used the novel as a convenient and popular springboard from which to launch his ideas on a multiplicity of subjects. The only political characters in his fiction who in any way can be considered as people rather than as spokesmen are Spandrell, the nihilist, and Illidge, the communist, both appearing in Huxley's finest novel, *Point Counter Point*—and even here, both tend to more "flat" than "round" characters.

Furthermore, to try to isolate Huxley's attitudes on politics, government, war, and peace is obviously to try to isolate but one color from his prismatic inclusiveness. His encyclopedic brain emitted waves on an ocean of subjects. Yet encyclopedias (incidentally, among his favorite reading) are divided into subjects, and Huxley's impact on our society can perhaps best be gauged by an analytic survey of the chief directions of his search for meaning. The direction I propose to investigate here is his search for sanity in the seemingly insane world of society. Inasmuch as Huxley's fiction, as already noted, is but a useful vehicle for the expression of his ideas, I shall not distinguish between his fiction and nonfiction. The central search in Huxley's works is for a life of meaning, a quest for the ultimate attainment of a transcendent union with divinity. In this search Huxley had to clear out the Augean stables of the drosses of time-centered and ego-oriented impedimenta; politics, economics, and social mores are part of this baggage.

It should be pointed out at the outset that there are essentially at least two Aldous Huxleys. One is the societal Huxley, who feels keenly the outrages of history and the deleterious distortions inflicted upon man by political, technological, and social-religious systems; this is the Huxley who looks at society, finds it wanting, and offers prescriptive cures for its amelioration. There is also the other Huxley, who, with the weariness of Ecclesiastes, knows that the more things change the more they remain the same, that man is Sisyphus, performing a futile and endless task, that activity tends to yield despair, and that the quest therefore should be directed toward self-transcendence in an attempt to gain a unity with the Godhead. Self-realization becomes self-effacement, and the problems of society attain a solution through a dissolution of time and place. In Huxley, as in Goethe's Faust, there are two forces contending for supremacy: the corporeal and sentient societal self and the transcendent self seeking unity with the divine spirit. Huxley wants to be a part of and apart from the human predicament. One of his wings is flapping toward earth; the other is soaring toward the Godhead. Although this paradoxical flight cannot gain much momentum if one wants to proceed in one direction, one should consider that paradox is the essential condition of man and that direction is not nearly so desirable as the drive for understanding.

Whereas musing on the arts occasionally gives Huxley some satisfaction, contemplation of the historical evolution of the various types of governments and the wars they have caused never gives him solace. His meditations on government have made him pessimistic; this pessimism is reflected in the many qualifications he attached to his proposals for the eradication of the evils generated by government. He seems to endorse Henry Ford's dictum that "history is bunk" and the belief in the cliché that the only thing we learn from history is that we never learn from history,[2] and yet Huxley believes that once we admit the difficulty, we are in a position to begin discussing the problems of government with comparative objectivity:

> As for the problems of government, they are not solved, and they can never be definitely solved, for the simple reason that societies change, and that the forces of government must change with them. There is no absolutely right kind of government. Men have come at last to realize this simple but important fact, with the result that, for the first time in history, the problems of government can be discussed in a relatively scientific and rational spirit. Even the divine rights parliamentarism and political democracy can now be questioned with impunity.[3]

Before we analyze the kind of government that Huxley advocates, let us see what kind of government he is against. First of all, he firmly accepts Lord Acton's belief that the more absolute the power, the more absolute the corruption. As early as 1921, in his first novel, *Crome Yellow*, he was already concerned with the dangers implicit in a government in which the leaders gathered unto themselves too much centralized power. One of the characters in the novel, Scogan, talks about the "Rational State" of the future and predicts that society will ultimately be divided into three groups: the Directing Intelligences, the Men of Faith, and the Herd. This classification of society resembles the "utopian" state in his *Brave New World*, published eleven years later. In this state of the future the power of the world has been centralized into the hands of ten directors. Every person is under the control of the government. Even his birth is carefully controlled so as to insure a proper proportion of Alphas, Betas, and so forth down to the lowly Epsilons. Under this centralized government, everybody is "happy." There are no neuroses, no psychoses, no complexes, no inhibitions, no diseases, no economic insecurity. Everything has become standardized and predictable. In this state of the year 2600, the only thing to fear is not fear itself, but the threat of unorthodoxy. All wisdom, all initiative, all creativity, all problems, have been assumed by the directors of this supergovernment. If the individual has lost his freedom and the nobility of individual action, and if the springs of the creative arts have become desiccated in the process, we must not shed too many idle tears. As Mustapha Mond, one of the directors, tells us, freedom, nobility, the arts, and religion have given people in the past merely the right to be unhappy, "not to mention the right to grow old and ugly and impotent; the right to have syphilis and cancer; the right to have too little to eat; the right to be lousy; the right to live in constant apprehension of what may happen to-morrow; the right to catch typhoid; the right to be tortured by unspeakable pains of every kind."[4]

It is obvious, however, that Huxley would not have us barter the trappings of "happiness" for meaning and value in life. He deprecates the evils of totalitarianism of both the right and the left not only in his novels but in his nonfiction works as well. In *Themes and Variations* and in *The Perennial Philosophy*, for example, he tells us that the religion of totalitarianism is "only an idolatrous *ersatz* for the genuine religion of unity on the personal and spiritual levels."[5] Totalitarianism leads to privileges for the few and enslavement of the many. The excessive privilege and power which flow into the hands of the few encourage greed, vanity, and cruelty in the leaders, and abysmal dedication to false ideals by the many. The greatest danger, moreover, is not the assumption by the dictators of all political power: "Tyrants cannot be satisfied until they wield direct psychological and physiological power. The third revolution is that which will subvert the individual in the depths of his organic and hyper-organic being, is that which will bring his body, his mind, his whole private life directly under the control of the ruling oligarchy."[6]

Huxley is careful to indicate that there is no preferred system of totalitarianism. He indicts communism, fascism, and socialism with almost equal vehemence. Let us look more analytically at his comments on these three manifestations of the centralization of power. First, he tells us that Karl Marx has been proved wrong in many ways. "The Proletariat as he [Marx] knew it had ceased—or, if that is too sweeping a statement, is ceasing—to exist in America and, to a less extent, industrialized Europe."[7] The working man, or the proletarian, as Marxists would prefer to call him, is no longer the victim of callous capitalists. Through agitation by labor, through a guilty feeling on the part of employers, and through the employers' realizing that a prosperous worker means a better consumer, the worker's salary has continued to increase until today the skilled and unskilled workers make as much as the professional people: "Given this transformation of the Proletariat into a branch of the bourgeoisie, given this equalization—at an unprecedentedly high level, and over an area unprecedentedly wide—of standard income, the doctrines of socialism lose most of their charm, and the communist revolution becomes rather pointless."[8]

And yet, although communism and socialism may have lost the justification of existence by the disappearance of economic exploitation, they have nevertheless continued to exist due to adroit manipulation by dictatorial governmental leaders of largely chimerical grievances; consequently, Huxley is more concerned with the more pragmatic problems of denouncing the evils springing from these forms of totalitarianism than with the comparatively academic question of exposing the obsolescence of Marxist predictions. Huxley objects to socialism because it "seems to be fatally committed to centralization and standardized urban mass production all round. Besides, I see too many occasions for bullying there—too many opportunities for bossy people to display their bossiness, for sluggish people to sit back and be slaves."[9] Communism he finds even more objectionable chiefly because it resorts to violence, whereas socialism presumably does not. In *Eyeless in Gaza*, he has several communists among the characters: Giesebrecht, a refugee from Hitler, and two people who are influenced by Giesebrecht to embrace temporarily the tenets of communism—Helen Amberley and Mark Staithes. Huxley's attitude toward communists is perhaps expressed by his comments on Helen's dialectical arguments:

> Helen's was the usual communist argument—no peace or social justice without a preliminary "liquidation" of capitalists, liberals

and so forth. As though you could use violent, unjust means and achieve peace and justice! Means determine ends; and must be like the ends proposed. Means intrinsically different from the ends proposed achieve ends like themselves, not like those they were meant to achieve.[10]

Little wonder, then, that Huxley has Anthony Beavis, the chief character in the novel, characterize communism as "organized hatred—it's not exactly attractive. Not what most people feel they really want to live for."[11]

Huxley's attacks on fascism are relatively fewer in number than his criticism of the evil of mechanization in our society, for example. Their comparative rarity, however, should not be interpreted as a silence of consent. Certainly, the points he makes about totalitarianism apply to fascism as well as to communism. Furthermore, in the character of Webley, whose prototype is the British fascist Sir Oswald Mosley, Huxley expresses his low regard for fascism as a way of life and for fascists as leaders of people. Like communists, they use violence and hatred to achieve their "ideal" society. Like communists, they, too, should be looked upon as false Messiahs.[12]

Since Huxley abhors totalitarianism, whether of the extreme left or of the extreme right, the reader might conclude that democracy then is the form of government which Huxley espouses. Such an assumption, however, even though partially valid, should be carefully qualified. It is true that Huxley favors democracy, but like E. M. Forster,[13] he has but two cheers for it. Whenever he mentions democracy in his books, he does so with comparatively little enthusiasm: "My prejudices happen to be in favor of democracy, self-determination, and all the rest of it. But political convictions are generally the fruit of chance rather than of deliberate choice. If I had been brought up a little differently, I might, I suppose, have been a Fascist and an apostle of the most full-blooded imperialism."[14] Similarly, when he compares the democracy of today with the kind of democracy that Godwin, Shelley, and other utopians dreamed about, he finds that "democracy in those days was not the bedraggled and rather whorish old slut she now is, but young and attractive."[15]

Huxley gives several reasons for his reservations about democracy. These he outlines in his essay "Political Democracy," published in *Proper Studies* in 1927. First of all, he believes that most people in a democracy are politically lethargic; they seem to become interested in the problems of government only when the policies of their government affect them adversely. Secondly, according to Huxley's observations, it is generally the incompetent charlatans who get into office; if competent people do manage to get into office, they do so either through accident or through undemocratic manipulations. Thirdly, the press in a democratic government usually wields tremendous power and sways the thinking and the votes of the electorate. Fourthly, inasmuch as in a democracy more people have control of the reins of government than in other forms of government, there are more opportunities for corruption.

In addition to the reasons he outlines in the essay "Political Democracy," other causes for his rather mild endorsement of democracy can be inferred from his other works. Thus, many of the major characters in his novels are somewhat uncomfortable when they try to practice the tenets of fraternity and equality. For example, Walter Bidlake in *Point Counter Point*, despite his liberal tendencies to help people, feels disgust as he mingles with some of the less savory representatives of the lower strata of society. Similarly, Anthony Beavis, in *Eyeless in Gaza*, suffers a rather rude jolt as he tries to spread the gospel of pacifism to the masses. There is something essentially aloof in Huxley's temperament (as in the temperament of his characters) which renders him more sympathetic to the discriminating exclusiveness of aristocracy than to the equalitarian spirit of democracy.

And yet he finds that democracy does have some benefits. Thus, he says with almost Whitmanesque glee that "democracy is, among other things, the ability to say No to the boss."[16] Similarly, he finds that in a democracy there are fewer opportunities for the rulers to exploit the many:

> In countries where democratic institutions exist and the executive is prepared to abide by the rules of the democratic game, the many can protect themselves against the ruling few by using their right to vote, to strike, to organize pressure groups, to petition the legislature, to hold meetings and conduct press campaigns in favor of reform.[17]

There is one twentieth-century aspect of both totalitarian and democratic governments that Huxley deprecates: This is the growth of the spirit of nationalism. He finds the growth of nationalism responsible for many evils. In *Beyond the Mexique Bay* he complains that nationalism has been responsible for endless and unnecessary red tape. "A mitigation of nationalism would save the world millions of hours of wasted time and an incalculable expense of spirit, physical energy, and money."[18] There are other evils emanating from nationalism which are even more regrettable: "One of the great attractions of patriotism—it fulfills our worst wishes. In the person of our nation we are able, vicariously, to bully and cheat. Bully and cheat, what's more, with a feeling that we're profoundly virtuous. Sweet and decorous to murder, lie, torture for the sake of the fatherland."[19]

Furthermore, nationalism has become a religion in itself. The internationalism of religion has been replaced by the tribalism of nationalism so that "in actual fact we worship, not one God, but fifty or sixty godlets each of whom is, by definition, the enemy, actual or potential, of all the rest."[20] The state has now become a god; however, it is not a benign deity, but an idolatrous entity which encourages greed, bestiality, and sacrifice of the decencies of life. Not that nationalism did not exist before the advent of the twentieth century. In previous eras of history, however, nationalism was confined solely to the sphere of politics. It did not hinder the exchange of ideas or the respect for artists of countries other than one's own:

> During the eighteenth century France and England exchanged ideas almost as freely as cannon balls. French scientific expeditions were allowed to pass in safety between the English fleets; Sterne was welcomed enthusiastically by his country's enemies. The tradition lingered on even into the eighteen hundreds. Napoleon gave medals to English men of science; and when, in 1813, Sir Humphry Davy asked for leave to travel on the Continent, his request was granted at once. He was received in Paris with the highest honours, was made a member of the Institute, and in spite of the intolerable rudeness and arrogance which he habitually displayed, he was treated throughout his stay in France with the most perfect courtesy. In our more enlightened twentieth century he would have been shot as a spy or interned.[21]

The chief evil caused by nationalism (although, as will be pointed out later, not by nationalism alone) is war. Huxley has never wavered in his opposition to war; he has changed his attitudes toward the arts, toward the life-worshiping philosophy of the Greeks, but never toward war. In his first novel, *Crome Yellow*, he writes sardonically that "those who had lost relations in the war might reasonably be expected to subscribe a sum equal to that which they would have had to pay in funeral expenses if the relative had died while at home."[22] In *Ape and Essence* the horrors of atomic warfare are made palpably evident; man has reverted to the savagery of the ape and the only "hope" left is the "ultimate and irremediable Detumescence."[23] War, Huxley finds, is the extreme evil because it has no redeeming qualities. "War always weakens and often completely shatters the crust of customary decency which constitutes a civilization."[24] He urges us to look at Goya's *"Desastres"* to find out what war really means—if we need any further reminders.

But it is not nationalism alone that brings about wars. The causes for wars are many and complex. Perhaps Huxley's fullest analysis of the intricate pattern of war is given in his essay "War," found in *Ends and Means*. First of all, he tries to shatter the myth that war is an instinctive part of human nature; in other words, it is not inevitable. He reminds us that the religions of Buddhism, Hinduism, and Confucianism have all regarded war as evil and peace as desirable. He tells us that only the western leaders (he singles out the Puritan Calvinists as being especially guilty in this respect) have preached a policy of "righteous indignation" and a consequent justification of war. War has existed only because human beings have wanted it to exist. They have encouraged the perpetuation of wars for a variety of reasons: War is an escape from the boredom of life —he notes that there are usually fewer suicides in times of war than in times of peace; war also provides a psychological outlet in which the suppressed antisocial tendencies of the people get the opportunity for either direct or vicarious expression; war also provides political leaders with the chance to secure strategic bases, additional armaments, and increased manpower; wars, such as the wars waged by Islam or the American Civil War, are fought for religious or political aggrandizement; the desire for economic gains—more land, natural resources, and profit arising from the manufacture of armaments—has also given impetus to the waging of wars. It should be remembered, however, that it is not one cause in isolation that brings about conflict but rather the combination of many influences.

That wars never result in the achievement of the goals for which they are allegedly fought is made quite clear. For example, as Eustace Barnack thinks of the wars of history, he is both amused and horrified at the futility of them all:

> He remembered his collection of Historical Jokes. A million casualties and the Gettysburg Address, and then those abject, frightened negroes one sees in the little towns of Georgia and Louisiana. The crusade for liberty, equality, fraternity, and then the rise of Napoleon; the crusade against Napoleon; and then the rise of German nationalism; the crusade against German nationalism, and now those unemployed men, standing, like half-animated corpses, at the corners of mean streets in the rain.[25]

In placing the responsibility of wars upon the leaders of governments, Huxley does not absolve the masses of people from guilt either. In *After*

Many a Summer Dies the Swan he notes that so long as people "go on thinking exclusively in terms of money and regarding money as the supreme good,"[26] so long as they continue to worship false values and false gods, so long will they be subject to the horrors of war. Similarly, in *Time Must Have a Stop* he writes that it is the gullibility and passivity of the bulk of people that have been responsible for the evils of mankind:

> Without Susan and Kenneth and Aunt Alice and all their kind, society would fall to pieces. With them, it was perpetually attempting suicide. They were the pillars, but they were also the dynamite; simultaneously the beams and the dry-rot. It was thanks to their goodness that the system worked as smoothly as it did; and thanks to their limitations that the system was fundamentally insane—so insane that Susan's three charming babies would almost certainly grow up to become cannon fodder, plane fodder, tank fodder, fodder for any one of the thousand bigger and better military gadgets with which bright young engineers like Kenneth would by that time have enriched the world.[27]

What are the solutions which Huxley proposes to counteract the evils of excessively powerful governments with their concomitants of nationalism and war? His remedies appear in nearly all his fiction and nonfiction works. The cures can be classified under three headings: (1) suggestions as to what the individual can do, (2) suggestions as to what can be done by reform groups working within a country, and (3) suggestions that can be effected by international movements.

First of all, the individual needs to be reminded that he is a force by himself, and not merely a puppet of external circumstances. "What is needed is a restatement of the Emersonian doctrine of self-reliance. . . ."[28] The individual should, by exercising his willpower, realize that he need not fall victim to the lure of false ideals. All of Huxley's "ideal" characters are self-sufficient. Thus, Mr. Propter, in *After Many a Summer Dies the Swan*, is skillful in farming and carpentry. Similarly, Bruno Rontini, in *Time Must Have a Stop*, owns a small bookstore, takes care of his own needs in his modest apartment, and does not fall victim to the temptations of the world of materialists. Furthermore, the individual should not shrink in the face of threats of brutal punishment. Anthony Beavis, in *Eyeless in Gaza*, knows that it is uncomfortably dangerous to continue his preaching of pacifism; yet, in spite of threats to his person, he continues his work. Similarly, Bruno Rontini, when faced with arrest by the Italian fascists, does not flinch in the face of punishment and accepts his fate with the resignation befitting his mystic philosophy.

If the individual is sufficiently strong-willed, he can transcend the limitations of customs and laws. The pages of history, Huxley reminds us, are replete with examples of people who escaped from the fetters of their times:

> Laws and precepts, ideals and conventions have a good deal less influence on private life than most educators would care to admit. Pepys grew to manhood under the Commonwealth; Bouchard, during the revival of French Catholicism after the close of the religious wars. Both were piously brought up; both had to listen to innumerable sermons and exhortations; both were assured that sexual irregularity would lead them infallibly to Hell. And each behaved like a typical case from the pages of Ellis or Ebing or Professor Kinsey.[29]

Huxley realizes, however, that strong-willed individuals like Pepys and Bouchard are the exceptions and that most people do succumb to the influences of their environment. He therefore outlines his program of reform in various sections of his novels and nonfiction works, realizing that the individual cannot wrestle with the evils of a centralized, standardized, and violence-ridden civilization by himself. What strikes the reader as he reads Huxley's suggestions for reform is the tone of moderation. His is not the passionate denunciation of D. H. Lawrence, who perhaps hated more than he loved.[30] He cautions us that reform must be undertaken under certain conditions: (1) Only those reforms that are absolutely needed should be attempted; (2) no reform should be undertaken if it is likely to provoke violent opposition; (3) reforms have greater chances of succeeding if the people are already familiar with and approve of the methods used in achieving them.[31]

These collective reforms should be attempted in several directions. One kind of reform might well be economic in nature:

> We need a new system of money that will deliver us from servitude to the banks and permit people to buy what they are able to produce; and we need a new system of ownership that will check the tendency towards monopoly in land and make it impossible for individuals to lay waste to planetary resources which belong to all mankind. But changes in social and economic organization are not enough, of themselves, to solve our problem. Production is inadequate to present population, and population, over large areas, is rapidly rising. A change in the laws governing the ownership of land will not change its quantity or quality. The equitable distribution of too little may satisfy men's desire for justice; it will not stay their hunger. In a world where population is growing at the rate of about fifty-six thousand a day, and where erosion is daily ruining an equal or

perhaps greater number of productive acres, our primary concern must be with reducing numbers and producing more food with less damage to the soil.[32]

In *Science, Liberty and Peace* he outlines more specifically the kinds of economic reform he would like to see implemented. He advocates a small, localized community in which the motivation would be mutual help and not individual profit. He would like to see the establishment of credit unions so that the individual can borrow money without increasing the influence of "the state or of commercial banks"; he would also favor the creation of "legal techniques, through which a community can protect itself against the profiteer who speculates in land values, which he has done nothing whatever to increase."[33]

Along with the decentralization of economic power should also come the decentralization of political power. He favors "federations of local and professional bodies, having wide powers of self-government."[34] The greater the power of the government, Huxley believes, the greater the opportunities of corruption and the less likely the possibility that ethical values will supplant expediency and efficiency as bases for conduct.

The decentralization of economic and political power is best achieved under a sociological system where most of the people live on farms rather than in cities. Cities, Huxley finds, breed the evils of mechanization and centralization of power; rural communities, on the other hand, encourage self-sufficiency and cooperation. In *After Many a Summer Dies the Swan* Mr. Propter, expounding his suggestions for the achievement of a more meaningful, human life, says that under the new system, society would consist mostly of peasants, "plus small machines and power. Which means that they're no longer peasants, except insofar as they're largely self-sufficient."[35] All Mr. Propter hopes for is that if he does his share in effecting an improvement in society, there will be some people who will be sufficiently interested to cooperate with him; he realizes that most people will not be content with living on small farms: "Frankly, then, I don't expect them to leave the cities, any more than I expect them to stop having wars and revolutions."[36]

Although the "ideal" governmental unit should preferably be small, Huxley is sufficiently aware that the world has grown so complex, that governments have waxed so centralized and powerful, that the best that might be accomplished is to bring about what he calls "goodness politics":

> The art of what may be called "goodness politics," as opposed to power politics, is the art of organizing on a large scale without sacrificing the ethical values which emerge only among individ-

uals and small groups. More specifically, it is the art of combining decentralization of government and industry, local and
functional autonomy and smallness of administrative units with
enough over-all efficiency to guarantee the smooth running of
the federated whole. Goodness politics have never been
attempted in any large society, and it may be doubted whether
such an attempt, if made, could achieve more than a partial success, so long as the majority of individuals concerned remain
unable or unwilling to transform their personalities by the only
method known to be effective. But though the attempt to substitute goodness politics for power politics may never be completely successful, it still remains true that the methods of
goodness politics combined with individual training in theocentric theory and contemplative practice alone provide the means
whereby human societies can become a little less unsatisfactory
than they have been up to the moment.[37]

I have already mentioned Huxley's lukewarm endorsement of democracy and his penchant for a kind of Miltonian aristocracy. In his essay
"Political Democracy," which appeared in Proper Studies, he writes that
the weaknesses of a political democracy can best be overcome by a government characterized by an aristocracy of minds and character. Governmental positions should be restricted to those who could pass rigid
educational and psychological tests. He indicates that in industry we
already have an aristocracy of leadership; why should we not have an
equivalent aristocracy of talent in government? Furthermore, in this kind
of government every individual should have the position to which he is
entitled by virtue of his mental and temperamental attributes:

> That every human being should be in his place—this is the ideal
> of the aristocratic as opposed to the democratic state. It is not
> merely a question of the organization of government, but of the
> organization of the whole of society. In society as it is organized
> at present enormous numbers of men and women are perform-
> ing functions which they are not naturally suited to perform.
> The misplacement of parts in the social machine leads to fric-
> tion and consequent waste of power; in the case of the individu-
> als concerned it leads to many varieties of suffering.[38]

It would seem, from the tone of this passage, that Huxley in 1927 was
not aware of the dangers befalling a society that emphasized efficiency
and competence at the expense of more human considerations. And yet
he was conscious of the limitations of a societal organization that put a
premium on efficiency alone. In the introduction to Proper Studies he

writes that "institutions which deny the facts of human nature either break down more or less violently, or else decay gradually into ineffectiveness."[39] Machinelike efficiency is not the supreme good. Furthermore, his espousal of an aristocracy of minds and character is later subjected to much modification. In 1937 he writes that "disciplinary arrangements may be of various kinds, but that the most educative form of organization is the democratic."[40] Thus, Huxley's attitude on the virtues of aristocracy is hardly monolithic; he realizes that "human nature" is such as to preclude absolute advocacy of any specific form of government; hence, his caution, his spirit of moderation, his philosophical resignation to the unlikelihood of the adoption or success of the reforms he writes about.

It is this skeptical caution that has perhaps made his attitude toward the adoption of a world government seem somewhat ambivalent. That he was long conscious of the need to transcend the limitations of national boundaries is evident even in his earlier writings. Thus, in *Ends and Means* he writes that "it is the business of educators and religious teachers to persuade individual men and women that bridge-building is desirable and to teach them at the same time how to translate mere theory and platonic good resolutions into actual practice."[41]

In *Science, Liberty and Peace*, published in 1946, he is not at all convinced that the bridge-building leading to the establishment of a world government will lead to an elimination of existing evils. He feels that even under a system of world government, "power lovers" will yield to the temptations of gratifying their lust for domination. In the essay "The Double Crisis," published in 1950 in *Themes and Variations*, he is willing to forgo his opposition to the establishment of a world government if it will facilitate "the relief of hunger and the conservation of our planetary resources, [a relief which] seems to offer the best and perhaps the only hope for peace and international co-operation."[42] It should be emphasized, however, that Huxley is more interested in feeding the hungry people of the world and in saving the world's natural resources than he is in the formation of a world government: "If . . . federation can be achieved by purely political means, so much the better. It does not matter which comes first, the political chicken or the technological egg. What is important is that, in some way or other, we should get both, and get them with the least possible delay."[43]

Although he never actually spells out in detail the kind of world government he would like to see established, he seems to support it in principle because it would eliminate one of the primary causes of war—what he calls "the demographic and ecological crisis." His interest in a world government stems from his desire to bring about the conditions of peace. He is even willing to forget his objection to the increased centralization which the establishment of a world government would encourage; he feels that if it is a choice between world government and peace on the one hand, and no world government and decentralization on the other hand, he would prefer the first alternative.

War, in other words, must be avoided at all costs. It is the maintenance of peace that is all-important. And yet Huxley is not so naïve as to believe that peace is the result of merely political federation. When Mr. Barnack asks his son under what conditions peace can become a reality, his son replies: "Peace doesn't come to those who merely work for peace—only as the by-product of something else."[44] That "something else," we are told, is "a metaphysic, which all accept and a few actually succeed in realizing."[45] This "metaphysic" is obtained only by "direct intuition."

Inasmuch as very few people are capable of obtaining peace through "direct intuition," Huxley, in his other books, outlines other remedies for the achievement of peace. First of all, we cannot have international peace unless we conduct our interpersonal relationships peacefully. He speaks of the "hyprocrisy and stupidity of those who advocate peace between states, while conducting private wars in business or the family."[46] Secondly, pacifism is not enough; it must be what he calls in *Eyeless in Gaza* "positive pacifism." It is true, as Huxley explains in the book, that in times of unemployment people are not easily swayed to fight wars; however, in such times, the people are easily persuaded to embrace either communism or fascism. It is therefore important to establish conditions of a more positive nature—not the condition of hunger and peace followed by the encroachment of totalitarianism, but a state of relative prosperity and peace.

A materialistic prosperity by itself is not sufficient for the permanence of peace. Materialistic pursuits themselves sometimes produce the conditions of war. What is needed above all is that philosophy of life which recognizes the ephemeral importance of material well-being and the permanence of a unitive knowledge and love of God:

> You can't preserve people from the horrors of war if they won't give up the pleasures of nationalism. You can't save them from slumps and depressions so long as they go on thinking exclusively in terms of money and regarding money as the supreme good. You can't avert revolution and enslavement if they *will* identify progress with the increase of centralization and prosperity with the intensifying of mass production. You can't preserve them from collective madness and suicide if they persist in paying divine honours to ideals which are merely pro-

jections of their own personalities—in other words, if they persist in worshipping themselves rather than God.[47]

Although Huxley has offered many suggestions to effect an "ideal" government and the establishment of peace, what underlies all his statements for reform is a current of pessimism about the ultimate efficiency of any attempt to ameliorate the evils of our society. This undercurrent of pessimism is perhaps responsible for the paradoxical juxtaposition of offering a cure in one book and then satirizing it in the next. Thus, for example, although he will advocate the creation of "bridge-builders" to bring about a better understanding of the various countries and philosphies of the world, he will satirize such a "bridge-builder" as De Vries in *Time Must Have a Stop*. Thus, although he mildly favors the establishment of a world government, he will say that what is needed is more decentralization: "Since genuine self-government is possible only in very small groups, societies on a national or super-national scale will always be ruled by oligarchical minorities, whose members come to power because they have a lust for power."[48] Thus, although he admires the efficiency of a government in which the elite would rule, he realizes that efficiency by itself is not the supreme good. Similarly, although he will deprecate the apparent inefficiency of democracy, he will mildly cheer its ability to withstand the tyranny of totalitarianism. And although he will preach the necessity of feeding the hungry people of the world, he will caution us that preoccupation with the material needs of life will lead to an atrophy of the soul and ultimately to the greedy savagery of war. He advocates reforms, but he admits that the achievement of reforms sometimes leads to other evils:

> Consider, for example, the results actually achieved by two reforms upon which well-intentioned people have placed the most enormous hopes—universal education and public ownership of the means of production. Universal education has proved to be the state's most effective instrument of universal regimentation and militarization, and has exposed millions, hitherto immune, to the influence of organized lying and the allurements of incessant, imbecile and debasing distractions. Public ownership of the means of production has been put into effect on a large scale only in Russia, where the results of the reform have been, not the elimination of oppression, but the replacement of one kind of oppression by another—of money power by political and bureaucratic power, of the tyranny of rich men by a tyranny of the police and the party.[49]

Despite the lack of finality and absolute certitude in the reforms he suggests, the impression that clearly emerges from the reading of his works written prior to *Island* is that government per se cannot possibly serve as a source of permanent value; he may be critical of the groping attempts of democracies to solve the ills of mankind, but he would hardly advocate looking to a centralized government as the god at whose shrine people should worship in self-abasement. Certainly, that is the message not only of *Brave New World* but of his other books as well. Granted that if we look at *human* affairs, we are faced with an almost insoluble dilemma: "In human affairs the extreme of messiness is anarchy; the extreme of tidiness, an army or a penitentiary."[50] When faced with such a dilemma, the best that can be achieved is a compromise between the horns of the two extremes: "The good life can be lived only in a society where tidiness is preached and practiced, but not too fanatically, and where efficiency is always haloed, as it were, by a tolerated aura of mess."[51] Little wonder that Huxley tried to resolve the mess of *human* problems by detaching himself from them; consequently, his penultimate solution for the problem which a consideration of government, war, and peace engenders is a life of mystical nonattachment and a striving for a unitive knowledge and love of God.

This gnawing pessimism that seems to erode many of his ameliorative suggestions also underlies his last published novel, *Island*. The very technological schemes that Huxley mocks in his 1932 novel, *Brave New World*, now become the altars before which he worships—almost. *Soma* has become the *moksha*-medicine, "the reality revealer, the truth-and-beauty pill."[52] Lovemaking, satirized in *Brave New World*, becomes one of the paths to a luminous bliss. In *Island*, on Pala, there are birth control, artificial insemination, classification of people into extroverts ("sheep-people"), introverts ("cat-people"), and activists ("Marten-people")—reminiscent of the earlier classifications of people into Alphas, Betas, and Epsilons. Again, people are conditioned for happiness in Pavlovian style: "pharmacology, sociology, physiology, not to mention pure and applied ontology, neurotheology, metachemistry, mycomysticism, and the ultimate science . . . the science that sooner or later we shall all have to be examined in—thanatology."[53] The guilt-oriented patterns for which St. Paul and Freud are held responsible have been exchanged for the guilt-free lives in which mind, body, and spirit are artificially synthesized into a harmonious unity. Yet somehow one realizes that "Paladise" is not Paradise. The book begins with the old cynicism of Huxley: "A moment later the bird on her shoulder joined in with peal upon peal of loud demonic laughter that filled the glade and echoed among the trees, so that the whole universe seemed to be fairly splitting its sides over the enormous joke of existence."[54] The book ends on a similarly pessimistic note. In spite of Will Farnaby's belief that he has gained "knowledgeless understanding and luminous bliss" as he enjoys the triune blessing of the *moksha*-medicine, Bach's Fourth Brandenburg Concerto, and the yoga of love that Susila offers him, his eyes still see the ugliness of a lizard and the copulation of two insects, and his ears hear the noise of "heavy vehicles" and "a few rifle shots," indicating that Pala's government has now been taken over by the western-oriented politicians, with all the attendant greed, materialism, and war which the Palanese had tried to eliminate. The last words in the book are "*Karuma, Karuma. . . .* Compassion." *Karuma* means "compassion," but "compassion" etymologically means "suffering with." The utopia of Pala turns out to be a *moksha*-inspired dream that vanishes when eyes are once again opened. Under the influence of *moksha* and the love of Susila, Will Farnaby thinks that "what he was seeing now was the paradox of opposites indissolubly wedded, of light shining out of darkness, of darkness at the very heart of light."[55] The reader emerges, however, feeling not that he has attended a wedding of indissoluble opposites, but that he has witnessed rather a reaffirmation of the spirit of Manichaeism.

Huxley died from cancer on the same day that President John F. Kennedy was slain. The assassination and the insane pattern of political behavior since then have given new meaning to the question that Will Farnaby raises in *Island*: "Which is better—to be born stupid into an intelligent society or intelligent into an insane one?"[56] Huxley in his last novel seems to feel—though with some reservations—that Pavlovian conditioning of individuals toward a sane society is preferable to letting society play Russian roulette by allowing each person relative freedom in developing his individuality. And yet the eroding question persists: Hasn't Huxley really embraced the very nightmare he was caustically rejecting in 1932 when he wrote his *Brave New World*? Hasn't he sacrificed the soul's freedom for a feckless fraternity and bartered individual man, created in the image of God, for a faceless citizen, created in the public image? Much as I admire Huxley's attempts to help bring sanity into a world veering into madness, I have to admit that Paradise should be made of sterner and more divine stuff. I am not yet ready to accept Dostoevski's Grand Inquisitor's panacea for the world's problems. What is missing from *Island* is the Savage from *Brave New World*.

As one glances back at Huxley's distinguished diversity, one can obviously find flaws; certainly his projected reforms for society can draw rebuttals from people of different political persuasions. His seeming inconsistencies, his almost complete about-face from *Brave New World* to *Island*, can excite scorn from logicians; and yet as a prophet (his *Brave New World*, like George Orwell's *1984*, still threatens to become fact), as a Jeremiah (note his lamentations that we are destroying ourselves through overpopulation and through exploitation of the world's natural resources), as essentially a humanist who chastizes man only to humanize him, as a man whose encyclopedic knowledge makes pseudo-Brobdingnagians feel like Lilliputians, Huxley stands almost alone in his majestic eclecticism.

NOTES

1. *Politics and the Novel* (Greenwich, Connecticut, 1957), p. 19.
2. See his essay "On the Charms of History and the Future of the Past," *Music at Night and Other Essays* (New York, 1931), pp. 119–136.
3. "Spinoza's Worm," *Do What You Will: Essays* (London, 1929), p. 90.
4. *Brave New World* (New York, 1950; copyright 1932), p. 288. For a comparison of this novel with George Orwell's *1984*, see Gaylord Le Roy, "A. F. 632 to 1984," *College English*, XII (December 1950), 135–138.
5. *The Perennial Philosophy* (New York and London, 1945), p. 11.
6. "Variations on a Philosopher," *Themes and Variations* (New York, 1950), p. 133.
7. "Revolutions," *Do What You Will*, p. 216.
8. *Ibid.*, p. 220.
9. *After Many a Summer Dies the Swan* (New York, 1954; copyright 1939), p. 122.
10. *Eyeless in Gaza* (New York, 1954; copyright 1936), p. 222.
11. *Ibid.*, p. 412.
12. As for the military "type," so frequently an adjunct of the totalitarian government, he has only satiric contempt. Spandrell's summary of his stepfather's military career could well symbolize Huxley's opinion of the military prototype: "Superannuated from Harrow . . . passed out from Sandhurst at the bottom of the list, he had a most distinguished career in the Army, rising during the war to a high post in the Military Intelligence Department. . . . If you look up 'Intelligence' in the new volumes of the Encyclopaedia Britannica . . . you'll find it classified under the following three heads: Intelligence, Human; Intelligence, Animal; Intelligence, Military. My stepfather's a present specimen of Intelligence, Military." *Point Counter Point* (New York, 1928), p. 99.
13. See E. M. Forster's discussion of the weaknesses as well as the strengths of democracy in his *Two Cheers for Democracy* (New York, 1951), pp. 69–76.
14. *Jesting Pilate: An Intellectual Holiday* (New York, 1926), p. 134.
15. "On the Charms of History and the Future of the Past," *Music at Night*, p. 134.
16. "The Double Crisis," *Themes and Variations*, p. 246.
17. *Science, Liberty and Peace* (New York, 1946), p. 4.
18. *Beyond the Mexique Bay* (New York, 1934), p. 186.

19. *Eyeless in Gaza*, p. 155.
20. "The Double Crisis," *Themes and Variations*, p. 244.
21. *Along the Road: Notes & Essays of a Tourist* (London, 1925), pp. 215–216.
22. *Crome Yellow* (New York, 1922), p. 181.
23. *Ape and Essence* (New York, 1948), p. 42.
24. "Variations on Goya," *Themes and Variations*, p. 227.
25. *Time Must Have a Stop* (New York, 1944), p. 193.
26. *After Many a Summer Dies the Swan*, p. 124.
27. *Time Must Have a Stop*, p. 279.
28. *Science, Liberty and Peace*, p. 56.
29. "Variations on a Philosopher," *Themes and Variations*, p. 75.
30. In the index to Huxley's edition of *The Letters of D. H. Lawrence* (New York, 1932), we find under "Hatreds": "aristocracy," "democracy," "the people," "the public," "society." Knud Merrild, in his *A Poet and Two Painters* (New York, 1939), pp. 239–240, tells us that Lawrence sometimes felt the urge to kill, not innocent animals, but "some of the beastly disdainful bankers, industrialists, lawyers, war makers and schemers of all kinds."
31. These three principles were obtained from his *Ends and Means: An Inquiry into the Nature of Ideals and into the Methods Employed for Their Realization* (New York, 1937), pp. 53–55.
32. "The Double Crisis," *Themes and Variations*, p. 251.
33. *Science, Liberty and Peace*, p. 57.
34. "Variations on a Philosopher," *Themes and Variations*, p. 58.
35. *After Many a Summer Dies the Swan*, p. 122.
36. *Ibid.*, p. 123.
37. *Grey Eminence: A Study in Religion and Politics* (New York, 1941), p. 312. He admits, somewhat sadly on the next page, that "society can never be greatly improved until such time as most of its members choose to become theocentric saints." The likelihood of most people's becoming "theocentric saints" does not leave much room for optimism.
38. "Political Democracy," *Proper Studies* (London, 1927), p. 166.
39. *Proper Studies*, Introduction, p. xii.
40. "Individual Work for Reform," *Ends and Means*, p. 156.
41. "Inequality," *Ends and Means*, p. 193. It is true that Huxley, with his usual inconsistency, occasionally laughs at these "bridge-builders." For example, notice how he satirizes the "bridge-building" of De Vries in *Time Must Have a Stop*.
42. "The Double Crisis," *Themes and Variations*, pp. 266–267.
43. *Ibid.*, p. 268.
44. *Time Must Have a Stop*, p. 308.
45. *Ibid.*
46. *Eyeless in Gaza*, p. 284.
47. *After Many a Summer Dies the Swan*, p. 124. See also his essay "Indian Philosophy of Peace," in Christopher Isherwood, ed., *Vedanta for Modern Man* (New York, 1951), pp. 294–296.
48. *The Perennial Philosophy*, p. 125.
49. *Grey Eminence*, pp. 305–306.
50. "Variations on *The Prisons*," *Themes and Variations*, p. 204.
51. *Ibid.*
52. *Island* (New York, 1962), p. 157.
53. *Ibid.*, pp. 163–164.

54. *Ibid.*, p. 15.
55. *Ibid.*, p. 327.
56. *Ibid.*, p. 216. Many of the ameliorative schemes that Huxley develops in *Island* he had already outlined in his Foreword to a reprinting of *Brave New World*. To the two horns of the dilemma he had analyzed in *Brave New World* (either a mindless, materialistic society or the withdrawal of the primitives in their Reservation) Huxley adds a preferable alternative: "In this community economics would be decentralist and Henry-Georgian, politics Kropotkinesque and co-operative. Science and technology would be used as though, like the Sabbath, they had been made for man, not (as at present and still more so in the Brave New World) as though man were to be adapted and enslaved to them. Religion would be the conscious and intelligent pursuit of man's Final End, the unitive knowledge of the immanent Tao or Logos, the transcendent Godhead or Brahman. And the prevailing philosophy of life would be a kind of Higher Utilitarianism, in which the Greatest Happiness principle would be secondary to the Final End principle—the first question to be asked and answered in every contingency of life being: 'How will this thought or action contribute to, or interfere with, the achievement, by me and the greatest possible number of other individuals, of man's Final End?' " *Brave New World* (New York, 1950; copyright 1932), Foreword, p. xxii.

GEORGE ORWELL
(1903-1950)

by Sir Richard Rees

IN 1947 GEORGE ORWELL wrote:

> What I have most wanted to do throughout the past ten years is
> to make political writing into an art. My starting point is always
> a feeling of partisanship, a sense of injustice. . . . And looking
> back through my work, I see that it is invariably where I lacked
> a *political* purpose that I wrote lifeless books and was betrayed
> into purple passages, sentences without meaning, decorative
> adjectives and humbug generally.[1]

This might be interpreted as a condemnation of most of his work before
The Road to Wigan Pier, which was published in 1937. His books before
1937 were *Down and Out in Paris and London* and three novels. We
shall return to the three novels, but it can be said at once of the other
book, which consists mainly of autobiographical reportage, that it is not
open to most of Orwell's implied criticisms, although it is true that it is
less lively than the first part of *The Road to Wigan Pier*, which it somewhat resembles.

Orwell's view of his own literary development can be summarized as
follows. He knew from a very early age, perhaps the age of five or six, he
says, that he was destined to be a writer. When he left school and
became a police official in Burma, he did so "with the consciousness that
I was outraging my true nature and that sooner or later I should have to
settle down and write books."[2] In 1927, when he was twenty-four, he
resigned from his job in Burma, suffering from a sense of guilt, which he

attributes to his having been a servant of British imperialism. At the time of his return to Europe he knew very little about European social, political, or economic conditions. He had formed a view of society which included only two classes, oppressors and victims; and in order to purge his sense of guilt he felt it necessary to identify himself with the victims by sharing their life. He appears to have regarded this action simply as a penance. He had no conscious revolutionary or political purpose, because he still saw himself as destined for a purely literary career. He saw no connection between literature and politics and he knew nothing about the European working classes. "When I thought of poverty I thought of it in terms of brute starvation. Therefore my mind turned immediately towards the extreme cases, the social outcasts: tramps, beggars, criminals, prostitutes."[3] He therefore became a dishwasher in Paris and later a tramp in and around London. He next got a poorly paying teaching job, followed by a job in a bookshop, and then gradually he began to make a little money by writing. Between 1933 and 1936 he produced three novels, but it was only when he became converted to socialism, after a tour of the distressed mining areas in Lancashire and Yorkshire, that he at last found himself as a writer, because, thanks to his political awakening, his pen had acquired the vitality which, in the conditions of the twentieth century, only a political purpose can inspire.

Such, in brief, is Orwell's own account of his development as a writer, and an examination of his work appears at first sight to confirm it. His writing certainly did acquire a startling new buoyancy and vigor in *The Road to Wigan Pier* (1937) and *Homage to Catalonia* (1938). But Orwell's explanation both of his resignation from the Imperial Police in 1927 and of the change in his writing in 1937 seems to me superficial. It underestimates the significance of his extraordinary decision in 1927 to become a down-and-out; and it overemphasizes the *political* aspect of the change in his writing from 1937 onward, though not the importance of the change.

It seems to me that some word other than "political" is needed to describe Orwell's writing, even when it is apparently concerned with topical political events, as in *Homage to Catalonia* and in some of his essays written during World War II. I would suggest "metapolitical," using that word to describe a kind of thinking which takes a pragmatic and empirical view of all political creeds and parties and whose concern with politics recalls Plato's reluctant philosopher-king, who sees politics as an unavoidable but unwelcome part of the task of educating the human soul. To begin with, we have already seen that in his own account, in 1947, of his politically inspired work Orwell says that his starting point "is always a feeling of partisanship, *a sense of injustice*" (my italics). And he tells us in *The Road to Wigan Pier* that at the age of twenty-four "I had carried my hatred of oppression to extraordinary lengths. At that time failure seemed to me to be the only virtue. Every suspicion of self-advancement, even to 'succeed' in life to the extent of making a few hundreds a year, seemed to me spiritually ugly, a species of bullying."[4] It appears that although he lacked, in those days, what he calls a political motive, he was already recognizably the potential creator of the world of *1984*, in which the only innocent people are the outcast proletarians and in which bullying is the principle upon which government is based.

In the three novels which he wrote between 1933 and 1936 his disinterested preoccupation with justice tends, as we shall see, to degenerate into a resentful sense of the injustices suffered by the novels' three protagonists, with all of whom Orwell to some extent identifies himself. And then, with startling suddenness, after his visit to the distressed mining areas and his conversion to socialism, the resentful complaining tone disappears completely and his writing strikes a new note of cheerfulness and of political aggressiveness and even of optimism. From then on he called himself a socialist, but his socialism was neither Marxist nor Fabian; it was entirely his own. It was not a cut-and-dried political or intellectual system but a rough-and-ready formulation of a profound psychological experience.

What had happened was that his visit to the coalfields had revealed to him the existence of the working class. Hitherto his mental picture of society had included little more than guilty oppressors on the one hand and half-starved coolies and down-and-outs and beggars on the other. But he now discovered a whole class of decent and self-respecting people who were economically depressed (to call them oppressed would be tendentious), who were neither down-and-out nor hopeless, and whose courage and cheerfulness and warmth were a revelation to him. One result of this was to exorcise his sense of loneliness and temporarily to mitigate his bitterness. He was no longer obsessed, as he had been in his first three novels, with the isolated tragedies of impoverished middle-class people in a world where the wicked are always triumphant. The world, he now knew, also contained a whole class of people who were neither oppressors nor hopeless human wrecks. And if this class were to achieve political power, might it not create a new and less unjust society? His experience of comradeship among the militiamen in the Spanish Civil War reinforced this hope. And a few years later, during World War II, he appears to have believed, as his anarchist and Trotskyist comrades in Spain had believed, that the war against Hitler was linked with a social revolution and that the success of each depended on the success of the other. But although the war speeded up many changes in European social life, the revolution failed to occur, so Orwell's revolutionary optimism was short-lived. In any case the socialism he hoped for was never anything more definite than an organization of society which would express the sense of justice, fairness, tolerance, and decency which he believed—after his experiences in the coalfields and in Spain—was characteristic of the common man. And when his pessimism reasserted itself, as it did even before the end of the war, it was because he had begun to fear that revolutions are always manipulated for their own ends by *un*-common power-seeking men.

His last two works of fiction, *Animal Farm* and *1984*, which are products of this pessimism, are sometimes regarded as recantations, because the first of them satirizes the Russian revolution and the second prophesies a similar and equally sinister revolution for the whole world. But these books do not recant any of Orwell's beliefs and ideals. They merely emphasize the fact that revolutions are not always for the better and may be very much for the worse; but because there had been occasions between 1939 and 1945 when Orwell was overoptimistic about the prospects of socialism, his reaction into pessimism was correspondingly extreme. Nevertheless, as a metapolitical thinker, he was much less liable than the typical intellectual leftist to change his opinions under the stress of disappointment, and he was immune to the follies of political fashion. He was never seduced, like so many of his contemporaries, by the glamour of revolutionary heroics or the thrill of vicarious violence.

Orwell would perhaps not have objected particularly to my gloss on his own account of his literary development. But he might have been surprised to see his interest in politics called Platonic in the sense of being related to the education of the human soul. And yet it is easy to support this view by quotations from his own work. For example, even when he is justifying the "materialism" of working-class politics, he is careful to put the word in quotes and he justifies it as follows: "How right [the workers] are to realise that the belly comes before the soul, *not in the scale of values*, but in point of time!"[5] And in general it is not the working-class socialist or the common man whom he accuses of materialism, but the Marxist intellectual and the middle-class socialist propagandist: "With their eyes glued to the economic facts, they have proceeded on the assumption that man has no soul and, explicitly or implicitly, they have set up the goal of a materialistic Utopia."[6] And again, in his essay on Arthur Koestler: "The real problem is how to restore a religious attitude while accepting death as final. Men can only be happy when they do not assume that the object of life is happiness."[7]

There is no question here of "the devil was sick, the devil a monk would be." Orwell did not write any of the above remarks during his last illness. They were written while his powers were still at their height and while he was an active supporter of the Labour party. The remark about a "religious attitude" shows that he could conceive the possibility of a religion so pure and disinterested as not to depend for its appeal upon the promise of personal immortality. And there is another glimpse of his ability to conceive an impersonal religion in the poem he dedicated to an Italian volunteer whom he believed to have been killed in Spain:

> Your name and your deeds were forgotten
> Before your bones were dry....
>
> .   .   .   .   .
>
> But the thing that I saw in your face
> No power can disinherit;
> No bomb that ever burst
> Shatters the crystal spirit.

There is, of course, nothing here that conflicts with Orwell's acceptance of death as final for the individual. What he conceives is an indestructible and eternal spirit, which can be manifested in any man's heroic life and death.

I emphasize this aspect of Orwell's thought because of its intrinsic importance and also because we cannot estimate his work as a political novelist unless we come to terms with it. And it is also necessary to give due weight to the extraordinary determination with which he set himself to experience the life of beggars and social outcasts. He himself, as we have seen, explains this as an attempt to purge himself of the guilt of imperialism: "Every suspicion of self-advancement, even to 'succeed' in life to the extent of making a few hundreds a year, seemed to me spiritually ugly, a species of bullying." But this feeling is not very far removed from world renunciation for the sake of a supreme and unformulable ideal of goodness and justice. The fact that Orwell was dominated for a time by such a feeling leads us to expect what we in fact find: namely, that when he begins to write about politics he shows a perspicacity and objectivity about fundamentals, which can hardly be attained by practical politicians because their preoccupation with day-to-day problems makes the necessary detachment almost impossible for them. Compared to their attitude, Orwell's can properly be described as metapolitical.

Looking at Orwell's first novel, *Burmese Days* (1934), from this point of view, one can see that his picture of imperialism, though its colors are harsh and bitter, is based upon a remarkably objective disinterestedness. It is only his attitude toward Flory, the hero, that is subjective and self-pitying. Flory's dislike of his fellow British officials and administrators is mainly personal irritation and has little to do with the evils of imperialism. Orwell understood very well, and was later to declare emphatically, that British imperialism had its good points and compared favorably with most other imperialisms. And it is not a British imperialist but a wicked Burmese who is the villain of the book. His villainy, of course, is successful; and the only two sympathetic characters, Flory and an Indian doctor who is his one friend in the place, are both ruined. The mood of the book is lonely self-pity, and the theme is the triumph of wickedness.

In *A Clergyman's Daughter* (1935) the gloom has not lifted; but instead of a lonely and harassed government official we have an overworked and impoverished clergyman's daughter who rejects the only escape from squalor that is open to her, which would have been to marry a disreputable middle-aged cynic with several illegitimate children. And in *Keep the Aspidistra Flying* we have an impoverished intellectual, a would-be poet, who is up against very much the same problems that Orwell himself was struggling with in the 1930's. In the end, in order to be able to marry, he gives up the struggle for independence and becomes a writer of advertising copy.

The moral of these novels is the same. The world is ruled by Mammon, whose favors go to the unscrupulous and ruthless. If you resist, you will finish either as a suicide, like Flory, or as a broken-down drudge, like the protagonists of the other two novels. Orwell is certainly identified to some extent with each of the three protagonists. Dorothy in *A Clergyman's Daughter* is given some of his own experiences. She becomes a schoolteacher and a hop-picker, and she spends a night on a bench in Trafalgar Square; there is an obvious similarity between Flory's life in Burma and Orwell's own; and the events and circumstances of the life of Gordon Comstock in *Keep the Aspidistra Flying* are to some extent autobiographical, though his character and behavior are a monstrous caricature of Orwell's. In all these three portraits there is an element of self-pity, and also of protest, which in the case of Gordon Comstock reaches an almost hysterical pitch of violence.

After *Keep the Aspidistra Flying* it was three years before Orwell produced another novel. And when it appeared, in 1939, it depicted an objective situation in no way less depressing than that of the first three novels. Indeed, it is in some ways worse because between 1936 and 1939 Orwell had learned a lot, much of it from personal experience in Spain, about communism, fascism, and international politics. The hero of this novel (*Coming Up for Air*) is a traveler for an insurance company and somewhat lower on the social scale than the protagonists of the earlier novels; and what is remarkable and unexpected is that the whole tone of the book, and in particular the character of its hero, George Bowling, is not only humorous but almost happy. George Bowling has a wretched job and a depressing, although virtuous, wife. His personal prospects are poor, and he is convinced—perfectly correctly, for the action of the novel takes place in the year before World War II— that there is a bad time coming for everybody; and yet his good humor and his spirits are undaunted.

There is very little humor in Orwell's first three novels, and anyone who had not read the two books that appeared between them and *Coming Up for Air* might be astonished by the difference. But, as we have already seen, the experiences he relates in the two intervening books, *The Road to Wigan Pier* and *Homage to Catalonia,* had given him a new feeling of buoyancy and of hopeful and even optimistic purposefulness. And they had stimulated his sense of humor. The criticism of bourgeois socialists in *The Road to Wigan Pier* is sometimes very amusing in a rather unsubtle way, and although the subject of *Homage to Catalonia* does not lend itself to humorous treatment, Orwell avoids undue heaviness and introduces humor when possible. It is sometimes a rather school-boyish humor, as, for example, in his reference to the Army and Navy Stores, a famous London department store. Speaking of the importance of food parcels from abroad during the Spanish war, he mentions that the only firm whose parcels of tea and biscuits safely reached him was the Army and Navy, and he continues, rather as though he was putting a banana skin under their feet: "Poor old Army and Navy! They did their duty nobly, but perhaps they might have felt happier if the stuff had been going to Franco's side of the barricade."[8]

But *Coming Up for Air* is humorous from beginning to end. The humor is still somewhat elementary compared to that of *Animal Farm,* which is the only book in which Orwell achieved an original blend of fantasy and humor. Nevertheless, *Coming Up for Air* is humorous in a very agreeable way, and the book is in other respects more characteristic than *Animal Farm* of Orwell at his best. It is a book that has not received all the appreciation it deserves. Its whole tone, as well as the character of its hero, convinces me that the principal result of Orwell's contact with unemployed miners and with his fellow militiamen in Spain had been a feeling of human encouragement rather than any particular political or intellectual revelation. It banished his feeling of isolation and it also, at least temporarily, mitigated his bitterness. What he had actually seen in the coalfields and in Spain had been grim; but the human beings he had met there had convinced him, or at least inspired the hope, that the idea of human brotherhood might after all be something more than a cant expression. He had discovered his ideal of the common man.

That he should have embodied this ideal in a character like George Bowling is a sign of his metapolitical objectivity. Bowling is nothing like the conventional hero of orthodox left-wing politics. He is neither a class-conscious idealistic progressive nor an intellectual; nor has he any sense of inferiority about not being one. He is a perfectly ordinary common man. So far from being by nature a revolutionary, he is instinc-

tively conservative and an individualist. But his outlook, like Orwell's
own, is metapolitical; and thanks to this, his natural kindliness and good-
will are fortified by a shrewdness and objectivity which make him
immune to political humbug, whether from the right or from the left. He
knows he is getting a shabby deal from society, and he has no illusions
about the company he works for; but he expects no salvation from either
Stalin or Hitler.

Orwell hoped—and for a time, especially during the war, appeared to
believe—that the Labour party could become the political instrument by
which the simple social ideals of people like George Bowling, the typical
common man, would be realized. But unfortunately the political intellectuals who frame party policies have little interest in or understanding of
the common man, and when Orwell returned to fiction after World War
II (which is on the point of breaking out in *Coming Up for Air*), he no
longer saw much hope of the sort of revolution that would fulfill the
ideals of George Bowling. He wrote a satire of the Russian Revolution in
Animal Farm and followed it four years later with a prophecy of what
the world would be like in 1984, which is an elaborate and horrifying
development of George Bowling's own presentiments when attending a
political meeting:

> The world we're going down into, the kind of hate-world, slo-
> gan-world. . . . And the processions and the posters with enor-
> mous faces, and the crowds of a million people all cheering for
> the Leader till they deafen themselves into thinking they really
> worship him, and all the time, underneath, they hate him so that
> they want to puke. It's all going to happen. Or isn't it? Some
> days I know it's impossible, other days I know it's inevitable.[9]

From a purely literary point of view, if there is such a thing, we
observe that the chief difference between *Coming Up for Air* and the earlier novels is that it is told in the first person by its hero, who is cheerful
while all the earlier heroes are miserable, and at least one of them,
Gordon Comstock in *Keep the Aspidistra Flying*, is almost pathologically
self-pitying. But is there any striking difference in literary technique?
And are the earlier characters "lifeless" in comparison with George Bowling—as they should be if Orwell's own view of the effect upon his writing
of having a conscious political purpose is correct?

I do not think so. Indeed, I think the hero of Orwell's first novel,
Burmese Days, is, if anything, more lifelike and less obviously a vehicle
for the author's ideas than any of the later heroes. But it is also true that
Burmese Days is more loaded than the other novels with deliberate fine
writing and purple passages. And in the next novel there is an elaborate
set piece of more than thirty pages describing by means of dramatic solil-

oquies a night spent in the open in Trafalgar Square by a group of down-and-outs, including the heroine.[10] It is somewhat labored and unimaginative and altogether unworthy of the author of *Animal Farm*. Indeed, except for *Animal Farm*, I think Orwell's writing is nearly always better in his critical and polemical essays than in his fiction. It is true, however, that the prose of his novels does develop from a rather conventional competence toward a powerful and impressive simplicity, and at its best it is almost as good as prose of its particular kind can be.

It is not, however, a sensitively imaginative kind of prose; so it is interesting to find Orwell, in *The Road to Wigan Pier*, commenting on a simile used by the most imaginative of all modern writers and suggesting an alternative which he prefers. He is looking at a snowy landscape in a coal-mining district and he says:

> I remembered that D. H. Lawrence, writing of this same landscape or another near by, said that the snow-covered hills rippled away into the distance "like muscle." It was not the simile that would have occurred to me. To my eye the snow and the black walls were more like a white dress with black piping running across it.[11]

Lawrence has, of course, often been criticized for his tendency to see wombs, loins, and muscles everywhere in nature, but Orwell is probably remembering here a beautiful passage in one of his letters:

> The upland is naked, white like silver, and moving far into the distance, strange and muscular, with gleams like skin. . . . The sheer, living, muscular white of the uplands absorbs everything. Only there is a tiny clump of trees bare on the hill-top—small beeches—writhing like iron in the blue sky.[12]

To set this passage alongside Orwell's white dress with black piping is an object lesson in the difference between imaginative and unimaginative prose.

Orwell's last book, *1984*, is written in the form of a novel. Its technique shows no striking advance on his earlier novels, except that his narrative style here almost reaches his ideal of a prose which should be as inconspicuous and transparent as a windowpane. Its psychology is simple and elementary, and most of the characters are cartoon figures; but like all Orwell's novels it is solid and very well constructed. It would be absurd, however, to judge the book simply as a novel. Just as *Animal Farm* is not a fairy story but a political satire, so *1984* is not a novel but a tract for the times and a desperate warning. It would be unfair to call it a prophecy, and if by the year 1984 we are not living under the sort of dictatorship the book describes, no one will have the right to laugh at Orwell as a false prophet. He describes a society ruled by a mysterious Big Brother, who is served by an Inner Party of bosses and an Outer Party of clerical and administrative drudges while the mass of outcast and powerless proletarians are left in their slums to run free like animals. But the point of the book does not depend upon the accuracy of this forecast nor upon the implausible sadistic philosophy which Orwell attributes to the Inner Party.

By paying too much attention to this aspect of the book and to the melodramatic tragedy of its hero and heroine, critics are in danger of missing the extraordinary perspicacity and realism with which Orwell has constructed the background of the story, the world situation within which the tragedy is enacted. He was able to do this, in my opinion, because he was primarily a metapolitical thinker. I do not know of any prophetic novel in which the general world situation is predicted with such horrifying plausibility as in *1984*. Neither Zamyatin's *We* nor Huxley's *Brave New World* nor any of H. G. Wells's utopias is equal to Orwell's novel in this respect, and Kipling's uncannily perceptive short story "As Easy as ABC" is too slight and light to be comparable. But admiration for the background should not blind us to the skill with which Orwell has invented the details of the foreground of *1984*. Within its limits, it is a powerful imaginative effort, even though much of it is only an exaggeration of the more depressing features of life in wartime London—canteen meals, shortages, general shabbiness and lack of repairs, and so on. Curiously enough, the one novel I know that predicts an England with a comparably claustrophobic atmosphere of impalpable, all-pervasive, and ineluctable tyranny employs the opposite method. This is Jane Lane's *A State of Mind*, which describes a prosperous and luxurious society in which sociological and psychiatric "progress" has evolved a sterile intellectual, moral, and psychological conformism from which there is no escape except by state-licensed euthanasia or banishment for life to a Hebridean island, which is isolated like a leper colony and where old-fashioned "religious superstitions" are allowed to survive. But in this novel, unlike Orwell's, the condition of the rest of the world is left undescribed.

Today, twenty years after the book was written, the main outlines of something very like the world of *1984* are already discernible. It is true that Orwell's three superstates—"Eastasia" (China and satellites), "Oceania" (the Americas, Australasia, and Britain), and "Eurasia" (Russia and Europe)—do not yet exist in exactly the form he gives them. Western Europe is still independent of Russia, and the relations between America, Britain, and western Europe are still fluid. But whether or not the whole

of Europe is ultimately taken over by the Soviet Union, the substantial
accuracy of Orwell's picture is already clear:

> In one combination or another, these three super-states are per-
> manently at war. . . . War, however, is no longer the desperate,
> annihilating struggle that it was in the early decades of the
> twentieth century. It is a warfare of limited aims between com-
> batants who are unable to destroy one another. . . . This is not to
> say that either the conduct of war, or the prevailing attitude
> towards it, has become less bloodthirsty or more chivalrous. On
> the contrary, war hysteria is continuous and universal in all
> countries, and such acts as raping, looting, the slaughter of chil-
> dren, the reduction of whole populations to slavery, and repri-
> sals against prisoners . . . are regarded as normal.[13]

The only things Orwell has missed are the political hijacking of planes,
and kidnappings and the arrests of alleged "spies" for use as hostages.

The continuous war waged by the three superstates is conducted in
parts of the world remote from the main centers of population (that is to
say, in places like Vietnam and central Africa), and for internal political
reasons none of them wants to bring it to an end. They cannot conquer
one another and would gain no advantage by doing so. "On the contrary,
so long as they remain in conflict they prop one another up like three
sheaves of corn."[14]

To have foreseen all this during the 1940's, when there was no sign as
yet of a split between Russian and Chinese communism, proves the perspicacity and detachment of Orwell's metapolitical outlook. Indeed, so
far as the general background of 1984 is concerned, I can find only one
point on which his perspicacity was at fault (or perhaps it was flagging
imaginative energy, for he was mortally ill by the time he finished the
book). In attempting to explain why the ruling class in all the three
superstates deliberately keeps the mass of the people in ignorance and
poverty, although it would be technically possible to provide them with
luxury and higher education, he gives two different reasons, neither of
which is very satisfactory. The first reason is psychologically implausible.
It is that the rulers are inspired exclusively by a sadistic philosophy
which makes them enjoy the infliction of humiliation and hardship upon
their subjects. The second reason is superficially plausible enough, as
well as being familiar and even hackneyed:

> If leisure and security were enjoyed by all alike, the great
> mass of human beings who are normally stupefied by poverty
> would become literate and would learn to think for themselves;
> and once they had done this, they would sooner or later realise

that the privileged minority had no function, and they would
sweep it away.[15]

But this old, familiar proposition begs a whole series of questions, and
it is odd to find it badly set forth, without comment, in *1984*. Admittedly,
however, it occurs in a book within the book and need not therefore be
taken to represent Orwell's own considered opinion. The book in which it
occurs is called *The Theory and Practice of Oligarchical Collectivism*, and
it is the secret gospel of Emmanuel Goldstein, the official and possibly
mythical traitor to the regime. Goldstein's position in relation to Big
Brother is similar to Trotsky's in relation to Stalin. It is possible, therefore, that by exhibiting Goldstein's naïveté Orwell meant to emphasize
the hopelessness of any resistance to the regime. For no one knew better
than Orwell that in a world in which everyone has learned to think for
himself the result of sweeping away a privileged minority is likely to be
its replacement by another privileged minority, and of that by another
one, and so on indefinitely. The fact that this may also happen by a
minority *coup d'état* in a state in which the majority are incapable of
thinking for themselves is irrelevant.

It still remains desirable, of course, that as many people as possible
should learn to think; but a world full of people thinking for, and of,
themselves will not be *ipso facto* an improvement upon the world of
1984. Orwell understood this perfectly, and few modern writers have
done more to dispel the illusion that people who have been educated to
"think for themselves" are more objective about their loves and hates and
desires than the less educated. Indeed, he thought them less so. Two of
his essays are devoted to this subject and, significantly, they have
received much less attention than most of the others. These two essays,
"Notes on Nationalism" and "Anti-Semitism in Britain," were both written
in 1945 and republished after his death in *England, Your England* (an
uncharacteristic title because it suggests precisely that derisive detachment which he disliked in the English intelligentsia and which he classi-
fies in the first of the two essays as a negative form of the nationalist
vice). In these two essays he makes a clear distinction between patriotism, which is an essentially peaceful attitude, perfectly compatible with,
and even conducive to, admiration for other countries and sympathy for
the patriotism felt by their inhabitants, and nationalism, which is always a
product of the restless, hungry, unsatisfied will to power. He demonstrates that, of all people, intellectuals are the typical and predestined
victims of the disease of nationalism and, further, that in its extreme form
this disease paralyzes all feeling for truth and all sense of reality.

Orwell's definition of nationalism is obviously much broader, but it is
also more refined and subtle, than the conventional one; and the reason

for the comparative unpopularity of these two essays becomes obvious when we look at some of the examples he gives of nationalistic feeling. These include the Celtic nationalisms, anti-Semitism, Zionism, communism, political Catholicism, pacifism, color feeling (either way), and class feeling (either way). And as if all that were not bad enough, he concludes the essay on anti-Semitism with the words "That anti-Semitism will be definitively *cured*, without curing the larger disease of nationalism, I do not believe."[16] Orwell was prepared, of course, to admit that vicious nationalistic loves and hatreds are part of the makeup of nearly everyone. But he was far more aware than most people that it is the so-called cultured classes who are their commonest victims. And since nationalism is a poison which vitiates thought, it cannot be cured by taking thought or by the naïve appeal to reason. Its cure is not so much an intellectual effort as, to use his own words, "essentially a *moral* effort."[17]

Orwell was repelled by the terminology of religion, but he was never afraid of using the word "morality," and he was as faithful as Kipling himself to the Gods of the Copy-Book Headings. This has led some critics to attribute to him a conformist tendency, and if they mean by this that he championed the normal, the attribution is well founded. One could even go further and say that military discipline had a certain appeal for him. But it is also true that he had a tenderness for cranks and eccentrics. In his essay on nationalism he refers to the lunatic fringe of Celtic nationalists who were so blinded by hatred of England that they contrived to be simultaneously pro-Nazi and pro-Russian during World War II. But although he was merciless toward their delusion that Ireland, Scotland, or Wales could survive unaided and that they owe nothing to England's protection, he would certainly have enjoyed meeting them and arguing the point, and he would have been up in arms against any threat to their freedom of expression.

Is there anything wrong in combining a love of discipline with a love of eccentricity? In Orwell's case it seems to me to prove that he possessed an exceptional breadth of mind. In any case, there is no doubt that he was exceptionally well aware that people thinking for themselves are liable to think very foolish thoughts, and that everything depends upon the use to which they put their capacity for thinking, which in turn depends upon character and upon will and upon motives, aims, and ideals. It seems to me, therefore, that the thesis of *1984* would have been strengthened if he had made the ruling party depend less upon brutal violence and more upon persuasive demagogy. A society that enjoys so-called freedom of thought but has no conception of what Orwell called "the religious attitude" can be manipulated by hedonistic progressive propaganda even more effectively than an ignorant mob can be coerced by brutal violence. And in the long run the "free-thinking" public will think itself into an even more pitiable state than the oppressed proletariat of *1984*—because "men can only be happy when they do not assume that the purpose of life is happiness." If Orwell were alive today, I am convinced he would be repeating this warning with all his characteristic virility and pungency.

And to this I feel free, thanks to a review by Miss Mary McCarthy in *The New York Review of Books* (January 30, 1969), to add a further word. Reviewing the four-volume edition of Orwell's *Collected Essays, Journalism and Letters*, Miss McCarthy expressed a very well founded doubt whether Orwell, if he were alive today, would be on her side in the Vietnam controversy. I knew Orwell intimately for the last twenty years of his life, but I always hesitate, after a friend's death, to make public guesses, based on the privilege of friendship, about his probable views on current events. But since Miss McCarthy has perceived, and had the rare honesty to state, something that should be obvious to every reader of Orwell, I feel justified in adding a further word about it. In my opinion it is practically certain that Orwell would have considered much of the propaganda against American involvement in Vietnam to be, at best, politically and morally imbecile. No doubt he would have agreed with some of the criticisms of America's handling of the problem, but it is certain that he would have had much more to say about the Soviet Union's handling of Czechoslovakia; and as for all those who talk about American "imperialism" and equate it, and even compare it unfavorably, with Chinese and Russian tyranny, they should congratulate themselves that he is no longer here to give them a piece of his mind. He was a pessimist, no doubt, but he would not have compared the western world of 1969 with the communist world. He would have known that 1969 is not yet *1984*.

NOTES

1. "Why I Write," in *England, Your England* (London, 1953), pp. 13, 16.
2. *Ibid.*, p. 7.
3. *The Road to Wigan Pier* (London, 1937), p. 181.
4. *Ibid.*, p. 180.
5. *England, Your England*, p. 175. Italics mine.

6. *The Road to Wigan Pier*, p. 246.
7. *Critical Essays* (London, 1945), p. 140.
8. *Homage to Catalcnia* (London, 1938), pp. 100–101.
9. *Coming Up for Air* (London, 1939), p. 184.
10. *A Clergyman's Daughter* (New York, 1936), pp. 164–198.
11. *The Road to Wigan Pier*, p. 19.
12. A. Huxley, ed., *The Letters of D. H. Lawrence* (London, 1932), p. 469.
13. *1984* (London, 1949), pp. 186–187.
14. *Ibid.*, p. 198.
15. *Ibid.*, p. 191.
16. *England, Your England*, p. 80.
17. *Ibid.*, p. 67.

GRAHAM GREENE
(1904-   )

by Marie-Béatrice Mesnet
(*Translated from the French by Richard J. Ricard*)

"DISLOYALTY IS OUR PRIVILEGE," wrote Graham Greene in 1948,[1] in an exchange of views on "the relation of the artist to society."

> I would emphasise once again the importance and the virtue of disloyalty. . . . If they [the writers] don't become loyal to a Church or a country, they are too apt to become loyal to some invented ideology of their own, until they are praised for consistency, for an unified view. Even despair can become a form of loyalty. . . . Loyalty confines us to accepted opinions: loyalty forbids us to comprehend sympathetically our dissident fellows; but disloyalty encourages us to roam experimentally through any human mind. . . .[2]

This idea, although troubling at first sight, is of fundamental importance. Greene has always denied being a deliberately committed writer—that is to say, writing in the service of a particular doctrine, in support of a particular cause, either political or religious. He has fought a running battle against the power of abstractions, the "isms" and "ocracies" that in our age have arrived to dominate politics, history, and economics. In a society organized either badly or too well, one in which technology, planning, and the growing power of government increasingly threaten individual freedom, one in which the totalitarian exploitation of men and ideas is widespread in both the communist state and the welfare state (although less noticeably so in the latter), Greene has argued that the writer's duty is "to accept no special privilege from the State."[3] He must at all costs maintain his independence, taking no orders from the state or from any party or creed.

This obligation does not mean that the writer, as a man, is dispensed from the obligations he shares with all his fellowmen, "our primitive duties as human beings.... If we do less than these we are so much the less human beings and therefore so much the less likely to be artists."[4] But his special responsibility is to "the establishment of justice," the "awakening of sympathy."

> Isn't it possibly the story-teller's task to act as the devil's advo-cate, to elicit sympathy and a measure of understanding for those who lie outside the boundaries of State sympathy? But remember that it is not necessarily the poor or the physically defenceless who lie there. The publicans and sinners belong to all classes and all economic levels.[5]

The writer's sympathy, then, must extend to all men. If he is Catholic, like Greene, he has to accept the idea that "doubt and even denial must be given their chance of self-expression." The task set for him is where lies his special exercise in charity toward others and is the prerequisite of his literary art: "The very act of re-creation for the novelist entails sym-pathy; the characters for whom he fails in sympathy have never been truly re-created."[6] He has, finally, another responsibility: "... to tell the truth as he sees it.... I don't mean anything flamboyant by the phrase 'telling the truth': I don't mean exposing anything. By truth I mean accu-racy—it is largely a matter of style."[7] For the writer, then, more than for anyone else, justice is inseparable from discipline. He must have the courage to tell what he sees. For to the extent that his account is an accu-rate one he can disclose man to himself and unmask the meaning of things and events.

This concern for justice and truth infuses all of Greene's work, giving the universe he creates the complex dimensions of reality. He has never quit fighting for mankind against the philosophies of determinism that undermine man's true stature. It is in this sense that Greene's works are political—political in the highest sense of the word, as it has been under-stood since the time of Plato's dialogues. Greene endorses Charlotte Brontë's observation:

> You will see that *Villette* touches on no matter of public inter-est. I cannot write books handling the topics of the day; it is no use trying it. Nor can I write a book for its moral. Nor can I take up a philanthropic scheme, though I honour philanthropy.

But he adds:

> Perhaps it was easier for Charlotte Brontë to believe that she
> had excluded public interest than it is for us. Public interest in
> her day was surely more separate from the private life. . . . It
> did not so colour the common life: with us, however consciously
> unconcerned we are, it obtrudes, through the cracks of our stor-
> ies, terribly persistent like grass through cement.[8]

Greene's novels are drawn from life as it is; his characters are grounded
in it. Just as we, they live, fall in love, toil, struggle, and die. We learn
their habits, their flaws and virtues, their weaknesses and acts of courage.
Each has his place in society, from the judge or policeman representing
the established order to the outlaw, murderer, or traitor challenging it,
and, in between, the industrialist and worker, writer, communist, and
priest. As a journalist, Greene traveled to almost every continent, collecting as he went the carefully detailed observations which were to become
the materials for his novels. Their scope is a global one; their backdrop,
the present, the history of our century. Its great human and social
dramas echo throughout Greene's works. He is, in one critic's words, "the
spokesman of tragic times."[9]

What, in fact, comes first to sight when one tries to capture reality as it
is? Violence, certainly. Violence is everywhere. It is in the oppressiveness
of social injustice, against which even conformity provides no secure
defense. It is in the very soul of man, who destroys himself when he gives
way to it. It is unleashed in war. War sets people against each other or
divides a nation. It turns man against his brother; it rends man and
woman when the sexes are confronted. It calls forth and precipitates
death. Greene's novels all culminate in a violent death, either murder, the
ultimate expression of violence against another, or suicide, the result of
frustrated violence turned inward against oneself. There is always at
least one victim; a gigantic tauromachy plays itself out. Death, in
Greene's works, exists as an abiding presence, as an inescapable part of
life. To Greene himself, it has long been a familiar companion: An often
cited essay, "The Revolver in the Corner Cupboard,"[10] recounts his own
adolescent attempts at suicide.

Violence and death, however, are only the fruits of evil, with which
Greene became acquainted at an early age, awakening in him a sense of
the religious. Every man's future begins unrolling from early childhood.
For Greene, it was the school at Berkhamsted, where his father was
headmaster and where he began his schooling, that furnished him with
his first and most vivid image of evil:

> In the land of the skyscrapers, of stone stairs and cracked bells
> ringing early, one was aware of fear and hate, a kind of lawless-
> ness. . . . One began to believe in heaven because one believed
> in hell, but for a long while it was only hell one could picture
> with a certain intimacy.[11]

At fourteen Greene realized his vocation when reading Marjorie Bowen's
The Viper of Milan:

> The future for better or worse really struck. . . . It was as if I
> had been supplied once and for all with a subject. . . . Goodness
> has only once found a perfect incarnation in a human body and
> never will again, but evil can always find a home there. Human
> nature is not black and white but black and grey.[12]

At twenty-two he converted to Catholicism. Although his works are no
more "Catholic" than they are "political," his faith gives his characters a
whole spiritual dimension lacking in the English novel since the death of
Henry James:

> With the death of Henry James the religious sense was lost to
> the English novel, and with the religious sense went the sense of
> the importance of the human act. It was as if the world of
> fiction had lost a dimension. . . . The novelist, perhaps uncon-
> sciously aware of his predicament, took refuge in the subjective
> novel. It was as if he thought that by mining into layers of per-
> sonality hitherto untouched he could unearth the secret of
> "importance," but in these mining operations he lost yet another
> dimension. The visible world for him ceased to exist as com-
> pletely as the spiritual.[13]

Only the sense of the invisible, in short, preserves the reality of the visible world, giving man his bearings in a way which psychology cannot.
Greene recognized this sensibility in François Mauriac, describing it in
terms which could well be applied to Greene himself: "[He] belongs to
the company of the great traditional novelists: he is a writer for whom
the visible world has not ceased to exist, whose characters have the solidity and importance of men with souls to save or lose."[14]

The demands of compassion and truth require, on the part of the novelist, considerable humility. "For to render the highest justice to corruption you must retain your innocence: you have to be conscious all the
time within yourself of treachery to something valuable."[15] Evil is just
such a treachery, a betrayal of our neighbor, of ourselves, of God.
Greene's novels are haunted by this theme. No cause to him is all good or
all evil. Our motives are never entirely pure. We are all traitors. It is not
our place, therefore, to sit in judgment either on ourselves or on others.

We can, however, condemn evil and error without condemning their per-petrators. This explains Greene's apparent and, at first sight, shocking suspension of judgment in the introduction he wrote for *My Silent War*, the autobiography of the English spy Kim Philby:

> "He betrayed his country"—yes, perhaps he did, but who among us has not committed treason to something or someone more important than a country? In Philby's own eyes, he was working for a shape of things to come from which his country would benefit.[16]

Philby himself has cited in self-justification the words of "D.," Greene's "confidential agent":

> "Do you believe," she said, "that *your* leaders are any better than L.'s?" . . . "No. Of course not. But I still prefer the people they lead—even if they lead them all wrong." "The poor, right or wrong," she scoffed. "It's no worse—is it?—than my country, right or wrong. You choose your side once for all—of course, it may be the wrong side. Only history can tell that."[17]

Philby's seeing himself in D. illustrates the symbolic and prophetic character of Greene's work. Greene arouses his reader, draws him in by his skill at storytelling, and thereby brings him face to face with things he would prefer not to see, asking him to read events and situations not just as they seem but as the signs of a deeper reality. Used in this way as a symbol, the particular is raised to the universal. "Cracked bells ringing" become the image of a lost childhood. The "sky-signs in Leicester Square, the 'tarts' in Bond Street, the smell of cooking greens off Tottenham Court Road, the motor salesmen in Great Portland Street,"[18] "the popu-lous foreshore of Brighton," are reminders of the "seediness of civilisation," of what man has made of man. Africa seems "not a particular place, but a shape, a strangeness, a wanting to know"[19] "at which point we went astray,"[20] just as it is also Pendélé, or paradise. The "Midget Make-Easy Air-Powered Suction Small Home Cleaner"[21] serves as symbol of the absurdities of our economic system. The most homely of words, "onions,"[22] can signify a whole world for two lovers. Andrews, Conrad Drover, Anthony Farrant, Pinkie, the whisky-priest, Scobie, Sarah Miles, Pyle, Querry, Brown—all the characters out of Greene's imagination are both unique individuals and human types. For Greene, the novelist cannot limit himself to recording modern man's contradictions, his sorrows and his joys; he must *be* that man. His task is "to draw his own likeness to any human being, the guilty as much as the innocent,"[23] connecting the drama within each man to that of all men. As Pierre Emmanuel wrote, "man's history begins anew in each of us."[24] It opens on eternity, which reveals its meaning. It is part of the mystery.

Now let us follow step by step Greene's pursuit of justice and truth and see what it reveals of our world, of our times, and of ourselves. Greene was born in 1904. In addition to several collections of essays and short stories, travel pieces, and magazine articles, he has published four plays and about twenty novels and "entertainments." As a novelist, his work spans forty years, from *The Man Within* (1929) to *Travels with My Aunt* (1969).[25] World War II was the major pivot point in his career. It coincided with Greene's maturity, a period from which came his great novels of directly Christian inspiration. His earlier novels are notable for the their striking evocation of the economic crisis of the 1930's and of the slide into world-shaking catastrophe. His later works are set under the sign of the cold war and so-called peaceful coexistence.

Greene's first three novels are youthful works, still bearing the stamp of romanticism. Nevertheless, they presage all the major themes which were to become the constants of his work.

The first is *The Man Within* (1929). Its story unfolds early in the nineteenth century in Sussex, where the local Pharisees, all "good and upright men," have crushed the poor and the unfortunate beneath them with contempt. The system of justice they have fashioned in their image is without compassion. In this land, Andrews, "friendless and alone, chased by harsh enemies through an uninterested world,"[26] lives afraid of life. "There's another man within me that's angry with me."[27] It is through Elisabeth, an idealized image of purity, courage, and faith, that he finally comes to know himself.

The Name of Action (1930), the story of an imaginary revolution in the 1920's, already shows Greene's interest in the problem of political involvement. Oliver Chant had "come to Trier with the intention of fighting for justice."[28] But on which side is justice? Freedom, he discovers, does not necessarily make men free. Although the revolution succeeds, it is for the wrong reasons, and his sympathies turn toward Demassener, the ousted dictator, who laughed at his defeat and who "carried his faith intact and hidden into a doubting world."[29]

Rumour at Nightfall (1931) carries us to Spain in the time of the Carlist War, in the second half of the last century. Caveda, a Carlist liberal who believes in the possibility of fashioning a world of justice and happiness, is the first of those spokesmen for atheism whom Greene has matched against Christian adversaries in many of his subsequent works.

Stamboul Train (1932) marks the beginning of a major series of social

novels condemning the smugness of the established order and the injustices of capitalism and of its so-called democratic institutions. The economic crisis then shaking the world had led liberal Europe into chaos:

> The world was chaotic; when the poor were starved and the
> rich were not happier for it; when the thief might be punished
> or rewarded with titles; when wheat was burned in Canada and
> coffee in Brazil, and the poor ... had no money for bread and
> froze to death in unheated rooms.[30]

As the first of several such women characters created by Greene, Coral
Musker seems to embody all the sweetness found in a cruel world and to
be marked by her goodness and vulnerability to end up its victim. Dr.
Czinner is a peasant's son brought up on Catholicism, who has convinced
himself that he has left his religion behind him. "Telling himself that God
was a fiction invented by the rich to keep the poor content,"[31] he seeks
to replace Him by a new faith. "I've tried to make things different ... I
am a Communist."[32] "How old-fashioned you are with your frontiers and
your patriotism. The aeroplane doesn't know a frontier; even your financiers don't recognize frontiers."[33] Those he fights for are the poor of the
world, with their "sad and beautiful faces, thin from bad food, old before
their time, resigned to despair."[34]

In *It's a Battlefield* (1934) Jim Drover, a London bus driver, kills a
policeman at a communist meeting. A decent, soft-spoken, honest man is
thus turned into a killer. "It's a battlefield," and its victims are chiefly the
poor, condemned by the workings of the economic and social system to
insecurity, to mechanized factories—"a hand to the left, a hand to the
right, the pressure of a foot"[35]—or to unemployment—"the beggar did not
beg because he would not work."[36] Justice is unjust, for "the laws were
made by property owners in defence of property."[37] Drover's communist
friends, for their part, ineffectually play at "making speeches ... recon-
structing England in theory, abolishing poverty on paper."[38] Surrogate,
the party intellectual, has no qualms about sacrificing Drover's life in
behalf of his own cherished abstractions. "The truth is, nobody cares
about anything but his own troubles. Everybody's too busy fighting his
own little battle to think of the, the next man."[39] If anyone heeds the
general war, it is perhaps the commissioner; he, however, is only a "mercenary," whose "work was simply to preserve the existing order."[40] Sometimes, though, "he dreamed of an organisation which he could serve for
higher reason than pay, an organisation which would enlist his fidelity
because of its inherent justice, its fair distribution of reward, its reason-
ableness."[41]

England Made Me (1935) is a cold and grim novel of the functional,

inhuman world of big business. It is a world in which man is dehumanized and enslaved, twisted into something like the fountain spouting
in front of the glass and steel box that houses the Krogh headquarters in
Stockholm. It is a totalitarian world Greene depicts. Kate Farrant has
made her way in it with cynical shrewdness: "We are all thieves. . . . No
brotherhood in our boat. Only who can cut the biggest dash and who can
swim."[42] Anthony, her twin brother, however, is part of "the refuse of a
changing world."[43] "It's because I'm not young enough and not old
enough: not young enough to believe in a juster world, not old enough
for the country, the king, the trenches to mean anything to me at all."[44]

Meanwhile, in Berlin, Hitler was rising to power. "On the ground,
among the Swastikas, one saw pain at every yard."[45]

> To-day our world seems peculiarly susceptible to brutality. . . .
> When one sees to what unhappiness, to what peril of extinction,
> centuries of cerebration have brought us, one sometimes has a
> curiosity to discover if one can from what we have come, to
> recall at which point we went astray.[46]

With this in mind, Greene set off for Liberia, "with Abyssinia the only
part of Africa where white men do not rule."[47] In the course of a long
Journey Without Maps (1936) he sought to return to "the old, the unfa-
miliar, the communal life beyond the clearing."[48] What he found in
"such a beginning, its terrors as well as its placidity, the power as well as
the gentleness,"[49] was "a kind of hope in human nature." "If one could
get back to this bareness, simplicity, instinctive friendliness, feeling rather
than thought, and start again."[50]

In the novels that followed, violence is more and more in the open; the
specter of war was drawing nearer. *A Gun for Sale* (1936) again attacks
the capitalist system. Raven, a poor, youngish man with a harelip, "the
badge of a class," is hired to assassinate the old Czech Minister of War.
His employer, the head of Midland Steel, counts on precipitating war
and selling armaments to save his floundering business. "A war won't do
people any harm," claims Raven. "It'll show them what's what, it'll give
them a taste of their own medicine. I know. There's always been a war
for me."[51] How can a war be averted to which everyone seems resigned?
Mather, "a member of the best police force," admits: "It doesn't matter to
me if there is a war. When it's over I'll still want to be going on with this
job. It's the organisation I like. I always want to be on the side that
organises."[52]

Of all Greene's novels, *Brighton Rock* (1938) is the most terrible. It is
also the first in which he explicitly seeks to trace the mysterious ways of
evil and of grace. "This is hell, nor are we out of it."[53] Evil is stripped

bare, for the battlefield is no longer only society; it is within man. Ida Arnold is ignorant; she does not know; she is just nothing. Pinkie, though only seventeen, already knows the world to be "the ravaged and disputed territory between two eternities."[54] He is a "Roman." He has known only poverty and crime, "a dark hole" from which he once thought of escaping by becoming a priest. Having become, too young, the leader of a gang of hoodlums, he finds himself trapped by an initial crime in a train of horrors without end. "You start and then you go on going on."[55] He wonders why he shouldn't "have had his chance like all the rest, seen his glimpse of Heaven if it was only a crack between the Brighton walls."[56] Rose's love offers him the chance: "She was good, he'd discovered that, and he was damned; they were made for each other.... Good and evil lived in the same country, spoke the same language."[57] Too late. Pinkie dies, "whipped away into zero—nothing."[58]

It is the Spanish Civil War that, barely disguised, serves as the backdrop for *The Confidential Agent* (1939). D. has chosen himself to fight the rich, in particular L., a dilettante aristocrat, a man able to appreciate the talents of an artist or scholar but who hadn't "the faintest conception of what it [meant] to love another human being."[59] In the past, D. observes, when Christianity held things together, one could move with more certainty, for "men were united by a common belief." Now commitment was more difficult. "Now there were so many varieties of economic materialism, so many initial letters."[60] The civil war seemed inevitably to destroy a part of oneself. "It was as if some code of faith and morality had been lost for centuries."[61] D. is skeptical both of the ideology professed by his leaders and of their integrity, but, like Kim Philby, he has chosen sides once and for all. It is really the poor for whom he is fighting. It is for Else, the fourteen-year-old chambermaid in a seedy London hotel. "If this was civilisation—the crowded prosperous streets ... and the sinking, drowning child—he preferred barbarity, the bombed streets and the food queues: a child there had nothing worse to look forward to than death."[62] Death is what he brings Else; he entrusts her with the future of his country's poor, and she pays the highest price.

Many intellectuals of Greene's generation joined the Communist party and then resigned, disillusioned by Stalin's reign of terror. Many went to fight in Spain. As a Catholic, Greene did neither,[63] but instead, in the spring of 1938, set out for Mexico.

> Less ideological, perhaps less courageous, writers chose corners where the violence was more moderate; but the hint of it had to be there to satisfy that moral craving for the just and reasonable expression of human nature left without belief.[64]

He arrived there toward the end of a period of religious persecution which had lasted over ten years. What he saw and described in an account of his travels, *The Lawless Roads*, was a totalitarian state where the practice of religion was proscribed by law.

> The State is in charge of everything. The State ... always the State. What idealisms have gone to the construction of that tyrant! ... No one any more is able to make the claim, "The State is I." The State is none of us. ... Perhaps the only body in the world to-day which consistently—and sometimes success-fully—opposes the totalitarian State is the Catholic Church.[65]

The social encyclicals of the Popes and the words of the apostle James, "'Go to now, ye rich men: weep and howl in your miseries which shall come upon you. ...' Those are the words of revolution."[66] In Mexico, the revolution succeeded despite the rich, by violence. But violence in itself is fruitless: "It's typical of Mexico, of the whole human race perhaps—violence in favour of an ideal and then the ideal lost and the violence just going on."[67]

Now let us narrow our field of vision from a country to one man, the priest without a name, the whisky-priest, whom Greene draws as an illus-tration of the "essential Christian paradox."[68] *The Power and the Glory* (1940) is the most classically conceived and the most finished of all Greene's works. In the tropical, godless state of Tabasco, every church was destroyed and "every priest was hunted down or shot, except one, who existed for ten years in the forests and the swamps, venturing out only at night."[69] "A small man dressed in a shabby dark city suit, carrying a small attaché case,"[70] he is pursued by the police. Once, when there was peace, "he had been comparatively innocent. ... Now in his corruption he had learnt."[71] Carrying with him forever the weight of his failings and the sense of his unworthiness, he had learned how to love: his daughter, the symbol of his sin, and even the half-caste who betrays him. His solitary wandering life "had peeled away from his memory every-thing but the simplest outline of the mystery."[72] However, he remained faithful to essentials, priest forever, consecrated in the service of man-kind. He "carries on." "God had decided. He had to go on."[73]

The young police lieutenant lives ascetically: no drink, no woman. A mystic in reverse, he pursues God out of hate. Those he loves are the children and the poor of his country; he wants "to begin the world again with them in a desert," "to give them the whole world."[74] He lets his heart, however, speak "at the end of a gun,"[75] which in the end finds its victim.

Two religions confront each other. The religion of man, denying God, is fundamentally flawed: It cannot be any better than the men who make it. "It's no good your working for your end unless you're a good man yourself."[76] It is willing to sacrifice men for the happiness of mankind or one class for another and can "stifle life from the best possible motives."[77] The religion of God, conversely, brings life. The weaknesses of men matter little to it, for God, in his "labyrinthine ways," uses men as they are. "It doesn't matter so much my being a coward—and all the rest. I can put God into a man's mouth just the same—and I can give him God's pardon."[78] Each individual man is deemed worthy of respect and love because he is made in God's image:

> That was the difference, he had always known, between his faith and theirs, the political leaders of the people who cared only for things like the State, the republic: this child was more important than a whole continent.[79]

Alone in his cell, forgetting his shortcomings and his fear of death, the priest weeps:

> It seemed to him, at that moment, that it would have been quite easy to have been a saint. It would only have needed a little self-restraint and a little courage. He felt like someone who has missed happiness by seconds at an appointed place. He knew now that at the end there was only one thing that counted—to be a saint.[80]

The last priest in Tabasco has been killed. But there is a knock on the door in the night: "My name is Father...."[81] A new priest has arrived.

"Mexico is a state of mind."[82] It only "started things in a small way while the world waited for the big event."[83] In September 1939 war came; within a year England was under bombardment. "Life there is what it ought to be. ... . An old dog-toothed civilization is breaking now."[84] The horror of those days is described in *The Ministry of Fear* (1943). Arthur Rowe, having killed his dying wife out of pity, finds that in the "torn landscape" of London, with the nightly raids and the "daily massacre," he "moved with familiarity; he was part of this destruction as he was no longer part of the past."[85] "It sounds like a thriller ... but the thrillers are like life. ... Spies, and murders, and violence, and wild motor-car chases ... that's real life: it's what we've all made of the world."[86] Rowe finds himself caught up in a great conspiracy, "directed, controlled, moulded," by a Nazi fifth column. "The Germans are wonderfully thorough. ... They formed, you know, a kind of Ministry of Fear.... It isn't only that they get a hold on certain people. It's the gen eral atmosphere they spread, so that you feel you can't depend on a soul."[87] Some people are brought in by blackmail, but for others the appeal is to their idealism. "The idealists don't see blood like you and I do. They aren't materialists. It's all statistics to them."[88] Our deepest yearnings are captured in the prayer Rowe chances upon one day in a Roman missal: "Let not man prevail."[89]

From 1941 to 1943 Greene was on duty with the British secret service, first in Lagos, then in Freetown. Not until 1948 did *The Heart of the Matter* appear. In the era of Belsen, open war is declared between the Christian and the world. Confronting a catastrophe which had shaken civilization to its foundations, "we saw ourselves, to borrow the words of Bossuet, and we were horrified by what we saw.... We have seen ... the mark of the nails."[90] Greene's personal exploration of the Christian conscience continued. If *The Power and the Glory* was written under the influence of Newman, *The Heart of the Matter* is based on Charles Péguy: "The sinner is at the very heart of Christianity.... No one knows more of what Christianity is about. No one, except perhaps the saint."[91] The collective sins of nations and the personal sins of men are the same in nature. The story Greene tells of Major Scobie is that of an upright man's slow disintegration. Its setting is a land of oppressive, irritating climate, where the whites have made themselves a refuge, "a home from home." The black natives, "the bloody niggers," who have been debased by the civilization brought to them, are generally detested. The war continues far away; corruption is commonplace. Only Scobie the Just, the deputy commissioner of the colony, is beyond reproach. But he, though keenly sensitive to responsibility, lacks the courage and humility needed to face the truth. Without this, no love is possible. Out of pity, not wanting to hurt his wife, he lies to her, and from this beginning everything starts slowly to crumble around him. "He felt his whole personality crumble with the slow disintegration of lies."[92] "He had no shape left."[93] Yet Scobie the sinner still prays, speaking to his God as never before. He ends in suicide, but, on the verge of death, "at the call of need, at the cry of a victim, Scobie strung himself to act. He dredged his consciousness up from an infinite distance in order to make some reply. He said aloud, 'Dear God, I love ...' "[94]

Sarah Miles's story, told in *The End of the Affair* (1951), also takes place during the war, in London, mostly in the time of the V-1 raids. An illicit love affairs culminates again in a death much resembling suicide. Sarah's metamorphosis, however, is in fact the very opposite of Scobie's. Her spirit does not destroy itself; instead, it grows. "Man has places in his heart," wrote Leon Bloy, "which do not yet exist, and into them enters suffering in order that they may have existence."[95] *The End of the Affair* is an impassioned novel in which love takes the place of pity. Sarah gives her love completely and with total trust: " 'I've never loved anybody or anything as I do you.' . . . We most of us hesitate to make so complete a statement. . . . She had no doubts."[96] This kind of love leads her into a spiritual wilderness, a place where selfhood dies. "It's as if we were working together on the same statue," Sarah writes in her diary, "cutting it out of each other's misery."[97] Eventually her hopeless love for Bendrix leads her to God. "There wasn't anything left, when we'd finished, but You. For either of us . . . You were there, teaching us to squander . . . so that one day we might have nothing left except this love of You."[98] Could Sarah be a saint, Bendrix wonders?

> The saints, one would suppose, in a sense create themselves. They come alive. They are capable of the surprising act or word. They stand outside the plot, unconditioned by it. But we have to be pushed around. We have the obstinacy of non-existence. We are . . . characters without poetry, without free will. . . . If *you* are a saint, it's not so difficult to be a saint.[99]

When the war ended, it left humanity wounded and the world divided. The story of Harry Lime, *The Third Man* (1950), written for the Korda film featuring Orson Welles, unfolds in "the smashed dreary city of Vienna divided up in zones among the four powers."[100] Although fiction, it is "based on a truth," the postwar trafficking in penicillin. "The war and the peace (if you can call it peace) let loose a great number of rackets, but none more vile than this one."[101] Immorality flourished as ever. Men just turned loose of their responsibilities. "They were one of a group, and if there was guilt, the leaders bore the guilt. A racket works very like a totalitarian party."[102] The leaders, for their part, evinced only a chilling cynicism. "It's the fashion. In these days, old man, nobody thinks in terms of human beings. Governments don't, so why should we?"[103]

To Greene, it seemed that "the democracies have been dosed with abstractions like a narcotic." Was Christian civilization itself in danger? Greene imagined the worst: "It is not impossible that we might see totalitarianism and atheism spread over the whole earth. . . . But even that would not mean the end,"[104] so long as even a single Christian remained.

In the aftermath of war the world found itself divided between East and West, with peace only an illusion. The battlefield had only been moved to the frontiers of the two power blocs. Greene, seeking as always to be on the battlefront, set out again on his travels. The revolts against colonial rule then developing were not, he came to believe, simply nationalist uprisings. As early as 1951 he felt that communism was the real enemy England was up against in Malaya. "We are back in the age of the religious wars," he said, adding:

> Communism is a threat to the rich and sometimes to the intellectual, but the poor and the illiterate have nothing to lose. There is only one man who is threatened by communism, whether he is rich or poor, educated or peasant, and that is the Christian.[105]

Recognizing the benefits European rule had brought to the colonies and sympathizing with the tragic situation of the white settlers, Greene deplored the indecision which seemed "part of the modern mind. We have lost the power of clear action because we have lost the ability to believe."[106] He criticized the "masochism of Europe," the idea that "we have brought it on ourselves."[107] He recognized from the outset, however, the necessity that the colonies be given their independence. What he hoped for was the development of indigenous Christian cultures to offset the attractions of communism, the same goal that the Bishop of Phat-Diem and the Eurasian colonel Jean Leroy were working toward in Indochina. Only Christianity, he believed, just as it might save Europe, could satisfy the real aspirations of these peoples, whether Kikuyu or Vietnamese. Only the priest and the commissar understood them. "Revolution can only be conquered by a revolutionary spirit."[108] Unfortunately, little true Christian spirit could be found in the deadlock of the cold war and "peaceful coexistence." The immediate victims of the global machinations of the great powers were the peoples trapped on the frontiers of the two camps, like pawns on a chessboard. They were truly the *nouveaux pauvres*.

It is in this context that we must read *The Quiet American* (1955), written after "four visits of three months each to Indo-China."[109] While the world was occupied with the war in Korea, Greene was with the French troops patrolling the rice-paddy front in Vietnam. In Saigon he observed "certain Americans dreaming of a Third Force." He recorded in 1954 that "the bar to-night was loud with innocent American voices and that was the worst disquiet. . . . They were there, one couldn't help being aware, to protect an investment."[110] He criticized the blunderings and the dangerous and misguided innocence of American policy in Indochina, just as he had earlier spoken out against the "campaign of uncharity" conducted by McCarthy's "witch-hunters," because "intolerance in any country wounds freedom throughout the world."[111] Despite Greene's disclaimer that *The Quiet American* is only "a story and not a piece of history," it has turned out to be as prophetic as it is symbolic. "How

many people have to die before you realise . . . that there's no such thing
as gratitude in politics?"[112]

Alden Pyle is young, pure, ignorant, silly. He believes in "being
involved," in doing good to the universe, in democracy, honor, and the
Third Force. His inspiration, as well as the source of his undoing, is York
Harding, a man who "gets hold of an idea and then alters every situation
to fit the idea."[113] Fowler, on the other hand, has neither faith nor hope
left and lives from day to day in the company of his girl Phuong and an
opium pipe. Pyle's lecturing and his theories only annoy him: "I never
knew a man who had better motives for all the trouble he caused."[114]
Fowler likes him nonetheless. "All the time that his innocence had
angered me, some judge within myself had summed up in his favour, had
compared his idealism . . . with my cynicism."[115] He wants to save Pyle,
to make him see that he is wrong:

> You and your like are trying to make a war with the help of
> people who just aren't interested. . . . They want enough rice. . . .
> They don't want to be shot at. . . . They don't want our white
> skins around telling them what they want. . . . Isms and ocracies.
> Give me facts. . . . The French are dying every day—that's not a
> mental concept.[116]

After the "bicycle bombs" incident Fowler tries to warn Pyle one last
time: "We are the old colonial peoples, Pyle, but we've learnt a bit of
reality, we've learned not to play with matches. . . . Go home with Phuong.
Forget the Third Force."[117] It is no use. When a bomb goes off in the
middle of the crowd, Fowler gives up, for Pyle "was impregnably
armoured by his good intentions and his ignorance."[118] Fowler betrays
him to the communists, but in so doing he himself sacrifices a man to an
idea, to "all I thought I hated in America."[119] "I've been blind to a lot of
things. . . . Was I so different from Pyle, I wondered? Must I too have my
foot thrust in the mess of life before I saw the pain?"[120] In the end, he
finds he can't forget the image of "a young man with a crew cut and a
black dog at his heels."[121] "Am I the only one who really cared for
Pyle?"[122]

Although *Our Man in Havana* (1958) is only "a fairy-story," it shows
Greene at his liveliest. The tale of Wormold's incredible adventures is
strewn with bitter and ironic reflections on the injustices and irrationali-
ties of our world. Business competition is made to seem remarkably like
international politics:

> We hear a lot nowadays about the cold war, but any trader will
> tell you that the war between two manufacturers of the same
> goods can be quite a hot war. Take Phastkleaners and Nu-

cleaners. There's not much difference between the two machines any more than there is between two human beings, one Russian—or German—and one British. There would be no competition and no war if it wasn't for the ambition of a few men in both firms.[123]

Cuba—then still the Cuba of Fulgencio Batista, with Fidel Castro's rebels up in the Sierra Maestra—serves as one of the garrisons in the western defense line, and "nobody cares what goes on in our prisons, or the prisons of Lisbon or Caracas."[124] Some people, observes the policeman whose own father had been tortured to death, belong to the "torturable class." "The poor in my own country, in any Latin American country. The poor of Central Europe and the Orient."[125]

By 1963 Cuba had had its revolution and the island was under American blockade. In Castro, Greene thought he recognized "a new voice in the Communist world": "Here in Cuba, it is possible to conceive a first breach in Marxist philosophy (not in Marxist economics)—that philosophy as dry as Bentham and as outdated as Ingersoll."[126] Here, coexistence with the Catholic Church seemed to Greene more promising than it had appeared to be, for example, in Poland.[127] Returning to Cuba in 1966, he saw the island as a veritable laboratory for communism, from which there might emerge an authentic kind of socialism allowing for real human freedom.

Not far from Cuba or from the United States, another traditionally Catholic country, Haiti, land of the voodoo, island of poets and painters, had conjured up the devil in the form of François Duvalier and his Tontons Macoute. The specter of Hitler haunts the pages of *The Comedians* (1966). The people of Haiti are obliged to endure Duvalier's reign of terror because Papa Doc is a "bulwark against Communism. There will be no Cuba and no Bay of Pigs here."[128] In "the wild world we live in now," what can one do? Become involved, like Dr. Magiot, "very big, very black," "born a Catholic," a man who "possessed great gentleness" and believed "in the future of Communism"? He explains to his friend Brown:

> But Communism, my friend, is more than Marxism. . . . There is a *mystique* as well as a *politique*. We are humanists, you and I. . . . Catholics and Communists have committed great crimes, but at least they have not stood aside, like an established society, and been indifferent. I would rather have blood on my hands than water like Pilate.[129]

For the present, one must learn to live. "Much courage and patience is needed to keep one's head."[130] In the end, however, Magiot falls victim to the Tontons Macoute, shot as an alleged spy for Castro, a tribute paid for the return of the American ambassador.

Brown, when he was a boy, had faith in the Christian God. Now that he approaches the end of his life, a "citizen of nowhere," it is only his sense of humor that enables him sometimes to believe in Him.[131] Brown counts himself among the world's "comedians," those who avoid involvements. The comedians, however, "the rootless," have their own kind of courage; they turn down "the temptation of sharing the security of a religious creed or a political faith."[132] They too are involved:

> We are the faithless; we admire the dedicated ... but through timidity, or through lack of sufficient zest, we find ourselves the only ones truly committed—committed to the whole world of evil and of good, to the wise and to the foolish, to the indifferent and to the mistaken. We have chosen nothing except to go on living, "rolled round in Earth's diurnal course, with rocks and stones and trees."[133]

Having lost everything, Brown no longer cares about his own future. Now, on his better days, he laughs.[134]

Querry is another who has learned to laugh. *A Burnt-Out Case* (1961) is "removed from world-politics." "This Congo is a region of the mind," a part of the continent "with the shape of a human heart" which the young Greene had explored in 1934. Here, at the edge of the world and the edge of time, Querry has come to the end of everything. Having lost his belief in God, in his art, and in love, he is left with nothing to say. There remains only a dullness within. "I've retired,"[135] he decides. He is a burnt-out case. "Self-expression is a hard and selfish thing. It eats everything, even the self. At the end you find you haven't even got a self to express. I have no interest in anything any more."[136] Indeed, "it needs a very strong man to survive an introspective and solitary vocation,"[137] as any artist knows. It occurs to Querry one day that he has never really loved anyone. "They use the phrase, 'make love,' don't they? But which of us are creative enough to 'make' love? We can only be loved—if we are lucky."[138] His respect for truth becomes his undoing—or salvation. "I won't pretend. All I have left in me is a certain regard for the truth. It was the best side of the small talent I had."[139] Dr. Colin, having worked fourteen years with the mission fathers caring for lepers, has also lost his faith in God. He believes in evolution and so goes on "from day to day," teaching Querry "to serve other people." Querry's native boy one day sets out into the jungle looking for Pendélé, the lost fountain of his youth. "It fell from the sky ... *Nous étions heureux.*"[140] Querry follows. And so he learns how to laugh, like the African natives in the moonlight, and also

how to suffer like them. "I am happy here." He is cured at last, released
from his inner prison. "The King is dead, long live the King."[141] But is
the king really dead? And this uneasiness of heart, as if he had lost someone he loved? God perhaps? Querry laughs and is shot by Rycker.
"Laughing at myself," he murmurs as he dies. "Absurd . . . this is absurd,
or else . . ."[142] Pendélé?

Which is the way to Pendélé? The cries of humanity sound around us
and within us, voices filled with anguish at a world gone awry. In all
Greene's novels the cries are echoed. He offers no theoretical solutions,
however, either political, moral, or religious. No political system is perfect, and evil is never entirely on one side. Democracy, for its part, has
failed in its mission of establishing the rule of justice and promoting the
public good. Too often, instead, it has served only the special interests of money and power, while remaining deaf to the voices of the poor.
Today it stands in danger of succumbing to a kind of technocratic totalitarianism. Communism, proclaiming itself the hope of the poor, has seen
fit to use any means to fulfill its dream. Such, then, is the kingdom of
man. Some have deliberately denied God's existence and founded an
entire system on that negation. Others have denied Him in fact, forgetting Him in their abandonment to their own pleasures, losing Him in a
system of anarchistic individualism or oppressive collectivism.

The kingdom of man culminates in a Hitler or a Stalin. Its cruelty
stretches from one end of the globe to the other—from Germany to
Haiti—and its strain of violence seems impossible to root out. We are in
the dark, "born in an age of doubt,"[143] as Oliver Chant puts it. We see
our familiar values overthrown and humanity itself threatened with destruction. Man has lost his roots or has cut them himself; he has turned
his personal responsibilities over to society. In so doing, he becomes a
cipher in a shapeless crowd, at the mercy of events or of the wisdom or
folly of his leaders, who are themselves only too often prisoners of the
established system. Meanwhile, the world exhausts itself in war and
revolution.

Political and social creeds have become veritable religions, but religion
in itself solves nothing. The new religions, moreover, made in the image
of man, are closed in on themselves and concerned with abstractions. The
world becomes less and less Christian. It has pronounced God dead. It
believes that it can manage without Him, that, in the words of Dr. Colin,
it has absorbed and explained Him: "Even the Christian myth is part of
the wave, and perhaps, who knows, it may be the most valuable part."[144]
In this process, though, man has lost his soul. Christians themselves abdi-
cate their responsibilities and toy with their doubts. Both believers and
half-believers are sharing the darkness with the atheists. They have for-

gotten the answers; they are not "sure." "Is it the same faith under another mask?" wonders Magiot.[145] The malaise and negation may, however, have a positive meaning. "In a mutual and humble awareness of our helplessness at attaining Him whose attraction is the source of our greatness," might we not, as Henri de Lubac hoped, become "mutually aware of our most fundamental brotherhood?"[146] Is it not on just this path that the whisky-priest and the lieutenant, Brown and Magiot, and Querry and Colin all have set out?

Greene observed in an essay he wrote in 1948 that a "troubled conscience, a sense of personal failure,"[147] was the major characteristic of Christian civilization. Greene's characters, from Andrews to Querry, all evidence this Christian conscience. Is it not man's only means to salvation, both for himself and for society? Behind all the parties and all the doctrines there stand individual men; it is in their hearts that violence has its roots. Each is separate, yet all bear a common responsibility. After Else's murder, D. remarks: "It was extraordinary how the whole world could alter after a single violent act."[148] Violence destroys man's soul, whether it is violence directed against himself or turned against others. The whisky-priest "carried a wound as though a whole world had died";[149] Scobie "mislaid his joy" among the Nissen huts;[150] Pinkie finds himself trapped in a fiendish circle; and Conrad Drover, after spending the night with Milly, has "a dull sense of an irrevocable injury which one of them had done to the other."[151] "The hurt is in the act of possession," Fowler remarks. "We are too small in mind and body to possess another person without pride or to be possessed without humiliation."[152] It is an observation true of all forms of violence, for the quest is always one of possessing, of exercising the will to power.

A true act of love is also a violent act capable of changing the world, but instead of destroying a man's soul, it strengthens it. Each of us has the capability of overcoming the violence within us and of transforming it into a positive force. Each of us is capable of the irrational act that brings release. Sarah "leaps" once and for all; Querry sets out on his quest for Deo Gratias in the Congo jungle; the whisky-priest answers every call. For this act, sometimes the most simple, all that is required is a little courage, trust in others, and faith. The journey leads into the wilderness, but there, like Querry, one finds a spring, the water that "fell from the sky." One learns to find joy in poverty, to experience tenderness, and in addition one discovers pleasure. Drawn from solitude by a concern for others, one rediscovers "a warm room with certainty."[153] Such is the case with Bendrix, holding Sarah close yet inaccessible in his arms, and with Brown and Martha, "approaching one another by words more nearly than they had ever approached by touch." To love and live, what is required is to accept the truth, to see it, to tell it, and to teach it to each other. As D. puts it:

> All over the world there were people like himself who didn't believe in being corrupted—simply because it made life impossible—as when a man or woman cannot tell the truth about anything. It wasn't so much a question of morality as a question of simply existing.[154]

It is Henry Callifer's retreat from the truth that condemns him to a life of sterility and silence.[155] It is, conversely, concern for truth that saves Rowe, Querry, Sarah, and the whisky-priest; for it is truthfulness that lays the foundation for any communication among men, between man and woman, or between man and God. The greatest good, then, that one man can do for another is to teach him to love the truth. As Sarah writes to Bendrix: "You taught me not to be sure. . . . You taught me to want the truth."[156] Only truth can lead to God; only it can give life and the power to transmit life, as Sarah, once dead, heals those who trust in her and as the whisky-priest continues to "pass life on."[157] It alone can bring about justice among men and among nations, even if it means dying for it.

Poor, stripped of all his belongings or having left them behind, like Brown, Querry, Sarah, or the whisky-priest, man learns humility. He recognizes his weakness yet still has the courage to continue living, to "carry on," humbly going about his daily work and helping his neighbor, who today, more than ever, is everyone and all peoples. Learning to trust, accepting each day what he is given, he becomes simpler. Learning not to take either himself or his earthly endeavors seriously, he recovers his sense of humor. He is free. Like Brown, like Querry, like the whisky-priest, he laughs.

NOTES

1. *Why Do I Write? An Exchange of Views Between Elisabeth Bowen, Graham Greene and V. S. Pritchett* (London, 1948), pp. 27–33.
2. *Ibid.*, pp. 47–48.
3. *Ibid.*, p. 30.
4. *Ibid.*

5. *Ibid.*, pp. 46–47.
6. *Ibid.*, p. 48.
7. *Ibid.*, p. 30.
8. *Ibid.*, p. 27.
9. Paul Rostenne, *Graham Greene, témoin des temps tragiques* (Paris, 1949).
10. "The Revolver in the Corner Cupboard," *The Lost Childhood and Other Essays* (London, 1951).
11. *The Lawless Roads*, uniform ed. (London, 1955), pp. 4–5.
12. *The Lost Childhood*, pp. 15–16.
13. "François Mauriac," *The Lost Childhood*, p. 69.
14. *Ibid.*, p. 70.
15. *The Lost Childhood*, p. 24.
16. Kim Philby, *My Silent War*, introd. by Graham Greene (London, 1968).
17. *The Confidential Agent*, uniform ed. (London, 1953), p. 71. Quoted by Kim Philby in his Foreword to *My Silent War*.
18. *Journey Without Maps*, uniform ed. (London, 1950), pp. 7–8.
19. *Ibid.*, p. 32.
20. *Ibid.*, p. 10.
21. *Our Man in Havana* (London, 1958), p. 10.
22. *The End of the Affair* (London, 1951), p. 48.
23. *Why Do I Write?*, p. 48.
24. Pierre Emmanuel, *Qui est cet homme, ou le singulier universel* (Paris, 1947), p. 225.
25. Both this novel and the *Collected Essays* appeared after the present study was written.
26. *The Man Within*, uniform ed. (London, 1952), p. 17.
27. *Ibid.* Epigraph quoted from Sir Thomas Browne.
28. *The Name of Action* (London, 1930), p. 293.
29. *Ibid.*, p. 343.
30. *Stamboul Train*, uniform ed. (London, 1948), p. 205.
31. *Ibid.*, p. 132.
32. *Ibid.*, p. 175.
33. *Ibid.*, p. 200.
34. *Ibid.*, p. 199.
35. *It's a Battlefield*, uniform ed. (London, 1948), p. 25.
36. *Ibid.*, p. 186.
37. *Ibid.*, p. 194.
38. *Ibid.*, p. 40.
39. *Ibid.*, p. 217.
40. *Ibid.*, p. 16.
41. *Ibid.*, p. 148.
42. *England Made Me*, uniform ed. (London, 1948), p. 274.
43. *Ibid.*, p. 238.
44. *Ibid.*
45. *Journey Without Maps*, p. 30.
46. *Ibid.*, p. 10.
47. *Ibid.*, p. 310.
48. *Ibid.*, p. 82.
49. *Ibid.*, p. 312.
50. *Ibid.*, p. 234.
51. *A Gun for Sale*, uniform ed. (London, 1947), p. 57.
52. *Ibid.*, p. 44.

53. *Brighton Rock*, uniform ed. (London, 1947), p. 281.
54. *Ibid.*, p. 185.
55. *Ibid.*, p. 272.
56. *Ibid.*, p. 306.
57. *Ibid.*, p. 168.
58. *Ibid.*, p. 327.
59. *The Confidential Agent*, p. 34.
60. *Ibid.*, p. 66.
61. *Ibid.*, p. 77.
62. *Ibid.*, p. 60.
63. In an interview with J. W. Lambert published in the *Sunday Times* (London), January 16, 1966, Greene discusses this point.
64. "At Home," *The Lost Childhood*, p. 190.
65. *The Lawless Roads*, p. 85.
66. *Ibid.*, p. 23.
67. *Ibid.*, p. 48.
68. "Paradoxes du christianisme," *Essais catholiques* (Paris, 1953). Most essays in this collection have never been published in English.
69. *The Lawless Roads*, p. 129.
70. *The Power and the Glory*, uniform ed. (London, 1949), p. 4.
71. *Ibid.*, pp. 179–180.
72. *Ibid.*, p. 80.
73. *Ibid.*, p. 179.
74. *Ibid.*, p. 257.
75. *Ibid.*, p. 258.
76. *Ibid.*, p. 252.
77. *Introductions to Three Novels* (Stockholm, 1962), p. 17.
78. *The Power and the Glory*, p. 253.
79. *Ibid.*, p. 103.
80. *Ibid.*, p. 273.
81. *Ibid.*, p. 288.
82. *The Lawless Roads*, p. 289.
83. "At Home," *The Lost Childhood*, p. 191.
84. *Ibid.*
85. *The Ministry of Fear*, library ed. (London, 1960), p. 39.
86. *Ibid.*, p. 72.
87. *Ibid.*, p. 140.
88. *Ibid.*
89. *Ibid.*, p. 83.
90. "Message aux catholiques français," *Essais catholiques*, p. 13.
91. *The Heart of the Matter*, uniform ed. (London, 1951), epigraph.
92. *Ibid.*, p. 250.
93. *Ibid.*, p. 300.
94. *Ibid.*, pp. 325–326.
95. *The End of the Affair*, epigraph.
96. *Ibid.*, p. 57.
97. *Ibid.*, p. 108.
98. *Ibid.*, p. 105.
99. *Ibid.*, pp. 229, 235.
100. *The Third Man* (New York, 1950), p. 14.
101. *Ibid.*, p. 105.
102. *Ibid.*, p. 106.

103. *Ibid.*, p. 139.
104. "La civilisation chrétienne est-elle en péril?" *Essais catholiques*, p. 32.
105. "Malaya, or the Forgotten War," *Life*, July 30, 1951.
106. "Mau Mau, the Black God," *Sunday Times* (London), October 4, 1953.
107. "Congo Journal," *In Search of a Character* (London, 1961), p. 83.
108. "Last Cards in Indo-China," *Sunday Times* (London), March 28, 1954; *The New Republic*, April 12, 1954.
109. *In Search of a Character*, p. 9.
110. "Return to Indo-China," *Sunday Times* (London), March 21, 1954; *The New Republic*, April 5, 1954.
111. "Dear Mr. Chaplin," *The New Republic*, October 13, 1952. See also "London Diary," *The New Statesman and Nation*, November 22, 1952. Greene disclosed that he had been "a probationary member of the Communist party for four weeks at the age of 19" when a student at Oxford in 1922. He wanted to show that "many innocent people, refugees from Central Europe," were excluded from the United States by the McCarran Act.
112. *The Quiet American* (London, 1955), p. 230.
113. *Ibid.*, p. 218.
114. *Ibid.*, p. 72.
115. *Ibid.*, pp. 204–205.
116. *Ibid.*, pp. 119–121.
117. *Ibid.*, p. 205.
118. *Ibid.*, p. 214.
119. *Ibid.*, p. 240.
120. *Ibid.*, pp. 242–243.
121. *Ibid.*, p. 246.
122. *Ibid.*, p. 19.
123. *Our Man in Havana*, p. 220.
124. *Ibid.*, p. 190.
125. *Ibid.*, p. 189.
126. *The New Republic*, November 2, 1963.
127. *Sunday Times* (London), January 8 and 15, 1956.
128. *The Comedians* (London, 1966), p. 252.
129. *Ibid.*, pp. 311–312.
130. *Ibid.*, p. 193.
131. *Ibid.*, p. 34.
132. *Ibid.*, p. 304.
133. *Ibid.*
134. *Ibid.*, p. 10.
135. *A Burnt-Out Case* (London, 1961), p. 42.
136. *Ibid.*, p. 52.
137. *Ibid.*, p. 156.
138. *Ibid.*, p. 144.
139. *Ibid.*, p. 187.
140. *Ibid.*, p. 95.
141. *Ibid.*, p. 205.
142. *Ibid.*, pp. 251–252.
143. *The Name of Action*, p. 283.
144. *A Burnt-Out Case*, p. 160.
145. *The Comedians*, p. 312.
146. Henri de Lubac, S.J., *Athéisme et sens de l'homme* (Paris, 1968), p. 88.
147. *Essais catholiques*, p. 21.

148. *The Confidential Agent*, p. 145.
149. *The Power and the Glory*, p. 85.
150. *The Heart of the Matter*, p. 191.
151. *It's a Battlefield*, p. 144.
152. *The Quiet American*, p. 153.
153. *The Name of Action*, p. 285.
154. *The Confidential Agent*, p. 37.
155. *The Potting Shed* (London, 1958).   See Marie-Béatrice Mesnet, "Le 'Potting Shed' de Graham Greene," *Etudes*, September 1958.
156. *The End of the Affair*, pp. 178–179.
157. *Introductions to Three Novels*, p. 17.

C. P. SNOW
(1905-   )

by G. S. Fraser

POLITICS, IN ONE of the stricter senses used by political scientists, has to do with the state or with the centers of authority in a society rather than with the shifting political loyalties, prejudices, and hopes and fears of that society at large. Most of us are at the receiving rather than the initiating end of the making of political decisions, which is the central activity with which pure politics is concerned. The attaining of power, which means, in practice, in the modern world, membership of decision-making committees, is an important part of pure politics, but it is secondary to the making of decisions.

Politics does not, of course, any more than art, exist for its own sake, and arguments about what decisions are to be made rest not only on a Hobbesian or Austinian concept of absolute state sovereignty or a Machiavellian concept of princely power—a power or sovereignty to be kept in existence at almost any cost as an alternative to anarchy or civil war—but also on the wider experience of members of committees or deciding groups as human beings, as ordinary members of society, and on the balances that come up in discussion between their social hopes and fears, on some concept assumed rather than arrived at by discussion of the "common good." Nevertheless, the committees by which our world is ruled are not Plato's guardians.

It is not, in the usual sense, that they are after personal power, and that power corrupts. There is an element of ambition, but it is no worse than the ambition of, say, a poet, a philosopher, an artist, or a teacher to use his powers to the full and to be a source rather than a channel.

There is such a thing or person as the naturally political man, to whom the processes of group discussion and arriving at firm decisions affecting a wide range of human activities offer the fullest possible scope for his interests and aptitudes. As the poet, for instance, has a special skill for distinguishing between the often muddled, private, and confused feelings which are at the roots of a poem and the proper public or universal shape which a poem ought to take, so the political man has a special skill in distinguishing between his personal likes and dislikes, hopes and fears, and, say, the most suitable person to appoint for a certain job (I dislike him but recognize his ability and approve of his policies) or the proper administrative decision to make (by sentiment and instinct I am, say, a Little Englander, but joining the Common Market seems, on balance, necessary for the future security and prosperity of my country).

The kind of judgments that lead to important political decisions tend, that is, to be balancing or disjunctive; some hunch or loyalty or impulse is always in some degree sacrificed, and some inner doubt remains about the decision that has been made. The final decisions are based on an estimate of general consequences, but such decisions are necessarily loose, vague, and speculative.

Political decisions differ from personal moral decisions in that the latter hardly consider consequences at all. It is right, for instance, to repay a loan when one has promised to do so, even though the person to whom one is repaying it may spend all the money on drink. It is right to rush a person with acute appendicitis to the hospital, even though there is some possibility that the inflammation, left to itself, will die down and that the operation will prove fatal. Ordinary moral behavior consists in doing what, without too much calculation, we feel to be decently expected of us. It has consequences, but the consequences of behaving or not behaving morally are felt mainly in one's own conscience; and I do not do a right action to keep my conscience quiet but, if I am behaving morally, in order to do the right thing. (Keeping my conscience quiet may, however, up to a point be one of my duties. And though it would not be a moral act to do something that my neighbors, colleagues, and students will approve of, simply because I desire their approval, it may be a sort of general duty to do up to a point the sort of thing that does not offend my neighbors.)

It may, in the political field, however, be paradoxically a duty to make decisions that leave my conscience hurt and offend some of my neighbors, because whereas in the personal life we usually, though not always, have some indefinite time before us to make a moral decision (not putting in for a job we would like because we think a colleague is more capable; arranging a marital separation because we think, on the whole, we are causing our spouse more pain than happiness by not separating;

giving up a habit, say smoking or drinking, which is associated with ideas of social pleasure but seems to lead to personal inefficiency; deciding not to publish a letter or article which has some scholarly or logical justification but might destroy a colleague's reputation; not committing adultery; and so on), in pure political activity decisions are rushed. The morally important thing in politics is that a decision should be made, not that it should be the certainly and absolutely right decision, which it never can be. It should nevertheless be as near right as it can be, based on what evidence there is, and those engaged in making it should, as far as possible, set aside their personal feelings (dislike of, or excessive liking for, other members of the decision-making committee and the possibility of personal advantage or disadvantage—promotion or demotion or being shelved—involved in the decision).

This little philosophy lesson, rather in the style of H. A. Prichard's *Moral Obligation*, may seem an odd preamble to a critical essay on a modern novelist. But it suits C. P. Snow. A scholarship boy from Alderman Newton's Grammar School in Leicester and the then very small Leicester University College, from 1928 his career, quite outside literature, has been one of mounting success: a research scholarship at Cambridge, a fellowship, work with Ernest Rutherford on molecular physics, high positions during and after World War II in the civil service, particularly on the civil service's and government's relationship with science, a knighthood, a life peerage, a ministerial post, and a seat in the House of Lords in Harold Wilson's first government. A man of extraordinary energy, Snow started writing novels and criticism, a detective story, a science-fiction story about a recipe for longevity, a Wellsian romance about the ideal of research; his long connected series of novels, *Strangers and Brothers*, was conceived as a whole before the outbreak of World War II, and the eponymous first novel was published in 1940.

Snow's great load of public duty meant that the second novel in the series was not published till 1947, but since then members of the series have been appearing every two or three years or so. The novels are not purely political. Some critics, like Robert Greacen, feel that those which deal with Lewis Eliot's personal troubles—his first marriage, the misfortunes of his friends—have a deeper resonance than those, *The Masters*, *The New Men*, *The Affair*, *The Corridors of Power*, which could be called, in the very narrow and exact sense in which I have attempted to delimit the term, novels of pure political activity; but it is with these four, clearly, that I shall be concerned.

Politics, in my sense here, is not of course confined to the sovereign national state: A Cambridge or Oxford college is a kind of miniature state; its senior fellows, its master, president, bursar, and so on are the state element in it; the undergraduates and junior fellows are the subjects or citizens or the back-bench M.P.'s. A large government-run research station, the scene of *The New Men*, has again this state/society dichotomy, though since it is working toward manufacturing the atomic bomb and exploring atomic power generally, the state must keep an eye on it. *The Masters* and *The Affair* are not the only university novels, but they are the ones of which the themes are most clearly political. *The Corridors of Power* is about cabinet and parliamentary government. Its hero is a young "new man" post-Suez minister, a Tory (but perhaps modeled a little on Wilson's attitude toward Hugh Gaitskell), who wants to cut British expenditures on producing and maintaining atomic weapons in collaboration with, and in subordination to, the United States; he fails. Snow has a strong feeling for noble failure, and, for all the success of his own career on three levels—a research scientist, a novelist and communicator of ideas, a politician (though there he was not very strikingly successful, as far as public reports on him went; he may, however, have been quietly successful behind the scenes)—one of the strongest things in his fiction is a puritanical self-questioning about the ethics and the guilt of success.

Leicester, the Midland mixed-light-industry city of Snow's birth, is still very much a Puritan and nonconformist city, distrustful of the arts, distrustful of pleasure and ostentation, but with a concern for social welfare and with a very long tradition (its Adult Education College, Vaughan College, is more than a hundred years old) of approving of education as a means of moral and intellectual self-improvement. In an old-fashioned way (it has some of the best grammar schools in England, and many of their best pupils get places, exhibitions, or scholarships at Oxford or Cambridge) Leicester still approves of achievement and emulation but not of cutthroat competition—it is a city of small, prosperous, traditional family businesses (textiles, hosiery, typewriters, silver polish, small machine-tools for the boot and shoe industry). Radical though it has been—for the Parliament in the civil wars, a Chartist center in the nineteenth century, three of its four M.P.'s now Labour, though on the whole right-wing Labour—Leicester exhibits the odd and in some ways fortunate homogeneity of English provincial social attitudes.

If there is a quietly unobtrusive patriciate, there is no smart set, and Leicester escaped, because of its diversified industries and because of its lack of one vulnerable heavy industry, both mass unemployment in the 1930's and mass bombing in the 1940's. It is decent, clean, slightly arid (a few fine old buildings but rather stuck in corners among anonymous brick); it has a proper civic pride. Snow is still a Leicester man. He has lived most of his life since his middle twenties in Cambridge and London, but he never acquired the finickiness and fastidiousness, the snobbery, which marks some Cambridge dons, or the gossipy, glancing malice which is typical of London as perhaps of all metropolitan literary life. Achievement and decision are for him centrally important; he aims at what seems to him the architectural core of life and is indifferent to (and does not provide in his novels) the external rhetorical gestures, the swags and flourishes. There is a Samuel Smiles side to him (local boy makes good). He is like a successful late-Victorian scholarship boy, without class hatred, because Leicester, flat and decent in its speaking voice, without ostentatious wealth or unbearable poverty, does not engender class hatred.

Snow has little sense of tonality in dialogue, because the central obsession with decision means that the dialogue should be in short, clipped sentences; at a moment of decision, and at the really hard moments (a mother dies, a wife leaves us, we are sacked from our job) we all talk in clichés. The apparent aridity of Snow's dialogue may be an aesthetic decision: He may have chosen to represent and record only the properly dramatic moments, the moments of choice.

But this concentration on moments of choice does mean that, compared to the two novelists who offer us a rather similar range of observation of social change in England over the last thirty or forty years, Angus Wilson and Anthony Powell, Snow lacks certain dimensions. There is a certain sick and angry feeling about contemporary England, a feeling of humbug, which Wilson conveys admirably by means of Dickensian exaggeration. Socially, Wilson is a radical, and the English class system, growingly nonfunctional, growingly taking refuge in fantasies, makes him sick. At moments, he seems to see the modern English as a nation of compulsive role-players, infantile and regressive. If Wilson is a little like Dickens, Powell is a little like William Thackeray: The sheer rumness and oddity of the English establishment, the loose London network in which everybody "knows" everybody else and in which bumbling and determined ineptitude like that of Widmerpool gets to the top, fascinates him, but a sense of comedy gets the better of any sense of furious indignation. He feels, and rightly feels, how full of irreducible individuality, how lacking in faceless men, the English scene still is. It is the fine failures, like Thackeray's Dobbin or Esmond or his own Stringham, the rogues and oddities who are not such bad rogues after all, the Rawdon Crawley or Captain Costigan types, the battered, worldly women with good hearts, like his Lady Molly, who interest him. Some of Powell's characters in The Music of Time could have met some of Snow's in Strangers and Brothers—the areas partly interact—but I do not know what they would have talked about.

I think Powell and Wilson together give a richer picture than Snow of what England has been like since 1935, say, but it is a picture of what England means to an intelligent man with a firm artist's bias, a wish to see life in a certain way, because that way suits his gifts. A much flatter writer than either of them, eschewing the delights of accumulation or resonance, Snow, like Stendhal (see Stendhal's letter to Honoré de Balzac about Balzac's flattering review of *La Chartreuse de Parme*), wishes to sacrifice "style," atmosphere, "fine writing," for the sake of "small facts." But his experience, the experience of a decision-maker, is more privileged but more limited than Stendhal's, of course. He has no passion for Italian opera; he is not, so far as one knows, perpetually in love. He did not retreat from Moscow or ever meet and talk with Byron. His attitude toward those members of the English aristocracy and gentry who still play an important part in English government is not at all like Stendhal's attitude toward the Ultras of the Restoration (why, indeed, should it be so?). Lewis Eliot, a man, like Snow himself, risen from the lower-middle classes, observes such characters with a certain reserve but notes that they are patriotic when it comes to the pinch; and anyway they are on the way out. Perhaps I am merely saying, in a roundabout way, that Snow's subject is the meritocracy; but such a label is less interesting than an attempt, even if a slightly ponderous one, to spell out its implications.

Politics to most people means something that is quite different from the politics of government, which is what it means to Snow: It means social politics, the politics of class struggle; it means what Lenin meant when he said in *The State and Revolution* that the central problem of politics is "Who whom?"—who, to put it coarsely, will bugger whom about? Most people who are passionately political are concerned with getting "our lot" on top. What our lot will do when they get on top is a minor question. One could not conduct an election on the basis of having a coalition government with the object of getting the most capable men into the most suitable jobs and consulting the real experts, the economists and scientists, say, on what the real priorities (beyond the range of understanding of the electorate) are. No Prime Minister would appear on television before a general election with the message: "Give yourselves up to the experts." Harold Wilson, to be sure, used to make occasional noises about technology, but they fell on cold ears.

There is a sense, then, in which the politics of committees and decision, with which Snow is mainly concerned in his novels, are, from the ordinary man's point of view, apolitical: They do not stir the blood. Yet the novels are important because very few novels have dealt so clearly, from an insider's point of view, with how the world is actually run. They are important also because Snow does not worship the state, which, as Nietzsche rightly said, is a cold idol. He knows that the machinery he describes, though it may be the best one can get—the British civil service, the governing mechanism of an Oxford or Cambridge college—is and must be slow and cumbrous and partly self-frustrating; it will arrive only at approximately correct decisions or approximately just ones (as in *The Affair*, where, as in the Dreyfus case, the victim of injustice is a cold and unsympathetic character, and his vindication brings no personal sense to Lewis Eliot of warmth or triumph). But it has at least a self-correcting mechanism built into it; it can learn by its mistakes. And Lewis Eliot does feel also, from time to time, how cold it all is and how little it is exactly predictable.

The title of his series of novels, *Strangers and Brothers*, suggests Snow's attitude toward human nature and social duty. He believes in fraternity (though Lewis Eliot and his brother Martin, at the end of *The New Men*, quarrel sharply). He believes in a certain essential loneliness in the human condition. F. R. Leavis, in his famous attack on Snow's Rede lecture on science and politics, mocked the Pascalian sentence: "We die alone." A few lucky people may still die in their homes, with wives and children around them; most people do die in hospital beds, taken away from all the surroundings that extended and perpetuated their personalities, treated no doubt humanely, but impersonally, as objects. Snow, not Leavis, was broadly right there.

And the hopes that Snow puts in science are, similarly, real but sharply limited. Science can, possibly, solve some of man's material problems (fear, hunger, the pressure of population, the dread of war, the dread of certain physical and mental diseases). It can free man from material pressures, not so much so that he can be happy (Snow is a very jovial and sociable man; he believes in enjoyment, but I am not sure that he is a happy man or even morally approves of happiness, a condition that may make one forget about one's social duties) as so that he may face the natural unhappiness, uncertainty, self-frustration, of the human condition with dignity.

Leavis saw Snow as the disciple of Bertrand Russell in his popular social books and of H. G. Wells (the Wells, I take it, of *A Modern Utopia* or *The World of William Clissold*, not the very disquieting Wells of *The Time Machine*, *The Island of Dr. Moreau*, or that awful late outburst, *Mind at the End of Its Tether*). But we live alone, as well as die alone; Lewis Eliot is a good administrator because he does not think that he has an intuitive, empathetic understanding of what people are like, because he thinks slowly and methodically, because he can always be surprised, and because the great commonplaces do not, for him, become clichés. I think Snow, a student of Marcel Proust and Stendhal, probably owes much less to Russell and Wells than to classical French moralists: the Blaise Pascal of the *Pensées* and Jean de La Bruyère.

One could make a case that Snow's view of life is in some ways a limited and arid one but not that it is ebulliently and naïvely romantic. I would think the natural bent of his mind is pessimistic. But he is a man of huge physical and mental energy, he has a dogged John Bullishness, and I think that the atmosphere of his native Leicester, a limited and arid place itself in many ways, but natively decent (the tradition of self-education, self-help, but also of freely given social service to the less fortunate, the poor, the old, the sick), has balanced the native pessimism with a wish to be useful. The total impression that his fictions make on one is in the end a bit bleak, but maybe the bleakness is the distinction.

This bleakness and a certain flatness of presentation are what Leavis attacks in the style of the novels in his famous diatribe against Snow's lecture on the Two Cultures. The very same qualities are praised—the austereness and functionalism of the prose and the dialogue—by a younger novelist, a friend and admirer of Snow's (though not in any sense technically a disciple), William Cooper. Cooper's own portrait of Snow—an affectionate comic portrait as the undergraduate Swann, a strange combination of physical clumsiness, absentmindedness, open-heartedness, and half-conscious social tact and adroitness—in his novel about Leicester University College in the 1920's, *Young People*, is in one sense a richer and rounder presentation than that of any of the characters who appear in the series *Strangers and Brothers*.

Snow has not the great gift, which very great novelists as different as Tolstoy, Dickens, Thackeray, and Proust and also some minor writers of talent like Arthur Conan Doyle or Edith Oenone Somerville and Ross Martin have, of creating a character whom we feel we would recognize—his appearance, costume, tone of voice, idiom, bearing—if he came into the room. Nor has he that related but different gift, the peculiarly individual tone of voice that makes us go on listening to Thackeray, Henry James, James Joyce, or Virginia Woolf when they are being self-indulgent: doodling, freewheeling, over-elaborating, filling up blanks with arabesques. More broadly than this, one could say that Snow (who seems to me, as a man, like Sydney Smith in Thomas Carlyle's description of him, to have a great and generous sense of fun but little sense of humor, little natural relish for the oddities and anfractuosities of human character as something intrinsically valuable, to be appreciated for their own sakes) avoids exaggerative humor, like Angus Wilson's, and even the slow-motion comedy of exaggerated precision, like Anthony Powell's, for the sake of the seriousness to him of his subject matter. His is a sort of puritan prose; he does not convey the oddly self-enjoying quality of human life half as much in his novels as he does in some of his prose memoirs. He writes, I think, good puritan, or perhaps good early Royal Society, prose: a naked, plain, and natural style. One wouldn't guess from reading him that, as a person, he is an exuberant, boisterous character, eager and clumsy: a touch of Falstaff, a touch of Dr. Johnson (he snorts and heaves himself about), a touch of Peter Bezhukhov.

The people Snow deals with are powerful but in a sense narrowly channeled people: often simple and limited, in emotion at least if not in intelligence. (I think, if he were a historian, he could handle very well characters like Lord Liverpool, possibly Viscount Castlereagh, but not Sir Stratford Canning, probably Calvin Coolidge and Richard Nixon but maybe not Warren Harding or John Kennedy, possibly John Adams and John Quincy Adams but not Thomas Jefferson, Viscount George Goschen but not Lord Randolph Churchill, the Younger but not the Elder Pitt, and so on: the functional rather than the picturesque characters. But I wish he would write an essay sometime on George Curzon, who was a kind of anticipation of a Snow character in his political efficiency and seriousness but who perpetually tripped himself up by his picturesqueness.) In novels like *The Masters, The New Men, The Affair,* and *Corridors of Power* Snow is dealing with centrally important questions of "pure" politics, in the sense that I have defined that: the relationships between knowledge and power (or knowledge and charisma), between expedience and justice, between one's affection for a certain person, say, and one's perception that another person, for whom one has little affection, is the better man for a certain job. These interests may possibly be "impoverished" in Leavis's connotational sense; Leavis feels that Snow's university characters seem to be indifferent to their subjects, as far as their conversation shows, but terribly keen about who shall be master, president, or whatever it may be. Professor Helen Gardner, on the other hand, seems to find the picture accurate enough; and if Snow's characters tend often to seem predictable and dim, so, to be sure, in my own experience, do many of one's university colleagues. They take internal politics seriously, as did the citizens of Florence in the Renaissance. Their inexpressiveness (the central figure in *The Affair,* a kind of transposition of the Dreyfus affair, *almost* certainly a victim and quite certainly a fellow traveler, is as unattractive as was Captain Alfred Dreyfus himself: The just seek justice generally, not just justice for people they find sympathetic)—their inexpressiveness has its own kind of "drama" and "life." Snow is not even residually a Christian, nor, I imagine, a philosophical theist. But the odd, fair flatness of his treatment of human character, his lack of "respect for persons" (a certain kind of favoritism for certain kinds of temperament), has something in common with certain concepts of Christian charity.

Institutional life is gray: weighing up arguments about how to cast one's vote, how to allow for one's prejudices (for and against), even, as in *The New Men,* about such an apparently trivial question as whether or not to write a letter to *The Times*. Yet it is only through the structure of institutions that the world has a continuing reasonably stable existence, and it is only through committees that the world, with some coarse approximation to justice and expediency, can be ruled. Professor L. C. Knights has a fine essay on one of the greatest of seventeenth-century historians and memorialists in England, Edward Hyde, Earl of Clarendon; he quotes and praises with special zest a passage of Hyde's on the usefulness of committees. Committee meetings are boring; they seem to go on forever; but the stupidest man on a committee may have a sudden insight, some piece of information, some relevant precedental experience, that is suddenly useful, and the cleverest man may be carried away by some sudden folly (an obsession, a dislike) that it needs his duller colleagues to correct. Nobody is negligible, nobody is infallible: In everybody, tiredness, ignorance, personal emotions, may produce error; and there is never enough time in committee meetings at the state level—there may sometimes be enough time in committee meetings at the university level—to have *all* the evidence fairly weighed. The bringing together of various types of expertise, the smoothing over or diminishing (which is Lewis Eliot's expertise) of intrapersonal touchiness by a good middleman—Lewis Eliot is essentially the good administrative middleman: not the planner but the bringer-together of those who are needed to concert the plan—may at least minimize the possibilities of fatal error. This kind of perception, rare in novelists, is common in good historians. I sometimes wish that Snow had been a historian. But his novels are at least unique in modern fiction in giving us a dry but accurate notion of how we are ruled and some quite deep insights into the consciences of our rulers. They are the novels, also, of a good man who sees how very easily the human race could, through its representative institutions, destroy itself and who is anxious to improve these institutions and prevent that from happening.

PART II

CONTINENTAL

NIKOS KAZANTZAKIS
(1883-1957)

by Peter Bien

I

No WRITER WHO lives in Greece can avoid politics. But it is one thing for an author to be personally involved in affairs of state or influenced by them in his work and quite another for him to be truly a political writer. By this I mean a writer whose most basic interests are in how men behave in groups, in societies: how (to go back to the root of the word itself) they build and maintain their cities, developing all the delicate compromises that enable masses of people to reside harmoniously together and prosper. Kazantzakis, of course, had such interests; moreover, he was personally involved in Greek—and world—politics at every step of his career, sometimes by choice, sometimes not, and his books lose much of their density if we fail to see how they reflect political events. Nevertheless, it would be wrong, I believe, to call him a political writer according to the above definition, for his most basic interests were not truly political: not directed toward how men behave in groups. We may speak, therefore, of "Kazantzakis and politics," but not of "Kazantzakis as a political writer"; failure to make this distinction is responsible for much of the misinformed and vituperative political controversy which, especially in Greece, still unfortunately surrounds both his personality and his writings.

What were his most basic interests, and why has he continually made his countrymen angry? These questions can perhaps best be answered by an anecdote. On April 21, 1967, the day of the Pattakos-Papadopoulos *coup d'état,* I happened to be in Athens. The next afternoon I visited a member of Kazantzakis's circle, a lady of refined taste and poetic sensibility, with whom I wished to discuss how the seventeen-syllable line of Kazantzakis's *Odyssey*, a line rare and eccentric in modern Greek poetry, sounds to cultivated native ears. We were pursuing this subject when the lady's nephew, a young man in his early twenties, entered the room. He sat politely in silence for a time, waiting for us to finish, but then he suddenly rose and interrupted us with what developed into a lengthy, vehement tirade. "How can you sit there chatting about prosody on this of all days?" he shouted. "And how can you be interested in Kazantzakis? For us [meaning the young], his work is dead and irrelevant!" Then, pointing to the street, which was still filled with tanks, he explained his anger: "Kazantzakis was a fake, a hypocrite. He presented himself as a great humanitarian; all forms of tyranny and injustice drew huge public tears from his eyes, but when you see through the facade, you realize that the really important things—political tyranny, social injustice, economic exploitation—interested him the least. Kazantzakis was imprisoned inside his own egomania, oblivious of the fate of others; the only things that really, basically, interested him were abstractions: God and his own salvation. Why should we, the young whose future has been cut off by yesterday's all-too-concrete events here on this earth, why should we be concerned with abstractions like salvation or God? And why should any Greek care about this egotistical, selfish man who because of his otherworldliness, his introversion, his refusal to devote himself first and foremost to the welfare of society—the *polis*—(think of Orwell! think of Malraux!) was un-Greek, outside Greek traditions, and therefore irrelevant to Greek reality?"

It is hard to rebut tirades with logic, and even harder in this case because the young man was correct about Kazantzakis's basic interests, though terribly mistaken, I believe, in his anger against Kazantzakis and in his rejection of him as a writer. True, Kazantzakis was not an Orwell, not a Malraux. His most basic concern was not the welfare of society but his own personal salvation; the proper rubric for his work is the one he himself chose from Dante: *Come l'uom s'eterna*—how man eternalizes himself, saves *himself* from death and despair.[1] In all this the young man was correct. His mistake, and the cause of his anger, was his unstated assumption that Kazantzakis was truly a political writer who at the same time betrayed everything political: thus the charges of "fake" and "hypocrite." If you really believe someone to be irrelevant to your own position, you ignore him; you do not become incensed. The problem here, as in all the similar accusations Kazantzakis faced during his lifetime, was a failure to make the crucial distinction between a man who is truly political and one who is sincerely involved in politics, yet for reasons that are "metapolitical." The problem, futhermore, was a failure to see that

Kazantzakis's political and non-political or metapolitical aspects were symbiotic. His critics continually analyzed him into two separate persons, the metaphysician and the politician, failing to see that neither "person" could exist independently of the other because the very method employed by Kazantzakis to win his salvation was political involvement (a political involvement which, by definition, could never be truly political).

The truth of Kazantzakis was this wholeness and this paradox. Thus the worst thing one could do in defending him against the accusers would be to split him apart, just as they did, and to argue that he was indeed either completely metaphysical or completely, truly political. By taking things out of context or by focusing only on specific moments of his career instead of on the whole, one could produce ample evidence to support either of these misleading responses. But both would be a distortion of the truth and would only serve to perpetuate the misunderstandings which have always surrounded him. If we try to assign priorities within the totality, saying, for example, that his basic interests were in God and his own salvation, we are already moving dangerously toward analytical distortion, though I believe justifiably so; if, however, we try to disentangle either Kazantzakis's politics or his metaphysics from the rest of him, we are creating a false man to suit our own convenience. Kazantzakis continually tried to grasp the totality. His politics grew out of his metaphysics, his metaphysics out of his politics. He did not leave one interest behind in order to proceed to the next, but, as Bergson taught, carried all his past interests with him while he accumulated new ones. The key words in his development are not "change" or "stage" but "continuity," "duration." His nationalism, for example, was a continuation of his aestheticism, his communism of his nationalism, his anticommunism of the very ingredients which produced his communism. And all his political positions were manifestations of certain continuing attitudes toward death, God, the bourgeoisie; of certain psychological needs; and of a metaphysical system which attempted to bequeath universal, cosmological significance to his drives and accomplishments.

We are left once more with a complex whole, a paradoxical tangle which defies logic but which is the only true Kazantzakis. Instead of responding analytically to the tirades by attempting to prove Kazantzakis's "true" political interests or accepting the charge that he is irrelevant to modern political problems or arguing that he was one thing at one time and another at another, we should try as best we can to comprehend synthetically the tangled wholeness which is his essence. If we at least try to do this, then perhaps we shall be forgiven if we also from time to time move away from the essential truth and consider Kazantzakis's politics as though they were a separate, autonomous category: in other words, move from the essential to the accidental and circumstantial. In either case, the important thing is how to eschew preconceptions and partisanship and to work from documented facts, avoiding the hysteria and misinformation which produced so many tirades against him while he lived and which still do today.

II

I should like to advance some generalizations about the essential totality of Kazantzakis and then about his circumstantial relationships to politics before demonstrating these assertions by discussing the crucial beginnings of his literary career.

Essentially, his politics reflected the needs of his creative personality; circumstantially, they were thrust upon him by his times or by the specific climate in Greece. In his creative personality he was very much like his own invention Odysseus, who travels the road of political participation in order to reach the destination of an individualist salvation dependent upon withdrawal from the concrete world into the spiritual world of the imagination. "Love all things on the bright earth yet stick to none" is Odysseus' motto,[2] and this is also an accurate description of his author, if we simply add: Stick nevertheless to your desire for personal meaningfulness—which, in Kazantzakis's thought-scheme, equals sanctification. Kazantzakis, like Odysseus, took the road of active political participation in order to arrive at a self-knowledge, meaningfulness, and sanctification which rejected—or transcended—such active participation and which therefore forgot the group in the interests of the self. He reminds us of James Joyce's Leopold Bloom and his "longest way round is the shortest way home" or—better still—of Stephen Dedalus's description of Shakespeare meeting robbers, wives, widows, brothers-in-love, all the forms of outward life, but really walking only through himself.[3] This describes Kazantzakis's creative personality perfectly and also indicates the precise path traveled by many of his characters. Politics was the method by which he actualized the nonpolitical potentialities within himself.

Turning now to the circumstantial ways in which Kazantzakis was associated with politics: He did seem to be truly political at times—that is, truly interested in the welfare of society as opposed to his own salvation—and this affected his ability to publish, all but closed to him the outlet of the Greek National Theater, sent him into self-exile periodically, and helped determine the subject matter of his works. He was abused by both the left and the right, mainly because he exasperated all regimes by being too complicated. Politics and paradox do not mix. Kazantzakis angered people because he seemed to embrace everything instead of defending one position consistently; or, even worse, because in his Olym-

pian detachment he seemed to embrace nothing. While the Greek communists could call him decadent, fascist, bourgeois, incurably religious,
and a warmonger, the Chinese communists could hail him as an apostle
of peace, the Orthodox Church could try to prosecute him for atheism,
the monarchists could see him as a bolshevik rabble-rouser, and the com-
munist-controlled resistance movement during the occupation could
reject him as a secret agent of German intelligence! As he himself realized, "There is no regime that can tolerate me—and very rightly so—
since there is no regime that I can tolerate."[4]

But Kazantzakis was not the passive victim of these attacks; in many
ways he encouraged them. For one thing, he seemed to think of himself
as a political writer, thus provoking others to expect him to behave like
one. True, he did not conceive of art as crude propaganda; nor, despite
external pressures, did he ever condescend to write in the mode of socialist realism. But still, he denigrated art for art's sake, considered beauty a
luxury our age could not afford, always felt that the artist must be committed—indeed, an agitator—and did not hesitate to express these views in
public. In 1957, for example, when an interviewer questioned him about
the relation between literature and politics and about how the writer
should respond to social injustice, Kazantzakis replied: "It is shameful to
remain unperturbed. . . . The writer . . . cannot repress his indignation or
shirk his responsibility. He is duty-bound not to sleep; he must keep his
people on the alert."[5] It is statements such as these that leave him open
to charges of being a fake and a hypocrite, especially when they are
taken out of context (as this one is). As we shall see at the very end of
this essay, however, Kazantzakis's full conception of himself as an agitator, far from being inconsistent with his refusal to write about specific
contemporary problems in the realistic mode, was actually dependent
upon that refusal. He knew what he wanted and did not misrepresent
himself, though he was continually misrepresented by others.

Another way in which Kazantzakis provoked the opposition and gave
ammunition to his critics was by confusing, in his own right, the circumstantial with the essential and by seeming to assert (though he really
knew better) that his life was *basically* one of distinct stages, each representing a new political allegiance. His life did indeed consist of stages,
but only circumstantially, never basically. This confusion is seen in *Report
to Greco* and also in his letters. In 1923, as he was entering his bolshevik
stage (circumstantially, not essentially!), he wrote to his first wife, Galateia: "I have been a *katharevousiános* [linguistic purist], nationalist,
demoticist, scholar, poet, socialist, religious fanatic, atheist, aesthete, and
now none of these can fool me any longer."[6] The implication is that he
had finally "arrived" because of his new allegiance to bolshevism. Thir-

teen years later, when he had renounced bolshevism for "metacommunism," he summarized his politics as follows:

> Until 1923, full of emotion and ardor, I passed through the nationalist camp. The shadow I felt beside me was Dragoumis. From approximately 1923 to 1933, with the same emotion and ardor, I was part of the left wing (never a communist . . . , I never caught that *intellectual* pox). The pale shadow I felt beside me was P. Istrati. Now I am passing through the third stage—will it be the last? I call it freedom. No shadow. Only my own. . . . I have ceased to identify my soul's fortunes—my salvation—with the fortunes of this or that idea. I know that ideas are inferior to a creative soul.[7]

This statement is misleading because it invokes stages and change instead of continuity. In truth, the so-called third stage was nothing new: It existed from the beginning, and indeed was at the core of the nationalism and left-wingism it supposedly replaced. We return to the complex, paradoxical tangle, the totality characterized by continuity of essential concerns (for example, freedom), and change only of circumstantial ones, of labels. Kazantzakis, in the above statement, encouraged the accusations and misunderstandings by making the circumstantial seem to be the essential and thus distorting the paradox and complexity which were the truth of his personality.

It is a shame that in certain of his pronouncements he encouraged and provoked those who wished to misunderstand him, because in many others he gave a more accurate sense of his creative personality: of the way in which the varied allegiances were means for him to remain stable, walking only through himself. A good example is a passage from *Zorba the Greek*, where Kazantzakis clearly speaks of his own experience through the character of the Boss: "I fell into the word 'eternity,' and afterwards into other words such as 'love,' 'hope,' 'country,' 'God.' Each time I thought that I had been saved, and continued on my way. But I had proceeded nowhere. I had simply changed words."[8] This is a useful statement because it treats the stages as accidental husks—mere words—which could be changed again and again while the essential kernel of Kazantzakis's personality remained unchanged inside them, proceeding nowhere. The stages are thus seen as they ought to be: a circling around self, an alteration surrounding duration.

Only when we have made this distinction between the circumstantial and the essential in Kazantzakis can we begin to comprehend the continuity of his true self. When I say that the essential Kazantzakis remained unchanged, proceeded nowhere, I do not mean that he stagnated but rather that in his movement he always carried his past with him. "Duration" is the proper word, and duration, as Henri Bergson tells us, is not stagnant inertia, but flux; it is the paradox of a stability which is constantly freshened and renewed, like a great river. D. H. Lawrence, in a famous letter, speaks of the human personality as a "radically unchanged element" such as carbon, which nevertheless undergoes allotropic changes into diamond or coal, depending on circumstantial conditions.[9] This describes Kazantzakis perfectly: The end of his career was a matured, mellowed allotrope of his beginnings; certain basic attitudes, psychological needs, and traits of personality endured throughout. Consider, for example, his continuing cry for freedom; I have already suggested that this was never a "third stage" but rather the kernel of various circumstantial allegiances: of his nationalism, communism, socialism, and metacommunism, not to mention nonpolitical allegiances such as aestheticism and Buddhism. The cry for freedom was at the core of all these, and at the core of the cry for freedom was a continuing, enduring dualism which ultimately must be attributed to Kazantzakis's temperament and personality. This dualism saw matter, and thus all forms of materialism (bourgeois affluence, Soviet five-year plans), as stifling the spirit, imprisoning it. Freedom, for him, meant an escape from the material into the spiritual or the imaginative; his obsession with freedom explains why, from the start of his career to the end, he was correspondingly obsessed with what he termed transubstantiating flesh into spirit. But this obsession, though enduring, did not remain static. His circumstantial allegiances, the walk he took through all the political and intellectual tendencies of the age, caused this essential element to be pressed into an allotrope of itself. One may think of his outward activities as the donkey traversing the circumference of a large circle (going the long way round) in order to turn the irrigation pump at the hub, which moves while at the same time proceeding nowhere. In this case, we advance from a derivative, quixotic idealism which loves the spirit and scorns a material reality it does not even know to an allotrope which is mature and chastened, the product now of Kazantzakis's own disillusioning experiences in the material world, and one which therefore has earned its right to champion man's "all-powerful spirit" as opposed to his weak, finite flesh. Kazantzakis's walk through political experience enabled him to meet himself: to actualize his own personal potentialities for mature, meaningful idealism; to understand his previous immaturity; and, through this understanding—which after all is a spiritual accomplishment—to fulfill his need to transcend the flesh and be free. By taking the long way round, he came home; by walking through others, he walked through himself. His critics could never appreciate that although he was essentially uninterested in the political movements of his age, he was at the same time never frivolous, irresponsible, or hypocritical in his various political enthusiasms. He desperately, sincerely wished to align himself, because only in this roundabout way—the circumstantial—could he come home to the essential problem of *come l'uom s'eterna*.

Further examples could be found to illustrate this paradoxical allotropic change in core elements which at the same time proceed nowhere, but I hope that I have conveyed at least some generalized notion of what was circumstantial in Kazantzakis's life, what was essential, and how the two interacted. At this point the reader should also have some generalized understanding of why it is necessary to pursue the topic "Kazantzakis and politics," even though we have concluded that Kazantzakis is not basically a political writer. Lastly, he should realize that Kazantzakis's career at any given point can be adequately comprehended only if we have some knowledge of its very beginnings, for at any given point he was carrying with him all that had gone before.

In order to demonstrate these assertions about continuity, the essential, and the circumstantial, I have therefore chosen to discuss the first four or five years of Kazantzakis's long career, treating them in relative detail.

III

Kazantzakis became interested in politics only after he commenced his graduate studies in Paris in October, 1907. His writings prior to this first foreign sojourn were largely nonpolitical, yet they exhibit themes and concerns which were to be subsequently repeated in a political context, giving us our first clear example of the continuity beneath the apparent stages and about-faces of his career. In the brief year and a half he spent as a professional writer in Athens before he left for Paris, he established himself as a *wunderkind*, publishing a highly acclaimed novella and writing a play which became the theatrical sensation of the 1907 season. The novella, *Snake and Lily* (1906), is remarkable even though undeniably derivative. Aping the manner of Gabriele D'Annunzio and the French Parnassians, it presents a protagonist who is a hero of sensitivity, devotee of the imagination, and worshiper of beauty. So obsessed is this young man with the ugliness of the mundane and the decay wrought by time that he prefers death to an antiaesthetic life. Thus he commits suicide with his beloved at their romance's acme yet before its physical consummation so that the beauty of the relationship may be eternally preserved from fleshly corruption and the ravages of time. Aesthete that he is, he chooses an appropriate method for his suicide: suffocation in the aroma of flowers!

Kazantzakis thus seems to have begun as a *fin de siècle* aesthete and idealist, a decadent romantic. To the modern sensibility this mode is unbearably dated (Kazantzakis later repudiated the novella), but for all its hysteria and artificiality, it expresses an attitude which does not date easily and which Kazantzakis, far from repudiating, cherished throughout his entire career. I mean, of course, the belief that perfection (including perfect freedom) cannot be attained in the finite. The enduring truth of this romantic belief lies, as Nikolai Berdyaev has said, "in its striving toward the infinite, in its dissatisfaction with all that is finite. In romanticism the truth of the 'subjective' is opposed to the falsity of the 'objective.' Romanticism does not believe that perfection is attainable in this world of objects."[10]

By following Kazantzakis's career, we shall see how this romantic zeal for perfection impelled him into radical political allegiances through which he dreamed of remaking the world, while at the same time it paradoxically eroded the very zeal it had engendered, since political action operates in the finite, objective realm: precisely where perfection, for a romantic, is impossible.

But the relevance of *Snake and Lily* to Kazantzakis's later career, and in particular to his politics, extends far beyond its romanticism. The novella, of course, inaugurates Kazantzakis's obsession with freedom, a freedom equated with the transubstantiation of flesh into spirit, and is also the first of many works that offer death, indeed suicide, as the only way to obtain this freedom and the only exit from a materialistic reality which, by definition, seeks to enslave us. Most interestingly of all, the novella presents a theory of history which became central to all of Kazantzakis's later political thinking: the theory of the transitional age. This may not be immediately evident in the text—that is, not until we have had the benefit of Kazantzakis's glosses. The essays published during this period throw a completely new light on the novella's protagonist. Whereas the text *in vacuo* might delude us into thinking that Kazantzakis sympathized with his protagonist, viewing him as a heroic champion of perfection, the essays suggest quite the opposite: that he meant the young aesthete to exemplify a sickness in our culture. In the essay "Le Mal de siècle" (1906)[11] Kazantzakis diagnoses the century's sickness as romantic melancholy. The victims of this disease are trapped and frustrated; their suicides—far from being heroic—are confirmations that "no exit" at all leads from the trap of this transitional age. He then goes on to explain all this by means of a cultural-historical theory and in the process turns his essay from a lament and a diagnosis into what seems to be a ringing manifesto. What we need to replace the effete, decadent beauty-worship of our times, says Kazantzakis, is a virile, youthful, amoral paganism. He hails the ancient Greek civilization in which Apollo reigned, melancholy was unknown, and beauty could be pursued naïvely, unimpeded by a Christian sense of sin or a narrow bourgeois morality. He then castigates Jesus as the destroyer of this pagan freshness. But what seems to be a clarion call to renewed pagan spontaneity (that is, something fully as escapist and juvenile as the decadent aestheticism we find in *Snake and Lily*) is actually something much more sober. It is an analysis. The *mal de siècle*, says Kazantzakis, arises because we are caught in the middle. On one side, we can no longer be pagans because of the degree to which Christianity has penetrated our civilization; on the other, we can no longer be Christians because science has destroyed the perfect spiritual world which is the necessary basis for Christian hope. Apollo is dead, but so is Jesus. We are trapped between loss of the spontaneous appreciation of this world's beauty and loss of faith in another world above. We are the melancholy, despairing victims of a transitional age, and our sensitivity, our natural instincts for beauty, our love of the imagination, all vent themselves in decadent, self-frustrating ways, such as those exemplified in the protagonist of *Snake and Lily*.

In order to appreciate the continuity of Kazantzakis's thought throughout the half century of his career, we simply need remember this novella, which shows that in his very first year as a professional writer he was already obsessed with these problems of death, freedom, spiritual fulfillment, and—especially—the transitional age. All his future permutations—his socialism, nationalism, communism, metacommunism—were conditioned by these obsessions, for in every case he was seeking an exit from transition, a new faith which would release the trap, cure the melancholic sickness of his age, and heal his own soul. Though he rarely admitted this, the hidden motif behind his political as well as his aesthetic and religious thought was how to win freedom from despair.

In the earliest years he naturally drew from his youthful, limited education and experience the love of the ancients which he acquired in high school; the shock of Darwinism, turning Christianity into a fairy tale; his platonic courting of the unconventional bluestocking Galateia (to whom *Snake and Lily* is dedicated); his clash with the restrictive bourgeois mores of provincial Heraklion, mores that had been rendered anachronistic and senseless in his mind by the removal of their only possible justification, reward in heaven. All these factors were incorporated into his next major work, the Ibsenesque play *Day Is Breaking*, which was written in 1906 and produced the following season with much fanfare, after having received highest praise in a prestigious dramatic competition (the judges refused, however, to award Kazantzakis the official laurel because of the play's shocking immorality). As in the novella, the setting is domestic, not political. The heroine, Lalo, falls in love with a romantic poet who happens to be her husband's brother. Her problem is: Should she go off with the brother and thus assert her right to be happy, or should she observe the restrictive and anachronistic morality which forbids adultery and commands her to maintain her dull marriage? Trapped by this predicament, she grows melancholy and—as we might have expected—chooses suicide as her exit. Around this sensational plot, Kazantzakis builds a drama of clashing ideas. His own spokesman is the heroine's doctor, a character very reminiscent of Tanner in Shaw's *Man and Superman*. With the ardor of a John the Baptist, he preaches the coming of a virile neopaganism where happiness will be not only a right but also a duty, and where neither bourgeois conventions nor flabby, decadent romanticism will threaten man's natural, healthy outlets. Against him in the intellectual plot stand Lalo's mother, an otherworldly Christian scandalized by the doctor's views, and the lover, a gushily romantic poet who believes in beauty and continually quotes Heinrich Heine. Lalo is thus tempted by two anachronistic falsehoods: If she stays, she capitulates to Christianity and provincial, bourgeois mores; if she goes, she symbolically embraces romantic decadence. The right way—the Truth—is represented by the doctor's virile defiance and joy, his sincerity, his strength. She knows what is right but cannot act upon it. Why? Because, born too early, she is caught in a transitional age and is thus alone, unaided, a "broken soul." More positively, she is like the dying hoplite of Marathon, for she "ran ahead of the others in order to proclaim the victory." Though she is collapsing, this does not matter. As she says in a doleful soliloquy: "Mortally wounded, I fall to the ground in war, dead. No matter. I have come to tell you that the light is winning, the sun is rising." She poisons herself and expires, her strength leaving her just as she attempts to embrace the dawn.[12]

This interesting play moves away from Kazantzakis's *mal de siècle* pessimism to the qualified optimism of Lalo's soliloquy: The night of Christianity, bourgeois morals, and romantic decadence is indeed being defeated by the day of the doctor's strong, pagan joy. But we are still in the transitional age; this day has not arrived. We have only an earnest of it: The sun is rising; "day is breaking." Optimistically, the play asserts that man can wriggle himself out of the trap, but only in his imagination. In other words, right thought is already possible in this transitional age. Pessimistically, however, the play asserts at the same time that right action is not yet possible. The truth can be known, but not followed, or not yet followed. Here we should recall what I said earlier about the romanticism which forms the basis of Kazantzakis's creative personality: the attitude that impelled him to seek perfection but at the same time taught him that perfection is attainable only in the subjective realm, not the objective—only in thought, not in act. Comparing *Day Is Breaking* with *Snake and Lily*, we see a move toward the optimistic pole; the play is governed in a qualified way by the impulsion toward perfection more

than by the belief in perfection's impossibility. The various political allegiances are a series of readjustments of balance between the same poles
of the same romanticism. In his nationalistic and early communistic
phases, Kazantzakis was impelled toward a belief that right action is
indeed possible. After this—that is, after his own frustrations in political
life—he returned to the more qualified optimism seen in *Day Is Breaking*
and created a series of protagonists who are marathon runners announcing the coming "day"—uttering their cry—but dying as a consequence. As
we shall see at the end of this essay, his vision became more and more
focused on the future (which is infinite), his faith more and more
anchored to the human imagination. But in order to return "home" in this
way to the idealism, indeed the aestheticism, of his beginnings, he traveled a very long way round. The death of the protagonists, for example,
was transformed during this journey from the weak response we see in
Day Is Breaking, where Lalo's suicide is the consequence of lack of
strength, to the very opposite: a strong response, indeed the proof of
strength. The obsession with death and suicide endured throughout his
career but underwent allotropic change. To die became paradoxically
the one way his political heroes could act positively, helping to transform
daybreak into a high noon sometime in the future. The later heroes are
no longer pinned mothlike to their transitional times—their fates—unable
to turn into lovely butterflies, yet too fine, too morally sincere, to become
beetles. They are no longer melancholy or passive. Instead, they wrestle
with fate and cheat it by selecting—with "pagan" exuberance, virility,
strength—what necessity itself would otherwise have forced upon them.
They are not trapped, simply because they walk into the trap knowingly,
of their own free will.

The ingredients for this political development—seen preeminently in
the heroes Nikephoros Phokas, Kapodistrias, Captain Michael, and
Father Yanaros (in *The Fratricides*)—are all present in the early, nonpolitical works. I have singled out the crucial obsession with the transitional age, the division between right action and right thought, the seesaw
between pessimism and optimism, the central role of death as an exit
from despair, the identification of freedom with escape from materiality,
and other motifs such as hatred of bourgeois inertia, exultation of pagan
virility and strength, belief in Spartan self-discipline, valuation of passion
as a good, indeed a duty.

All these were the essential concerns which endured when Kazantzakis
went to Paris in October 1907 and—circumstantially—entered his first
political phase. Walking through the events and people he encountered
there, he became a ferocious nationalist, ready to sacrifice everything for
the sake of his race. But in reality—essentially—he was walking only

through himself: seeking, as always, his own salvation, his own exit from meaninglessness and despair.

Though the sojourn in Paris lasted only twelve months, its effect upon Kazantzakis was extraordinary. As published evidence we have a series of newspaper dispatches, his doctoral dissertation on Nietzsche, the novel *Broken Souls*, and the play *The Masterbuilder*. In addition, Kazantzakis probably wrote a monograph (now lost) on William James during this period, and he most certainly amassed the material for his 1912 treatise on Bergson—all this while attending courses in law and philosophy. The year in Paris left its mark on his entire personality, not just on his mind. Coming as he had from the provincialism of Heraklion and Athens, he was able to broaden his experience in many sectors: education, politics, women, art; and this in turn seems to have made him more pragmatic and mature. For example, immediately after leaving Paris he could say of D'Annunzio, whom he himself had imitated several years earlier: "He excites a few youths who, before knowing life, quite naturally seek from it very much more than it can give."[13] This does not mean that he went to the other extreme and became a positivist or a cynic. He remained a romantic dreamer, but he tried to become a hardheaded one, spinning his dreams from the stuff of reality (historical forces, realpolitik, biology, Darwinism, the nature of the human analytic reason) rather than from romantic poetry or soft, wishful thinking.

Matured in this way, he developed an increasing interest not so much in the dream itself as in its application (an interest carried with him, of course, from *Day Is Breaking*); in short, he veered more and more toward action, and because of the nature of his studies in law and in Nietzsche's theory of the state, plus the particular social ferment he encountered in Paris, the actions which attracted him were political in nature: those affecting the fortunes of entire societies. From the very first, he attended political congresses and parliamentary debates, coming away with admiration for the reforming spirit he observed. He was particularly impressed by the socialists. In his earliest newspaper reports he describes their desire to have all land belong to the state and asserts that this is the beginning of the new society.[14] He then tries to view socialism with his new hardheadedness, scientifically: The socialists address themselves to the needs of contemporary man because they base their program on the death of Christian otherworldliness. They attempt to improve this life since none other exists; they are the new apostles of the new religion which corresponds to the new needs arising after the French Revolution, etc., etc.[15] Here we have a splendid example of the continuity of Kazantzakis's thought, the way in which he dressed the same basic concerns in new clothes designed by external fashion. He is still seeking an exit to the frustration and despair of our transitional age; the new set of clothing, like the old, covers the same essential obsession with the vacuum left by the demise of Christianity. The difference is that his previous (somewhat juvenile) paganism in *Day Is Breaking*—the doctor's call to sun-worship and freedom for the instincts—has given way to a hardheaded interest in land ownership and economic theory. Romantic rhetoric and derivative Ibsenesque naughtiness have been replaced by empiricism, scholarship, and personal observation.

But the socialists did not appeal to Kazantzakis for long. Though he liked their atheism, in many ways they did not satisfy the needs and interests he had brought with him from Greece. We should remember in particular his belief in struggle, passion, strength, and self-discipline. Confirmed in these Spartan inclinations by his readings in Auguste Barrès and especially in Nietzsche, he soon began to view the socialists as degenerate and feminine. Whereas Nietzsche taught that the vitality of strong young nations is expressed by their expansion at the expense of weaker neighbors, the socialists were pacifistic and internationalist; whereas Nietzsche preached passion which is severely disciplined, the socialists, according to Kazantzakis, were rationalistic, and insofar as they believed in the instincts, they invited license, abuse, and anarchy.[16] Thus, he soon began writing in his newspaper dispatches of a France "made flabby by the premature and consequently criminal internationalism of various intellectuals" and of the feeling of Greek students in Paris that they must not return home as "socialist or internationalist windbags" but rather as youths who have learned "how fierce is the battle of life."[17]

It is not surprising that his new allegiance to a virile nationalism à la Barrès, Giosuè Carducci, and Kipling (all of whom he invoked) should have pressed him to turn his gaze more and more away from France and back toward Greece. His articles grew increasingly chauvinistic. He objected to the condescending attitude of monstrous France toward tiny Greece, and he called up the vision of "Great Hellas,"[18] the "Great Idea" of a revived Greek empire with Constantinople once more its capital. All this was a new—yet at the same time familiar—search for an exit to humiliation and despair, a continuation, altered by circumstances, of his earlier paganism. Thinking specifically of Greece, he ferociously declared:

> Nations ... must become egotistical and hard in order to trample the corpses of their opponents and *to advance strong and happy in the sun-bathed, manly intoxication of life.* The voice of our ancestors [presumably the Spartans] joins the voice of science [Darwinism] in commanding us ... to be beautiful and strong, to hate our enemies and ... , released from the Christian

ideals of the crippled and diseased, to hold high the Selfhood of the race.[19]

Kazantzakis's new ferocity understandably led him to despise French art—that of Claude Debussy, for example—as displaying the "death-bring-ing smirk of thrice-delicate irony," the "tubercular, aristocratic grace of withering organisms," whereas in the barbarity and primitivism of a Rich-ard Wagner or of a certain modern Greek sculptor, he saw individual rays of hope which, if only they could merge (note his language here), would constitute the "Great Daybreak."[20] Nor is it surprising that he should have begun to worship the strong men of history: Napoleon, Cesare Borgia, Benvenuto Cellini, "all the hard and strong stalwarts who ... left upon life the traces of their insatiable and rapacious desires." How magnifi-cent, he sighs, were Florence's past rulers, with their power, ambition, and heroism, and how miserable are that city's "democratizing and social-izing" children of today![21]

In these scattered remarks we have the attitudes which were to domi-nate the next decade of Kazantzakis's life. If they must have a label, we can call them "aristocratic nationalism," but I have tried to demonstrate that they are continuations of the seemingly different attitudes which preceded them. By the same token, we should realize that they are not essentially different from the seemingly very different attitudes and alle-giances which followed them. When Kazantzakis abandoned aristocratic nationalism in the early 1920's, he appeared to make an about-face, align-ing himself with the internationalist, antiaristocratic communists. If we spy beneath the surface, however, we see that his communism was simply one more expression—brought on by changed external circumstances—of his theory of the transitional age, his search for an exit, his worship of pagan strength, the strong man, passion, and youth. This is why, unlike other communists, he could admire Mussolini at the same time that he admired Lenin. If we stuff him inside of neatly ticketed allegiances, his inconsistencies only make us angry; if we do not, we realize that all his seemingly contradictory enthusiasms were consistent manifestations of a personality intent on finding itself—achieving its own personal salvation—by walking the long way round through all the major political tendencies of his times.

When Kazantzakis returned to Greece to announce the "daylight" of aristocratic nationalism, he was not—this time—a marathon runner who had arrived ahead of all the others. Nor was he condemned to the frus-tration and death of those who possess right thought but have been born too early for right action. On the contrary, his nationalism coincided with a huge movement which had already begun to dominate his countrymen. Returning to Heraklion in April 1909, he found a Greece which had fully recovered from its humiliating defeat by the Turks in 1897 and was already in the midst of a patriotic zeal and euphoria destined to dominate intellectual as well as political circles for over a decade, swelling and swelling until it burst in the Asia Minor catastrophe of 1922. During this period the Greeks emerged victorious in the Balkan Wars and World War I. Their breasts, as Demetrios Glynos has written, were "proudly swelled by colossal self-confidence. The bards of the race commenced grandiloquently to sing Hellenism's modern glories alongside the ancient."[22] What the poets and intellectuals helped formulate was not a thoughtless expansionism but a sophisticated ideology that spoke to a whole generation of Greeks of all classes and all political persuasions. This was the revived "Great Idea," the age-old dream of the enslaved Greeks of the Ottoman Empire, a dream which had always been Greece's consolation and hope, a psychological compensation for Hellenism in decline. The Great Idea, as described by Ion Dragoumis in 1909, was "a memory which has remained deeply nestled in the soul of the Greek ever since the Turks captured Constantinople in 1453. It is the memory that Greeks, with Constantinople as their capital, ruled the east in the past."[23]

When Kazantzakis arrived home from Paris, this memory already cried out for practical action. The dream seemed to have become realizable. Psychologically, instead of being just a compensation for a nation in decline, it had become a force awakening the Greeks to a higher plane of life and action, to new and superior accomplishments in all fields. Politically, instead of being just a vague hope, it had solidified into very specific and hardheaded goals. When Eleutherios Venizelos pleaded Greece's cause at the Versailles Conference, he presented a table showing the distribution of the "Hellenic nation": Only 55 percent resided in Greece; the remainder—almost four million people—lived outside, chiefly in Thrace, in Constantinople, in Asia Minor, and in the Caucasus (also in the United States).[24] The hardheaded objectives of the Great Idea were to free all these Greeks who were still "enslaved," to acquire the territories in the Balkans and Asia Minor to which Greece believed it had rights, and—as a logical, inevitable extension of all this—to fulfill Hellenism's "manifest destiny" by eventually reestablishing the Byzantine Empire, which meant a Greek king enthroned at Constantinople and a Greek patriarch once again in Hagia Sophia.

It is obvious that Kazantzakis returned to an ideological climate where action was the great cry: The Greeks had dreamed long enough. He returned to a country full of optimism and soon formed decisive friendships with strongly optimistic personalities such as Dragoumis and (after

1914) Sikelianos. All this encouraged him to apply the activist theories he had brought back with him from Paris. As I stressed earlier, he remained a dreamer, but his interests veered from the dreams themselves to their application. This change manifested itself in his own actions on behalf of Hellenism, notably his crusading demoticism, his involvement in educational reform, and his mission in 1919 to the Caucasus to free 150,000 of the "Hellenic nation" from persecution by the Bolsheviks. But the change had already manifested itself, and very starkly, in the writings he had brought back with him from Paris—specifically, in the difference between the novel *Broken Souls* and the play *The Masterbuilder*. Both are addressed to his fellow Greeks, and both are political in message, though the novel is at the same time introverted and psychological. But whereas the "broken souls" lack Spartan discipline and do not base their dreams on reality,[25] the virile masterbuilder remedies these defects. Though he dreams, he does not overlook the Darwinian nature of life; though he has great impulses, he controls them, directs them with ruthless logic, and thereby conquers fate itself and is ready to move to the next great exploit, the next hardheaded, practical achievement of the impossible. One might even say, with just a little imagination: He is ready to recapture Constantinople! The "broken souls" were drawn from certain flabby, decadent Greek students Kazantzakis met in Paris and also from his own past self. The masterbuilder, dreaming, yet knowing "how fierce is the battle of life," was his new self and a healthily optimistic, virile Greece.[26]

These works are, of course, much richer than I indicate; they bring to a new fusion all the negative and positive concerns we have seen in Kazantzakis's early career: suicide, romanticism, love, the transitional age, the role of the exceptional man in history, the need to sacrifice sentiment and happiness to the "great work." Most important, however, they take us from a "broken" hero who is capable only of right thought to a virile and healthy one who proceeds ruthlessly from right thoughts to right acts. Daybreak has become Day.

Having said this, I must immediately voice a caution. Whether we consider Kazantzakis's writings or his direct political activities, we should not let his activism deceive us. I have tried to stress that he never really changed, that he always carried his whole past with him. Speaking in general terms about his nationalism and also about his subsequent communism, I suggested that although he seemed to have become truly political at last—interested in conquering and molding concrete reality so that whole societies could prosper—he was most basically still seeking an exit from personal despair and was acting not out of a belief that reality can actually be molded but rather in spite of his belief that it cannot. His activism and his seeming optimism always lie within the framework of a thoroughgoing philosophical and temperamental pessimism.

These generalizations receive their corroboration in a nationalistic manifesto which he published in 1910.[27] On the surface this is a ringing call to youth to join the good fight and support the Great Idea, but Kazantzakis undercuts himself—and of course at the same time demonstrates his intellectual honesty—by saying, for example, that it really does not matter whether we choose nationalism over internationally minded socialism, because both are subjective and relative. Since one is no truer than the other, we should simply choose the ideology which best suits our personality. The document goes on to suggest that we should act in spite of ourselves, *as if* we believed. The superior man, says our supposedly political Kazantzakis, will "see the vanity of all things, and at the same time . . . the need to clutch at various unbaptized ideas . . . and name them *truths*. And they really are truths—subjective ones." Here, as always, the emphasis swings away from the objective to the subjective, away from the group and toward the psychological necessities of the man who is supposedly devoting himself to the group. He acts because he must escape his vision of universal vanity and the net of despair which this vision will otherwise cast over him: because he must save himself. The only "objective" good or truth becomes his own subjective self-discipline, the willfulness which enables him to perform gratuitous, purposeless acts with fervor and dedication. As Kazantzakis wrote seventeen years later, looking back on his mission to the Caucasus: "The words 'Greece,' 'mission' and 'duty' are meaningless. But it is beautiful to sacrifice ourselves, willfully, for these nothings." "I believe that there is no religion more in accord with man's deepest hardihood than the cultivation of purposeless heroism."[28]

IV

This view, expressed so nakedly in 1927, was already the foundation of Kazantzakis's "political" thinking in 1910, the fourth year of his long career as a writer and doer. In all the subsequent circumstantial allegiances, the same ground base of *come l'uom s'eterna* remained. Kazantzakis's ferocious nationalism began to die in 1920 when Venizelos fell from power and Dragoumis was assassinated. In 1922 it died completely, for the Turks had sacked Smyrna, driven the Greeks into the sea, and brought a definitive, catastrophic end to the Great Idea. Kazantzakis had already begun to look to Russia. His communism, as I have already suggested and as can be conclusively demonstrated from his letters and manifestos, was a continuation of previous needs; he saw in the Bolsheviks the same pagan energy, discipline, passion, antirationalism, and barbaric youthfulness that he had seen in the nationalistic Greeks a decade earlier. Moreover, his responses followed a predictable cycle. Once again we observe the initial, momentary euphoria, the seeming belief in concrete action, the seeming interest in others. But this was then undercut by his pessimistic world view. The emphasis, just as in his nationalistic period, moved toward the subject and away from the object: toward the struggle itself and away from the goal. At the same time, Kazantzakis could not be the same person he had been ten or fifteen years before. More experienced, more mature, he was better able to respond creatively to the disillusion which greeted him whenever he attempted to participate in political life. As I indicated in my general discussion, instead of tilting against one "objective" windmill after another, he began to return to his initial aestheticism and idealism—with the crucial difference that he now had earned the right, through experience, to assert that perfection cannot be obtained in the finite world of objects. We see him once again projecting right act into some unspecified (and thus infinite) future. Whereas he at first declared Russian communism to be the daylight marking the end of the transitional age, the new idea *and pragmatic fact* replacing Christianity, by 1929 he considered the Russians part of the transition: Even this youthful society, originally so admired by Kazantzakis, was not yet ready for right act. Furthermore, in projecting right act into some unspecified and infinite future, Kazantzakis was also naturally inclined to conceive of this act in spiritual rather than in concrete terms. Whereas he had originally spoken hardheadedly about specific educational programs, the abolition of hunger, etc., he now spoke more vaguely of a postbolshevik age in which society would honor spiritual values. He called his new hope "metacommunism."

In all of Kazantzakis's political writings from this time on, and especially in the great novels, the key words were "future" and "spiritual." In his personal life he still devoted himself in fits and starts to immediate, concrete problems: From 1940 onward he joined other Greek intellectuals in a resurgent nationalism occasioned by the Albanian campaign and the German occupation; in 1945 he led a socialist coalition; in the 1950's, though embittered by his exile, he spoke out publicly for Greek aspirations in Cyprus. But despite all this, the key words "future" and "spiritual" came to dominate his personal life as well as his writings. This is because he had finally reconciled himself with his own temperament and had consciously accepted the fate which made him not a man of affairs, directly molding contemporary reality, but a prophetic artist dedicated to man's infinite potential.

All this would seem to confirm the view expressed in the tirade cited at the opening of this essay: that Kazantzakis is irrelevant to the concrete problems of the here and now, problems such as the tanks which on April 21, 1967, rolled into the streets of Athens, bringing the end of democratic liberty. Kazantzakis's pessimistic nihilism, entrenched in him by his repeated failures and disillusionments in the political arena, prevented him, it is true, from confronting such problems in their own terms: concretely, contemporaneously. Nevertheless, he considered himself a committed political writer and even an agitator. "The writer," we will recall him declaring, "cannot repress his indignation or shirk his responsibility."

Out of context, this declaration of commitment may seem hypocritical and inconsistent, yet it is not. Kazantzakis was truly, honestly committed. But taught by his experience in political affairs, he was committed to the only things worthy of his *continuing* allegiance: the future and the spiritual. He insisted that this did not make him irrelevant to the present and the concrete. His work derived from the present and concrete, from his walk through all the political tendencies of his age, and it was meant to speak to the present, concrete needs of the oppressed. Its method, however, was not propagandistic, but prophetic. His job as a committed writer was initially to divine the nature of the present age, acting as a kind of seismograph or "early warning system" both for its tremors of dissolution and for the first faint voices of future renewal, the rays of future "day." This done, his next job was to formulate that future by creating archetypal embodiments of truth and heroism and preeminently by voicing a *kravghí*, a cry. As he himself has said, "Driven by [my] duty as agitator, I compel myself in my work to set heroic models before the people. ... They alone incarnate the claims and the hopes of the famished and the persecuted, and are capable of showing the people the way toward salvation."[29]

In this way, though seemingly turning his back on contemporary political reality, the writer can serve it well. He serves it, according to Kazantzakis, by helping the spirit—man's imaginative conceptions—to stay out ahead, like a bag of fodder in front of a horse. Thus he inspires reality to catch up, and even more: He helps determine the direction which reality will take, for the cry or fictional model will hopefully function as a riverbed into which material life will flow when it is ready.

By writing prophetic books, Kazantzakis managed to reconcile the pessimistic and optimistic needs of his temperament. The purposeless heroism of his protagonists has a purpose after all, for these heroes are models of spiritual achievement, encouraging reality to reach them in some undefined (and constantly receding) future. They die and sometimes in dying help to inspire others to live better and make better societies, but probably even more important than this, they voice—and leave behind them—a cry. This, though intangible and spiritual, is their right act, the one that will do most to bring an end to the injustices and chaos of the transitional age.

As far as Kazantzakis himself was concerned, this spiritual right act was the composition of plays, epics, and novels. Here was the "freedom" he invoked in 1936 as his "third stage." It was not, however, a third stage in an essential sense but rather a continuation, an allotropic form, of Kazantzakis's abiding identification of freedom with the human imagination, his romantic conviction that the concrete world is by definition one of finite restriction and enslavement. His imaginative writings are his *kravghí*, and his *kravghí*—while constituting a riverbed into which future reality will hopefully flow—is, more importantly, his spiritual understanding of his own external experiences: It is the imposition of meaningfulness upon his outward life and thus his inward life's salvation. In this way, his books are circumstantially political, essentially unpolitical. They trace the long road of participation taken in order to reach the home of personal salvation; in them, Kazantzakis the political agitator fuses with the Kazantzakis whose basic concern was *come l'uom s'eterna*.

None of this may satisfy people who consider themselves truly political and who truly believe in the establishment of concrete justice and freedom for human society in the here and now. But Kazantzakis amalgamated his political urges as best he could into a temperament which from the very start was basically devoted to the imagination. He may anger both the left and the right and be unacceptable to all regimes, but what he achieved is just as important.

NOTES

1. Inferno, XV, 85. See Kazantzakis's diary for 1915, cited in *Tetrakosia Grammata tou Kazantzaki ston Prevelaki* (Athens, 1965), p. 9, and in Helen Kazantzakis, *Nikos Kazantzakis* (New York, 1968), p. 60.
2. *The Odyssey: A Modern Sequel* (New York, 1958), IX, 691.
3. *Ulysses* (New York, 1961), pp. 377, 213.
4. Helen Kazantzakis, pp. 401, 402.
5. *Ibid.*, p. 529.
6. Nikos Kazantzakis, *Epistoles pros ti Galateia* (Athens, 1958), p. 184.
7. *Tetrakosia Grammata*, pp. 464–465. Cited in English in Pandelis Prevelakis, *Nikos Kazantzakis and His Odyssey* (New York, 1961), p. 160, and in Nikos

Kazantzakis, *The Saviors of God* (New York, 1960), p. 33. The word "intellectual" (*pnevmatiki*) is underlined by Kazantzakis in the original. As Prevelakis has noted, it refers to Marx's doctrine of historical materialism.

8. Cited by Kimon Friar in his Introduction to *The Saviors of God*, pp. 33–34. *Zorba the Greek* (New York, 1953), pp. 174–175.

9. Letter to Edward Garnett, June 5, 1914, in Diana Trilling, ed., *The Selected Letters of D. H. Lawrence* (New York, 1958), p. 75.

10. *The Beginning and the End* (New York, 1957), p. 190.

11. "I Arrosteia tou aionos," in *Pinakothiki* (Athens), March–April–May 1906, pp. 8–11, 26–27, 46–47, reprinted in *Nea Estia*, May 1, 1958, pp. 691–696. Similar ideas can be found in "Nostalgia," *Pinakothiki*, June 1907, and in "Christougenniatiko," *Pinakothiki*, January 1908.

12. The glosses are (a) an article in Kazantzakis's regular column "Chronographimata," in the newspaper *Akropolis* (Athens), May 8, 1907, reprinted in *Nea Estia*, May 15, 1958, p. 753, and (b) a letter to the editor of *Pinakothiki*, dated August 22, 1906, and published in "Anekdota grammata tou Nikou Kazantzaki," *Kainouria Epochi* (Athens), Fall 1959, pp. 31–32. The play itself exists only in Kazantzakis's original manuscript, now in the possession of Helen Kazantzakis. The phrase "broken soul" occurs in Act III, Scene vi, and the marathon-runner soliloquy in Act III, Scene viii. Some short excerpts from the text were published in *Pinakothiki*, August 1907, and in *Pantelideios Dramatikos Agon* (Athens, 1907), pp. 48–59. See the reprints in *Nea Estia*, May 15, 1958, pp. 746–749.

13. "Taxeidiotikai Entyposeis: Eis tin Florentian," *Neon Asty*, April 10, 1909, reprinted in *Nea Estia*, September 1, 1958, p. 1292.

14. "Epistolai apo to Parisi: I Poikilia pantou," *Neon Asty*, October 25, 1907, reprinted in *Nea Estia*, August 15, 1958, pp. 1210–1212.

15. "Parisina Grammata: I Exegersis tou sosialismou," *Neon Asty*, November 6, 1907, reprinted in *Nea Estia*, August 15, 1958, pp. 1212–1213.

16. *Ibid.*

17. "Epistolai apo to Parisi: Oi Ellines spoudastai," *Neon Asty*, March 8, 1908, reprinted in *Nea Estia*, September 1, 1958, pp. 1284–1285.

18. *Ibid.*

19. *Ibid.* Italics mine.

20. "Apo to Parisi: O Ellin Glyptis," *Neon Asty*, June 26, 1908, reprinted in *Nea Estia*, September 1, 1958, pp. 1285–1288.

21. "Taxeidiotikai Entyposeis: Eis tin Florentian," *Neon Asty*, April 10, 1909, reprinted in *Nea Estia*, September 1, 1958, pp. 1291–1292.

22. In *Neoi Protoporoi*, February 1935. Cited by L. Tasolampros, *I Symphiliosi kai oi pnevmatikoi igetes* (Athens, 1947), pp. 50–51. The ideas in the remainder of this paragraph and some of the next are paraphrased from Giorgos Theotokas, "Ta Provlimata tou aionos: i oxytati ideologiki krisis tis epochis mas," *To Vima*, September 21, 1958, p. 1.

23. *Noumas*, October 11, 1909, p. 6.

24. This table is in the Venizelos archives at the Benaki Museum, Athens.

25. This interpretation, clear enough in the text itself, is confirmed by Kazantzakis's gloss in *Noumas*, September 27, 1909, p. 2, reprinted in *Nea Estia*, October 1, 1958, p. 1498.

26. For a fine discussion of the political climate and how it affected *The Masterbuilder* and comparable plays by Kostes Palamas, Spyros Melas, Nirvanas,

etc., see V. Laourdas, *I Epochi tis "Trisevgenis"* (Thessalonika, 1964) (#2 in the 1963–1964 lecture series of the State Theater of Northern Greece).

27. "Kritika meletimata: gia tous neous mas," *Nea Zoe* (Alexandria), February–April 1910, pp. 232–239. The passages I cite are from pp. 236 and 238.

28. "Ó Giannis Stavridakis," *Neoellinika Grammata* (Heraklion), May 1927, pp. 364, 369. The words of the first passage I cite are placed in the mouth of Stavridakis, but the sentiments are obviously those of Kazantzakis himself.

29. Helen Kazantzakis, p. 530. For a more comprehensive exposition of Kazantzakis's conception of the artist's role, see *Spain* (New York, 1963), pp. 100–102, and also his article "To Drama kai o simerinos anthropos," *Nea Estia*, November 15, 1954, pp. 1636–1638, which is inadequately recapitulated in *England* (New York, 1966), p. 227.

GEORGES BERNANOS
(1888-1948)

by W. M. Frohock

GEORGES BERNANOS'S POLITICS are inextricable from his religion. He believed very simply what he had learned in the Lyons Catechism: Supernatural evil really exists; Satan wanders through the world seeking the ruin of souls; and the world is in dire, constantly renewed need of salvation. He is not the only modern French writer to make the devil a character in a novel, since the latter also has a somewhat ambiguous role in Gide's *Counterfeiters*, but he is alone in believing literally in the one he put in his book. When the hero of *The Star of Satan* spends part of a night wrestling with the Father of Lies—who is lightly disguised as a horse trader for the occasion—there is no chance in the world that the novelist intends an allegory; the future saint is at real grips with the real Prince of Darkness.

Such literalness puts off, of course, readers who can accept such beliefs only as metaphor. Even among Bernanos's fellow Catholics, committed though they are to a doctrine of eternal punishment, hell and its proprietor are not particularly popular subjects. Reference to the pangs of damnation persists in the act of contrition, and mention of Christ's descent into hell is still part of the Nicene Creed, but the Archangel Michael is no longer beseeched at the end of Mass to "be our safeguard against the wickedness and snares of the devil," and sermons like the one that frightened the lights out of young Stephen Dedalus are out of style. "Hell must exist," the fashionable Abbé Meugnier is reported to have said, "but doubtless God is too good to send anybody there."

Bernanos did not agree. Not only an individual but also a whole community, or even a country, can go to hell. The villages in which he sets his best novels, *The Open Mind (Monsieur Ouine)* and *The Diary of a Country Priest*, are what he calls "concentrations" of the modern world, examples of what can happen. He says this explicitly in his correspondence. They are little foretastes of hell because God is absent and they are emptied of love and joy; the ceremony of innocence is drowned.

A world on the brink of perdition overwhelms, rejects, and destroys his heroes—or would do so if they were not the instruments of divine grace. The nameless narrator of the *Diary*, Abbé Chevance, of *The Imposture*, the curé of Fenouil, in *The Open Mind*, are weak or ill, easily confused, tactless, in bad odor with their superiors, and detested by the people they have the vocation to serve and save. Chevance and the curé of the *Diary* die of natural diseases, but with the world snapping at their heels. The curé of Fenouil is utterly defeated by a town where his futile effort at regeneration only compounds chaos. Everywhere evil takes the form of mindless violence and hatred. The novels are full of murders, suicides, rapes, cynical seductions, homosexuality, and drug addiction. People have lost the elementary human capacity to respect and love the human in themselves. The fate of Bernanos's heroes and saints can be only martyrdom of one kind or another. Chantal de Clergerie, the pure heroine of *Joy*, is murdered for no more of a motive than that her murderer has seen her saying her prayers.

These are not the only victims. There are also those like Mouchette, in *The Star of Satan*, whom the world pushes into sin and crime, and who murders her lover and cuts her own throat; like Simone Alfieri, in *The Crime*, who moves inexorably from narcotics and other vices to murder; like the other Mouchette, in *Mouchette*, who lets herself be seduced and then drowns herself in a pond. They have sinned, but they have been vilely sinned against; Bernanos calls them "the humiliated." They are the objects of his great pity; their plight stirs his loudest wrath.

This humiliation is the work of the modern state and those who serve it: the civil functionaries, the teachers who purvey the state's secular education, the doctors who substitute science for religious faith, the practical politicians, and the rest who preach the modernity of the modern world; they create the climate of the devil. The ill they do is not necessarily intentional, but their believing what they say only increases and intensifies the havoc. The worst are filled with passionate intensity.

And meanwhile the best lack all conviction. Nominally Catholics, they have tried disastrously to compromise between their religion and the world. They failed, after 1870, to take control of the state. They obeyed the order of a mistaken Pope to "accept" and live at peace with the Third Republic. They want the honors and esteem that the modern world offers: Bishop Espelette, in *The Imposture*, would sell his soul to keep his reputation for liberalism; Clergerie, in *Joy*, will sacrifice anything for election to the academy. Bernanos calls these people *les bien-pensants*—the respectable middle class, characterized by their mediocrity and their vanity, the stupidity that lets them be so often duped, their hope that they can somehow get the goods of this world without losing those of the next, their immense desire to offend no one. In this category he puts most of the Catholic bourgeoisie, a majority of the French clergy, and so many intellectuals that at times this Catholic sounds like no one more than the Jew Julien Benda, in his *Treason of the Intellectuals*.

Such is the universe of his novels, as well as the view of life that underlies his vociferous, incoherent, polemic essays. His admirers claim that he was in essence an apolitical man, and in a sense they are right. He never contrived to put together a coherent statement of his political position, even during the years when he was an active member of the Action Française. Yet it is obvious that his novels are full of political implications and that his entire adult life, from the aftermath of the Dreyfus case to the aftermath of World War II, was engaged in political issues.

Within the general limits of the frame here outlined he varied immensely. Most of the specific stands he took he later abandoned or contradicted himself about. As late as 1932 he had been violently anti-Semitic, but he was completely revolted by Hitler's treatment of the Jews; he spent years working for the Action Française but later became one of the most eloquent adversaries of the group's leader, Charles Maurras; he welcomed the revolt of Mora and Franco but wrote *A Diary of My Times* (*Les Grands Cimetières sous la lune*) in protest against the brutal cruelty of Franco's "holy" war; he had been a lifelong royalist but put his immense talent at the disposal of Charles de Gaulle; *La Grande Peur des bien-pensants* is a defense and glorification of the archreactionary Edouard Drumont, but at the end of his life he was suggesting that memorial masses be said for Drumont's fiercest political enemy, Georges Clemenceau. This may make him look less consistent than he was, of course: De Gaulle, for example, may have seemed to promise the return of a "Christian France," such as some royalists claimed had existed under the old kings. But superficially, at least, consistency was not his forte.

Yet the inconsistencies themselves emphasize how much politics was a constant part of his life, and his novels can be understood fully only in the light of his more openly political books. His study of Drumont holds the key to *The Imposture* and *Joy*, just as *The Diary of a Country Priest* and *The Open Mind* also condemn, though indirectly, a political situation.

Throughout the welter of varying opinions, one factor remains constant—his hatred of the injustice he called "humiliation." As in the novels, the word has the special sense of taking criminal advantage of those unable to defend themselves—like the Mallorcan peasants herded into trucks and taken to be shot on mere suspicion. And again as in the novels a world capable of such injustice is wrong. He made the common French assumption that "world" and "France" are synonyms, and modern France, for him, meant the Third Republic.

Bernanos came by this disposition honestly. His conservative family, living in Paris, had started him in school at the Jesuit establishment in Vaugirard. His childhood coincided with the anticlerical campaigns of the Combes and Waldeck-Rousseau ministries that ended with the banning of the "unauthorized" teaching orders. He seems to have been unhappy in school and low on the schoolboy pecking order, but his letters show that he formed friendships with some of his teachers which endured over long years. Eventually his family took him out of Paris to finish secondary school under other priests near their home at Fressin, in the department of the Pas-de-Calais. Photographs taken in his home show that there, as well as at school, he was surrounded by priests. It was only natural if he considered these friends the victims of a hostile (and worse, atheistic) government. Nor does it surprise that when he returned to Paris to take up law studies at the university he should have joined the antirepublican Action Française.

This society of radical dissidents had been founded during the Dreyfus case by a schoolteacher named Henri Vaugeois, himself a republican with violent patriotic—hence proarmy—leanings, whose fame was shortly obscured by that of one of his early recruits, the picturesque poet-journalist Charles Maurras. Maurras shortly took over leadership and retinted the society, politically, with his own beliefs. He was antirepublican, "integrally" nationalist, pro-Catholic (because to be Catholic was to be French), and advocated the restoration to the French throne of the traditional monarchy, represented by the house of the ducs de Guise. He was against the Protestants, the Free Masons, and the centralized state educational system, because these in his view were the chief supports of the Republic, and against the Jews because Jewish bankers, as Drumont had claimed, constituted an international plutocracy inimical to French interests. In his moments of literary criticism he favored traditional French classicism for the same reason he favored the Catholic Church: It was part of the prerevolutionary, monarchic French tradition. (It may be added that he was not a practicing Christian and that his verse was not particularly remniscent of Jean de La Fontaine or Jean Racine.)

Maurras in turn gathered around himself a gifted group of talents including the immensely gifted Léon Daudet, the critics Henri Massis and Pierre Lasserre, and, ultimately, the young historian Jacques Bainville. The daily newspaper they founded was so violently polemical that it could not have existed had there been a viable libel law, but it was at the same time intelligent and extremely witty, so that it quickly became known as the liveliest reading offered by the Paris press.

Subsidiary to the Action Française proper was an activist youth organization, some of whose members were to turn up later as leaders of the pro-Nazi *milice*—a paramilitary police body—in the occupied France of World War II. Its members, calling themselves Camelots du Roi, did everything from selling the Action Française newspaper, through parading and occasional street fighting, to breaking up the meetings of opposing political groups. Bernanos became a Camelot, participated with enthusiasm in its operations, and in 1908 was one of a party who erupted in a solemn meeting at the Sorbonne so violently that one of them pulled the venerable dean, the classicist Alfred Croiset, about the rostrum by the beard. Bernanos served a brief term in jail for his part in the disturbance.

No one doubts that Maurras was one of the decisive influences in Bernanos's life. (The other was the French Benedictine Dom Besse, whom he met somewhat later.) Bernanos had always been a royalist; Maurras offered him a coherent system of beliefs consistent with royalism—a complete politics and an attitude toward the totality of French life. In 1913–1914 Bernanos manned the Action Française outpost at Rouen, editing the weekly *Avant-Garde de Normandie,* in which he attacked, among others, the noted local philosopher Alain. He remained a member of the Action Française until 1919, when he resigned in a disagreement over parliamentary policy, but continued to contribute to its publications for a decade after that.

Yet the alliance of the intensely Catholic Christian and the freethinking Maurras was bound from the start to be uneasy. It survived the condemnation of Maurras by the Vatican and the prohibition of his newspaper as habitual reading for Catholics (1926)—a fact that witnesses to Bernanos's readiness to follow his own conscience rather than directions from Rome—but at length the strain became too great. After a violent polemic in *Figaro* against Maurras and Daudet, he severed all connections in 1932. (For details see *Bulletin de la société des amis de Georges Bernanos,* nos. 17-20, which are devoted entirely to the break with Maurras. In the absence of a biography, the *Bulletin* is the principal source of information regarding the episodes in Bernanos's life.)

Does all this make Bernanos a reactionary? Surely it does not make him the opposite of one. No man living in the first half of the twentieth century whose political ideal was the traditional French monarchy as it existed before the rise to power of the bourgeoisie could hope to avoid the label, and Bernanos did not seriously try to avoid it. But if by reactionary we mean someone willing to sacrifice the welfare of the working class to that of the others or capable of preferring a victory of the Nazis to an alteration of the existing political structure such as would put power in the hands of the workers, he did not fully merit the term. He insisted, himself, that he was "neither of the Right or of the Left," and (elsewhere) that even in his days with the Action Française he and his co-workers had favored a coalition of aristocracy and working class as a counterpoise to the overweening power of the bourgeoisie.

In this respect, at least, Bernanos is hardly the lonely figure among French writers he sometimes proclaimed himself to be. Of the generation of novelists whose work appears to have had the greatest impact on the French reading public during the decade just before World War II, for example, four others revealed as complete an alienation from the going middle-class culture as he did, each in his own way: André Malraux, Louis-Ferdinand Céline, Jean Giono, and Henry de Montherlant each "gave back his ticket" and declared his "estrangement." We are fairly sure, in retrospect, that much of the outcry that arose against several of these writers after the war, the accusations of collaboration with the occupiers, reflected the resentment of a bourgeoisie whose values the writers had felt no obligation to defend.

Like the others, Bernanos created his own complex myth to make his position tenable in his own eyes. At its core is the vision of a Christian France under a Catholic king, strong because of the harmony of its social organization, blessed with national integrity and justice, the center of Christendom. Just when this happy state existed is not important: His Christian monarch sounds at times like a mixture of the best in Saint Louis with the more admirable qualities of Henry of Navarre—for whom, one remembers, Paris was "well worth one mass." What counts is that this France had "honor." It is difficult, reading Bernanos, not to feel a similarity with the at-last-harmoniously ordered but also imaginary France celebrated by Paul Claudel in the last act of *The Tidings Brought to Mary*.

This France was finally betrayed by a Christian middle class that abdicated its vocation, which was to defend the commonwealth against the natural enemies of "honor," the anticlericals, radicals, socialists, and radical-socialists. The latter had taken over the country by default, through the cowardice of the "imbeciles" of the conservative Catholic persuasion, the complacent compromisers who could have restored the monarchy in 1789 instead of letting the enemy walk off with the fruits of the revolution and who missed another opportunity in the aftermath of 1871. All their compromising has ever achieved is their own political bankruptcy.

The hope of France thus has to be a working class which has retained its traditional virtues of loyalty, sobriety, industry, and common sense. In an alliance between this group and the royalist remnant, under a firm king, lies the one hope of defending the national "honor" against both the enemy within and the enemy without. For Bernanos myth requires an external enemy also.

Hence France is constantly endangered by an international conspiracy of rich Jews who control her finances and invariably put their own interests above hers. Their money is a source of continual corruption because it serves their interest to keep the country in a weakened condition.

As myths go, this one seems more vulnerable than most. Bernanos's vision of a Christian monarchy is probably not much more out of contact with reality than the Marxist vision of the Withering State—but the Marxist one at least looks into the open future rather than a closed past. Just how Bernanos's monarchy would have coped with the Industrial Revolution, the emergence of an industrial proletariat, and the problems posed by the ownership of the means of production is never very clear. (He seems at times to have thought of a Proudhonian socialism under royal auspices.) If he dwelt on such matters much, this does not show in his work.

Nor does his vision of a faithful, enduring bon peuple reveal a greater concern with current fact. The stereotype recurs persistently in modern French literature. The poetic system of Charles Péguy, for example—see the marching pilgrims in "Présentation de la Beauce à Notre-Dame de Chartres"—would collapse without it; and even so sophisticated a writer as Jacques Maritain resurrected it in France, My Country, the noble little essay he wrote just after the invasion and defeat of 1940. For all the purveyors of this cliché, the bon peuple is rural rather than urban, peasant rather than industrial. Bernanos is no exception: His working class sounds more like the farmers of Jean Francois Millet than factory hands capable of walking off their jobs on orders from the Confédération de Travail!

There is even a slight unreality about the role he attributes to the bourgeois bien-pensants. The tradition of berating the middle-class conservative is, of course, well and long established in France: Few subjects lend themselves better to caricature. But not even Gustave Flaubert leaves quite so much blame at his door. To make him responsible for everything that has gone wrong in France for a century, as Bernanos does, testifies less to respect for historical truth than to a need for scapegoats.

So does his anti-Semitism. Belief in a Jewish conspiracy was a fundamental tenet of the Action Française and doubtless explains the group's appeal for many adherents who could live without the restoration of the ducs de Guise but blamed Jewish bankers for their own losses in the large-scale swindles that had plagued the Third Republic. Bernanos held it for gospel. In the years since his death his admirers have had understandably little to say about it, but he was still expressing it openly on the eve of World War II, and I know no evidence that he ever repudiated it, much as he hated the abominations of Hitler. Yet this myth informs his novels as well as his books of polemic.

La Grande Peur des bien-pensants appeared in 1930, when the long association with the Action Française was coming to a close. *The Star of Satan, The Imposture,* and *Joy* had already established him as a novelist, but the second and third novels had not done as well as the first; he was short of money to feed his family. Elementary prudence might have told him to get on with his next novel and sustain his reputation rather than take time to write a book about an unpopular figure, which would appeal at best to a small group of political sympathizers. It is a measure of Bernanos's character, as well as of his indifference to practical affairs, that he chose to do the book on Drumont.

Drumont himself had been a curious figure. A journalist with an abundant gift for vituperation, he lived by pen and sword: The sword—he worked regularly with a fencing master—was used to defend himself in duels when he was called out by the victims of his pen. He was distinguished, even among his fellow reactionaries, as the most rabid Jew-baiter of his time and was so intemperate in expression that even many who agreed with his views eventually tired of him. This loss of popularity alone, in Bernanos's eyes, would have been enough to make him a martyr. Drumont remained, even on the eve of World War II, the novelist's "master." His most famous book was *La France juive.*

This book (two volumes, nearly 1,300 pages) is a classic example of its dubious type. A first part establishes a composite picture of *the* Jew as sociological and psychological type; the second traces the influence of Jews, generally harmful, on the history of France; the conclusion proposes a politics based on a program of resistance to the Jewish "conspiracy" and the exclusion of Jews from all political power. There is, in Drumont's theory, very little that varies from the ideas of Houston Stewart Chamberlain: Any paranoid could use them to justify the institution of extermination camps.

In a short piece called *Scandale de la vérité,* written as the Introduction to a projected anthology of Drumont's writings and dated 1939, Bernanos declares his persistent adherence to Drumont's beliefs. The published version passes rapidly over the subject of anti-Semitism, but a long passage which was finally excluded from the text reaffirms Bernanos's stand: The Jews are a separate race who *want* to be a separate race, hot after power, making a weapon of wealth, and dangerous because of an inability to attach themselves to any interests but their own. He never repudiated this view, and there is no sign that he ever changed it.

Some of the best-informed students of Bernanos believe, however, that what made the subject of *La Grande Peur* so appealing to him was less

Drumont's anti-Semitism than the pretext he provided for an all-out on-slaught on the conservative bourgeoisie. They may be right: The title of the book suggests as much; and when, later, he calls *A Diary of My Times* a continuation of *La Grande Peur*, the connecting theme is clearly that of the great failure of nerve. These people had failed to take up what Drumont had offered them.

In a way, this preoccupation with politics may be an explanation of the failure (at least relative) of Bernanos's second and third novels. *The Imposture* is supposedly the story of a priest who fails his vocation through intellectual pride. But a whole section of the four-section story puts this man far in the background while it pictures a typical group of *bien-pensants*: a liberal bishop who is courting the favor of a perverse and sickly writer, a lady-poet, an old conciliatory Catholic publicist, and a young journalist of the same general persuasion whom the others are busily throwing to the wolves for his "indiscretions" in an article touching upon the *mauvais prêtre*. The young man's name is Pernichon, a word that inevitably brings up the French verb for "snivel." All he has done to endanger the conservative cause and ruin his own career is to have spoken the truth, for once, unguardedly. An unforewarned reader is at a loss to explain just what this long scene has to do with the rest of the novel.

He has a similar difficulty with *Joy*, which forms a sequel. Here the principal story is about a girl who manages to live a saintly life in a social setting marked by spiritual sloth, in a climate of hidden but loath-some evil. Yet a disproportionate amount of attention is given the girl's father, a historian whose great ambition is to be elected to the academy. As a potential candidate he has to frequent and court the favor of men whose views he cannot possibly agree with. One gets the impression that the pure and saintly Chantal is finally murdered no more because the evil Russian chauffeur cannot abide her purity than because her father wants a chair among the Forty. The novel, like *The Imposture*, leaves the effect of incoherence.

This example seems to bear out the interpreters who hold that the unity of Bernanos's work must be sought outside his novels. It also com-mends the view of students of fiction who believe that his progress as a novelist can be measured by the evidence of his learning, late indeed, how to separate his polemic from his imaginative writing or, at least, how to keep his beliefs from wracking and disrupting his fictions. We understand what, for Bernanos, was wrong with the historian Clergerie and the liberal Bishop Espelette, not from the novels but from *La Grande Peur*.

We know enough about Bernanos to suspect the nature of the evolu-tion of the street-fighter of the years before World War I into the prophet of doom of the early 1930's. He had matured with passing time, of course; his religion had deepened and intensified under the influence of Dom Besse; he had taken on the responsibilities of supporting (as an insurance man) a wife and family; and he had lived through two major crises induced by outside events. One was the war itself, the other the condemnation of the Action Française by the Pope.

Bernanos had enlisted in 1914 and was on active duty in the trenches throughout the hostilities. He had been, by his own account, a clumsy but faithful soldier. He had accepted the war as a relief from the "odious monotony of life" and had hoped that the sacrifices of his generation in all the death and stench and mud would somehow expiate the sins of his countrymen, restore national honor, and bring about a moral regeneration. What the soldiers found when they got back from fighting was a population eager to forget all the inconveniences and to return to the easy pleasures that had been interrupted. His indignant surprise rapidly turned to indignant alienation. It is clear that this hurt never ceased to rankle.

In 1926 Archbishop Andrieu, of Bordeaux, complained to Rome about the association of Catholics with confirmed neopagans in the Action Française. Rome returned an interdict forbidding regular participation in the organization by Catholics and the habitual reading of its papers. Bernanos had dropped his membership earlier but now, with his old friends in deep trouble, returned to their side.

He was caught between his loyalty and his faith. The issue was not one of faith and morals, those subjects on which Catholics believe papal teachings ex cathedra to be infallible, but of obedience. Obviously, if the prohibition held up, he would have to accept it—or find himself at permanent odds with Rome. But meanwhile he could protest.

Maurras and the others, he argued, had done signal services to the Church in France that the hierarchy had acknowledged. What had happened to change their disposition? What was wrong now that had not been wrong earlier? He would obey, indeed, but he would like a clear statement of what he had to obey and why obedience was required. Not unsurprisingly, no word came from the Pope admitting that he had been misinformed. For the Catholic Bernanos an eventual break was inevitable.

It would have had to come anyhow, even if the situation had not created new tensions within the organization itself, and even if Maurras and his circle had not given up their earlier view of the desirability of a strong labor movement. It may be overstatement to suggest that the Vatican may have pushed the Action Française toward fascism; other forces were also working in that direction, but there is no doubt that Bernanos's interpretation of what had happened was in nature political: The Vatican

had produced a new order for a *ralliement* with the Republic by destroying the principal opponent of the politics of the conservative bourgeoisie.

Bernanos became, after the break with Maurras of 1932, a reactionary
without a party, and those who accuse him of the sin of despair are
right; if it is a sin to be without *political* hope, he committed it. And he
began to talk more and more frequently of staying faithful to *"le petit
garçon que je fus"* and of the "dawn" of death. Physical misfortunes and
a worsening financial situation were to darken his spirit still further. But
he was not yet finished with the *bien-pensants*.

He was living in Palma de Mallorca when the Spanish Civil War broke
out. He saw the early fighting on the island. His son was already a
member of the Falange. Here at last, so he thought, was a conservative
group ready to fight sooner than compromise. But then he also saw the
brutal repression, the regime of fear, the sadism, and the needless slaughter. And he saw the Archbishop of Mallorca bless the slaughterers. This
was the genesis of *A Diary of My Times*.

It was the fault of the archbishop in question and of the Spanish hierarchy generally that they had allowed a civil insurrection to develop into
a holy war. But the Spaniards had at least the excuse of being close to
the scenes of combat and perhaps blinded, by nearness, to some of the
realities. What bothered Bernanos even more was that a large section of
the French hierarchy and the *bien-pensants* who followed their lead
were ready to lend their blessing also. *A Diary of My Times* consists of
233 pages of recrimination, bordering on invective, against the "imbeciles." No few consider this book his masterpiece.

Shortly he left France for South America and in time set himself up in
a hacienda in Brazil. "I can't pray for France, anymore," he explained,
and he added elsewhere that he had come to *"cuver sa honte,"* an expression that may well be translated by "hide his shame." He intended, it
seems, to live out his life as a rancher. Munich was still some months in
the offing.

By this time he was cut off from most of his former friends and associates. Over the years since 1932 he had broken off relations with Maurras;
with Léon Daudet, whose enthusiastic critical article had launched the
success of his first novel; with Jacques Maritain, who had accepted the
same novel for the publisher Plon; with Henri Massis, whose criticism
had helped his work hold the attention of the public; with Paul Claudel;
and with many more. Came the war, and he was cut off from home in a
physical sense also.

There was no question of where his sympathy lay: He detested the dic-
tatorships, although perhaps hardly more than he detested the Third
Republic, but the Third Republic was only a state, not his country, not
France. He went to work in the one way he could, for the Free French,

De Gaulle, and the Resistance. A flood of articles, scripts for radio broad-
casts, moral propaganda of all sorts, passed from the backcountry of
Brazil through the British State Office in Rio, to be fed into France from
London. About Henri Pétain and Vichy his position was clear: They were
the last refuge of the "imbeciles," the ultimate compromise.

For some time after his death, this period of Bernanos's life was not
well known. His writings had necessarily been occasional and were scattered; some were not even signed. Questions about what happened to
Bernanos, politically, arise in some minds even now. After his return to
France, summoned by De Gaulle following the liberation, he met and
formed a close friendship with the scholar-critic Albert Béguin. Béguin
was entrusted with Bernanos's papers after the novelist's death in 1948
and during the remainder of his own life devoted much of his time to
collecting and publishing in the *Bulletin de la société des amis de
Georges Bernanos* the various *disjecta membra*, including no little correspondence. It was the conviction of the Bernanos family, and a necessity
for Béguin, that the materials should be fed to the public piecemeal.

Béguin himself was closely linked with the group of Personalist-
Catholics, once led by Emmanuel Mounier, who published the review
Esprit. In many respects his political leanings were those of a Christian
Democrat. It was only a matter of time before someone should accuse
him of suppressing some of Bernanos's writing in order to leave the
impression that during the war the novelist had come around to a democratic disposition. Béguin indignantly repudiated the charge, and what
he went on publishing, in the time left him to live, bears him out. The
fact that the family and the Société des Amis decided after his death
that it was still too early to publish the two-thousand-odd letters of Bernanos he had collected leaves final proof still pending.

Since the decision against publishing, even qualified students have
been denied access to the files, and no one is authorized to publish any
that he may have seen and copied before the prohibition was in effect.
This special circumstance may justify a personal testimony. I was permitted by Béguin himself to examine and copy or take notes of all the letters
that were in his possession in the winter of 1950–1951, many of which
have since been published in the *Bulletin*, although many others have
not. I can thus testify from firsthand knowledge that nothing I saw led
even to the suspicion that Bernanos had changed his essential political
beliefs—quite the contrary. Béguin could not, had he wanted, have
tampered with the truth without there being an outcry—of some volume,
since I am certainly not the only one to have seen the letters. There was
none, for the simple reason that the late Albert Béguin was a man of
complete integrity.

An essential stumbling block would have prevented Bernanos's joining the Catholic partisans of social justice in any case: He simply did not believe in the alleviation of poverty. He had been abjectly poor himself, though largely because of his epic mismanagement of his own affairs, and had come to see poverty as the fundamental virtue of the great saints. The kind of justice he wanted would have involved no concession to the materialism of the times.

He may have hoped that the politically inexperienced de Gaulle could pull France together and lift her out of the slough, reviving, though not Christian monarchy, at least the civic virtues—summed up in the word "honor"—that he associated with the monarchic tradition. If so, the hopes evaporated rapidly: The Fourth Republic turned out no better, to his eyes, than the Third. Just as, at the beginning of the war, he had consciously renounced writing fiction and given himself wholly to what the French call literature of combat, he now forsook this kind of writing in order to devote what time remained to the life of Christ he had long wanted to undertake. Remembering his book on Drumont, it is tempting to speculate on what the political implications of this final book might have been. He did not live to write it.

Once again he had turned his back on home and gone off, this time to Tunisia, where he planned to live and write. He was discouraged, tired, and already ill. In the early summer of 1948 he returned suddenly to Paris for an emergency operation and died on July 5 at the American Hospital in Neuilly. At his funeral only one other French writer came to join the mourners, André Malraux.

Such was the political life of a self-styled apolitical man. Some of his admirers call him a prophet. If he was one, it was in the manner of a Jeremiah. He foretold doom, and as he aged, doom seemed more and more certain. He had a prophet's capacity for indignation. His followers were not disturbed by his having, also, a prophet's capacity for incoherence.

He was, it should be added, emotionally ill. Repeatedly through his adult years he required treatment for anxiety crises. Those who knew him say that he was subject to seizures of paralyzing wrath. The wrath—the verbal rhythms of anger—recur persistently in his style, characterizing the tone of what has been called his "prophetic voice."

Prophet or not, the principles of his anachronistic, visionary politics had not changed. It was after the war that he wrote of his continuing distrust of human "mediocrities," a term which in his vocabulary was still synonymous with "imbeciles," meaning the conservative middle class. It was also after the war that he called democracy a "dictatorship of the mediocre" and told General de Gaulle that national union could not be founded on the "median opinion of average men," adding, to the general's face, that the "mediocre" would end by defeating him, "because the mediocre win out over everyone." The Resistance, he thought, had been exploited for cheap political ends, in another instance of Péguy's law that everything begins in mystique but ends in politics. The modern state, he believed, was too strong in techniques, too deficient in moral fiber, and the world was hastening toward a new, mindless, universal totalitarianism. Nothing in all this is inconsistent with the views he expressed earlier in life.

At times he was absurd. There was something absurd in his adulation of Drumont and something frighteningly so in his racism. And anyone not French-born must smile, however tolerantly, at his conviction that France was divinely called to be the repository of political virtue and had abdicated her responsibility. But he was not absurd when he attacked the French and Spanish clergy of his own church or foresaw in the rightist bourgeoisie the bastions of eventual fascism. And one does not smile at his belief that politics should be based on principle rather than expediency and is something nobler than the mere art of the possible.

ANDRÉ MALRAUX
(1901-   )

by Montgomery Belgion

I

ANDRÉ MALRAUX, whose novel *La Condition humaine* (1933) was awarded the Prix Goncourt—the outstanding French annual literary prize—and was translated into eighteen languages,[1] is, of course, far more than a successful novelist. From 1960 to 1969 he was French Minister of Cultural Affairs; in the earlier administration of General de Gaulle he was Minister of Information. He has made a name as a sensational traveler, as an archaeologist, as a seeker after Eastern sculptures. He has organized a remarkable and widely known series of art books. He is the author of a notable study of Goya. In 1933 he and André Gide, who was awarded the Nobel Prize for literature, took to Berlin a petition of protest against the incrimination of Dimitroff in the Reichstag fire which followed the arrival of the German National Socialists to power. In the Spanish Civil War he set up and led the foreign aviation on the republican side. During the German occupation of France he conducted sabotage by dynamite and commanded the Alsace-Lorraine brigade of the Resistance.

What further helps to make him not only a versatile but also an arresting figure of our century is that at the same time as he has lived politically, politics enters into a majority of his novels, and political presuppositions figure in some of his other books. I mean that he has found material for those novels in his own political activity, an activity inspired by his fullhearted support of first one political cause and then another.

La Condition humaine is his most ambitious work of imagination. It is both the most substantial and the best constructed. Its story is set amid the actual attempt made in 1927 by the communist wing of the Kuomintang to wrest the city and port of Shanghai from under the sway of Chiang Kai-shek, the Kuomintang leader. An earlier novel, *Les Conquérants*,[2] has its scene laid in China too, during the Chinese strike of 1925 against the European presence, a strike that was meant to bring business to a standstill outside Canton, in Hankow, and on the island of Hong Kong. The prime mover in the operation is the fictitious character, half Russian, half Swiss, of Garine, a man of action who looks upon Marxism as a mere means, and for whom energy is a supreme value. For him, another of the characters, Chang-Dai, an advocate of nonviolence, is but "a noble figure anxious to show up well in his biography." The unscrupulousness of Hong, the terrorist, who acts out of hatred of those who weighed him down in the past, he understands better. But Borodin, the Russian indoctrinator of communism in Canton, has Hong executed as too self-willed. Borodin is imported into the novel from real life. At Canton he was director of army and navy services. He was a Latvian Jew originally named Braunstein or something like that. He did not allow displays of conscience. The intention of the agitators in 1925 was to prevent any European vessel from coming up the river to Canton and to keep every Chinese vessel out of Hong Kong harbor. Like the communist attack on Shanghai in 1927, the strike in August 1925 did not succeed. The power of the whites was curtailed; they were not driven away. The British are still in Hong Kong today. But Malraux had the prescience to perceive that the strike presaged the twilight of white or European domination.

Neither novel could have been written without firsthand acquaintance with the Far East or without realizing that the East was in ferment. In 1923, when only twenty-two, Malraux had just married and left Paris with his bride on an archaeological expedition to Indochina, duly authorized by the French government on condition he paid his way himself. There, with the blessing of the French School of Archaeology, he and a friend named Chevasson took a convoy of bullock carts about twenty miles north of Angkor Wat. There, in the jungle, they chiseled away from the walls certain bas-reliefs and in a fortnight were back at their starting point, ready to have their spoils loaded on board ship. Instead the spoils were impounded, and the two young men were arrested, although not put into custody. Their trial took place in July 1924 at Phnom Penh, capital of Cambodia, before a French judge named Jodin. Malraux and Chevasson were both found guilty; Malraux was sentenced to three years' imprisonment and Chevasson to a lesser term. Both were given leave to appeal, and on appeal the verdict of guilty was maintained, but the prison sentences were reduced. Malraux seems then to have returned to Paris, where his case came before the court of cassation, the supreme court of France. His first wife says she drew up a petition in his favor which was signed by eminent French writers, among them André Gide, François Mauriac, André Maurois, Max Jacob, Gaston Gallimard (the publisher), André Breton (chief of the surrealists).[3] It got Malraux off. Thereupon he was offered the editorship of an independent biweekly in Saigon, call L'Indochine. He set out for the East a second time.

Apparently this newspaper became so outspoken about alleged misdeeds of French rule in the protectorates and colonies of Indochina that in 1926 Malraux was driven to slip away from Saigon to Hong Kong, and thence he went on to Canton. How long he stayed in Canton and what he did there remains obscure. In 1926 a committee of twelve operated there. Did Malraux belong to it? Years ago he gave me to understand that he had worked in Canton with Borodin. Yet it must not be forgotten that Malraux never joined the Communist party, a fact upon which he has had to insist repeatedly. There was a communist wing in Canton in 1925 all right, and communist propaganda was being spread in the neighboring provinces of Kwangsi and Kwangtung.

According to Walter Langlois, Malraux returned to Saigon later in 1926 and revived his newspaper under the new title of L'Indochine enchaînée.[4] This kept up a steady attack on French officialdom. His outspoken criticism was directed at what he regarded as French exploitation of the native, even as Henry de Montherlant has attacked French officialdom in North Africa, and particularly in Morocco, in his novel La Rose de Sable (full version, 1968). Incidentally, Montherlant enthusiastically praised Malraux's novel L'Espoir, the scene of which is Spain, a country Montherlant knows well. In 1926 Malraux was antibourgeois. For him, a bourgeois was not simply middle-class; he was above all a man who made an idol of respectability. (I translate as "respectability" Malraux's word considération.)

As early as those days in Indochina he felt that belief in communism—which is distinct from the doctrine itself—was transforming the life of even the lowliest coolie, and his feeling has since been expressed by the Chinese communist leaders also. They are convinced that the communist goal, however distant it may be, endows Chinese teamwork with a significance and value which fill the life of the humblest with a sense of purpose, a sense of mattering.

In 1927 Malraux left the Far East for good and back in France wrote the two novels which his firsthand experiences had suggested. Earlier, in 1926, he had published in Paris La Tentation de l'Occident, in which eastern and western cultures are contrasted and compared by means of an exchange of letters between a young Chinese in Paris and a Frenchman in China. This, too, could not have been written without acquaintance with the Far East to draw upon. The book illustrates the close connection between what happened to the author and what he wrote.

But *La Tentation de l'Occident* has not the political implications of the two novels *Les Conquérants* and *La Condition humaine*. The latter, it is notable, justifies its title. It is a serious effort to delineate the true nature of the human situation today.[5] The scene is during a period of violence because, in the author's view, it is then, at such a period, that the stark facts of life have to be frankly confronted, at such moments that a man decides what he may do with that priceless gift—his one life. A man may deliberately choose to lay down his life, and thereby he will have given his life meaning and direction. He does not prize his life less because he risks it. In the shadow of death life gives forth its full sweetness. At the approach of certain death friendship can show itself to be absolute.

In *La Condition humaine* other features of being alive are made vivid. The cruelty and inhumanity of man, the depths of human ignominy which anybody may plumb when he realizes how the infliction of torture and pain upon a fellowman is fascinating to watch or to read about, how we all disregard the feelings of others now and then, the senseless spell exercised by gambling—all these and more are exemplified in the narrative. Chiefly, however, it is a man's efforts somehow to transcend his mortality that make the novels representative of our day and age. For Malraux, religion is not dead. He is ready to admit that this terrestrial life may be succeeded by another. What he insists upon, however, is that no human society any longer treats Christianity as a life-giving force. Man has emancipated himself. Upon him alone individually now lies the task of replacing a discarded providence.

In short, politics in *La Condition humaine* as in *Les Conquérants* is background. It furnishes the context in which the characters grapple not with political systems but with life itself. There is no question of weighing the validity or invalidity of communist arguments. The whole point lies in the power of communism as a faith, whether the faith is valid or invalid, to quicken its converts into more intense living, into a sharper self-consciousness.

II

Malraux's literary activities and his continuing preoccupation with the access of the poor and disinherited into a sense of their individual reality and actual existence did not exhaust his own appetite for enterprise. What carried him to Indochina in the first place was, as I have said, archaeology—specifically, Khmer art, sculptures of a remote past. It was sculptures that he then proposed to bring home. Now, in 1930, he made another Eastern expedition. He made for the Pamir desert, hitherto the preserve to some extent of Sir Aurel Stein, and brought back statuary, including heads that strangely matched archaic Greek and European medieval sculptures. He emphasized the kinship of what he had retrieved from the highlands of Central Asia with, for instance, the reliefs of the wise and foolish virgins on the great west doors of Strasbourg Cathedral. The sculptures were exhibited first in Paris and then in New York.

Next, in 1934, he and a friend, Corniglion-Molinier, flew over the Sinai desert in the region of the reputed capital of the queen of Sheba, Rub' al Khali, and brought back from Kabul stucco heads which in their turn were put on exhibition. This excursion gained additional publicity through being disputed in the French press.

III

Before the exhibition politics had again seized the attention of the world. In 1933 Marshal Paul von Hindenburg, President of the German republic, invited Adolf Hitler to be chancellor. As the German National Socialists took power, there occurred almost simultaneously a fire in the Reichstag. Two scapegoats were found—Ernst Thälmann and Dimitroff. The evidence against them, if there was any, was not published. Malraux became chairman of a world committee against fascism, and a monster petition was drawn up protesting against the incrimination of the two men. Malraux, with André Gide, took it to Berlin. Hitler did not receive them.

Those were early days for knowing what incarceration by the Nazis involved. But Malraux was already led to write his third novel—the short Le Temps du Mépris (1935). The central character, Kassner, has been arrested and put into a cell. He makes no secret of being a communist. He overhears another prisoner not far away being knocked about. And then it is his turn. He is not interrogated. He hasn't the chance to refuse to answer. As though according to a routine, he is simply knocked down, struck, and kicked. Next he is put into a circular cell without windows. He is questioned and denies he is married. Actually he is torn with anxiety over his wife. Will she wait for him till he is at large again? Suddenly he is set free. He is told that another man has given himself up, saying it is he who is really Kassner. His wife turns out to have remained true and loyal to him. Le Temps du Mépris has not been reprinted, save for an illustrated edition. It has been said of the novel that it made known to a heedless world the existence of a German resistance movement to Nazidom and the horrible reality of the concentration camps.[6] But ten years were to elapse and World War II had to be fought and won before the world understood what was meant.

Then, in January 1936, Franco brought a contingent of soldiers from Morocco into Spain and set up a provisional capital at Burgos. The Spanish Civil War had begun. The event must have stirred Malraux profoundly. This time there was no question of merely editing a newspaper or even of helping to disseminate propaganda. This time there was no question of just delivering a petition. Malraux showed that he was no fighter on paper only. He enlisted with the Spanish republicans. In August 1936 he took command of the España air squadron, which he had helped to recruit, and at the Battle of Medellin he was commanding the whole of the republican air force. The next year he was wounded, and upon recovery he toured the United States and Canada, lecturing and raising funds for the republican cause.

For literature, the fruit of this further experience was the novel *L'Espoir* (1937), which grew out of a film he made with the same title. This novel, translated into English first as *Man's Hope* and then (1968) as *Days of Hope*, is a sequence of vignettes of the waging of war on the republican side. The atmosphere is splendidly rendered. The untrained soldiers, who remain civilians in mind, the lack of a highly professional chain of command, fighting in the snow, the evacuation of the wounded—all that is made vivid with action and movement. There are great set pieces of battle description that need a diagram to be properly followed. Manuel, Hernandez, García, and Magnin, who commands the international air force—their names grow familiar, and yet it is too much to say that they achieve flesh and blood for the reader, as Chen and Kyo, Katow and Gisors, do in *La Condition humaine*. Perhaps that does not matter. Many incidents are unforgettable. At the Alcazar Hernandez allows the enemy commander to send a message to his wife. And one night there is a wounded man crying out in pain and despair in the dark. Three German volunteers go out to bring him in. If a Verey light goes up, they will draw a hail of bullets upon themselves. Before they lose their way or reach their man, he stops crying out. The reader is left to suppose he has succumbed.

In reading *L'Espoir* the reader is not to worry over the ultimate defeat of the republicans or about the true worth of their claims; he is not to worry about what he may have read of the divisions among the republican politicians, divisions which the novelist honestly refers to in passing and which Don Salvador de Madariaga, for example, has dwelt upon. The reader has to let himself be carried away by the strength of conviction, the fanaticism even, with which the protagonists in their losing struggle wage their sectional battles, see to the wounded, collect prisoners, and so on. For although it is impossible to underrate the fervor with which Malraux himself espoused the aim of the Spanish republicans, neither politics nor any political creed is at the center of the novel. As in

Les Conquérants and as in *La Condition humaine*, the prerequisite of the drama is not the validity of a political ideology but the power that such an ideology can exert over its adherents, rousing them to more intense living. In reality Malraux is no politician in the accepted sense. He is a social philosopher, a writer anxious to bring home to his readers the excitement of being faced with the infinite potentialities of actual life.

IV

After years of bitter fighting, General Franco, in the spring of 1939, proclaimed the defeat of the republicans and at last the civil war was brought to an end. On its heels came World War II. A French conscript, Malraux was called to the colors as a private in the tanks. He was wounded and taken prisoner. He has described how he found himself in the cathedral of Chartres, which the Germans had transformed into a casualty clearing-station for prisoners of war. He was moved into an open-air camp, from which he escaped. In due course he joined the French Resistance. A private in the French army before the armistice, in the Resistance he became a colonel and took the name of Berger. An Alsace-Lorraine brigade was raised and in Alsace he took command of it. Then he was in the southwest, took part in dynamiting some German works, and in 1944 received the surrender of a German regular unit. That summer he was again wounded and fell into German hands. The German army handed him over to the Gestapo. In Toulouse, with his arms handcuffed behind his back, he was about to be interrogated and presumably tortured when his captors discovered that headquarters in Paris had sent the wrong file, that of his younger brother, Roland. His interrogation was accordingly put off. A day or two later came the liberation. The prisoners whom the Germans were holding had but to walk out into freedom.

During the war Malraux had written another novel, *La Lutte avec l'ange* (Jacob's wrestle with the angel). He says that the Gestapo destroyed the manuscript except for the first part and that "one does not rewrite a novel." Accordingly he issued the first part in Switzerland, and then had a second edition in France, under the title *Les Noyers de l'Altenburg.*[7] It is more of a discussion piece than a conventional novel, reminiscent of Bernard Shaw's *Heartbreak House* or of his *Misalliance*. There is a magnificent account of a gas attack on the Russian front in World War I. The politics that comes into the narrative is entirely practical, exclusively Turkish and Arab. The narrative begins autobiographically with the author's own captivity at Chartres in 1940. The Turkish politics comes in as part of the life of the narrator's father. The narrator, I ought to say, bears Malraux's *nom de guerre* in the French Resistance—Berger. Much of *Les Noyers* is reproduced in his latest book, *Antimé-*

moires (1967). (Three other volumes of *Antimémoires* will, it is announced, be published after the author's death.)

The Turkish and Arab politics of *Les Noyers* is not included in the portions of the novel reproduced in *Antimémoires*. Nevertheless, the politics is referred to in some of the books that have been written about Malraux and his works. *Les Noyers* is out of print and copies are hard to come by.

The narrator's father, Vincent Berger, is an Alsatian and therefore in 1910 is officially a German. At about that date he becomes involved with the Young Turks, led by Enver Pasha, who later commanded the Turkish armed forces against the Allies in World War I. One thing Berger realizes is that Pan-Islamism cannot serve Germany, for if Germany were an ally of the Muslims, they could hardly pretend that they were waging a holy war under the caliph. As for Germany, at the time Berger expects socialism to come out on top there. Owing to an indiscretion on his part, he loses credit with the Germans but retains Enver's confidence and friendship. When Enver takes command in Tripoli in the war against the Italians in 1911, Berger goes there also. The war ended, of course, in the defeat of the Turks.

Next Berger has plans for getting into touch with the Muslims of Central Asia. He believes that Turanians will side in a kind of holy war. He goes to Afghanistan and learns that no Turanian race, tribe, or nation exists. He is badly disappointed. He has wanted to establish a direct tie with the emirs of Bukhara and the Kurds of Russian Turkestan. The mission which has brought him to Kabul is a fiasco. He loses faith. He is stricken with fever. Enver and he meet a last time. Enver resents the failure of the mission. Their association ends, and Vincent Berger returns to his home in Alsace. Soon afterward he kills himself.

All this is unquestionably political, but it hardly fits in with the political elements so pronounced in earlier novels. At most it may be held to prefigure in some way the revolt of Asia against European interference and claims to superiority. As we have seen, Malraux has shown himself to be rather in sympathy with this revolt, at least for the sake of its quickening effect on the poor and disinherited.

V

Since the appearance of *Les Noyers de l'Altenburg*, Malraux has brought out no further fiction as such. But in *Antimémoires* three of the five sections into which it is divided bear the titles of previous novels—"Les Noyers de l'Altenburg," "La Voie royale," and "La Condition humaine." I have said that the section called "Les Noyers" is a reprint of portions of the novel or a fraction of the novel of that name. The other two sections contain original matter. The one entitled "La Condition humaine" contains nothing previously printed. It begins by recalling the author's visit to Hong Kong in 1926 in quest of type with which the newspaper he then edited at Saigon, *L'Indochine*, might go on being set at a moment when the French colonial authorities had succeeded in preventing any printer in the capital of Cochin China from producing it. He implies that they feared an exposure of what he calls *les spoliations de Baclieu*. Bac-lieu is a sea town in Cochin China, southwest of Saigon. What the *spoliations* were I do not know.[8] *Antimémoires* then passes to an account of the Long March of the Chinese communists. Only 20,000, he says, survived it. In January 1929 Nanking had 100,000 troops and Mao only 40,000. Yet in two months the national army had been routed. Malraux describes his recent visit to the Museum of the Revolution in Canton, and next he reports his successive audiences with, first, Chou En-lai and then with Mao Tse-tung and the President of the People's Republic, Liu Shao-chi, who were together to receive him. To the president he brought a letter from General de Gaulle. Although he notes that for Marshal Chen-yi, Minister of Foreign Affairs, who received him before any of the others, the United States is not the country that twice in this century rescued the liberty of Europeans but the country that backs Chiang Kai-shek, the minister showed, he says, a confidence and knowledge of the facts such as evidently animated the Chinese leaders concerning their vast country. And not only the leaders, by all accounts, but also and especially the common people. When Malraux attended a performance of the play *The East Is Red*, in a theater with five thousand seats, he shared the enthusiasm which the crude propaganda evoked. It evoked that enthusiasm because, crude as it was, it accurately mirrored the hopes which were inspiring groups and teams of the Chinese masses. As he is at pains to insist—in the novel *La Condition humaine* itself—the Chinese are not individualists in the way Europeans are. They not only live and act collectively, they also think collectively, and this is partly why communism suits them as a political program; why they respond to a policy of renovation, of ousting grasping landlords and moneylenders, of industrializing the economy, of modernizing agriculture. Yet, unavoidably, the chief Orientals in *La Condition humaine* are highly individual.

VI

In a moment I shall reach that section in *Antimémoires* called "La Voie royale," remembering that so far I have said nothing of the novel from which the section heading is taken. First let me turn to the section in *Antimémoires* entitled "La Tentation de l'Occident," from the name of the book which in 1926 proved a forerunner of the novels, the book in which, as I have said, western and eastern cultures are contrasted and compared by means of an exchange of letters distantly reminiscent of Montesquieu's *Lettres persanes*. In this section the contrast is resumed. After describing a visit in 1965 to Benares, while accomplishing the mission to the East upon which he was sent by General de Gaulle, Malraux carries the reader back to himself inside a tank at the French front in 1940. The East and the West sure enough! Next he is reporting meetings and conversations with Pandit Jawaharlal Nehru that took place during the same visit to the East. He had met Nehru earlier more than once, the first time in Paris in 1935, as Nehru recalls in his autobiography. Malraux on that occasion asked him, he says, to explain how Hinduism had succeeded in expelling Buddhism from India. The matter was too complex for an oral reply. The values most prized in the West, Malraux now told him, were happiness and individual freedom. He points out to the reader that he was not forgetting the photographs he had seen taken during the exchange of populations, when Pakistan and India were newly formed and Hindus and Muslims were being sorted—photographs of the piles of corpses on baggage trolleys, of pregnant women being carried on the backs of men, of little children in the arms of older children, of mattresses being borne on the head, of camps overtaken by flood, of a cholera hospital heaped high with dead, of untouchables warding off the vultures as they sheared human corpses of their rags. And yet India is building atomic reactors, as in this conversation both Nehru and Malraux himself recognized.

While he was in prison, Nehru had dreamed of what he would do for India if he ever had the power. But most of that, he confided, he had not been able to carry out. He was, Malraux says, a most agreeable conversationalist, a charming host, and, as it seemed to his interlocutor, he was living up to the picture he must have had in his head of an English gentleman. Thorny topics like Kashmir were not alluded to.

By comparison Mao Tse-tung was to keep his distance.

To understand Malraux's after-war feelings about politics, we do well to go to his account in *Antimémoires* of his first meeting with General de Gaulle. One of Malraux's acquaintances called one evening to tell him that the general wished to know if he was willing to help him. He was given an appointment at the Ministry of War in Paris. This was their first meeting.[9] The general asked him to sum up his past. He said he had thrown himself into the struggle to obtain social justice, or rather—realizing no doubt the ambiguity of the phrase—to secure that every person should have his opportunity. He now regarded the Soviet Union as all-too-plainly imperialistically minded. "In the domain of history the outstanding capital fact of the last twenty years is, in my view, the primacy of the nation. Different from nationalism. The nation as particular, not as superior." He was in Russia, he went on, at the time the "Internationale" became the equivalent of a Russian national anthem, and it was simultaneously that *Pravda* began referring to "our Soviet fatherland." The claim to fair treatment, the claim to social justice, was perhaps due to the weakening of the organized religions. "Politics means the creation, and then the action, of a state. Without a state, policy is in the future tense and becomes more or less an ethics." Literature was not enough; it was too diffuse. He believed, he said further, that the parliamentary game was played out.

"What struck you on coming back to Paris?" the general asked.

"The falsehoods," he replied.

However, General de Gaulle never invited him to cooperate overtly on policy. The ministerial posts that Malraux has held have not involved his political convictions, except indirectly. As minister, it is in cultural affairs that he had the opportunity of fulfilling his bent. He organized official exhibitions of paintings and sculptures both at home and abroad. He transformed the look of French cities by having the facades of public buildings cleaned. He ensured that in the towns of the French provinces both drama and musical entertainment were available. He had festival halls built for that express purpose.

The task cannot have made him feel he was being sidetracked. For—to stress the point again—what he feels deeply about is not this or that political ideology in itself; it is the effect upon men of holding a political faith that stirs them, whether they hold it as individuals or as teams.

I have still, it will be remembered, one of his novels to deal with. It is *La Voie royale* (*The Royal Way*), published in 1930, a novel unfolding a story that certainly depends on politics—on the fact that at the time, the northern part of Laos was unsubdued and the tribesmen hostile to the French—and yet a story of the lives of two private persons, Perken and Grabot—Perken especially, the man who prizes his life and yet boldly risks it. Like Malraux himself a decade earlier, Perken penetrates into the jungle and comes across ancient sculptures lying alongside the royal way. Let a man be blinded and castrated and put to turning a mill by means of pushing a wooden bar round and round in an eternal circle and he will still cling to life. Malraux is arguing that the instinct of self-preservation will make a man put up with conditions such that if in advance he could picture them he would gladly die to avoid them. Herbert Spencer is only one European philosopher to have asserted that most men would not renounce life because their conditions grew worse.

La Voie royale, as I say, contains no direct politics. It is rather the call to live one's life as intensely as one can, realizing the marvel it is to be alive. In *Antimémoires* Malraux discloses that Perken was modeled on a man called Mayrena. He was king of a tribe called the Sedangs. In the section of *Antimémoires* entitled "La Voie royale" we learn quite a bit about him. The first page of the section is headed "Singapore." The author states that in that city he was put up at the French consulate general and that an early visitor was "Baron de Clappique." The introduction of such a figure as real is a mild literary hoax, for there never was a Clappique. He is an important character in *La Condition humaine*. That novel opens abruptly by showing Chen standing in the bedroom of a Shanghai hotel. On the bed is a man Chen has murdered while the man slept. Chen is getting hold of certain unspecified documents. It is for these the murder was committed. Chen is a fanatic. He feels he has lived with a purpose and that his life gains significance when he throws himself under a motorcar with a bomb in his hand. The bomb blows both him and the car to pieces. He has fancied Chiang Kai-shek would be in the car, but it carries no passenger. Chen is the adopted son of the Frenchman Gisors, who also has by a Japanese mother a true son called Kyoshi, or Kyo. The latter, too, feels that he gives his life purpose and meaning by sacrificing it for communism. In imagination men often have richer and more vivid experiences than they have in actual life. König, Chiang Kai-shek's chief of police in Shanghai, gives Kyo a chance to change sides. Kyo scorns the idea. It is Clappique who, in behalf of his father, tries to intercede for him. Chiang's police round up a number of the agitators. Kyo is able to avoid execution by killing himself with cyanide. But in such desperate moments some men, we are shown, are capable of immense generosity. Katow gives his cyanide to two fellow prisoners, and he is left to his fate, which, he fears, is to be thrown alive into a blazing furnace. König warns Clappique to make himself scarce. He gambles away his passage money and is reduced to being a stowaway.

In *Antimémoires* the imaginary Clappique gives Malraux details of a film scenario he says he has composed about Mayrena. It is called *The Reign of the Evil One*. Malraux writes that he was led to imagine Perken and Perken's torture and mutilation thanks to what he learned about Mayrena, and Mayrena's idea of himself, and about his terrible struggle with death. Here, as elsewhere, the intimation is that a man intensifies his life by risking death but that nevertheless each of us has only one life to live.[10]

I said to begin with that Malraux has organized, edited, and partly written a remarkable and now widely known series of art books. They are books filled with reproductions of works of fine art. They have been a notable publishing success. They constitute one more indication that the reason Malraux has been preoccupied with political creeds and with actual political struggles is that the best political regime in his view is one that allows the widest opportunity to as many human beings as possible for each to make something of his one life and its infinite potentialities. Logically, of course, those he labels fascists can find in their cause as much as those he calls communists or those he calls patriots can find in theirs. Ultimately what particular cause is embraced cannot in this respect matter. But he invariably writes with the bowels of compassion. He writes in favor of the emancipation of the oppressed and the release of those under an invader's heel.

VII

When in 1944 the Gestapo asked Malraux to state his religion, he replied "Catholic." We have all been christened, he once said in conversation. It is, to his mind, a mere sign of normality, like going to school. At one place in *L'Espoir* Manuel sits at the organ in a church, notwithstanding that the republicans made war on the church, and plays from memory Palestrina's *Kyrie*. The church is full of wreckage, but the voice of the next world takes possession of it. Malraux is not against religion. He merely points out that the organized religions, and in particular the Christian religion, no longer matter nationally anywhere. Today everybody is theoretically master of his fate. He can always shape it to a greater or lesser extent, but normally he cannot perpetuate it. No man can elude his mortality. No man? In the art books Malraux invites the world to recognize the special situation of the artist, a situation shared to an extent, he says (and this is his novelty), by the spectator.

In order to designate the new universal accessibility of works of art, thanks to the wonderful progress made in reproduction processes, so that we may every one of us view works drawn from the four corners of the earth, he coined a phrase which he made into the title of the first of the three volumes which he produced under the embracing title of *La Psychologie de l'art*. The phrase is *Le Musée imaginaire*. For the English translation Stuart Gilbert substituted for the phrase another: *The Museum Without Walls*. Of the other volumes the French titles are *La Création artistique* and *La Monnaie de l'absolu*. The aim of this profusely illustrated work in three volumes is to bear into the individual home some notion of the rich and varied heritage of the plastic arts. The works reproduced are not confined to the West; the wide world has been held to tribute.

Malraux points out that the public is no longer bound to visit museums in order to be acquainted with art. Their contents, and also the treasures of private owners, can now be viewed in admirable reproduction in the peace and quiet of the home. Successful art is worth studying for its own sake. But that is not why Malraux welcomes the popularization of art. If we examine a single specimen of successful art, we shall see as much as we may see by examining a great number. But by examining a great number we grasp what, no matter their variety of origin, they all have in common. The artist in the act of making succeeds in transcending the all-too-mortal flesh; he steps out of time and triumphs over the limitation of his days.

Malraux's views here have met with vigorous and substantial disagreement. Apart from philosophers such as Étienne Gilson, who contend that no reproduction can be equivalent to the work itself, there is Georges Duthuit, who in his *Le Musée inimaginable*,[11] opposes the already existing thrall of the museum. The museum, he says, is not made more beneficial in being transformed from a warehouse into a temple. But regarding what Malraux is actually advancing, this seems to be beside the point. Of course, the museum may be deplored from several standpoints. Works of art are not produced *in vacuo*. Each is related to its time and to the circumstances of the artist's environment. Severed from its origins it must lose much of its significance. Or works of art may be regarded as ancillary to religion or to a philosophy of life. Once collected in a museum, works of art lose that relation, and, if it is really a live relation, they are made so much the poorer. But none of this affects Malraux's case.

While he invites examination of a great quantity of specimens of art, his claim for art in general refers to whatever is achieved in the fashioning of a single work as much as it is in hundreds. The perdurable is attained in a single artistic act. He holds further that, as mysteriously, the sense of permanence is communicated by the work to the spectator. Of course, the actual physical work is liable to perish, like all things material. But that cannot spoil the quality of the very act of making.

Finally, since the war Malraux has produced his book on Goya and on those works of Goya's that are gathered in the Prado. It is called *Saturne* (1950). The choice of painter was not fortuitous. Goya reacted with his whole being against the presence on Spanish soil of Napoleon's soldiery even as Malraux was unable to stomach the presence of Hitler's troops in France. So it is that the novels are invariably related to the experiences of an author who has himself lived to the full. Quite possibly there are readers persuaded in advance that the politics must be wrongheaded. After all, every question has two sides. But any such refusal to agree is irrelevant. What matters in the novels is the evidence of the generous human impulse which they contain. Let me insist again that the political element, although it figures so largely, is background. In front of that background are various human figures face to face with the task of each shaping his own destiny unsustained by religious faith and, as the price of his autonomy, constantly face to face with the gravity of death.

NOTES

1. Translated into English first as *Man's Fate* and then (1968) as *Man's Estate*.
2. Translated into English as *The Conquerors*.
3. Clara Malraux, *Le Bruit de nos pas* (Paris, 1966).
4. Walter C. Langlois, *André Malraux: The Indo-China Adventure* (London, 1966). In 1913 Clemenceau ran a daily newspaper in Paris called *L'Homme libre*. It was suppressed by the French government of the day. He was able at once to revive it. He simply changed its name to *L'Homme enchaîné*.
5. To translate *la condition humaine* as "the human condition" betrays an imperfect grasp of English idiom.
6. Pierre de Boisdeffre, *André Malraux* (Paris, 1960), p. 26.
7. The English translation is called *The Walnut Trees of the Altenburg*.
8. I have not seen Langlois mention them.
9. The story that the general came upon him in Alsace in 1944 or before and then repeated (unconsciously?) Napoleon's remark after meeting Goethe is apocryphal.
10. In an article in *Figaro littéraire* (Paris) for July 15–21, 1968, Henri Muller writes of Baron Clappique (called Baron *de* Clappique in *Antimémoires*) and contends that this fictional character was suggested to the novelist by a French Jew he knew moderately well in Paris—René Guetta, almost a dwarf, who died suddenly just after the war.
11. 3 vols., Paris, 1956.

ALBERT CAMUS
(1913-1960)

by Philip Thody

> And, to conclude, it is not the struggle which makes us into artists, but art which compels us to join in the struggle. By his very calling, the artist stands witness for liberty, and this is a justification for which he can be required to pay dearly. By his very calling, he is involved in the thickest depths of history, at the place where the very flesh of man struggles to find breath.[1]

IN THUS STATING, almost exactly halfway through his literary career, the primacy which he gave to the idea of art, Albert Camus was issuing more than a general declaration of independence. He was describing what his own experience had been as a writer who had begun with essentially individualist concerns but who was now playing an important part in the political and ideological contests of his time. Ten years earlier, in 1938, he had taken very little interest, as a writer, in the wider political issues of his day. Committed though he was, through his work on the left-wing newspaper *Alger-République*, to a policy which sought to correct the abuses of French policy in Algeria, and sympathetic though he was to the republican side in the Spanish Civil War, he nevertheless kept the books which he wrote between 1936 and 1942 remarkably free from politics. *L'Envers et l'endroit* (*Betwixt and Between*) and *Noces* (*Nuptials*), the two books of essays which he published in 1937 and 1939 respectively, dealt with the individual's relationship to the universal experiences of death, poverty, illness, and nature.

Nowhere did these essays suggest that either the happiness or the unhappiness which they describe could be influenced by political events, and nowhere did they do more than hint at the presence of racial conflict or social injustice in the sometimes blissfully pagan society they evoke. Camus certainly knew of the many imperfections that existed in his native Algeria and wrote about them at length in *Alger-Républicain*.[2] He does not, however, seem to have thought that they could inspire a work of art. *L'Etranger* (*The Stranger*) and *Le Mythe de Sisyphe* (*The Myth of Sisyphus*), published in occupied Paris in 1942 and 1943, were equally free from political or social considerations. Meursault, the hero of *The Stranger*, is as indifferent to politics as he is to love, ambition, or friendship, and the only political fact to be noted about *The Myth of Sisyphus* is the obligation imposed upon Gallimard, in 1943, to remove the essay on Franz Kafka on the grounds that it dealt with a non-Aryan author.[3] The similarity between Caligula, the hero of the play which Camus completed in its original version as early as 1938, and the mad emperors whose tyrannies ravaged Europe in the 1940's was apparently quite fortuitous, and there is no political significance to be attached to the fact that *Le Malentendu* (*Cross Purpose*), the gloomiest of Camus's plays, is set in Czechoslovakia.

It would nevertheless be wrong to use this virtual absence of political themes from Camus's early work to argue that nothing links the apparently detached nihilist who wrote *The Stranger* to the earnest moralist who uses *La Peste* (*The Plague*) and *L'Homme révolté* (*The Rebel*) to put forward some essentially political ideas. Admittedly, the Camus of *The Stranger* or *The Myth of Sisyphus* seems to be studiously avoiding anything that might be construed as moral or social comment. Nevertheless, he obviously prefers Meursault's almost aggressive honesty to the hypocrisy of the legalistic bourgeois society with which he comes into contact in the second part of the book, and he is clearly on Meursault's side when his hero rejects the consolations of religion on the grounds that he can appreciate only physical realities. Similarly, when he encourages the reader of *The Myth of Sisyphus* to prefer the truth he can grasp in human terms to the intoxicating rhetoric of religious philosophers, Camus is providing a semiphilosophical basis for the more ethical views expressed in his later work. Both *The Stranger* and *The Myth of Sisyphus*, like the lyrical essays which provide so appropriate a commentary on them, imply a view of man and of the human condition that Camus refined and developed but never fundamentally altered. Man alone is the measure of all things, and any intellectual system which requires physical realities or intellectual consistency to be sacrificed to some "higher good" must be rejected. Though there is no God and no natural pattern in the universe to compel morality, man is still expected to keep certain rules: Meursault refuses to lie about his feelings, is loyal to his friends, and is always kind to the old. Nature is a source of infinite delights as well as of mysterious dangers, but these delights are granted fully only to the man who can strip himself of the social husk and confront them as a naked, existing individual. The spirit of man, which stifles under the weight of abstract ideologies, is the only source of truth in the world, while his flesh, perpetually threatened by the natural phenomena of disease and old age, as well as by human violence and political tyrannies, is the only means which he has of establishing contact with the universe. If his mind is held in a straitjacket of religious or political doctrines, then no judgment of true or false can ever be made.

The moral implications of this basically humanist position were not, however, extended to cover other people until Camus argued, in an essay published in 1945 and entitled "La Remarque sur la révolte" ("A Remark on Revolt"), that each man had the duty to see that the integrity of his neighbor's personality was respected. By that time, his own political commitment was much deeper than it had been in the prewar days when he had used his opportunities as a journalist to ensure that René Hodent, a government agent wrongly dismissed for alleged dishonesty, was given a fair trial and restored to his original position.[4] From 1942 onward, he had been active in the Resistance movement, and his *Lettres à un ami allemand* (*Letters to a German Friend*), first published clandestinely and appearing in book form in 1944, had laid the foundation for the attitude which was to inspire his four most openly political works: *The Plague*, *L'Etat de siège* (*State of Siege*), *Les Justes* (*The Just Assassins*), and *The Rebel*. This attitude, sketched out in "A Remark on Revolt" and presented in its final intellectualized form in *The Rebel* was one that Camus always referred to as *"la révolte"* (revolt). His use of this word, however, does not mean that he recommended either the rejection of all law or a violent revolution against society. Violent though Caligula's rejection was of a world in which "Men die and are not happy,"[5] there is no doubt that, by the time Camus's play was staged in 1945, he was presenting the main character as an example to be avoided, not imitated. The right answer to the problems of injustice, absurdity, and unhappiness was not, Camus argued in his *Letters to a German Friend*, to increase their intensity by the cruelty of power politics. It was to bring into being those specifically human qualities of order and justice so lacking in the natural state of the universe.

For the Camus of "A Remark on Revolt," the original movement of revolt stemmed from an instinctive refusal to see another human being unjustly treated, and he quoted, as an example to illustrate his thesis, the "protest suicides" of certain prisoners in the slave labor camps of prerevolutionary Russia against the excessive ill-treatment of some of their fellows. Even in these depths, Camus maintained, a protest movement presupposed the existence of some limit which even the worst tyrant could be required to respect. Thus, in its very origins, the movement of revolt established as its principal aim the idea that there were limits valid for all men, and no political movement which claimed to be inspired by man's protest against the injustice of his condition could justifiably claim to ignore them. These limits were what revolt set out to defend, and in the Europe of the 1940's they were threatened by what Camus always called "totalitarianisms of the left and right": fascism and communism. And what was worse, the second of these totalitarian movements claimed to be inspired by revolt itself.

It is significant that, like almost all the authors of his generation, Camus devoted little time and energy to attacking fascism. Alone among his works, the play State of Siege contains an out-and-out denunciation of a right-wing dictatorship—the one established in Franco's Spain as a result of the civil war of 1936 to 1939—and whose admission to UNESCO in 1952 provoked Camus's immediate departure from that organization. So few French intellectuals were attracted to fascism, especially after 1940, that it scarcely seemed worthwhile attacking. Even in the 1930's, the political aims of fascism were so obviously bad that the problem was always one of strategy and tactics rather than of fundamental aims. How could fascism be best contained; was an alliance with Russia the best barrier against it; how could the democracies be persuaded to abandon the doctrines of appeasement and "nonintervention"? At that time, Camus was too involved with the immediate issues of Algerian politics, too interested in the theater and in his own writing, too unsure of the importance of international politics, to play an important part in such debates. He did, it is true, base his first play, Révolte dans les Asturies (Revolt in Asturia), on the repression of the Oviedo miners' rebellion in 1934, and he did give up his membership in the Algerian Communist party after Pierre Laval's visit to Moscow in 1935 had, in the name of a common front against fascism, led to a reduction in the support which French communists were prepared to give to the campaign on behalf of the Arabs. But it was not until the threat of fascism in Europe had virtually disappeared that he became seriously involved in politics and was led to confront what he and many others saw as the greatest threat to liberty in Europe: the expansion of communism and the attraction that it exercised not only over trade-union leaders and ordinary voters but also over writers and intellectuals.

It is this attraction which, perhaps more than anything else, explains why Camus should have given the books which he wrote in the 1940's so important a political content, with the implicit denunciation of totalitarian communism in The Plague and the more open attack on it in The Just Assassins and The Rebel. Unlike fascism, communism has always retained, even in its most tyrannical forms, a strong idealistic appeal: the creation of a just and egalitarian society, the use of science and industry in the service of mankind as a whole and not for the benefit of a privileged group, the end of the exploitation of man by man, the end of alienation, the humanization of human history. And, unlike the form which parliamentary socialism has taken in France, the French Communist party has always shown a steadfastness of purpose, a cult of discipline and efficiency, and an apparently genuine devotion to working-class interests, which explain why the French working class continues to vote Communist almost to a man in both local and national elections.

For the intellectuals, the appeal of communism was even stronger. It offered an apparently comprehensive philosophy, capable of giving fruitful and interesting results when applied to history, art, and literature, as well as to economic and social questions, and it was also remarkably successful in the 1930's and 1940's in attracting writers, artists, and intellectuals to its ranks. Louis Aragon, Paul Eluard, Pablo Picasso, Frédéric Joliot-Curie, Roger Vailland, and Claude Roy were card-carrying members; Sartre and the Temps Modernes group were already, in the late 1940's, beginning to move toward some kind of alliance with the communists; intellectuals were numerous among the fellow travelers who read *France-Observateur* or who wrote articles for it; and the Communist party had not only its own daily newspaper in *L'Humanité* but also the weekly *Les Lettres françaises* and the monthly *La Pensée*. Intellectually, communism was a force in the France of the 1940's that compared not unfavorably with what republicanism had been in the 1840's or radicalism in the 1890's. To many, it seemed the incarnation of the way that history was moving, and the philosophy of historical inevitability that Marx had at least partly borrowed from Georg Hegel lent strong support to this view. It was, for such thinkers, revolt triumphant.

For a variety of reasons, however, Camus was not attracted by communism. To him, it seemed to have taken over many of the worst features of fascism and to have kept its humanistic appeal as a mere facade. The cult of history, he argued, not only led to the sacrifice of those individuals who stood, or appeared to stand, in its way; it also encouraged dogmatism, a refusal to face facts, a readiness to neglect present realities in the name of a hypothetical future, and a tendency to declare that, because his victory showed him to have the approval of history, the victor was always right. Those intellectuals who were attracted to communism in the name of revolt, he maintained in *The Rebel*, were in fact betraying its origins. Because the end they were pursuing was an absolute, they had no time for limits or for moral rules. If an individual stood in the path of history, he was wrong and had to be removed. The creation of a classless society was an end so good as to justify the use of all means, and there were no limits to what could be done to bring it about.

Anyone daring to suggest that this end might not be obtainable or that the means used in its pursuit were morally unjustified or tactically incorrect was immediately denounced as a traitor. In the form which it took in the 1940's, Camus argued in *The Rebel*, communism had taken over the worst features of the two national traditions inspiring it: From Germany it had adopted the idea of historical inevitability essential to Hegelianism and already used by the Nazis, and from Russia it had taken the nihilism and denial of all moral values already detectable in the socialism of the nineteenth century and denounced at the time by Dostoevski.

The Rebel, the longest book that Camus wrote and his major attempt at political philosophy, was an attempt to use these criticisms to discourage French people, and in particular French intellectuals, from joining or supporting the Communist party. Whether or not it succeeded, in the sense that Sartre is said to have succeeded in at least one aspect of his political writing by having "saved a number of Lucien Fleuriers from letting their mustaches grow,"[6] is not easy to decide. Too many other, more specifically political events, such as the repression of the Hungarian revolt in 1956, helped to reduce the attraction of communism in the 1950's for us to be able to attribute a particular influence to any one book. It is not, from an artistic or intellectual point of view, one of Camus's most successful works and suffers particularly from two faults that almost all the critics noticed as soon as it was published in 1951: a tendency to overexaggerate the role played by ideas in influencing political action, and a paucity of practical suggestions. The first of these is less serious than the second, for Camus was, after all, concerned with what had happened now that at least a part of the Platonic tradition had come true and the philosophers were kings. The fact, however, that he can suggest as an alternative to communism only a vague admiration for the achievements of the Scandinavian democracies or a return to the anarcho-syndicalist tradition is almost an acknowledgment that, in 1951, only the Communist party did represent the genuine aspirations of the French working class.

By 1951, the syndicalist idea of craft trade unions was represented only by a very small minority of the French working class, and Sartre's criticism of the positive recommendations of *The Rebel* as largely irrelevant to the problems of French society was justified. A similar charge was also leveled at *The Just Assassins*, the play that Camus had produced in 1949 and in which he puts forward one of the central arguments of *The Rebel*: that if the needs of revolt oblige a rebel to kill he should demonstrate the moral unacceptability of his act by committing suicide or allowing himself to be killed immediately afterward. This, in fact, is what the terrorist Kaliayev does in Camus's play, and the relevance of his behavior to the preoccupations which inspired Camus in almost all his political writing is brought out when, in *The Rebel*, his act of killing the Grand Duke Serge is described as being both "necessary and inexcusable."[7] For it is essentially with killing, and more particularly with killing for an idea, that Camus is concerned when he talks about politics.

This may, at first sight, seem to give his work a rather limited appeal within the Anglo-Saxon, and especially the English, political tradition. Philip Toynbee, reviewing the English translation of Volume II of Camus's *Carnets*, quoted Camus's remark "I am unsuited to politics since I am unable to wish for or accept my opponent's death" and commented: "Impossible not to think of Mr. Wilson and Mr. Heath *looking* daggers, no doubt, across the floor of the House, but surely never tempted to use them."[8] In the Europe of the 1940's, however, with the example of the Moscow state trials of the 1930's and of the trials and executions in eastern European countries since the ending of World War II very much in everybody's mind, it was more difficult to share Mr. Toynbee's detachment. Camus was living in a country whose first revolution had established a tradition of executing political opponents, and there was every reason to feel that the French Communist party would follow it. Moreover, Camus himself felt a particular disgust for the death penalty in general and for its political use in particular. This disgust, he explained in what is perhaps his most intensely committed social essay, "Réflexions sur la guillotine," had a very personal origin. All he knew of his father, who was killed at the first battle of the Marne before Camus was a year old, was that he once went to see a murderer guillotined and came back so revolted by the spectacle that he could do nothing but lie on his bed and vomit. Camus gave Meursault, the hero of *The Stranger*, exactly the same memory of his father, and for all its apparent lack of social awareness, this novel contains a powerful emotional attack against the death penalty. It is what Camus acknowledged as a personal obsession which inspired much of the journalism that he wrote in the 1940's— the articles "Ni victimes ni bourreaux" ("Neither Victims nor Executioners"), for example, published in *Combat* in November 1946[9]—and which occurs as a leitmotif in almost everything he wrote.

It is true that, compared to the Arthur Koestler of *Darkness at Noon*, to the Malraux of *La Condition humaine*, to the Orwell of *1984* or of the essays on Mahatma Gandhi and Burnham, or to the Sartre of *Les Mains sales* or *Les Séquestrés d'Altona*, Camus does tend, because of this obsession, to look at politics from a very narrow angle. He sees little but the problem of violence, and always in the highly generalized terms of a philosophy which, in his view, justifies killing in the name of historical inevitability. He offers nothing of Sartre's or Koestler's feeling for the complexity and unpredictability of history, little of Orwell's detailed analysis of how doctrines and attitudes change in response to different situations, none of Malraux's ability to dramatize the wide general sweep of the historical process and thus make it emotionally as well as intellectually comprehensible. But if he sees things narrowly, Camus also sees them sharply. The concern for the living individual already implicit in his early work, and essential to his view of the artist's calling, recurs in its most intense and moving form in those books and articles in which he is striving to protect men against the two worst things an ideology can do to them: kill them outright or deprive them of their individuality. It is this concern to protect the individual against both these dangers which inspires what is, from a political standpoint, his most complex and probably his most satisfying work: *The Plague.*

From the moment of its publication, in 1947, this novel was interpreted in political terms: as an allegory of the German occupation and French Resistance movement and as an interpretation of this movement presented by a man once involved in it, as a more general description of totalitarianism in action, and as a novel that recommended, though without leaving the plane of allegory, a certain form of political behavior. While it is on the first level that its transposition of the definite ambitions of the Nazi movement into the more impersonal activity of the plague is most open to criticism, it is nevertheless here that its immediate appeal to the 1947 reader was to be found. Objections can indeed be made to the assimilation of the Resistance movement to the fight of a small but united minority against an external oppressor. Insofar as there were Frenchmen prepared to collaborate with the Germans, it was a kind of civil war, and the rivalries between the various Resistance groups also emphasized this characteristic of the struggle. Unlike the volunteer who helped fight the plague in Oran by carrying stretchers or helping the doctors, the Resistance fighter knew that his attack against a German sentry meant not only the death of that particular man but also quite probably the execution of innocent hostages as well. And, unlike the fight against the inexplicable epidemic which invades Oran, the fight against the Germans in occupied France did give verifiable results. Nevertheless, as Camus pointed out in answer to these and similar objections when they were formulated by the critic Roland Barthes,[10] everyone in Europe did recognize the applicability of *The Plague* to the ordeal which they had just undergone, and the novel thus fulfills what Sartre himself considered in *What Is Literature?* as the first condition of any "committed" novel: It speaks to its readers about their own immediate or most recent experience.

It is, however, at its second and third levels that the novel maintains a more permanent relevance to the problems of society, and that Camus's success in merging his concerns as a political writer with his ambitions as an artist is most marked. Indeed, there is even a way in which a deeper reading of the novel provides a very convincing answer to the objections raised by Roland Barthes and other critics: It invites us to see both Germans and French, invaders and invaded, executioners and victims, as afflicted by the same malady, alienated and persecuted by the same tendency toward abstraction and depersonalization which characterizes the plague. In this respect, the novel offers an explanation of what might be called the Eichmann experience, if by that we mean the mixture of horror and pity which came over so many people who saw photographs of him in the dock. Here was a man guilty of murdering hundreds of thousands of people and whom one ought, in principle, to long to punish as the very embodiment of evil. Yet all one saw was a little man so obviously ordinary and mediocre that he could not be held personally responsible for so great a crime. He too, like the Jews he had sent to the gas chamber, was the victim of a virus; he too had been carried away by a terrible illness whose nature he did not understand. Now that the scourge which he had incarnated in Europe was defeated, there was no point in hating him or wanting to kill him, as a person, at all. The only thing that could be done was to fight against the illness which he personified: the spirit of intolerance, of abstraction, of totalitarianism. This is the kind of reply that Camus suggests in *The Plague*, and it is perhaps the greatest measure of his success as a political writer in this particular novel that considerations such as this should occur almost spontaneously as soon as his account of Hitler's tyranny is compared to the view which we have of it today.

The most immediate message of *The Plague*, however, in the political atmosphere of France in 1947, was concerned more with communism than with fascism. It is contained in the section of the novel generally referred to as Tarrou's confession, where the attack upon the death penalty is specifically related to political killings. Just as fascism had massacred Jews, seeing them only as representatives of a race and not as human beings, so communism uses the death penalty to eliminate all its opponents, describing as "objectively counterrevolutionary" even acts inspired by the best revolutionary motives. This is Camus's great objection to it, and it is put forward in this passage with great emotional force. There is, however, another criticism of totalitarianism which shows itself just as clearly in the prose used to describe the other events as in the particular section of Tarrou's confession. What characterizes the invasion of Oran by the plague is the gradual reduction of everything to the same level, the elimination of individual experiences and their replacement by a universal feeling of loneliness and separation. As the plague comes to power, verbs in the third person singular are replaced either by impersonal expressions or by verbs in the third person plural. Individuality disappears under the weight of abstraction, and it is the repetition of this word that emphasizes the link between the impersonality of the disease and the tendency to ignore individuals which characterizes totalitarianism. People who accept any all-embracing philosophy rapidly cease to see things as they really are, and in thus inviting his readers to identify the effects of totalitarianism with those of the plague, Camus is suggesting why communism, for all its apparent attractions to the progressive intellectual, is not an acceptable political doctrine: It ignores the essential, living human beings with whom it pretends to deal. Like the plague, it kills, and this similarity is underlined by Tarrou when he says: "It seems to me that history has borne me out; today there's a sort of competition who will kill the most. They're all mad crazy over murder and they couldn't stop killing men even if they wanted to."[11]

Camus does not, however, limit himself to suggesting why communism is unsatisfactory. In making the central character in the novel, Doctor Rieux, introduce an important distinction between his role of seeking to improve health and the priest's role of helping men attain salvation, he is implying that a similar difference exists in political matters. Salvation is an absolute, the equivalent to the solution of all economic and social problems through the creation of the classless society. Health, in contrast, is a relative thing, and the person who is prepared to introduce piecemeal social reforms in the body politic is like the doctor who seeks a remedy for a specific illness and not a fundamental change in the psychophysiological makeup of his patient. Fundamental to this implied comparison there is, of course, the totally un-Marxist assumption that western society is basically all right, and that its defects can best be remedied without the drastic surgery of total revolution. At least the elements of this idea can be found in Camus's early career, when he was able to use the legal machinery of bourgeois society in order to remedy the specific abuses of René Hodent's imprisonment, and except for one or two of the articles which he published in the Resistance newspaper *Combat* in 1944, he never seems to have been a revolutionary in any meaningful sense of the word. What he is recommending in *The Plague* is a kind of reformist democracy, in which excessive measures are eschewed for the harm they do to others as well as for the degree of abstraction which they involve. But there is also, in the phrase about the worst of all vices being that of "the ignorance which thinks it knows everything and then assumes the right to kill,"[12] another reason that we should reject a political philosophy that authorizes such extreme measures as killing: The degree of certainty which they imply is just not available to man.

For all the sympathy which he had for certain aspects of the Christian ideal and for all the interest which Christian thinkers have shown in his ideas, it is nonetheless true to say that Camus was, in many aspects of his personality, one of nature's agnostics. The inspiration of his early work, with its insistence upon the finality of death and the overriding importance of the body, is thoroughly pagan, and it is significant that when he made a favorable mention of Voltaire in the second volume of his *Carnets*, it was to point out that he had "suspected almost everything."[13] He also said that *The Plague* was the most anti-Christian of his works,[14] and one of its many virtues is that it expresses an essentially agnostic attitude with the fervor usually found only in proselytizing books. Part of its attack on Christianity lies in the fact that Paneloux, in his first sermon, at any rate, is guilty of the same kind of abstract thinking which is used to justify totalitarianism. He sees the plague as a punishment sent directly by God to punish the inhabitants of Oran for their ungodliness, just as the Vichy authorities presented the defeat of France in 1940 as the direct consequence of the selfishness, materialism, and frivolity of the French nation.

But if he begins by neglecting the individuals who suffer from the vengeful and generalized intervention of God in history, he is soon brought face to face with what suffering means. Together with Rieux, he is present when a child dies in agony from the plague, and he can find no rational answer to the doctor's objection that the child, at least. was innocent. It is then that he preaches his second sermon and recommends an attitude of total submission to the will of God, "a humiliation to which the person humiliated gave full assent."[15] He is, in fact, forced to confront the dilemma which Camus himself presents, in *The Rebel* and elsewhere, as the major objection to Christianity: that if God is all-powerful and all-good, it is impossible to understand why he should allow the innocent to suffer through natural causes. Such considerations are, of course, only tangentially relevant to the political content of the novel. No philosopher of history, however providential his vision, has maintained that absolutely everything is for the best, and that the progress of the dialectic knoweth even the fall of the sparrow. What the introduction of these wider issues does illustrate, however, is the extent to which the Camus of *The Plague* avoids the major pitfalls of the political novel: relevance to only one period and to only one problem.

The Plague treats the problem of totalitarianism from a number of different angles, and it also recommends an attitude of tolerant agnosticism in political matters. But it is also a novel of the human condition, an attempt to show the problem of suffering in a metaphysical as well as in a political context. It may well be that, with the passage of time, its immediate applicability to the problems confronting France or Europe in the 1940's will become less immediately visible. It is already difficult for young readers to grasp the references to the German occupation and to the Resistance movement, and the gradual liberalization of even the

French Communist party will make Camus's attack on totalitarianism increasingly difficult to understand. Nevertheless, three aspects of *The Plague* will more than outweigh these possible disadvantages: the excellence of Camus's prose, especially in the imagery which serves to emphasize both the naturalness of the plague and the delights of the natural life; the criticism of all forms of abstract thought; and the plea for tolerance, which has a far wider applicability than the immediate circumstances for which Camus was writing.

On March 7, 1951, Camus noted in his *Carnets* that he had completed the first version of *The Rebel* and remarked that this book "brings to an end the first two cycles." In asking, immediately afterward, whether creation "can now be free,"[16] he gives the impression that he had been writing political works such as *The Plague* or *The Rebel* more out of a sense of duty than as a spontaneous expression of his personality or a desire to create works of art. His insistence, in his Nobel Prize speeches of 1957, that he was first and foremost an artist is also an indication that he never considered politics as one of his major concerns, and that he would, ideally, have liked to write books with as little political content as *Nuptials* or *The Myth of Sisyphus*. Nevertheless, as he recognized in the article which he wrote in 1948, art itself compelled him to join in the struggle, and this remained almost as true after the publication of *The Rebel* as it had been in the 1940's. Then he had clearly felt that the freedom essential to the artist's calling could be defended only if totalitarianism were defeated, and that it was his duty to take part in the struggle. Now totalitarianism seemed to him to present itself in France in a slightly different form, and one that needed a more indirect treatment than the open criticism of it in *The Rebel*. The three literary works which he wrote in the 1950's and which do have a political content—the novel *La Chute (The Fall)*, the short story "Le Renégat ou l'esprit confus" ("The Renegade"), and the adaptation of Dostoevski's *The Possessed*—are much less obviously political in inspiration than *State of Siege, The Rebel,* or even *The Plague*. They are also more directly satirical of the French intellectual and artistic establishment than any of his earlier works, and the moral fervor of *The Rebel* or *The Plague* is replaced by a shriller, more virulent tone which does not always add to their literary value. The origin for this different tone undoubtedly lies as much in the controversies which followed the publication of *The Rebel* as in Camus's own intense personal reaction to the conflict which broke out in his native Algeria in 1954.

Camus had already, before 1951, engaged in a number of public arguments in the press. In 1944, for example, he had defended the policy of punishing collaborators with the Vichy regime against the objections formulated by François Mauriac and in 1945 had protested in *Combat* against the charge that his work, like that of Sartre and Malraux, was excessively pessimistic. In 1948, he conducted a lengthy argument in the pages of the review *Caliban* with the left-wing journalist Emmanuel d'Astier de la Vigerie, and in December of the same year he wrote a public letter justifying his decision to place the action of *State of Siege* in Spain.[17] However, it was not until 1951 that he was involved in a really major intellectual controversy and experienced the full intensity of the intellectual climate which he once compared to that of the Brazilian rivers where the fish can strip a man of his flesh in seconds.[18] After the publication of *The Rebel*, he had to defend himself against two main charges: those advanced by André Breton and the other representatives of the surrealist movement, who maintained that he had totally misinterpreted the revolt of writers such as Arthur Rimbaud and Lautréamont; and those put forward by Sartre and the Temps Modernes group, who contended that his book was so critical of revolutionary movements as virtually to preclude any attempt to change the status quo. Both accusations seemed to Camus to be based on a deliberate misreading of his book, and the articles by Sartre and Francis Jeanson caused him particular annoyance by their presuppositions that all bourgeois writers were so caught up in the general wickedness of bourgeois society as to have forfeited any right to criticize the revolutionary movements of the left. It is this idea that recurs in a slightly exaggerated form in *The Fall* and which gives a political flavor to the atmosphere of that novel.

Like *The Stranger*, *The Fall* is told in the first person, but its central character, Jean-Baptiste Clamence, has none of the innocence and simplicity of Meursault. He is a sometime Parisian lawyer who hangs around the bars of Amsterdam and gets into conversation with visiting Frenchmen. Intrigued by his facile speech and rather peculiar manner, they listen to his life story and discover how he fell from an illusory state of moral grace to a recognition of his own fundamental wickedness. He had thought, when devoting his talent to defending widows and orphans, that he was inspired by noble sentiments; in fact, as he now realizes, he was seeking merely to flatter his vanity and feed his sense of superiority. By telling his listeners how wicked he is, Jean-Baptiste gradually manages to convince them that they are just the same, that "we are all in the soup together."[19] However, he still retains his superiority. By injecting his own feeling of guilt into his listener, he deprives the latter of both his innocence and his freedom. For, he argues, this listener will fall into such anguish that he will be prepared to accept the rigorous discipline of any orthodoxy which offers him a way out of his guilt. Jean-Baptiste describes himself as "an enlightened advocate of slavery," and it is his aim to persuade all men that they are too ridden with guilt ever to deserve either happiness or freedom.

Thus reduced to its bare bones, the plot of The Fall sounds a little far-fetched. It depends, perhaps more than any other work by Camus, on the subtlety of his technique of narration and on the many deliberate ambiguities which make it what Sartre—who almost certainly did not agree with its political implications—called the finest as well as the least under-stood of his books.[20] Its political meaning is linked to a particular interpretation of why bourgeois intellectuals are attracted by the absolute discipline of the Communist party which seems to have occurred to Camus during the controversies over The Rebel. They feel guilty at the privileges and freedom which they enjoy in a society where so many others are neither rich nor free, and they lack the strength of character to adopt a reasonable attitude toward their guilt. Acceptance of communism enables them to see this guilt as a necessary phenomenon and also offers them a way of escaping from it through the highly disciplined revolution-ary struggle for a classless society. This meaning is not, however, some-thing that leaps immediately to the eye, and it has never been as widely discussed as the relevance of The Plague to the German occupation. Indeed, it could even be argued that it is so well disguised by the other aspects of the novel, and especially by the light which The Fall casts upon Camus's attitude to Christianity, that a political interpretation is almost a classic example of the intentionalist fallacy.

Because Camus remarked in an interview in 1954 that "many modern writers, and among them the atheist existentialists, have denied the exist-ence of God; but they have kept the notion of original sin. People have insisted too much on the innocence of creation; now they want to crush us with the feeling of our own guilt,"[21] it seems legitimate to interpret The Fall in the light of this general accusation. This seems even more justified when it is remembered that Camus placed a quotation from Mikhail Lermontov, to the effect that his hero was "an aggregate of the vices of our whole generation in their fullest expression," at the front of the English translation of this book and thus directly invited at least his Anglo-Saxon if not his French readers to see Jean-Baptiste Clamence as more than just another fictional character.

For all these statements, however, the political meaning of The Fall is clear only to the reader who has been told that it is there, and the book is much less obviously a political novel than The Plague. There is no point in being committed unless people can see what you are being committed about, and the same criticism of relative obscurity can also be leveled at the short story "The Renegade," whose political implications are apparent only to someone with a fair understanding of The Rebel. In this story, a priest makes a complete *volte-face* from a missionary fervor to convert the heathen to an equally fervent readiness to serve their cause. He thus illustrates, within the context of *The Rebel*, another of the reasons which Camus gives for the popularity of totalitarianism: the readiness with which violent opponents of all systems of political organizations—the French surrealists, for example—can pass to an equally absolute adoration of party discipline. *The Fall* and "The Renegade" are thus concerned, like *The Plague*, with totalitarianism, and both recommend, as did Camus's earlier novel, the same attitude of moderation: We must guard against exaggerating either our sinfulness or our initial revolt, lest we become infected with the intolerance and lust for power which characterize the bacillus of the plague.

All three works express the same agnostic humanism, but the second two are particularly open to the criticism that the diagnosis which they offer involves a considerable oversimplification of the issues involved. For example, it is a truism that bourgeois intellectuals feel guilty about the society in which they live, and that many of them have, in the past, been attracted to communism because it helped them to feel less guilty. Similarly, it is true that the kind of personality which is attracted by extremes will be tempted both by total revolt and by total submission to a disciplined plan for revolution. George Orwell made a similar point when he commented, in his essay "Lear, Tolstoy and the Fool," on the tendency toward intellectual intolerance that shows itself in anarchists and other extreme "libertarian" thinkers. Where *The Fall* and "The Renegade" are vulnerable to criticism is in the absence of any suggestion that the political attitudes which Camus is denouncing have any origin other than the desire to rule or the longing for extremes. It is surely fair comment to say that communism is not only a means of assuaging guilt or establishing dictatorships, and that both its defects and its popularity are due to technical, political, or economic factors. The great criticism which political scientists have always leveled against literary men who dabble in politics is that they are inclined to accept facile rather than complex explanations. Literary men, in turn, have justified this tendency by pointing out that works of art are already sufficiently complex, and that there is no room in them for the minutiae of technical political analysis. Valid though this reply may be in some cases, it is acceptable only insofar as the work does not deliberately exclude these more technical factors. There is more obviously room for them in *The Plague* than in *The Fall*, and more in "The Renegade" than in his stage adaptation of Dostoevski's *The Possessed*, which Camus himself directed in 1959.

As the quotation from Luke 8:32–36 which he places at the beginning of his novel implies, Dostoevski saw the revolutionaries of his day as being, quite literally, possessed of the devil. The chapters in *The Rebel*

which deal with the Russian socialists of the nineteenth century all seem
to assume that Dostoevski's analysis of their mentality in *The Possessed*
was wholly valid, and this assumption recurs in the various texts which
Camus wrote about Dostoevski when he adapted this novel to the stage.
Thus when he said that *The Possessed* was "a prophetic book . . . because
it foreshadows our nihilism" and that Dostoevski, while being the man
who had "given the most profound expression to our historical destiny,"
also refused to accept "a socialism that was not religious in the widest
sense of the word,"[22] he even seems to be sympathetic toward
Dostoevski's rather peculiar theocratic solution to Russia's problems, as
well as to his diagnosis of what was wrong with the socialism of his day.
What is so curious about the tendency to dismiss all modern socialists as
nihilists, which shows itself in these remarks on Dostoevski, is that
Camus himself seems to have fallen victim to the vice which he
denounced so convincingly in *The Plague*. He, too, is guilty of abstraction, in that he fails to appreciate the complexity of human beings and
political movements, apparently refusing to see that socialism contains
anything but the desire to deify man, which he had analyzed in *The
Rebel*.

However limited *The Fall*, "The Renegade," and the stage adaptation of
The Possessed may seem as political analysis, they are all nevertheless
extremely successful as works of art. *The Possessed*, especially, achieves a
tour de force of making the extremely complex plot of Dostoevski's novel
immediately comprehensible, while both *The Fall* and "The Renegade"
are brilliant examples of the use of style to create both character and what
D. H. Lawrence called "the spirit of place." It could also be argued that
their political content, for all its oversimplification, is now wholly irrelevant to their aesthetic value. Émile Zola thought that he was writing, in
the Rougon-Macquart series, a thoroughly scientific novel, when in fact he
was producing a modern epic. Yet the theories of Claude Bernard which
he took as his starting point do contribute to his final achievement in the
sense that they provided him with a basic intellectual framework within
whch his essentially poetic vision could operate. Reluctant though Camus
was, as the remarks which he made in 1948 indicate, to recognize that
the political struggle could inspire an artist, it does nevertheless seem
that he was driven on, especially in *The Fall* and *The Possessed*, as much
by the desire to illustrate a political idea as by more exclusively aesthetic
motives.

In the 1950's, as in the 1940's, Camus also took part in politics through
journalism. In 1955, for example, he wrote articles for the weekly periodical *L'Express* in support of the election campaign of Pierre Mendès-
France, and he made constant attempts, between 1954 and the year of his
death, to mitigate the horrors of the Algerian war by appealing to both

sides to respect the civilian population. Unlike Sartre, however, and unlike many of the intellectuals with whom he had been associated during his more left-wing days on *Combat,* he did not side with the Arab F.L.N. against the European Algerians. Neither did he join in the many campaigns of protest against the use of torture by French troops in Algeria, and when challenged on this abstention during a press conference at Stockholm in 1957, he replied that he loved justice but that he also loved his mother. Catherine Camus was, in fact, living in her native Algeria at the time (she died in 1960, shortly after her son), and it was impossible for him not to be more intensely divided in his loyalties than any other French writer. He was, of course, widely criticized for his attitude, and its essentially apolitical nature came out in 1958 when he was one of the few French writers not to take sides either for or against the return to power of General de Gaulle. What is perhaps more significant is that his concern over the Algerian war, unlike his opposition to communism in the 1940's, did not show itself in any literary or philosophical work. The articles "Neither Victims nor Executioners" are directly related, with their attack on totalitarianism and the death penalty, to *The Plague.* No such link attaches the Algerian Reports in *Actuelles III* to *The Fall* or to the stage adaptations either of Dostoevski's *The Possessed* or of Faulkner's *Requiem for a Nun,* and in this respect they mark a return to the separation between politics and literature which characterized his early work.

Almost everything which Camus says about politics in the two volumes of his *Carnets* that have so far been published indicates that he took part in politics only reluctantly and always tried to give priority to artistic considerations. Had he been born in a different age, when political questions presented themselves with less urgency, there is little doubt that he would have remained a more detached artist, and that his work would have reflected more of his declared ambition to write prose as Mozart composed music. In a way, this would have been a pity. The great appeal which Camus made in the 1940's was as a moralist, and his intense concern for ethical questions fitted in remarkably well with the political mood of the time. The excellence of *The Plague* lies precisely in the way that this encounter between his conscience and the political atmosphere of postwar France gives rise to considerations that are applicable to the permanent problems of political action and not solely to one period. Without the impact that politics made on Camus in the 1940's, we should be poorer by a masterpiece; and without the political concerns that continued to inspire part of his work in the 1950's, we should lack the opportunity of seeing how some very good books can be written under the inspiration of some rather limited ideas.

NOTES

1. Albert Camus, *The Witness for Liberty*, December 1948.
2. Thus in June 1939 he wrote eleven articles describing the extreme poverty in Kabylia. A number of these articles were reprinted in book form in *Actuelles III*, in 1958.
3. See the Pléiade edition of Camus's *Essais* (Paris, 1965), p. 1415.
4. Details of the Hodent case are given in Emmett Parker, *Albert Camus: The Artist in the Arena* (Madison, Wisconsin, 1965).
5. See *Théâtre, récits, nouvelles*, Pléiade ed. (Paris, 1962), p. 16, and *"Caligula" and Three Other Plays* (New York, 1958), p. 8.
6. See Michel-Antoine Burnier, *Les Existentialistes et la politique* (Paris, 1966), p. 186. The reference is to Sartre's early short story "L'Enfance d'un chef," in which a young man adopts fascist ideas and lets his moustache grow to symbolize this supposed virility.
7. *L'Homme révolté, Essais*, p. 575.
8. *The Observer* (London), February 27, 1966.
9. These articles were reprinted in *Actuelles I* in 1950 and included in the Pléiade edition of the *Essais*. "Réflexions sur la guillotine" was published in the *Nouvelle Nouvelle Revue française*, June and July 1957, and in book form together with Arthur Koestler's "Reflections on Hanging" (Paris, 1957). Justin O'Brien's translation *Resistance, Rebellion and Death* (New York, 1961) contains the attack on capital punishment.
10. Roland Barthes's article, like Camus's reply, appeared in *Club* in 1955. Camus's reply is also printed in the Pléiade edition of *Théâtre, récits, nouvelles*.
11. *Théâtre, récits, nouvelles*, p. 1423.
12. *Ibid.*, p. 1324.
13. *Carnets II* (Paris, 1964), p. 319.
14. *Théâtre, récits, nouvelles*, p. 1978.
15. *Ibid.*, p. 1401.
16. *Carnets II*, p. 345.
17. See *Actuelles I, Essais*, pp. 391–396. His replies to Mauriac were published in *Combat*, October 20 and 25.
18. *Carnets II*, p. 321.
19. *Théâtre, récits, nouvelles*, p. 1545.
20. See Sartre's article on Camus's death in *France-Observateur*, January 7, 1960.
21. *La Gazette de Lausanne*, March 28, 1954.
22. *Théâtre, récits, nouvelles*, pp. 1877–1880.

ALEXANDER SOLZHENITSYN
(1918-   )

by Sergei Levitzky

SELDOM IS the Nobel Prize for literature awarded to a writer who fully deserves this honor. Neither Leo Tolstoy nor Anton Chekhov was awarded a Nobel Prize, and some decisions of the Nobel Committee have been dictated by nonliterary considerations.

There have been, of course, exceptions when the literary worth of a writer and the decisions of the literary judges coincide. As with Thomas Mann, Albert Camus, Eugene O'Neill, William Faulkner, and other laureates, such was the case of Boris Pasternak. Such is also the case of Alexander Solzhenitsyn, who was characterized by one Swedish critic four days before the awarding of the Nobel Prize as "a giant of world literature and a giant of moral courage."

The value of each great writer is measured by the degree and the originality of his artistic vision. The ethical element, with which this essay will deal in relation to Solzhenitsyn's literary works, is not clearly or equally present in all writers of caliber. In fact, it is quite possible for one to be a great writer and yet to lack an ethical pathos. Such is the case with the naturalistic writers—with Émile Zola, for example. Similarly, no particular ethical pathos is noticeable in the case of such a master of literary form as Vladimir Nabokov, who, with his too skillful "toying with the plot," knows how to make reality grotesque and the grotesque real. There are also writers who, because of their moral intuition, can visualize the ethical essence of their heroes—the most striking example being, of course, Leo Tolstoy.

In some western critical reviews of the literary work of Solzhenitsyn his affinity with Dostoevski has been stressed; he is, in fact, called a modern Dostoevski. As far as the theme of human suffering and tragedy is concerned, this observation is undoubtedly true. If we take literary methods into account, however, then Solzhenitsyn is closer to Tolstoy.

The basic fact is that Solzhenitsyn is a writer of his own vision and might. Too persistent analogies drawn between him and the Russian literary titans actually do disservice to Solzhenitsyn. His own originality is thus somewhat overshadowed by two supershadows, but if we compare—and compare we must in literary criticism—then, to be sure, he is closer to Tolstoy, primarily because Solzhenitsyn, like Tolstoy, belongs to the writers who are endowed with the moral intuition that borders on ethical clairvoyance. He can read the souls of his heroes as one reads an open book.

There are two dimensions of moral vision in art; these may be called clairvoyance and prophecy. Both these ethical dimensions penetrate into the moral and the spiritual essence of man, but their approach is different. Dostoevski, "the visionary of the spirit," penetrates into metaphysical and mystical depths. Tolstoy visualizes, behind the social masks of his heroes, their predominantly moral essence. (What expert on Tolstoy could deny that the sage of Yasnaia Poliana had an aversion to all forms of mysticism?)

Both the prophet and the moral clairvoyant perceive the Eternal in man, but the prophet, as the word itself indicates, is a seer of Eternity through the dimension of the future. The moral clairvoyant, on the other hand, sees the souls and minds of men in the dimension of the present. Of course, a prophet may be figuratively called a clairvoyant of the future, but it would be somewhat unnatural to call a clairvoyant a prophet of the present. Needless to say, each prophet is a clairvoyant to a certain degree, and each clairvoyant may also be a prophet. At the same time it must be stressed that one must not think in absolute categories except when one thinks about the Absolute—God.

While following in his own incomparable way the naturalistic traditions in the description of the way of life in the concentration camp in *One Day in the Life of Ivan Denisovich*, Solzhenitsyn also knows how to compel us to see that the soul of his unsophisticated hero lives not by bread alone. Apart from the tremendously vital stamina of Ivan Denisovich and his good-natured, peasant cunning, we feel in him a man of goodwill whose spirit is not filled with bitterness, despite the crying injustice of his punishment and despite, too, the inhuman conditions of life in the so-called corrective labor camp. On the contrary, his soul is radiated by his belief in humanity, by the ease with which he establishes human contacts.

How sympathetically Solzhenitsyn also depicts the other inmate, Alyosha. The latter overhears Ivan Denisovich's words before retiring to bed, "'So, God thanks, the day is over.'" In the subsequent text we read the following: "Alyosha heard Shukhov thank the Lord and turned to him. 'Look here, Ivan Denisovich, your soul wants to pray to God, so why do you not let it have its way?'" Furthermore, Ivan Denisovich says that he prayed for a speedy release from the camp. Whereupon Alyosha answers: "'The only things of this earth the Lord has ordered us to pray for is our daily bread. What do you want your freedom for? Rejoice that you are in prison. Here you can think of your soul.'" One would not necessarily conclude that Solzhenitsyn shares the religious convictions of Alyosha, but it is both obvious and revealing that he sympathizes with them.

The late Russian author and critic Korneil Chukovski, after having read *One Day in the Life of Ivan Denisovich*, called Solzhenitsyn a "literary miracle." One cannot know what he would have said had he read *The First Circle*, but Solzhenitsyn's best works really do convey the impression of being literary miracles, achieved through a rare combination of naturalness, deep insights, and incomparability of artistic talent—talent denied in a tone of aggressive hypocrisy by those in power in the Soviet Union. Indeed, the phenomenon of Solzhenitsyn is not only a literary miracle but also a spiritual miracle.

The ethical element appears in an especially dramatic way in two main novels by Solzhenitsyn, *Cancer Ward* and *The First Circle*. The ethical aspect of these novels can be considered under three headings: Solzhenitsyn's exposition of the negative ethical essence of some of his heroes, his skill in detecting the sparks of goodness even in the souls of his negative (though not hopelessly so) heroes, and his ethical views, expressed when the author speaks through his positive heroes or in the form of author's remarks.

With respect to the element of remorse, we can find it in the case of Rusanov, from *Cancer Ward*. Rusanov is a hardened Stalinist, although personally he is not cruel, and he even makes a good husband and father. In his youth he was a worker; later, joining the Red Army, he made a career of being a minor party-leader. Eventually he became the head of a questionnaire department in the secret police. Then, quite unexpectedly, he becomes a victim of cancer, and we find him in the novel in the "cancer ward." He gets a series of strong injections. His sleep becomes unquiet, and he often has bad dreams.

Quite involuntarily, he begins to see the victims of his former denunciations in these dreams. (He was a secret informer in the earlier days of his career.) For example, he informed on his former colleague, Mrs. Elchanskaia, who was arrested and whose little daughter was delivered to an orphanage. In his bad nights this woman persistently appears before him. She asks him, in a very quiet but firm tone, about the where-abouts of her daughter, requesting realistically detailed information.

"Rusanov was lying in bed and remembered that he even liked Elchanskaia. He had no evil intentions toward her. Why did he inform on her? He could not even remember." By these remarks Solzhenitsyn obviously wants to indicate that his negative hero had no remorse in the classical sense of the word, for it was, so to speak, suppressed into his subconscious and manifested indirectly in the persistent appearance of his victims in his bad dreams.

From the petty negative hero let us now proceed to the negative hero of gigantic caliber, the striking description of Stalin in the novel *The First Circle*. Thus, we turn from Stalinist to Stalin himself. In this novel Stalin, who suffers from insomnia, has the habit of receiving his closest subordinates after midnight. He has just received the head of N.K.V.D., Abakumov (the latter is also a real-life figure who was finally executed).

Stalin is personally interested in the so-called secret telephony, a tech-nical device that would enable him automatically to determine the iden-tities of telephone voices on the basis of their vocal peculiarities and into-nations. He needs this device in order to detect the secret "enemies of the people." He has plenty of other, no less important worries, however, and therefore he forgets to ask Abakumov about the progress of the "secret telephony" business.

Solzhenitsyn uses this opportunity to penetrate into the inner world of the aging dictator. In the chapter entitled "Old Age" we read the follow-ing:

> The master of half the world, dressed in the tunic of a gen-eralissimo, slowly ran his finger along the shelves, passing his enemies in review.
>
> And as he turned from the last shelf, he saw the telephone on his desk. Something which had been evading him all night slipped from his memory again like the tip of a snake's tail.
>
> He had wanted to ask Abakumov something. Had Gomulka been arrested?
>
> He had it. Shuffling in his boots, he made his way to the writ-ing desk, took the pen, and wrote on his calendar—"Secret telephony." . . .
>
> He staggered and sat down, not in his own armchair, but on a small chair next to the desk.
>
> The left side of his head seemed to be tightening at the temple and pulling in that direction. His chain of thoughts disintegrated. With an empty stare he circled the room, hardly seeing the walls.
>
> Growing old like a dog. An old age without friends. An old age without love. An old age without faith. An old age without desire.

He did not even need his beloved daughter any longer, and she was permitted to see him only on holidays.

The sensation of fading memory, of failing mind, of loneliness advancing on him like a paralysis, filled him with helpless terror.

Death has already made its nest in him, and he refused to believe it.

So, without a single word of the external condemnation of a tyrant, Solzhenitsyn makes us feel the inner nemesis of the mania of total power. This nemesis is the absolute solitude, aggravated by the inner foreboding of a close, inevitable end. Men who commit evil deeds but whose conscience is still alive usually feel remorse. No trace of this is to be found in Stalin, however, as presented through the magic prism of Solzhenitsyn's art. There is not a trace of the prick of conscience, because leaders like Hitler and Stalin are full of the evil will with which they identify themselves. They strangle their own conscience. Indeed, how could they feel any pricks of an already dead conscience?

It is claimed that the essence of *The First Circle* lies in the unmasking of the evils of Stalinism. This claim is, of course, true, but to see this as the central meaning of the novel would mean a gross politicizing of Solzhenitsyn's creativity. The very idea of *The First Circle* does indeed have an intrinsically political aspect, but Solzhenitsyn is primarily concerned with denouncing the spiritual evil of Stalinism: the lives mutilated by a regime of terror, the bleeding wounds of human souls—in short, the external triumph of evil. In a comparable way, incidentally, even though not on such a stratospheric level, another anti-Soviet Soviet writer, Valery Tarsis, while depicting the Stalin period and describing a hard-core Stalinist, made the following remark: "The very word 'soul' sounded to him as something anti-Soviet." All this, even though it is closely connected with politics, transcends its domain. In his *Doctor Zhivago* Pasternak wrote that the strength of the artistic portrayal of Raskolnikov's crime in Dostoevski's *Crime and Punishment* strikes us even more than the very crime of Raskolnikov. Something analogous can also be said about Solzhenitsyn's *The First Circle*.

After these generalizations we can turn briefly to the more specific aspects of this novel, and particularly, at this point, to the still unextinguished spark of goodness which exists in the soul of one of the major heroes, Volodin. He is a foreign-service diplomat, a typical career man, Soviet-style, a soft-spoken opportunist, and, as he sometimes privately admits, even an "Epicurean."

Yet something remains sacred for him: the memory of his deceased mother, who was in her youth a typical representative of prerevolutionary intelligentsia, with its impracticability and high ethical standards. Volodin learns that the hard-core Communists are planning an evil trick on the old professor of medicine, Dobroumov, who happened to be his mother's personal physician. Knowing that Professor Dobroumov has made an important medical discovery, as yet unpublished, the top K.G.B. agents want to provoke him to disclose this discovery to an old French colleague. (Dobroumov is to take part in a pending medical conference in Paris.)

Learning about this plot, Volodin decides to make an anonymous telephone call to Dobroumov in order to warn him about this perfidy, but to his dismay the old professor's pedantic and rather mean wife takes the receiver. She refuses to call her husband unless Volodin discloses his identity and tells her the exact reason for his call. This protracts the hectic conversation—a circumstance that eventually proves fatal, with disastrous consequences for Volodin. (At one point the telephone line is even broken.)

Of course, this telephone conversation is wire-tapped. The tape is then given to two experts in the privileged concentration camp—an electronics engineer and a linguist. They get a special emergency assignment to identify the anonymous telephone voice (the "secret telephony"). In this task they succeed, as seen near the end of the novel. Volodin is then arrested and thrown into prison.

Commenting on Volodin's decision to discard his fears temporarily and to take the risk of warning the old medical professor, Solzhenitsyn utters a memorable aphorism that crystallizes the main message of the novel and is expressed with classical brevity: "Yes, life is given to us only once. But then conscience, too, is given to us only once."

A few words are necessary about the ethical views of Solzhenitsyn as they are expressed in *Cancer Ward*, with reference to be made, in this connection, to only one of several important conversations between patients that involve the practical problems of ethics. At the end the novel's principal hero, Kostoglotov, the author's alter ego, is preparing for his release from the hospital. He exchanges remarks with another patient, Shulubin. A promising scientist in his youth, Shulubin was wise enough not to try to make any career during Stalin's famous purges in the 1930's, and he became an insignificant clerk. This decision probably saved him from being purged; besides, he knew how to keep his mouth shut. Being endowed with a keen and observant mind, however, he accumulated a lot of bitter thoughts, and trusting Kostoglotov, he discarded his usual restraint. In the conversation Shulubin at last gives free vent to his secret creed. He utters a long tirade and, among other things, says the following:

> "At the end of the last century Tolstoy decided to spread practical Christianity through society, but his ideals turned out to be impossible for his contemporaries to live with. His

preaching had no link with reality. I should say for Russia in particular, with our repentances, confessions, and revolts, our Dostoevski, Tolstoy, and Kropotkin—there's only one true Socialism, and that's ETHICAL SOCIALISM. That is something completely realistic."

Kostoglotov screwed up his eyes. "But this 'Ethical Socialism,' how should we envisage it? What should it be like?"

"It is not very difficult to imagine," said Shulubin. "We have to show the world a society in which all relationships, fundamental principles, and laws flow directly from ethics, and from them alone. Ethical demands should determine all considerations— how to bring up children, what to train them . . ., to what end the work of grownups should be directed. . . . For example, Vladimir Solovyov argues rather convincingly that even economy could and should be built on an ethical basis. . . . So, you see, that's what Ethical Socialism is. One should never direct people toward happiness, because happiness too is an idol of the marketplace. One should direct them toward mutual affection. A beast gnawing at its prey can be happy, too. But only human beings can feel affection for each other, and this is the highest achievement they can aspire to."

Let it be noted that Vladimir Solovyov, who died in 1900, was a most prominent Russian philosopher. He tried to reconcilè philosophy, art, and science on a religious and ethical basis. He aspired for an all-embracing synthesis that he called Pan-Unity. (Most students of Russian literature know Solovyov mainly as a mystic and a poet who glorified the Eternal Femininity and taught the doctrine of Holy Sophia, or God's wisdom. This aspect of his thought exerted a strong influence on great Russian poets of the twentieth century, particuarly on Alexander Blok and on Andrei Bely.) Speaking about Solovyov's "Pan-Ethicism," Shulubin does not name any specific work by him, but for all experts on Solovyov it should be clear that the book in question is *Justification of Goodness* (1896), in which Solovyov, while polemicizing against Tolstoy's doctrine of nonresistance, tries to show that morality must become the basis of all human endeavors, both practical and theoretical. Yet according to Solovyov, morality, while being a common denominator of all religions, grows from a religious soil and is nourished by religious inspiration. One cannot conclude from *Cancer Ward* that Solzhenitsyn really shares this view of Vladimir Solovyov, but by reading between the lines and by taking into account the manner in which Solzhenitsyn conveys Shulubin's ideas, the reader can feel the profound religiosity of the author, hidden and obvious at the same time.

On the basis of the quotations cited above and, more so, of the overall impression of Solzhenitsyn's creativity, there can be no doubt about the presence of a deep ethical pathos in the writer and that his moral intuition borders on ethical clairvoyance. In our time it is often the fashion to discredit moral values, and the very word "morality" is often placed in quotation marks. Against this negative background, it is to Solzhenitsyn's great merit that, by his literary works, in which he so boldly denounces an externally triumphant immorality, he has contributed greatly to the rehabilitation of ethics. There is a deep and urgent need for this rehabilitation today. Solzhenitsyn reminds his readers of that which makes men human: of their ethical essence, of the Eternal in man.

GÜNTER GRASS

(1927-   )

by Norris W. Yates

I

WHEN A WRITER has taken a definite political stand, a question that arises is, How, if at all, has his politics affected his art? In the case of Günter Grass, an even more pertinent question is, How has his active participation in politics—unprecedented among German writers since Walther von der Vogelweide rode through the dukedoms, urging support for Kaiser Friedrich II in his struggle to become Holy Roman Emperor—strengthened or weakened or otherwise altered his creative powers? As a step in answering this question, three propositions are offered here:

1. Nearly all of Grass's fiction is rich in political themes and implications, even when it seems least concerned with political matters. To a large extent this was true long before his direct involvement in politics as a citizen.

2. This involvement has been a logical and psychological culmination of an interest that began, not surprisingly, in 1945 during Grass's days as a prisoner of war and grew steadily until fiction, poetry, and drama no longer satisfied him as means of effective political expression.

3. Since he first developed this interest in politics, Grass's ideological orientation has not changed. He believes now, as he did in the late 1940's, in a modified parliamentary socialism with considerable freedom for capitalist enterprise; he supports, without belonging to, the Social Democratic party, and above all he is against doctrinaire absolutism. The Germans' greatest enemy, he recently wrote, is *Idealismus*, because it

encourages totalitarian ambitions in both the left and the right (*Der Spiegel*, August 11, 1969, p. 94).

In the grossest and most brutal way, political developments affected Grass's life course, as they did that of most European youth. The son of a shopkeeper who was also a minor Nazi party official in the then Free City of Danzig, Grass was raised amid lower-middle-class surroundings, but the mixed background of the family—Polish and Kashubian, as well as German—helped make him something of an outsider in his relationship to German society. Twelve years old when Danzig fell to the Third Reich, Grass was eventually drafted into the armed services, where he served competently but without enthusiasm the purposes of Hitler and his General Staff. From a POW camp Grass, still under eighteen, went back to school, where in a small and negative way, he rebelled openly against the establishment for the first but not the last time: When the history teacher recited the names of German wars, battles, and national holidays, Grass abruptly quit school without a diploma.[1]

During the hungry postwar years, Grass worked as a potash miner, a stonecutter, a cook, and a musician. Shortly after the currency reform of 1948, when the West German "economic miracle" is said to have begun, Grass began the formal study of sculpture and painting; he had made a name as painter, sculptor, poet, playwright, and writer of scenarios for ballet before he finished writing *The Tin Drum*. In 1957, when that novel was still in progress, Grass became affiliated with Gruppe 47, an informal organization of writers drawn together in 1947 partly through a mutual conviction that the German language, prostituted during twelve years of Hitlerism, needed purification and revitalizing.[2] The Gruppe met regularly to hear readings of new work by members or outsiders; the novelists Heinrich Böll, Uwe Johnson, and Gisela Elsner and the poet Hans Magnus Enzensberger have been among the participants.

As J. P. Bauke has put it, "They [the Gruppe] had to learn that the responsibility of the writer extends beyond words and becomes a moral and ultimately a human commitment."[3] Grass learned that lesson thoroughly. In 1958 he settled permanently in West Berlin, primarily because he felt that contemporary realities were most clearly reflected in that city;[4] presumably he also hoped that writers and artists in the two Berlins could eventually become a single cultural center that would help to reunify his split country. In May 1961 he attended a writers' congress in East Germany and there made an "impassioned plea" for literary freedom; he was immediately expelled from the gathering.[5] In August of that year, while the Berlin wall was under construction, Grass published two "open letters," one to Anna Seghers, a prominent Marxist writer whose antifascist novel *The Seventh Cross* had inspired him during his youth, and the other to the German Writers' Association in East Berlin. Both letters insisted on the responsibility of writers to speak out boldly against force and suppression.[6]

According to one source, Grass first became interested in the Social Democratic party through conversations with a co-worker in a potash mine, and he first considered campaigning actively for Willy Brandt, then mayor of Berlin, because of the systematic vilification to which Brandt had been subjected. In 1965 Grass made nearly sixty speeches and published several essays on behalf of Brandt's candidacy for chancellorship of the Bundesrepublik.[7] People all over West Germany, he recalled later, were "shocked" by his active participation, but, as he told a reporter for *The New York Times*, "We are all affected by the results of politics. Why shouldn't we all take part?"[8]

After the election, Grass concentrated on strengthening the ties between writers and artists in the West and in the Soviet-dominated nations. In 1967 a "Manifesto" in protest against the suppression of writers and artists in Czechoslovakia was purportedly signed by 329 intellectuals of the West, including Grass; this document was soon exposed as the fraudulent concoction of a literary adventurer. Grass denied any part in it but criticized the restrictions imposed on creative artists in both the West and the East blocs; his statement touched off a series of letters amounting to an "East-West dialogue" in *Die Zeit*, the prestigious political and cultural weekly of Hamburg, between Grass and Pavel Kohout, a prominent Czech playwright and producer. In these letters, Grass reaffirmed his opposition to doctrinaire dialectics and defended the evolutionary and parliamentary brand of socialism which he felt was likely to dominate western Europe, although he blamed the West almost equally with the East for the *pervertierter Koexistenz*—that is, the armed truce which inhibited the creative arts on both sides and encouraged both to exploit rather than to help the underdeveloped nations of the Third World.[9]

During the 1965 campaign, Grass had often spoken under Social Democratic auspices, but he reserved the freedom to make independent appearances and to criticize the party and its leaders. He even wrote a one-act play, *POUM* (published in *Monat*, XVII [June 1965], 33–38), in which the party leadership was satirized for, among other things, their obsession with public-opinion polls. During the elections of 1969, Grass co-founded the "Social Democratic Voters' Initiative," which stressed informal discussion meetings and likewise operated harmoniously with, but independently of, the tightly structured Social Democratic party. Under the auspices of this group Grass hit the campaign trail on behalf of Willy Brandt for over four months before other West German politicians began their electioneering; in over one hundred appearances he aimed mainly at nonparty voters, declaring that "people leave too much to the parties. What we need is a more active citizenship."[10] Considering the closeness of the vote, the Social Democrats surely owed something to Grass's strenuous efforts, but he has insisted that he wants no office and prefers to remain, as *Time* magazine has called him, "an unofficial catalyst of political action."[11]

Grass's position on most issues would in the United States be vaguely categorized as liberal. He has consistently advocated acceptance of the Oder-Neisse line as the boundary between Poland and Germany, the eventual reunification of the two Germanies, more flexible relations with East Germany, certain domestic social reforms—especially lowering of the voting age to eighteen and legalizing abortion[12]—and interaction between the older, ruling generation and the generation born since the war and impatient with their elders' guilt and conservatism. Accused of communist leanings, Grass has insisted that *"ich bleibe Sozialdemo-krat"*[13]—in spite of the *aufgewärmte Räte-Republik* (warmed-over Soviet Republic) favored by Rudi Dutschke and the persuasive arguments against democracy advanced by Herbert Marcuse: *"Solange die legalen Wege frei sind, auf evolutionäre Weise die parliamentarische Demo-kratie wiederherzustellen, bedarf es keiner Revolution"*[14] ("As long as legal ways remain open for us to get back on the evolutionary track toward parliamentary democracy, no revolution is necessary"). Grass has assiduously promoted such legal methods; in addition, one of his favorite adjectives for himself is *bürgerlich*, and he once suggested to the Russian novelist Konstantin Simonov that, in the interest of freedom, "publishing houses in the Soviet Union should become private enterprises again."[15]

Accused of turning to politics because he was burned out as a writer, Grass has said that Germans treat their writers as if they were priests of some sort: "First they [Germans] make them more noble than they are; then they can safely ignore them"[16] and "when a man engages in politics, he isn't defining his position as a writer but as a citizen. . . . As a citizen I write articles not meant for eternity."[17] Further, it is not enough for the writer as citizen merely to state formally his general principles: "I'm against intellectuals who publish manifestoes. You don't change anything that way. If you want to change something, you have to work hard at specific things."[18] Grass sees himself as a pragmatic activist, western style, rather than as an ideologue.

Accused of propagating a "new nationalism," Grass has endeavored to distinguish between the "fake kind of nationalism" in East Germany and the "empty materialism" of the West; he has rejected both in favor of a "natural" sort of nationalism which would consist in part of a nation's knowing itself.[19] By implication, this would include Germany's facing up to its ghastly past, an ordeal which Grass has encouraged in all his fiction.

II

Grass has claimed that he does not deliberately try to put across his ideology in his fiction, but "my beliefs will naturally permeate anything I write. It could be about fleas."[20] *The Tin Drum* (1959) is about a dwarf named Oskar who was born in Danzig in 1924 and who, at the age of thirty, lies in a mental hospital writing and "drumming" his life story. Grass writes in the leisurely, ample form of the *Bildungsroman,* and in addition to re-creating the sights, the sounds, the smells, the history, and the folklore of the Danzig area, he depicts in full the flabby religion, ethnic bigotries, petty corruption, and ostrichlike insularity of the lower-middle classes in this region. All this documentary goes far to make understandable the at first insidious, then accelerating, infiltration of Hit-lerism into a city-state with a proud history. Indeed, the rise and fall of the Third Reich is a unifying element in the novel, although it pervades mainly the background of a narrative the focus of which is consistently on Oskar's life and on the lives of the minor characters around him. The emphasis is most often biographical and apolitical, and yet, paradoxi-cally, the book is political in a fundamental sense: Nearly every incident is explicitly or implicitly related to either the growth, the collapse, or the aftermath of the Nazi regime. As one reviewer noted, *The Tin Drum* is an incisive attempt *"die Beziehungen zwischen Kleinbürgerei und den Abenteuer der Diktatur festzuhalten"*[21] ("to depict the relationships between the petite bourgeoisie and the enterprise of dictatorship").

When Hitlerism breaks into the foreground—that is, when it directly affects the lives of Oskar, his family, and their acquaintances—Grass treats it with satire that ranges from the whimsical to the grotesque. Matzerath, Oskar's putative father, is promoted in the Nazi party; the family celebrates with a skat game and by hanging a picture of Hitler opposite that of Beethoven. "So began the most sinister of all confronta-tions: Hitler and the genius, face to face and eye to eye. Neither of them was very happy about it."[22] In contrast to this pointed whimsy is the gro-tesque conclusion to Matzerath's career in the party: Fearing that posses-sion of his party badge may incriminate him, he tries to swallow it, and when it chokes him, his convulsions alarm his Russian captors into shoot-ing him. The grotesque element is augmented when Oskar, "while my presumptive father was swallowing the Party and dying," involuntarily squashes a louse that he has just caught on the Kalmuck who has been holding him. The grotesquerie and the grimness are compounded yet fur-ther when the Galician Jew who takes over the shop is shown the still unburied body of Matzerath. Making a gesture that is part of the stereo-typed comic Jew, Mr. Fajngold claps his hands over his head just as the toy-shop keeper who had provided Oskar with his drums used to do before he was murdered, and (p. 398)

> he called not only Luba his wife, but his whole family into the cellar, and there is no doubt that he saw them all coming, for he called them by name: Luba, Lev, Jakub, Berek, Leon, Mendel, and Sonya. He explained to them all who it was who was lying there dead and went on to tell us that all those he had just summoned as well as his sister-in-law and her other brother-in-law who had five children had lain in the same way, before being taken to the crematoria of Treblinka, and the whole lot of them had been lying there—except for him because he had had to strew lime on them.

Less grotesque and more directly satirical is Oskar's breaking up a party rally with his drumming, not because he is anti-Nazi but simply because he has been denied what he feels is his rightful place on the rostrum (p. 118); and verging on farce is the attempt made in 1954 by a pair of former Nazi "executioners" to murder a onetime Polish civilian soldier on the authority of a death warrant dated October 5, 1939. "I vote for Adenauer just the same as you do," one of them explains to Oskar and his disciple Vittlar. "But this execution order is still valid; we've consulted the highest authorities. We are simply doing our duty" (p. 574). The would-be assassins are comic-strip types, with their green hats and black hatbands, and the episode borders on farce because their attempt is foiled, but their rationalization is a *reductio ad absurdum* of the basic defense of many war criminals and also includes a hint that the postwar Christian Democratic regime receives support from, and even cooperates with, such unsavory elements.

Nor are such elements confined to the Nazi party. Wehrmacht Corporal Lankes, who mildly protests but finally obeys the order to slaughter the nuns on the beach, is merely a soldier who obeys his superiors. A list of active or passive collaborators would include almost every character in the novel except for the Dusters—"The Dusters were against everything" (p. 368). These teen-age thieves, muggers, and rapists are a nihilistic caricature of the system against which they rebel, and they, like the more conventionally disillusioned youth in the German world, are willing and even eager to follow a false messiah—in this case, Oskar-as-Jesus—who leads them to destruction.

Satire, then, especially in the grotesque mode, prevails in Grass's treatment of the more blatantly political subject matter in this novel. But Grass is protean in his use of other materials and devices. Closely related to the author's views on Hitlerism is his emphasis on history: Through historical summary, anecdote, place legends, superstitious lore, allegory, myth, and symbolism, Grass tries to convey the reality of living through a certain continuity of events in historical space and time—"great" events which in their totality are no more but no less real than the mishaps and the fortunes of the individuals in the historical continuum. To cite only two examples in which several of the elements listed above appear in combination: The killing of the nuns on the beach is rendered in the form of a morality play; the concrete pillbox, with its puppy entombed alive in the foundations, and the symbolic epigraph written on the pillbox, "Barbaric, Mystical, Bored" (p. 337), become an allegory of the Third Reich, and Lieutenant Herzog, Corporal Lankes, and his squad are a microcosm of the German war machine. Bebra and his troupe similarly represent that portion of German culture which debased itself through acquiescence in mass murder. That the sensuality and sentimentality rampant in this culture persisted into the postwar years is the message of "In the Onion Cellar" (pp. 519 ff.), delivered through satirical fantasy in which the lowly onion becomes the grotesque cause and symbol of the easy tears shed over song, love, and grief by a populace that collaborated in the slaughter of millions for whom they shed no tears.

Another effective way in which Grass makes the historical background a part of the action is his frequent and usually ironic correlation in time of historical events with incidents in the lives of Oskar and other characters. While the Boer War was in progress, Oskar's mother was conceived (p. 24); "at the end of July 1900—they were just deciding to double the imperial naval building program—my mother was born under the sign of Leo" (p. 25); while the Wehrmacht swept over Poland, Oskar worried because he was "running out of drums" (p. 258); "while V-1 and V-2 rockets were winging their way to England" (p. 372), Oskar's glass-shattering voice was winging over rooftops on behalf of the Dusters; while two aircraft carriers sank each other and the armies of Koniev and Zhukov prepared to resume their drive through Poland, Oskar refused to betray himself during the Dusters' trial (p. 384). (In Book Three, which takes place after the war, such correlations are rarer. History is not moving so fast or spectacularly and less need exists for making it part of the foreground.)

Making the characters a part of history forces Grass to raise, at least indirectly, the question of whether they have free will or are moved by social and political currents beyond their control and in consequence bear no moral responsibility for their actions. In The Tin Drum, unlike his stance in Dog Years and in The Plebeians Rehearse the Uprising, Grass evades giving a clear-cut answer to the question by presenting the entire narrative as the artistic re-creation of a possibly disordered and certainly immature mind. In a novel which, regardless of the elaborate pose of objectivity, is one long *j'accuse*, this evasion is a moral inconsistency and possibly an artistic flaw. However, two arguments may be advanced in defense of this evasion. First, Oskar has been called a moral monster; he is not one, but he may be schizoid, as is implied by the frequent shifts in viewpoint between the first and third person, and throughout most of the book he is definitely a child who, when he reaches thirty, is still far from being full-grown, physically and mentally. Childlike changes of mood and indifference to facts abound in his creative reminiscence; for example, at one point Oskar refers to the death of Matzerath as fate putting on its act (p. 394), and shortly thereafter he relates that "Oskar owned to himself that he had killed Matzerath deliberately" because he had intended that "he put the Party in his mouth and choke on it" (p. 404). But no indication is given here or elsewhere that Oskar had any clues enabling him to foresee Matzerath's putting the badge in his mouth; in the process of drumming up his past, Oskar is projecting a belated guilt feeling backward in time. This projection, along with his somber resolution to leave the hospital and go forth into the world once more, suggests that at least he is willing to assume a degree of moral responsibility, whether or not such willingness can be objectively justified in the matter of his father's death.

Second, despite his concern with history, Grass presents history as meaningful only in its effect on individuals. In one of his essays he criticizes Hegel's theory of history as a "fatal guide,"[23] and in his fiction he is indifferent to any alleged laws or principles of historical development that might lighten the individual's load of responsibility. This indifference is consistent with his general distrust of systematic ideologies.

This distrust is part of his artistic as well as his political credo. He felt no obligation to present positive alternatives to the situation of Oskar and his society. In suggesting that involvement is better than withdrawal, Grass scarcely goes beyond Camus's *The Stranger*. He has insisted that in spite of the satire and fantasy in *The Tin Drum*, "this is a realistic novel. . . ."[24] But his friend, the poet and critic Walter Höllerer, has pointed out that *The Tin Drum* is *"ein poetisches Buch,"* and that "poetic" means, among other things, a hint of many potentialities in the characters beyond the single actuality in each individual portrait (*"Und 'poetisch' meint unter anderem: in den einzelnen Bildern is die Möglichkeit von vielen Aspekten vorhanden, nicht nur einem"*).[25] Oskar must go out and face the black witch of evil, but he has come to recognize that this evil is in himself as well as in society. Although he has fearfully guessed at some of his potentialities for both good and evil action, the final utterance in his manuscript is a laughter no more fearful than defiant.

III

The theme of involvement and withdrawal likewise dominates *Cat and Mouse,* a novella in which, as in *The Tin Drum,* the problem involves religious belief as well as psychological growing up. But the political element is always present, though often submerged. Again Grass has constructed his tale in the form of a reminiscence written long afterward by a major character, a framework that allows the author to present all judgments as provisional. Heini Pilenz, the narrator, is never sure which of the motivations for his friend Joachim Mahlke's long-planned withdrawal is most important: the over-sized Adam's apple, narrow idolizing of the Virgin Mary, betrayal by the school officials, an urge to emulate a father who died heroically, or the need of the compulsive performer for an audience. Certainly of minor importance is dislike of the National Socialist regime; Mahlke is thrown out of the Young Folk but serves in the Hitler Youth as a "colorless unknown quantity,"[26] and, in the army, he wins the Knight's Cross. His doubts about the war come later, and the actively rebellious phases of his withdrawal are associated less with the state and the party than with the Conradinum school.

Possibly because of Grass's disgust with the postwar atmosphere in his own school, the gymnasium in all his novels tends to be a microcosm of the venal, authoritarian society which it supports. In *Cat and Mouse* Dr. Klohse, the principal (who has also become a party official), is not only a little dictator but an adept at using the velvety rhetoric of pedagogical authority to veil the iron fist. Dr. Mallenbrandt is another, cruder bully; Dr. Brunies reads sentimental poetry to his classes while openly eating the vitamin tablets he is supposed to have distributed to them. The reaction of the staff as a whole to the theft of a war hero's medal by Mahlke resembles that of storm troopers or an S.S. squad, though without the truncheons. This same crew of pedagogues listens worshipfully when decorated war veterans lecture to the students in language which parodies the obsession with overprecise detail, the catchphrases of German nationalism, and the hypocritical sentimentality characteristic of public rhetoric in the Third Reich. When a U-boat commander says of a sunset, "So it must be, when birds and angels bleed to death" (p. 62), switches to a detailed account of the sinking of a merchant ship, and follows this with a sugary genre painting in words, "Christmas on a submarine" (p. 63), one understands why Grass shared the desire of Gruppe 47 to revitalize conventional language.

Mahlke's total withdrawal ends in probable self-destruction, but he stimulates the end of innocence and the growth of maturity in Heini Pilenz. Perhaps as important a character as Mahlke, Pilenz is motivated largely by reason, skepticism, and guilt. "What began with cat and mouse torments me today" (p. 126)—because he feels he may have started his friend on the way through clowning and rebellion to withdrawal by holding a cat against the "mouse" on Joachim's neck. Mahlke's adoration of the Virgin and his paradoxical skepticism about the existence of God stimulate Pilenz's own nascent skepticism, while in matters of conduct Mahlke easily resists the other's "tedious appeals to reason" (p. 110). Pilenz too is no anti-Nazi, but because of Mahlke, he stands aloof from the acquisitive materialism of the postwar period, living a contemplative life, working in a settlement house, and trying to write. In his mature commitment to art and to pragmatic social action for modest but attainable ends, Pilenz seems the closest to Grass of any of this author's characters.

For whatever the correlation is worth, Grass wrote *Dog Years* during 1960–1963, a period when his direct involvement in politics was increasing but still consisted mainly in attending writers' meetings, in composing "open letters," and in participating in informal discussion; similarly, the overtly political content of *Dog Years* is greater than in his two previous novels. As a whole, the work still lies within the tradition of the realistic, panoramic novel, but the political and religious allegory tends to dehumanize the characters; their voices tend to merge into the single voice of the author. Moreover, much of the social and political satire is aimed at language and ideas rather than at actions—for example, the many parodies of Martin Heidegger. In an author less brilliant at re-creating scenes with vivid, sensuous detail, the increase in allegory and parody might be a gain; in Grass it is a net loss.

This tendency to talk and allegorize more and to re-create less may have developed because Grass's increasingly political orientation drew him into a task beyond even his powers, nothing less than awakening the consciousness and conscience of the entire German people by offering a cross-sectional history of the German middle class before, during, and after the war. To that end, Grass once again presents a reminiscence written in the first person, but this time there are three narrators, each of whom represents a significant German type: Eddi Amsel, a businessman supposedly tainted with Jewish blood; Harry Liebenau, a bureaucrat with a "file-card memory" (p. 468) who nourishes a passive, Wertherlike love for his predatory cousin Tulla; and Walter Matern, a perpetually disappointed idealist who is addicted to violence in support of and in rejection of his ideals—first communism, then Hitlerism, then Catholicism, finally becoming, in his journey of vengeance, a postwar antifascist who, as Grass has said recently, pursues *"mit faschistischen Methoden seine Art Antifaschismus."*[27] Matern's portion of the narrative includes the most effective satire, but Amsel, who commissioned the other two characters to write their portions of the narrative and who dominates both men, is at once the most significant and the most complex of the three. The main theme of the book is not the fortunes of Hitler's black dog but the blood-brotherhood of Eddi and Walter—that is to say, of Jew and Gentile. Amsel manifests several traits used by the Gentile mind to stereotype Jews: He is clever, corpulent, canny about cash, expert at manipulating people to serve his own ends, and supple at role-playing—at various times he turns up as Haseloff the impresario, Goldmouth the black marketeer, and Brauxel (or Brauksel or Brauchsel) the mine owner. He is also aggressive in trying to get accepted at the Nazi-controlled athletic club and in other Gentile circles. Above all, he manages to wrest some advantage from every situation; after Matern has knocked out his teeth he flees Danzig, where his days were numbered anyway, and turns up in Berlin as a prosperous ballet master. However, his ancestry is half Gentile and may be entirely so. This ambiguity of background and his ritual brotherhood with Walter suggest that he is not different from millions of "Aryans."

In addition to being an industrial magnate and mine owner, Brauxel is a satirical artist. As a boy he made scarecrows ridiculing his neighbors and enemies, and as a man he runs a scarecrow factory in a former potash mine—deep underground, symbolically in the depths of the past, where the Germany of the future is in production. Grass seems to imply that one ingredient of the new Germany is art perverted by technology and industry, which, thus perverted, helps to create a grotesque, materialistic caricature of what a society should be. The social and political satire of the postwar leaders who base their policies on the predictions of the mealworms is specific and relatively good-natured; the satirical allegory of the scarecrow mine is far-reaching, savage, and much more radical than anything Grass has said in his nonliterary speeches and writings.

IV

Since the 1965 campaign, Grass's art has come progressively closer to undiluted political discussion—with results not altogether pleasing. *The Plebeians Rehearse the Uprising* (1966) had a promising theme: a theatrical producer and playwright (inspired by, but not a portrait of, Bertold Brecht) who refuses to support the East German workers' uprising in 1953 partly because it is badly planned and partly because it is not good theater. However, like Brecht's weaker plays, *The Plebeians* bogs down in long-winded discussion, and it was coolly received by reviewers and audiences. *Davor* (*Therefore*), which opened in West Berlin early in 1969, is reportedly little more than a series of interconnected dialogues, largely on political and philosophical themes. *Davor* was incorporated, with some modifications, into the middle section of Grass's latest novel, *Local Anesthetic* (*Örtliche Betäubt*), published in August 1969. Once more the basic situation is highly evocative: Störtebeker, the leader of the nihilistic Dusters in *The Tin Drum*, has become Herr Starusch, a strictly pragmatic liberal and a respected teacher in a gymnasium. Much of the book consists of conversations between Starusch and his dentist, a simplistic utopian who feels that what society needs most is a worldwide system of "Sickcare."[28] His endless and inclusive efforts to reconstruct the patient's teeth allegorize any doctrinaire attempt to remake the world. Significantly, he is unsuccessful, and the last words of the novel are *"immer neue Schmerzen"* ("always new pain").

Interspersed with these conversations are episodes involving, among other characters, a student militant whom Starusch finally persuades not to burn his dog as a gesture of protest and a former general in the Wehrmacht who has never gotten over his defeat in battle. Though the juxtapositions of episodes and dental conversations are often comic in their incongruity, the speech and narrative lack the baroque richness and excitement of Grass's prose in *The Tin Drum* or even in parts of *Dog Years*. Moreover, *Local Anesthetic* lacks the multidimensionality of his earlier fiction: *The Tin Drum* was a religious and a picaresque novel as well as a political novel and a *Bildungsroman*. Finally, as reviewers of *Local Anesthetic* have noted, Grass is here too often content to state his views in discussion rather than to embody them in description, action, or characterization.[29] For social implications, there is little in his latest work to match the description—citing only one example—of the police kennels' orderly room in *Dog Years* (p. 139):

> Behind the desk and Lieutenant Mirchau's back hung, again symmetrically echeloned, six framed and glassed paper rectangles, illegible from where I was sitting. To judge by the type and sizes of the lettering, they must have been certificates in Gothic print with gold embossing, seals, and raised stamps. Probably dogs, who had served with the police, who had been drilled in the Langfuhr-Hochstriess police kennels, had won first, second, or even third prize at inter-regional police dog meets. On the desk, to the right of the inclined part, slowly moving back and forth over the lieutenant's work, stood in tense posture a bronze, or perhaps only plaster shepherd about the height of a dachshund, who, as any dog fancier could see at a glance, was cow-hocked and let his croup, to the onset of the tail, slope much too steeply.

In visualizing the cluttered, ersatz-baroque interior of a minor power center within the German establishment, Grass demonstrates rather than comments on the bad taste, the officiousness, the obsession with trivia, the glorification of animals at the expense of humans, and behind it all the dog teeth of brute force.

James Russell Lowell wrote of himself, in "A Fable for Critics" (ll. 234–235):

> The top of the hill he will ne'er come nigh reaching,
> Till he learns the distinction 'twix singing and preaching.

At one time Grass understood this distinction very well; in his poem "Diana—or the Objects," he declared:

> I have always refused
> to let my shadow-casting body
> be hurt by a shadowless idea.[30]

And in an essay published in 1957, "Der Inhalt als Widerstand" ("Content as Resistance"), he maintained that for the artist content is prior to form; one begins with content and finds form by overcoming its resistance.[31] The content, or substance, of Grass's work has always included ideas consonant with his belief in practical reform rather than in doctrinaire programs of either the left or the right. One commits a logical fallacy in saying that Grass's increasing preoccupation with the role of the artist as militant citizen has led him to overstress political themes in his work with the enthusiasm of the doctrinaire liberal and to impose the form of political discussion on his raw material quite arbitrarily rather than making a genuine attempt to overcome its "resistance"—that is, doing full justice to the complexities, nuances, and grotesque elements latent in that material and which he actualized so effectively in *The Tin Drum*. But whatever the causes of this doctrinaire imposition, the effect has been a debilitation of his art.

NOTES

1. J. P. Bauke, "A Talk with Günter Grass," *The New York Times*, May 31, 1964, Sec. III, p. 16.
2. *Ibid.* For further information on Gruppe 47, see Hans Werner Richter and Walter Manzen, eds., *Almanach der Gruppe 47* (Neuwied, 1962).
3. Bauke, p. 16.
4. Keith Botsford, "Günter Grass Is a Different Drummer," *The New York Times*, May 8, 1966, Sec. VII, p. 76.
5. Franz Spelman, "Günter Grass: A Big New Talent," *Show*, III (January 1963), 85.

228

6. Reprinted in *Die Mauer, oder der 13 August*, Hans Werner Richter, ed. (Hamburg, 1961), pp. 62–64, 65–66. The second letter was done in collaboration with Wolfgang Schnurre.

7. Some of Grass's 1965 campaign speeches and articles, along with some later material, have been published in his *Über das Selbstverständliche* (Neuwied and Berlin, 1968). Information about the beginnings of his political interests can be found in "Grass: Sowas durchmachen," *Der Spiegel*, August 11, 1969, p. 89.

8. Botsford, p. 28.

9. Günter Grass and Pavel Kohout, *Briefe über die Grenze: Versuch eines Ost-West-Dialogs* (Hamburg, 1968), pp. 46–47, 72–74. The fraudulent manifesto is on pp. 99–103.

10. "Grass at the Roots," *Time*, September 5, 1969, p. 29. See also "Grass: Sowas durchmachen" and David Binder, "Independent Citizens' Movement Enlivening German Campaign," *The New York Times*, September 10, 1969, p. 12.

11. *Time*, September 5, 1969, p. 29.

12. *Über das Selbstverständliche*, pp. 66–68.

13. *Ibid.*, p. 228.

14. *Ibid.*, pp. 226–227.

15. Günter Grass and Uwe Johnson, "Conversation with Simonov," *Encounter*, XXIV (January 1965), 90.

16. Botsford, p. 63.

17. "Grass Speaks," *Le Monde*, reprinted in *Atlas*, XI (April 1966), 250.

18. *Ibid.*

19. Botsford, p. 76.

20. Michael Stone, untitled interview with Günter Grass, *Saturday Review*, XLVIII (May 29, 1965), 26.

21. Joachim Kaiser, "Oskars getrommelte Bekenntnisse," *Süddeutsche Zeitung* (Munich), reprinted in *Von Buch zu Buch—Günter Grass in der Kritik: Eine Dokumentation*, Gert Loschütz, ed. (Neuwied and Berlin, 1968), p. 14.

22. *The Tin Drum*, trans. by Ralph Manheim (New York, 1962), p. 116. All citations in the text are from this edition.

23. *Über das Selbstverständliche*, p. 215.

24. Spelman, p. 85.

25. Walter Höllerer, "Roman in Kreuzfeuer," *Der Tagesspiegel* (Berlin), reprinted in *Von Buch zu Buch*, p. 16.

26. *Cat and Mouse*, trans. by Ralph Manheim (New York, 1964), p. 25. All citations in the text are from this edition. All citations from *Dog Years* are from the Harcourt, Brace & World ed. (New York, 1965), trans. by Ralph Manheim.

27. Günter Grass, "Unser Grundübel ist der Idealismus," *Der Spiegel*, August 11, 1969, p. 94.

28. Günter Grass, *Örtliche Betäubt* (Neuwied and Berlin, 1969), p. 110. See also *Local Anesthetic*, trans. by Ralph Manheim (New York, 1970), pp. 86–87.

29. For example, Rolf Becker, "Mässig mit Malzbonbons," *Der Spiegel*, August 11, 1969, pp. 102–103.

30. *Selected Poems* (New York, 1966), p. 51. This poem was translated by Christopher Middleton.

31. Günter Grass, "Der Inhalt als Widerstand," *Akzente*, IV (June 1957), 229–235.

PART III

AMERICAN

THEODORE DREISER
(1871-1945)

by Sheldon Norman Grebstein

IF BY A WRITER's political beliefs we also mean his social beliefs—and surely the two are indistinguishable—then Theodore Dreiser's political beliefs were of fundamental importance to his career. Indeed, few major American writers have given themselves more fervently or frequently to sociopolitical thought and utterance than Dreiser. Strictly speaking, the subject of politics—that is, the concern with the relationship of governments and governed, with the origins, applications, and consequences of power, with the respective social roles of individuals and institutions—inspired three polemical books: *Dreiser Looks at Russia* (1928), *Tragic America* (1932), and *America Is Worth Saving* ('1941). The same subject is treated in passing in Dreiser's four autobiographical volumes: *A Traveler at Forty* (1913), *A Hoosier Holiday* (1916), *A Book About Myself* (1922), and *Dawn* (1931). Politics, strictly defined, assumes an important role in the narratives of three of Dreiser's novels: *The Financier* (1912), *The Titan* (1914), and *An American Tragedy* (1925). And politics, more broadly defined as the portrayal of social and economic conditions, enters into most of the remainder of Dreiser's work, especially *Sister Carrie* (1900) and *Jennie Gerhardt* (1911). There even appears a special sort of political interest in such seemingly unpolemical and personal novels as *The Genius* (1915) and *The Bulwark* (1946).

Obviously, so important a facet of Dreiser's career has not gone unremarked. In the three volumes of Dreiser's letters edited by Robert Elias and in the biographies by Elias and W. A. Swanberg we have abundant evidence of Dreiser's personal commitment to political activities, especially in the last fifteen years of his life. F. O. Matthiessen devoted one chapter of his critical biography to Dreiser's politics, while Dorothy Dudley was obsessed by the subject in her early study. The same matter receives attention in Charles Shapiro's book and in essays by various critics. All who have attempted to explain Dreiser's *Weltanschauung* have of necessity also considered his politics, either directly or by implication. Perhaps the most eloquent attack on Dreiser, Lionel Trilling's essay "Reality in America," focuses specifically on the problem of Dreiser's political convictions as they affect his qualities as an artist. In summary, W. A. Swanberg provides this patronizing, sardonic, yet essentially accurate account of Dreiser's "eclectic political ideology":

> A burning hatred for the rich, for capitalists.
> A tender sympathy for the masses in the abstract.
> A simultaneous suspicion of the masses in actuality.
> A Nietzschean belief in the superman, complicated by the conviction that he was one of them.
> A fear that his supermanship was unrecognized, that he was sinking into financial, artistic, and social failure.
> A resulting compulsion to leap before the public in articles, lectures and statements often ill-advised, bellicose, and misinformed.[1]

With so well-examined a subject, then, as Dreiser's politics, what remains to be said? I intend to discuss three phases of the problem which, despite the work of previous critics, either have not been stated emphatically enough, have been viewed through perspectives other than those I will employ, or have not been studied at all.

The first point concerns politics in the strict sense and concerns Dreiser's portrayal of political events in his novels as conspiracies in which the private interests and motives of the select few prevail over professed common ideals and public welfare. The second, paradoxically, is Dreiser's depiction of social opinion, especially the opinion regarding sexual behavior, as a relentless force impinging upon individual conduct; or, in other words, social opinion as an exercise of political power. Finally, there is Dreiser's ambivalent treatment of the relative influence of heredity and environment in human nature, a treatment which produced a confusion between class and caste in the portrayal of his characters and confounded a liberal's hope of individual and social progress with a fatalist's sense of futility in the face of overwhelming biological forces. That is to say, we will confront, at last, the paradox of Dreiser's portrayal of man as a political being.

I. The Politics of Conspiracy

In *A Book About Myself*, later more accurately retitled *Newspaper Days*, Dreiser provides a trenchant account of his own political education, or, better, his political disillusionment. During his approximately three years as a newspaperman in Chicago, St. Louis, Pittsburgh, and New York, 1892–1894, he formed that concept of politics as a conspiracy of the few (rich and powerful) against the many (poor and weak) which he later dramatized in the Cowperwood trilogy and *An American Tragedy*, and which remained his deep personal conviction to the end of his life. Under the tutorship of older, seasoned reporters, men no longer bemused by "moralistic mush," and instructed by his own direct observation, Dreiser came to regard the politician with utter cynicism as a man "out for himself, a trickster artfully juggling with the moods and passions and ignorance of the public." On one occasion in Pittsburgh he interviewed Thomas B. Reed, Speaker of the House, on the significance of Coxey's "Army." Reed denounced Coxey and his band as revolutionaries and concluded with a sentiment still potent in American politics: "It doesn't matter what their grievance is. . . . This is a government of law and prescribed political procedure. Our people must abide by that." Dreiser's response had already been conditioned by his comparison of the steel workers' hovels at Homestead with the magnificent houses of the rich:

> I was ready to agree, only I was thinking of the easy manner in which delegates and elected representatives everywhere were ignoring the interests if not the mandates of the body politic at large and listening to the advice and needs of financiers and trust builders. Already the air was full of complaints against monopoly. Trusts and combinations of every kind were being organized, and the people were being taxed accordingly. All property, however come by, was sacred in America. The least protest of the mass anywhere was revolutionary, or at least the upwellings of worthless and never-to-be countenanced malcontents. I could not believe this. I firmly believed then, as I do now, that the chains wherewith a rapidly developing financial oligarchy or autocracy meant to bind a liberty-deluded mass were then and there being forged. I felt then, as I do now, that the people of that day should have been more alive to their interests, that they should have compelled, at Washington or elsewhere, by peaceable political means if possible, by dire and threatening uprisings if necessary, a more careful concern for their interests than any congressman or governor or President, at that time or since, was giving them.[2]

But before Dreiser had set down these conclusions in discursive prose, he had already embodied them in *The Financier* and *The Titan*. The fortunes of Frank Cowperwood follow exactly the directions implicit in this description of the politics of conspiracy. That is, in *The Financier* Cowperwood's rapid ascension to great wealth and power in Philadelphia begins in his association with an elected official, Stener, and his use of public funds to finance his operations—with Stener's complicity and to Stener's profit. Likewise, Cowperwood's empire crashes when this conspiracy is exposed and public sentiment aroused. Public outrage conjoins with the machinations of Cowperwood's rivals and enemies, another set of conspirators, to ruin Cowperwood temporarily and send him to prison. Later, when public concern ebbs and Cowperwood's chief antagonist dies, a pardon is arranged for him and he is freed to recoup his fortunes.

As Dreiser constructs the novel and formulates the character of Cowperwood, man's behavior, his political behavior included, is almost wholly determined by material forces: power, money, sex. The lust for beauty, an important factor in the later novels of the Cowperwood trilogy, scarcely appears in *The Financier*. Dreiser permits only one vital nonmaterial impulse to operate efficaciously in the narrative: Butler's paternal feeling for his daughter Aileen, a feeling strong enough to turn his mild friendship for Cowperwood into implacable hatred. But even this paternal feeling has a materialistic aspect: Butler's bitterness at the damage to his personal and family reputation.

In short, as Dreiser makes clear in his novel, and as John J. McAleer has recently noted in his valuable little study of Dreiser, the dominant characteristic of Cowperwood and the major theme of the narrative which concerns him is *force*. For force we may read power, and power is synonymous with politics. Cowperwood's first and most profound deduction about the nature of life is essentially a political deduction: that given the basic principles of existence, "Things lived on each other"; those creatures with the best weapons win. And with an ironic subtlety Dreiser is supposedly incapable of, he concludes the opening chapter—in which the young Cowperwood has witnessed the conflict between lobster and squid and has formed the conclusion just cited—with repeated reference to the washing of Cowperwood's hands, followed by these lines: "From seeing his father count money, he was sure that he would like banking; and Third Street, where his father's office was, seemed to him the cleanest, most fascinating street in the world." Here Dreiser suggests the paradox by which "civilized" man lives: Although he is a part of nature, red in tooth and claw, he fights with clean hands and in an arena not of jungle but of streets, banks, offices.

The occasional but significant images that highlight Dreiser's blocky style are appropriately those of birds, beasts, conflict. Thus stock traders are "gulls and stormy petrels, hanging on the lee of the wind, hungry and anxious to snap up any unwary fish." Mollenhauer and Simpson, two of the men who conspire against Cowperwood, are likened to massive tiger and quick, lean cat. Judge Payderson, the party hack who tries Cowperwood for embezzlement, is characterized as "a lean herring of a man"; and herrings, as we know, are school fish. Cowperwood's attitude toward the law, expressed in a thickly metaphorical passage, views it for the weak as a hampering fog or the space between the millstones of force or chance; while for the strong the law serves as a sword and shield, a trap for one's pursuers, dust in the eyes of enemies, the spider's mesh for one's prey. One employs lawyers simply as weapons of combat, knives and clubs.

This wholly cynical political attitude receives even greater emphasis in the second book of the trilogy, The Titan. Completely hardened by his experiences in Philadelphia, Cowperwood employs the politics of conspiracy on a grand scale in Chicago. The subtle and selective bribery of a few public officials, as described in The Financier, no longer suffices for Cowperwood's great design: to control the public transportation system of Chicago. He must attempt to buy political power wholesale. Early in the novel he secures the services of John J. McKenty, "patron saint of the political and social underworld of Chicago," whose credentials Dreiser describes: "Even as a stripling what things he had not learned—robbery, ballot-box stuffing, the sales of votes, the appointive power of leaders, graft, nepotism, vice exploitation—all the things that go to make up (or did) the American world of politics and financial and social strife." And through McKenty Cowperwood does for a time exert the necessary influence, until his antagonists compete with even larger bribes and slimier tactics. In fact, the graph of Cowperwood's financial career in Chicago must be charted in political terms, for as the novel proceeds, Cowperwood's financial efforts become largely dependent upon his political intrigues. Much of the conflict in the novel consists of Cowperwood's struggle to control the political power necessary to his master plan, as he attempts to buy the Chicago City Council, the Illinois State Legislature, and even the governor. The latter character provides one of the few glimmers of idealism in the prevailingly dark scene of Dreiser's politics; out of principle he refuses Cowperwood's open bribe of $300,000. Nowhere in American fiction does there exist a more vivid demonstration of the relationship between money and politics than in The Titan, the power of each increasing in geometrical ratio to the other.

Appropriately, the concept of force again determines the novel's imagery, far more pervasively than in The Financier. It is embodied early and recurrently in specifically military terms. As Cowperwood begins his operations in Chicago, Dreiser compares him to Hamilcar Barca and Hannibal. Cowperwood engages among his first subordinates a veteran of the Civil War, General Van Sickle, who falls into the habit of addressing Cowperwood as "Captain." Cowperwood's financial opponents are always named "the enemy," and Cowperwood conceives of each new monetary ploy as "invading the enemies' country." The novel's chapter titles frequently utilize a military vocabulary or allude to conflict; the title of Chapter 26, for example, succinctly repeats the novel's major themes: "Love and War." In the book's climactic episodes, those concerning Cowperwood's final battle to capture the fifty-year franchises vital to his transportation lines (Chapters 58–61), Dreiser renders the atmosphere of Chicago as that of a warring state. These chapters contain the most nervous and electric writing Dreiser had yet done. In them he combines his usual narrative method of the omniscient and panoramic with, for him, the rare technique of direct dramatic scene. The language, too, is much more highly charged than usual, especially with military images, animal and jungle-combat references ("life knife in hand, life . . . dripping at the jaws with hunger"), contrasts of storm and calm, noise and silence, light and dark. Indeed, some of the best passages of both *The Titan* and *The Financier* derive directly from Dreiser's treatment of the politics of conspiracy.

Characteristic of the general inferiority of the trilogy's last novel to its predecessors, there is no such treatment of politics in *The Stoic* and an attendant loss of verisimilitude and vitality. Although much of the data of *The Financier* and *The Titan* had been based on Dreiser's research into the career of Cowperwood's prototype, Charles T. Yerkes, the raw data had been transformed into the stuff of art by the urgency of Dreiser's feelings about American life and the authority of his own observations—especially as concerned with the power of money and the role of politics. In shifting the scene of *The Stoic* to England, Dreiser remained faithful to the course of Yerkes's career, but at the expense of separating himself from his own artistic roots. Strangely enough, almost none of the anglophobia which permeates another of Dreiser's last books, *America Is Worth Saving*, creeps into *The Stoic*, other than Dreiser's observation that Parliament, too, has its price in such matters as granting public-utilities franchises to private speculators. To the contrary, Cowperwood praises the English for their greater tolerance of individual foibles and their reluctance to make invidious judgments about one's behavior. Cowperwood also says: "People over here make way for intelligence and beauty in a way that has never yet been dreamed of at home."

Perhaps the most trenchant political idea in *The Stoic*, political in the broadest sense, comes forward in the aging Cowperwood's musings during a visit to the cathedral at Canterbury, reflections that summarize his own world view and undoubtedly something of Dreiser's as well (p. 137):

> Was any man noble? Had there ever been such a thing as an indubitably noble soul? He was scarcely prepared to believe it. Men killed to live—all of them—and wallowed in lust in order to reproduce themselves. In fact, wars, vanities, pretenses, cruelties, greeds, lusts, murder, spelled their true history, with only the weak running to a mythical saviour or god for aid. And the strong using this belief in a god to further the conquest of the weak.

An equally bleak view of man prevails in Dreiser's masterpiece, *An American Tragedy*, one of the great American novels of the twentieth century. The same novel also contains Dreiser's most poignant and vivid treatment of the politics of conspiracy. To put it bluntly, Clyde Griffiths is murdered by a sociopolitical process far more deliberate and ruthless than his behavior in causing the death of Roberta Alden. Just as Clyde sacrifices Roberta to his will to live (that is, will to succeed), so Clyde is sacrificed to the political ambitions of the district attorney, Mason, who sees the case as the chance to revive his flagging political fortunes. Furthermore, from the moment Roberta's body is discovered, all the functionaries of the law are motivated in part by the possibility of political or material advantage, and all participate in the legal conspiracy that finally annihilates Clyde. The entire process serves as another illustration, this one grimly ironic, of Dreiser's thesis that man kills to live.

To some degree Mason, Clyde's "killer," stands as a kind of ironic double of Clyde. Both are of impoverished backgrounds, both are of "romantic and emotional" nature, both are marred by what Dreiser calls a "psychic sex scar"—although Mason's is external, a disfigured nose, while Clyde's is internal, a disfigured ego. The major differences between them are Mason's cunning, toughness, and ability to succeed within given social norms. Again drawing on the data of real events, the Chester Gillette–Grace Brown case of 1906–1908, Dreiser casts Clyde's arrest and trial against the background of an impending election. For Clyde the ideal had been the money and social position attainable through marriage to the wealthy and beautiful Sondra Finchley. His dreams of Sondra and his revulsion against poor, pregnant Roberta cannot be separated from his dreams of success; nor are Mason's political ambitions separable from his pursuit and conviction of Clyde. Although Dreiser permits Mason and the others honest feelings of indignation, pity, and righteous anger, just as he permits Clyde to feel something like love, in Dreiser's view tangible and immediate forces prevail. For Mason, in short, the ideal is likewise the money and position to be gained with the judgeship that is his reward for Clyde's conviction. Dreiser never allows the reader to forget this, as he interlines his narrative through much of Book III with allusions to the political implications of the crime. One might say that for Dreiser politics hovers over the action much as the writers of older literature visualized Fate or God.

Another illustration of the politics of conspiracy as it favors the rich is the complete suppression of Sondra's name during the trial. Neither the defense nor prosecution hesitates to expose every aspect of Clyde's past and motivation, but Sondra, vital as she is to Clyde's conduct, enters only as Miss "X." This is all quietly arranged before the trial by Sondra's father, who communicates with a highly placed official of Mason's party, who in turn confers with Mason. Not only is Sondra's name suppressed but also her letters to Clyde—significant evidence. From such episodes we can surmise that were it Gilbert Griffiths, heir to the family fortune, being tried rather than his poor relation Clyde, both the conduct and the outcome of the case would have been different. Dreiser further emphasizes the inequality of the rich and the poor before the law by pointing out that Clyde's attorney, Belknap, had in his youth faced a similar situation but was saved from desperate action by the exercise of his family's money and influence. *An American Tragedy*, then, leaves us with this paradox: The pursuit of wealth engenders crime; the possession of wealth circumvents punishment.

II. Public Opinion as Determinant

There are a few instances in Dreiser's work which testify to man's capacity to love and to act selflessly in love, as exemplified in Jennie Gerhardt's love for Lester Kane or Solon Barnes's love for his wife and children. Thus Dreiser the naturalist does sometimes allow for a dimension of human character that has nothing to do with chemisms. Then, too, Dreiser obviously believes in luck or chance, although this may well express itself as a material force. But other than those, Dreiser's work consistently records only two nonmaterial factors which impinge on the fates of his characters: the general collective factor of public opinion and the particular individual factor of the lust for beauty. (I should note, however, that Dreiser's descriptions of the beauty instinct often utilize his favorite physical-chemical terms and present it as a kind of tropism.) Oddly enough—and this is among the paradoxes of Dreiser's world view—he demonstrates emphatically how the general ethos of public opinion is comprised of the sum of individual moral judgments fostered by and collected in various institutions, especially the church. Yet the lust for beauty remains in Dreiser's conception an individual trait, apparently as urgent and necessary for some humans as food and drink but never institutionalized and always finally a mystique, an unattainable ideal. The conflict arises because, in Dreiser's view, only the exceptional person has a fully developed instinct for beauty and because the instinct is often expressed—notably in Dreiser's men—as a sexual quest. The mass is, by Dreiser's definition, either incapable of or hostile to all individual quests which do not abide by collective norms. Of course, the mass is capable of sex-as-chemism, but this impulse, too, must follow approved directions.

The problem has another side. Collective norms are not only Christian, they are capitalistic. That is, they defend the ideal of private property, whether or not the small men who compose the mass have any such property. This ideal impels the common man to oppose bitterly anyone who threatens his imagined share. Further, Dreiser pointed out that these religious and economic ideals conjoin to produce our hypocritical but ironclad insistence on virginity and marital fidelity as the foundations of the social order, for both denote virtuous conduct and the sanctity of private property. Add to this ironic conception Dreiser's fluctuating identification first with the common man and then with the aberrant, superior individual, and there arises a paradoxical politics indeed.

But although in Dreiser's view such common norms are absurd when tested against the amoral flux of the universe, we witness in his novels a serious, consistent, and respectful treatment of public opinion as a determinant in the destinies of his individual characters. Whether weakling like Clyde Griffiths or superman like Frank Cowperwood, no Dreiser protagonist is immune to it. In some cases it can decide the difference between success and failure, life and death. And it functions efficaciously even in such nonpolitical novels as *Jennie Gerhardt*, *The Genius*, and *The Bulwark*.

The force of public opinion upon the fate of Clyde Griffiths has already been implied; it creates an atmosphere more appropriate to a lynching than a trial. Although the weight of evidence against Clyde would have resulted in conviction even under cooler circumstances, the intensity of feeling against him not only as Roberta's murderer but also as the thief of her virginity demands the death penalty rather than the long prison sentence which would have been just. Mason's conduct of the state's case deliberately appeals as much to the jury's sentiment as to its reason, and the jury discharges its felt role as spokesman for the community's norms by finding Clyde guilty of murder in the first degree. The one juror in doubt surrenders to the threats of the others and accedes in the unanimous verdict: "We'll fix you. You won't get by with this without the public knowing exactly where you stand." Clyde's last hope for life, an appeal to the governor for clemency, disappears when the governor—who we are told is a good man—refuses to grant it, in part because the court decisions seem sound, in part because he observes that public opinion wants the sentence executed. Thus Clyde's death in the electric chair satisfies the common feeling, voiced by a spectator during the trial: "Why don't they kill the God-damned bastard and be done with him?"

Public opinion materially alters the career of Frank Cowperwood in *The Financier* and *The Titan*, superman though he is. In fact, it keeps him from his most cherished ambitions. In *The Financier* Cowperwood might have escaped the consequences of his own misdeeds and the plots of his enemies, except that a now-alert community represented by the "Citizens Municipal Reform Association" demands his punishment. After his release he knows that public opinion will forever hamper his movements in Philadelphia, and that he must follow his career elsewhere.

The Titan records an even more significant instance of the superman's collision with the mass and the mass's triumph. Actually Cowperwood suffers two defeats. The first is a subtle social defeat in which rumors of his past and the fact of his marriage to Aileen, who is, ironically, "too common," bar him from admission to the circle of Chicago's elite. His wealth, charm, grand house, and art collection do not suffice to overcome public opinion. The "public" in this case consists of the few families who act as social arbiters.

Cowperwood's second defeat is the sudden and dramatic confrontation between the interests of the superman and the community, with the community joined by Cowperwood's enemies and rivals, themselves lesser supermen. Yet the real force belongs not to the conspirators, despite their wealth and their control of the newspapers, but to the mass, the little men speaking in unison. At last, Cowperwood's shrewdest plans and most lavish bribes are negated by the mass: "Hungry aldermen and councilmen might be venal and greedy enough to do anything he should ask, provided he was willing to pay enough, but even the thickest-hided, the most voracious and corrupt politician could scarcely withstand the searching glare of publicity and the infuriated rage of a possibly aroused public opinion."

Appropriately, Dreiser dramatizes public opinion in *The Financier* and *The Titan*, as he was later to do in *An American Tragedy*, by trial scenes. The scenes in *The Financier* and *An American Tragedy* are actual trials, with the jury serving both a real and a representative role. In *The Titan* the "trial" is cast as a meeting of the Chicago City Council attended by a crowd of citizens, half crusading army with banners and drums, half lynch mob, but wholly the loud and irresistible voice of the people. In their presence Cowperwood's bought aldermen can only bend before the mass. In *An American Tragedy* the crowd's strength is depicted not by the aural and martial images of *The Titan* but by the constant pressure of its eyes. Under the audience's and jury's implacable stare Clyde's sensitive face and involuntary gestures become part of the evidence against him. Moreover, in all three novels the trial scenes occur at crucial junctures in the narrative structure, at just those points where they constitute climaxes. From them flow the denouements. In structure as well as in theme the trial functions as a kind of apotheosis of public opinion and as the ultimate demonstration of its effect upon individual destinies.

A contributing factor to Cowperwood's defeat in *The Titan* is his unquenchable sexuality, in part a mode of conquest and an expression of the same drive that builds financial empires, in part an impulse toward beauty, but in any case a force that forever sets him apart from ordinary men and exposes him to their enmity. But although the intensity of Cowperwood's sexuality is unparalleled in Dreiser's other characters, he is linked to them by it: victims like Clyde and Hurstwood, those of superior ability like Lester Kane and Eugene Witla, the promising but tragically fated Stewart Barnes. Throughout Dreiser's work the avenging demon of public opinion relentlessly pursues those who disobey its commandments of virginity and fidelity.

Because Hurstwood has violated the community's code in his infatuation for Carrie, he becomes vulnerable to his wife's claims in a divorce action and thus stripped of his substance. Without it, and without the vitality or self-confidence of youth, his end is foredoomed. As he sinks Carrie rises, her success as an actress a paradoxical illustration of the public's power to exalt as well as to condemn. Ironically, the role that brings her fame is one that exploits her air of quizzical innocence.

No character in Dreiser's fictional world better deserves reward for her sweetness and loyalty than Jennie Gerhardt, yet she, too, must forever live beyond the pale because of her transgressions with Senator Brander, out of gratitude, and Lester Kane, out of love. Sneering public opinion invades her home with Lester in Hyde Park, just when a secure and stable life seems at hand. And outraged public opinion, manifested in the stipulations of his father's will, humbles even so proud and seemingly independent a man as Lester. When his security is threatened, he takes the practical step of marrying the socially prominent Letty Gerald. To persist in his love and thereby risk poverty is for Lester, as for the majority of Dreiser's characters, an intolerable danger.

As we know from Dreiser's biography, the fear of public opinion as a consequence of sexual conduct was in part transcribed from his own experience. Indeed, the major episode in *The Genius* closely parallels a phase of the author's life. Just as one of Dreiser's romances led to his dismissal from a lucrative and important position with Butterick Publications, so Eugene Witla's relationship with Suzanne Dale causes his discharge by the United Magazines Corporation. Although the relationship was consummated neither in life nor in literature, the very fact of a married man's desire for a virginal girl was in itself sufficient proof of guilt. In this case public opinion becomes the club which Suzanne's irate mother brandishes over the heads of Witla's employers, threatening public exposure to the firm's female readers unless the offender is dismissed.

Finally, in *The Bulwark* Stewart Barnes kills himself because he cannot face the public disgrace his actions have brought upon his family, although he realizes that in the forthcoming trial he might well escape the law's full severity. Only in this last and most mystical of Dreiser's books does the artist approach an admission of something like sin, the existence of an inner moral force, conscience. Yet, ironic to the last, *The Bulwark* demonstrates simultaneously the beauty of a truly noble soul, the force and the validity of conscience, and the wreckage produced by love and virtue if applied too strongly to a world neither all-loving nor all-good. Solon Barnes is unmistakably a saint, but judged by the destinies of the majority of his children, he is also a fool. The conflict in all Dreiser's preceding novels derives from situations in which the individual is less good than public opinion would have him; the conflict in *The Bulwark* arises because he is too good.

I find this apt summary of Dreiser's attitude in the passage which begins the epilogue to *The Titan*. Echoed in many places and in various versions throughout Dreiser's work, it stands as the expression of one of his basic beliefs:

> The world is dosed with too much religion. Life is to be learned from life, and the professional moralist is at best a manufacturer of shoddy wares. At the ultimate remove, God or the life force, if anything, is an equation, and at its nearest expression for men—the contract social—it is that also. Its method of expression appears to be that of generating the individual, in all his glittering variety and scope, and through him progressing to the mass with its problems. In the end a balance is invariably struck wherein the mass subdues the individual or the individual the mass—for the time being. For, behold, the sea is ever dancing or raging.

III.   Caste, Class, and Social Reform

Theodore Dreiser gave much of his energy during the last fifteen years of his life to active involvement in social causes and projects for reform. Just before his death he culminated a long relationship with the Communist party by finally taking membership in it. From his pen there came a steady stream of letters, broadsides, and communications to his readers, colleagues, the newspapers, and such heads of state as Stalin and Franklin Roosevelt. He investigated labor conditions in the Kentucky mines; he became an advocate of technocracy; he visited Spain and undertook a relief project for Spanish civilians; he agitated for Tom Mooney's release; he participated in various conferences; and, shy as he was before an audience, he even took to the lecture platform.

Dreiser's activism seems to have been engendered by his visit to Russia, November 1927–January 1928, which, despite his complaints at the time and the reservations recorded in *Dreiser Looks at Russia*, apparently had enormous impact upon his thinking. Thereafter he tended to evoke Russia as an exemplum of the ideal, and in *Tragic America* he argued for the transplantation and adaptation of Russian communism to American soil (although later in the 1930's he changed his mind about its efficacy for our national problems). Furthermore, behind the hysterical tone, the distortions, and the crude prose of *Tragic America* one can discern a genuinely liberal intention. Dreiser's proposals that social organization should become the chief subject of study in American schools, that Americans must use the ballot to reform the social order, and that we must establish a system of "equity" permitting the individual's full contribution to, and benefit from, the social order all stem from a conviction that we can be better than we are. In short, the fundamental premise behind Dreiser's polemical writing and personal activism must be called a liberal premise.

By definition the liberal believes that human nature and the social destiny contingent upon human nature are not inalterably fixed at or before birth; that man's lot can be changed, improved, ameliorated. Such a belief permits a recognition of class, one's particular rung on the social ladder as decided by such variable conditions as earning capacity, education, tastes; it does not permit a belief in caste, one's birth-to-death station in the social order as fixed by irrevocable physical, mental, and moral characteristics. For the liberal the key factor is environment. Through the control and the improvement of environment, man may compensate for the defects in himself and in the given scheme of things. Without such a belief there can be no hope of reform. Clearly, then, in this sense Dreiser was a liberal, at least in the last phase of his life.

Yet with the paradoxicalness that seems to be the ruling principle of his politics, the preponderant view of character in his novels—the only documents that really matter—is not liberal but reactionary, that is, fatalistic. As Dreiser's characters come into life, so for the most part do they live it and leave. With few exceptions the politics of Dreiser's novels is not that of John Locke but of Thomas Hobbes: an inflexibly ordered and ranked society dominated by the individual divinely preordained as superior.

This paradox has hardly escaped attention. Many years ago Robert Elias, the first serious student of Dreiser's career, wrote to him asking how he could reconcile his personal, liberal activism with his fatalism as an artist. Dreiser's response was typically ambivalent:

> Since I started in observing my world and writing about it, I have been interested in the effects of social systems on individuals. And although I didn't take any really active part in reform programs until the 1920's and after, my feelings have almost always gravitated toward sympathy with what I regarded as the underdog. At the same time, though I may sympathize with the unwilled, helpless, seemingly undeserved suffering which becomes the lot of the many, I am forced to realize that the strong do rule "the weak." Even determinists where and when sympathetic and taking part in social reform for the benefit of "the weak" are to some extent helpless. When I take part in Communist activities and write *Tragic America*, I am still a helpless victim of my own feelings and sympathies. . . .
> You must see for yourself, that one cannot help wanting to do and doing "something about our oppressors" as you put it, and yet realizing that success in the matter may not permanently abolish mental or strength differences. The hope is that all—or at least a majority—will reach that mental level at which planned inequity by a few will no longer be tolerated or possible. I shall continue to argue for that though inequity may not disappear.[3]

Dreiser's reply may be admirable in its dedication to a splendidly impossible cause, but like many of Dreiser's statements it seems less convincing than the attitudes conveyed by his art. In sum, we perceive in Dreiser's fiction not only a confusion between caste and class but also an implicit preference for caste and an underlying identification with the strong, however deep and genuine his pity for the weak. I will argue this point and conclude this study with reference to Dreiser's three best novels, *Sister Carrie*, *The Financier*, and *An American Tragedy*.

Dreiser's first novel, the one furthest removed in time from his personal activism, is paradoxically his most liberal. That is to say, the society portrayed in *Sister Carrie* has perhaps more fluidity, more room for human development, than that depicted in most of Dreiser's work. The naïve, insensitive, somewhat amorphous country girl at the novel's beginning becomes in just a few years the poised, aware, and successful actress whom we leave at the narrative's conclusion gazing philosophically out into the universe. Although Carrie's natural beauty and charm, her caste characteristics, are crucial to her success, it is also true that the learning process, the acquisition of grace, sophistication, manners, taste in dress—"class," in several forms—are likewise instrumental. The social refinement acquired under the influence of Drouet, Hurstwood, and Mrs. Vance passes Carrie through the school of hard knocks. Alone, she might not have graduated. And as the novel concludes she has just met the man who will school her mind, Ames, whose very name suggests self-improvement. Further, Ames, an electrical engineer, represents a new generation of technician-intellectual whose endeavors will transform both the natural and the social environments. Although he is more metaphor than fully-fleshed character, his appearance in the novel's closing pages suggests Dreiser's faith in progress, man-made. Dreiser may not permit Carrie the attainment of ultimate happiness or wisdom as he leaves her wistfully rocking, but she has already gained much in the social sphere. She is interesting to us precisely because Dreiser has given her the capacity to change and grow. Without it, she would be dull and flat. Jennie Gerhardt, her literary sister, is far more lovable but also far less intriguing.

If Carrie's rise typifies one aspect of class, Hurstwood's fall represents another. When we first encounter Hurstwood and as we view him through Carrie's perspective, he seems to be a superior man enjoying a properly affluent social station. Yet no man of truly superior caste could plummet so quickly to so miserable an end. Dreiser attempts to account for Hurstwood's decline in terms of social as well as biological determinism, showing him deprived of both his money and his youth. But although many critics have found the portrayal of Hurstwood's fate the best thing in the novel, and while it is true that the Hurstwood narrative inspires some of Dreiser's best scenes, I would propose that Hurstwood's fall is perhaps more vivid than credible. In spite of Dreiser's invocation of various forces and contingencies to explain it, and notwithstanding the masterly treatment of victim-psychology it elicits, the fact is that Hurstwood's destiny pivots upon a piece of pure invention and factitious melodrama—the *deus ex machina* closing of the safe door. As a consequence the reader, at least this reader, takes away from *Sister Carrie* a memory not primarily of man mangled by the teeth of inexorable forces but rather of a fluid social scene in which brains, talent, pluck, and beauty, sharpened and strengthened by education and experience, decide one's life. Appropriately, in Carrie's case the characteristic associative scenes and images are social: indoor scenes, money, clothes, personal accouterments, apartments, vehicles, furniture, artificial light. For Hurstwood we begin with such scenes and images during his prosperity and then shift during the narrative of disintegration to the naturalistic: outdoors, cold, snow, winter, darkness.

In contrast to the frequent reference in *Sister Carrie* to traits of class, the presentation of characters in *The Financier* depends heavily upon images of caste; that is, Dreiser's vocabulary constantly stresses unchangeable physical qualities, what is given, not acquired. We have already observed the novel's use of animal references and its treatment of Cowperwood in terms of force. But Dreiser also uses a less obvious method, a form of incremental repetition, and that is the steady, cumulative allusion to Cowperwood's physical presence, vigor, well-being, alertness, acuity. In the first four chapters alone there are nine such references; a tabulation of the whole novel would reveal hundreds. Dreiser also bestows upon his protagonist a kind of special power, most often expressed as visual, a psychokinetic energy of the eye. From the beginning Cowperwood's clear, gray, inscrutable eyes are made essential to the reader's concept of him.

Nor does Dreiser allow us to forget the presence of Cowperwood's mind. In describing the young Cowperwood's performance in his first job, Dreiser employs the most ordinary terms of common speech, *to know* and *to see*, which are at the same time exemplary of Cowperwood's innate qualities. During the five paragraphs depicting Cowperwood's first week's work (Chapter 4), Dreiser refers to mental process—knowing, seeing, deciding—*fifteen* times. But despite its frequency, this aspect of style is neither labored nor spectacular. It operates naturally in context, is integrated within the larger body and normal vocabulary of Dreiser's prose, and functions as part of the basic, heavy rhythm of his style.

Other men of force in the novel are likewise characterized by means of their physical attributes and presence. Butler, though elderly, is "hale and strong like seasoned hickory, tanned by wind and rain." Mollenhauer is "tall and heavy and shrewd and cold," massive of head and of imposing visage. Simpson is small and frail in appearance but has his strength in his eyes: "deep, strange, receding cavernous eyes which contemplated you as might those of a cat looking out of a dark hole."

In contrast to men like these, who would obviously dominate any social order, there is the weakling type as represented by Stener. Such men as Stener may enjoy a temporary ascent in fortune and social status, taking on the concomitant superficial characteristics of success: finer clothes, more flesh, heartier manner. But the weakling can never alter his essential being, his inferior substance. Accordingly, Dreiser's recurrent portrayals of Stener picture his mediocrity in physical terms. The reader's first glance at Stener perceives him immediately to be one of the losers:

"eye of vague gray-blue ... stomach the least bit protuberant." Of course, when trouble hits, the characters' relative responses have been foreshadowed. The strong grow stronger; the weak, like Stener, collapse into little mounds of quivering protoplasm. Dreiser's perspective in *The Financier* reminds us of the argument we modern environmentalists would have with our elders: "You can be better," Arthur Miller's hero shouts at his father in *All My Sons*. "It's in the blood," our elders, and Dreiser, would reply.

In part because of the relative simplicity of Dreiser's treatment of caste and class in *Sister Carrie* and *The Financier*, they are less complex and searching novels than *An American Tragedy*. The reader never meets Carrie's parents; she enters the novel already a young woman. Dreiser does sketch in Cowperwood's family background with some detail, but Cowperwood's genius is plainly not explicable by heredity, although it is well nurtured in an atmosphere of plenty. In *An American Tragedy*, however, the entire first book of the novel records with scrupulous care the formative influences on Clyde Griffiths, and in an earlier manuscript version the treatment was even more exhaustive. The depiction of environment offers no problems. Dreiser demonstrates fully how and why Clyde is deprived and in what ways his later behavior is predictable from such deprivation. What we cannot understand, because Dreiser himself did not understand it, is the peculiar admixture or confusion of class and caste traits, that determined by environment and that determined by heredity, which go to make up the whole nature of Clyde Griffiths.

Accordingly, Dreiser's portrayal merges, blends, and confounds aspects of personality, or social attributes, with attributes of body and mind. For example, the first description of the father stresses the social, although the eyes and body are again telltale clues: "the impractical and materially inefficient texture of the father, whose weak blue eyes and rather flabby but poorly-clothed figure bespoke more of failure than anything else." The mother's description, in contrast, embodies almost purely Darwinian terms: "The mother alone stood out as having that force and determination which, however blind, or erroneous, makes for self-preservation, if not success in life." Soon again Dreiser treats the father, beginning with a quasi-scientific vocabulary but then straying into slippery and subjective terms: "Asa Griffiths, the father, was one of those poorly integrated and correlated organisms, the product of an environment and a religious theory, but with no guiding or mental insight of his own, yet sensitive and therefore highly emotional and without any practical sense whatsoever." This is not at all the objective description it pretends to be, but instead a series of judgments in which the author's values completely override his attempted scientism. There has never existed an "organism" simultaneously "poorly integrated" and "sensitive," without mental capacity yet "highly emotional" withal. Intelligence is precisely the capacity for sensitivity and keen response. It all adds up to Dreiser's version of caste, a mysterious series of givens.

Clyde, too, despite the elaborate environmental detail of Dreiser's presentation, partakes more of mystery than of science, as these early descriptions indicate: "A tall and as yet slight figure, surmounted by an interesting head and face—white skin, dark hair—he seemed more keenly observant and decidedly more sensitive than most of the others . . . his mind much too responsive to phases of beauty and pleasure. . . . The youth, aside from a certain emotionalism and exotic sense of romance which characterized him and which he took more from his father than from his mother, brought a more vivid and intelligent imagination to things. . . . For Clyde was as vain and proud as he was poor. He was one of those interesting individuals who looked upon himself as a thing apart." Even by caste standards Clyde's difference from his parents—his mental acuity, for example, and his good looks—can only be explained as a sort of mutation or, in literary terms, by the flower-in-the-rubbish-heap theory of naturalism.

The same sense of caste infiltrates virtually all the character descriptions in the novel, and it structures all the character relationships as well. Although from start to finish Dreiser graphically documents those flaws and imbalances in the social system which might be amenable to reform—especially, as we have seen, the whole matter of crime and punishment—society itself appears to have been ordained by laws beyond human reach. Those who command do so, for the most part, by virtue of their innate superiority; those who obey are born to obey. Consider how Dreiser's conviction of caste manifests itself in this passage (Chapter 6, Book Two):

And after dinner he made his way out into the principal thoroughfares of Lycurgus, only to observe such a crowd of nondescript mill-workers as, judging these streets by day, he would not have fancied swarmed here by night—girls and boys, men and women of various nationalities, and types—Americans, Poles, Hungarians, French, English—and for the most part—if not entirely touched with a peculiar something—ignorance or thickness of mind or body, or with a certain lack of taste and alertness or daring, which seemed to mark them one and all as of the basement world which he had seen only this afternoon. Yet in some streets and stores, particularly those nearer Wykeagy Avenue, a better type of girl and young man who might have been and no doubt were of the various office groups of the companies over the river—neat and active.

The key word here and elsewhere in the novel in Dreiser's descriptions of the working class is "thickness," a built-in quality seemingly immutable. Or does one become less thick with the advantages of money or high station? There is no explicit answer in Dreiser's work. The implicit answer appears to be No. For Dreiser, the blue-collar worker seems to belong not to a rank but to a race: "meaty," "stodgy," "coarse," "animal," are some of his habitual adjectives.

In caste terms, then, Clyde's tragedy, the American tragedy, is not solely —as a liberal reading of the novel would suggest—a tragedy of social injustice, repression, mistaken values, and "inequity," to use Dreiser's favorite word of the 1930's. It is a tragedy of hubris as well, except that the hero falls not from high to low but from low to lowest. Clyde's flaw is to resemble the master but think like the slave, to feel the desires of the superman but possess the capacity of the weakling. The strong man would have achieved his desires either by avoiding murder or successfully committing it and escaping punishment. Clyde is not fundamentally betrayed by his lack of money or influence but by the essence of his nature, that "certain emotionalism and exotic sense of romance" that makes him first the subject of our interest and then the object of our pity. He may school himself sufficiently in the social graces to win favor from his rich uncle, the smart set of Lycurgus, and even the prettiest girl in town, but he can never acquire the toughness, courage, ruthlessness, and sharp intelligence which forever characterize the Frank Cowperwoods of the world. Those qualities are in the blood, as Dreiser forces us to conclude from the testimony of his work. However much he may have hated what Jefferson called the "artificial aristocrats," he could not help believing that the artificial and the natural aristocrat are one.

Perhaps it can even be speculated that much of the power and durability of Dreiser's best work, as in *An American Tragedy*, derives precisely from this final paradox of Dreiser's politics: that he was able to create a tangible social world, historically authentic, solidly and accurately specified; that he responded to the world passionately both as man and as writer; but that his deepest truths concern not the temporal social order but the larger permanent condition of mankind. Dreiser will finally come to stand for us, I think, neither as literary pioneer nor chronicler of the way it was but as an essentially religious writer, an artist engaged and forever baffled by the eternal mysteries.

NOTES

1. *Dreiser* (New York, 1965), p. 416.
2. *Newspaper Days*, p. 408.
3. *Letters of Theodore Dreiser*, pp. 784–785.

SHERWOOD ANDERSON
(1876-1941)

by Ray Lewis White

FEW AMERICAN NOVELS achieve the artistic purity of *Winesburg, Ohio.*
Since publication in 1919, Sherwood Anderson's masterpiece has been
studied as a realistic, possibly naturalistic, document. Readers have
finished the book feeling that they know the entire life fabrics of the
Winesburg citizenry. They have seen the Reverend Curtis Hartman
creep through winter streets to his church steeple to spy upon Kate Swift
in her bedroom. They have seen Alice Hindman run naked into
a dark street in frustrated search for the sex act. They have learned
from misanthropic Doctor Parcival that "everyone in the world is Christ
and they are all crucified." And they have come to the ironic knowledge
that "many people must live and die alone, even in Winesburg."

Only the very thoughtful reader is aware that he has seen in *Winesburg, Ohio* the mere fringes of the town's emotional patterns. In spite of
the prefatory town map, the inclusion of revelatory minor personages,
and the amazing integrity of imagery and character, *Winesburg, Ohio* is
by no means a complete picture of a midwestern American town in the
late nineteenth century. Emphasizing the "grotesques," beautiful as they
are in their suffering, Sherwood Anderson deliberately omits the average
and the routine, essential in life but not in art. The people of Winesburg
are thus seldom social, usually bewildered, and never political, for
Winesburg, Ohio is the perfection of the middle period in Sherwood
Anderson's creative years, a time of pure artistry preceded and followed
by deeply contrasting periods of intense political concern.

I

Although Sherwood Anderson created *Winesburg, Ohio* from his imagination, he based the town on memories of his boyhood in Clyde, Ohio. The Anderson family circumstances in Clyde foreshadowed much of Sherwood Anderson's later political and social interest. The father, an undistinguished veteran of the Civil War, began his adult life as an ambitious harness-maker and slowly lost business enthusiasm as he assumed the burdens of marriage and children. As Irwin Anderson realized the increasing inanity of his family responsibilities, he escaped from them into the easy refuge of the late frontier tradition—the self-indulgence of the storyteller. According to his tales, Irwin Anderson was the rightly rebellious son of a noble southern family, married to a fine if poor woman. He claimed to be a hero of Union Army exploits, the owner of downtown Cleveland, and a good provider for his family of seven children. Actually, his colorful improvidence lost his harness shop, jobs in various towns, and the respect of his children. If Irwin Anderson was later to be immortalized in fiction by his second son as a careless loafer and braggart fool, he never deserved even that generous recognition, for at life he was that most ordinary of small-town types in nineteenth-century America—a failure.

His wife, Emma Smith Anderson, was surely a comparable failure. Set to hard work at an early age, she knew little of the good life and expected less from her improvident husband. Stern, overworked, under-educated, Emma Anderson bore her children, ignored her husband's neglect, and supported her brood by frugal living and the older children's earnings. Only a sentimental Sherwood Anderson could look back upon this most ordinary of women as an extraordinarily tender mother, doomed to an unwelcome death in 1895. From her, Anderson claimed to inherit his lifelong sympathy for the poor of the working class; from his father, he appropriated the role of tale-teller escapist from unpleasant realities. Ordinary parents both, their son Sherwood remained very ordinary for his first thirty-five years.

Growing up in a small Ohio town in the 1880's and 1890's meant assuming the verities of the almost-Calvinist social milieu. Sherwood Anderson as a young boy with impoverished parents was encouraged to work hard, to recognize that prosperity and morality were officially yoked, to admire the financially successful citizens of Clyde. In rebellion against his father's ways and in compensation for his mother's suffering, young Sherwood Anderson determined that he must have money, status, and security. As Clyde, Ohio, became industrialized, there were chances to get ahead provincially; but Anderson responded after his mother's death to that loudest of calls in the Midwest—the promise of Chicago.

For Sherwood Anderson the reality of Chicago was hours of hard labor rolling barrels in a cold-storage warehouse, dividing his small salary with younger brothers, and carrying out the maxim "Education's the thing" by fitfully attending classes at the Lewis Institute. Chicago had money and security for many, but not for an ill-educated small-town boy from Ohio. For Anderson any escape would do; his was the call to arms for the bogus Spanish-American War. Entering enthusiastically, determined to emerge alive and heroic, Sherwood Anderson saw the South, listened to the rhythm of marching feet, missed all combat, and thoroughly enjoyed the irresponsibility of army life. Only the sound of men marching and firsthand experience of United States imperialism in Cuba remained with Anderson. Forty years later he could recall the battle slogan *"Cuba libre"* and wish his nation had meant its war call.

The war over and additional maturity gained, Anderson decided to follow still the conventional road to success. By attending Wittenberg Academy in 1898–1899, he attained the equivalent of high-school education and thus began the linked events which led to the most famous personal rebellion in American literature. For a successful graduation speech at Wittenberg led to work in a Chicago advertising firm, that most ostentatious subform of American business. As Anderson became adept at the mechanics of buying and selling, he automatically acquired the next necessities—a wife and his own company.

From 1907 to late 1912, Sherwood Anderson controlled, reorganized, expanded, and profited from small distribution companies in Cleveland and Elyria, Ohio. He was making good on ground near his poor boyhood hometown. But the companies brought responsibilities, the marriage brought three children, and increasing worry over the meaning of life brought Anderson to a serious but wonderful emotional turning point: On November 27, 1912, after explaining to his secretary that his feet were wet and cold, Sherwood Anderson walked from his office, wandered for three days in amnesia, and within two months abandoned his unhappy middle-class life for the excitement of Chicago—by 1912 the voice of renaissance in all American literature.

II

To reconstruct Sherwood Anderson's political mind in his Ohio business years is a difficult task, tangled as the scarce facts are with the gigantic myths. Anderson's prosperity may have been deceiving "paper profits"; but he did join a country club, attend literary discussions, impress bankers, and play golf with "the boys." Apparently, it was the hypocritical business and personal ethics of these "boys" which drove Anderson into his first political activity. The philosophy of "service to the public"—used as an all-rationalizing code by American industry—led Sherwood Anderson into extreme reaction against his own business activities.

Although there is absolutely no objective corroborating evidence, Anderson's later accounts of his "Commercial Democracy" scheme are probably accurate in spirit. Accepting "public service" literally, with little practical acumen, Anderson tried to interest various manufacturers, distributors, and salesmen in his plan to produce goods well and cheaply for consumption at an almost nonprofit rate. The profit motive in American businessmen, Anderson assumed, was to diffuse into a hazy atmosphere of "each according to his needs." When this vague scheme interested no one but Sherwood Anderson, the worried Elyria businessman took the only step then possible: he wrote a book called *Why I Am a Socialist* (no copies ever found) and at least two novels (published later in Chicago after the "liberation") detailing fictionally the amateur author's own political confusions.

Windy McPherson's Son (1916) and *Marching Men* (1917) are Anderson's apprentice novels, formed on the frustrated businessman's idea of what novels should be, although both works show autobiographical origins. Sam McPherson and Beaut McGregor, the protagonists, are small-town boys who mature into pursuit of Darwinian economic ethics and emerge after debacles with most impractical humanitarian impulses.

Sam McPherson, ashamed of his foolish, storytelling father, escapes from Caxton, Iowa, to financial success in Chicago industry. His childless marriage and his morale deteriorate when he suffers psychic rebellion in the exact pattern of Sherwood Anderson. To achieve "innocence" McPherson travels and learns about humanity and himself. Determined to care, to order his life usefully, he adopts several children and returns to his unfulfilled wife, ready to be of true "service."

Similarly reenacting Anderson's own youthful poverty and drive to success, Beaut McGregor, of *Marching Men*, rebels against the brutality of a small Pennsylvania mining town, hates all mankind in compensation for his "cracked" father, and becomes financially secure. But in McGregor reversal comes from Anderson's fascination with massed marchers in his army days: McGregor organizes thousands of working people to march stoutly to and from their factory gates, thus frightening industrialists into sharing both means and profits. Both the plan of the marching men and Anderson's novel dissolve into confusion.

These heroes' attempts to regain Adamic innocence in order to serve

mankind are pitiful efforts at real storytelling by Anderson the businessman; the 1912 breakdown and escape into Chicago's artistic circles led
Sherwood Anderson to better art and a peculiar but necessary unconcern
with politics.

Even Sherwood Anderson could never adequately describe his ecstasy
at meeting serious artists and writers in Chicago. The founding of
Poetry: A Magazine of Verse and *The Little Review*, the publication of
Carl Sandburg's *Chicago Poems* and Edgar Lee Masters's *Spoon River
Anthology*—these great events were more or less coeval with Anderson's
welcome into the Chicago renaissance. While supporting himself (until
1923) with halfhearted advertising writing, Anderson met the unknown,
struggling, naïve "little children of the arts" as well as the famed—Floyd
Dell, Ben Hecht, Francis Hackett, Margaret Anderson, Harriet Monroe,
Sandburg, and Masters. All of these people cared intensely about genuine
achievement in the arts; many of them recognized in the shy, middle-
aged Sherwood Anderson a great need to write sincerely and originally.
Under their encouragement Anderson first wrote of "real" people, confused and hurt and "grotesque"—and *Winesburg, Ohio* took form in the
winter of 1915–1916.

Most of the Chicago artists were unconcerned with politics, even when
World War I threatened to draw the United States into battle. However,
by 1917 Anderson had met a new group of literary friends; and with
them he showed mild concern over the European war. In New York
Anderson had come to know Van Wyck Brooks, John Reed, Paul Rosenfeld, Waldo Frank, and Randolph Bourne. These men, by opposing
American involvement, caused Sherwood Anderson to work out his own
attitude toward the foreign war.

In April 1917 he wrote to Waldo Frank, "In a dim way I am trying to
feel that the war has meaning. That it is mankind's stupid way of working something out, a terrible house cleaning." But still glorying in his
new acceptance into a small society that truly cared about his writing,
Anderson began to see the war as a personal threat. By August he was
writing to Frank: "One feels now that the difficulties are greater than in
ordinary times. What a terrible enervating effect this war must be having
on all art and on all expression thru art. It is the time of stupid action
now and the noise of guns and the windy wordiness of men intrudes
upon everything."

In fear of being drafted into military service (he was forty-one; the
age limit was forty-five) and yet hoping that he would somehow lose his
advertising job and "go adventuring," Sherwood Anderson by September
1917 became "every day ... more convinced that the war and all the distracting things that arise from the war are not going to upset me and the

work I want to do. . . . I know that it, with all its bad thinking and with all the distracting influences that are at work, is after all only the same old clatter raised to a roar. Let it roar." The war did roar on, but Anderson followed his own advice that "the great thing is to keep alive the spirit of men at work in the more delicate and subtle things. The whole other business must as far as possible be treated as a right-minded elephant would treat the fact of a bee lodged under his ear."

The armistice finally signed, Anderson continued throughout the 1920's to live his belief in apolitical art. He visited Europe in 1921 and in 1926, there met Gertrude Stein and James Joyce, and fell under the spell of Joyce's prose and D. H. Lawrence's philosophy. He wrote autobiographies, poetry, and two novels, one of which (*Dark Laughter*, 1925) sold well enough to let him join briefly in the wealth of the fabulous 1920's. Personal fulfillment and creative work were the bases of Anderson's way of life, eloquently stated in his long letter (to Paul Kellogg, of *Survey*) of December 14, 1920:

> When I look within myself and ask myself what I most want to see come to life in America, I have to answer "a leisure class." That, I take it, is pretty un-American. . . .
>
> You see, people—not things—interest the novelist, and I am afraid it has come to the place with me that I care nothing at all about who owns the factories, what wages men get, where their children go to school. . . .
>
> I want my leisure class, and I want it now. I want men and women who, at any physical cost to themselves and others, will refuse to continue to work as we understand the word work. . . .
>
> When all the world is crying out for more production at less cost and when the workers are striving for a greater share in industrial management, I want some of the best blood of the country to quit work (in the old sense) entirely.
>
> What I suppose I am asking for is a surplus of energy that doesn't have to farm farms, tend machines in factories or buy or sell anything. . . . I want to hear less about the future splendid physical growth of towns, factories or farms and more about trees, dogs, race horses and people.
>
> It is my notion that if we can in America by some method, fair or foul, create a leisure class, something surprising may come out of it. Such men and women are bound to begin looking about and asking questions. They will wonder why every other person met on the streets is tired or nervous. When they have had time to look about a little and have bottled up within themselves some surplus energy that need not be expended in making anything at all to feed, clothe or house other people, most anything in the world may happen. It is even conceivable that under the influence of such people and with some such sur-

plus energy loose among us, we may begin to do some of the things that now seem entirely out of our reach. We may begin to make towns, houses, books, pictures, gardens, even cities that have beauty and meaning.

And so you see I want a body of healthy, young men and women to agree to quit working—to loaf, to refuse to be hurried, or try to get on in the world—in short, to become intense individualists. Something of the kind must happen if we are ever to bring color and a flair into our modern life. Naturally I believe that the growth of such a class would do more than anything else to make this a better world to live in.

Sherwood Anderson firmly maintained this detached, aesthetic state of mind. In 1921 he explained to Paul Rosenfeld that *Windy McPherson's Son* and *Marching Men* had shown

the effects of a reaction from business men back to my former associates the workers. I believe now it was a false reaction and carried with it something else ... sentimental liberalism. For a time I did dream of a new world to come out of some revolutionary movement that would spring up out of the mass of people. That went. A break came. . . . [Now] I take these little ugly factory towns, these big sprawling cities into something. . . . I pour a dream over it, consciously, intentionally, for a purpose. I want to write beautifully, create beautifully, not outside but in this thing in which I am born, in this place where in the midst of ugly towns, cities, Fords, moving pictures, I have always lived, must live.

Should his writing have political intent? No, according to a 1923 comment to Roger Sergel: "As to the social implications of a story—my own mind simply does not work in that channel. . . . I think story telling worth while in itself—for the sake just of story telling." Should the writer speak publicly on political issues? No, not in the abstract, as Anderson wrote in 1926 to the International Committee for Political Prisoners: "As a matter of fact I know nothing on the subject [of the Italian dictatorship] and for me to write on it would be a good deal like my writing on the affairs of Mars. I have never been in Italy, have read very little on the subject and have no political turn of mind. To be frank I feel entirely incapable of doing anything that would be of any value." Finally, should the writer even identify with causes of the common people? No, as Anderson informed J. J. Lankes in January 1929:

I think one of our weaknesses in this country is, that we artists have been afraid or ashamed to belong to our own class.

We are definitely a class by ourselves and might as well accept it.

As between the Industrial and Laborer there is no choice for us. We have to feed our life and give back what we can and when we want any closeness we have to get it from each other.

But within a year the stock market had crashed, the United States was in a desperate economic depression, and Sherwood Anderson's isolation from politics had ended.

III

Sherwood Anderson's time of most intense political activity had a quiet beginning and a quiet ending. In 1929 Anderson tired of directly managing his country newspapers in Marion, Virginia. The pastoral newspaper episode in southwest Virginia (see *Return to Winesburg*, 1967) had been part of Anderson's attempt to regain close association with small-town and rural America—the source of his best writing. The Marion newspapers were decidedly apolitical, as was Sherwood Anderson's effort in 1929 to break away from the isolation of the Virginia Highlands. Traveling widely and observing the common American, Anderson wrote highly perceptive human-interest articles for his papers. This travel, in the first year of the Depression, combined in 1930 with Anderson's love for Eleanor Copenhaver, of Marion, national industrial secretary of the Young Women's Christian Association, led the writer into his first direct political move.

On January 2, 1930, Anderson declared that he was "through with the ordinary problem of middle-class people in love, etc." His vital new interest was in "working people—in the mills, particularly the working people, the poor whites in the mills in the south." Recognizing his recurrent sympathy in his own boyhood poverty and his idealized image of his suffering mother, Anderson acknowledged that in social concerns he was "an incurable sentimentalist about working people. They seem so much nicer than the rest of us." But the "niceness" might end: "The industrialists are pushing the thing to the limit. Every year there are more people thrown out of work by the perfection of the machines. It's beginning to bite in and will bite in more and more."

Anderson's earlier reaction to mechanization, best expressed in *Poor White* (1920), had been to lament the passing of the old craftsmen—men who cared about their small-scale businesses and who invested personality into their crafting. Now, under Eleanor's benign influence, Anderson wanted to examine a new relationship between machine and man. Planning to write of southern cigarette factories and cotton mills, he wanted to "take the readers inside the factory in a new way, to make them really conscious of the insides of factories." How? "I want to do the job I have in mind without any social theories. When I wrote *Winesburg*, I had no social theories about the small town. I just wanted to get a picture of life in the small town as I felt it, and I would like to do that for the factories, now, if I can." Anderson's resulting articles led him inevitably to close identification with the working class and eager espousal of their causes.

As the economic crisis became more obviously catastrophic in the United States, Anderson reversed his earlier philosophy of aesthetic detachment to declare in the summer of 1930: "An artist cannot help being affected by the mood of his time. With every breath he breathes he takes it in. We have now, in our cities, really hard times. . . ." Without money by 1931, his sympathy fixed, Anderson took political action: In January 1931 he spoke to ten thousand strikers and organizers at a cotton-mill dispute in Danville, Virginia. Knowing the strike was bound to fail, Anderson spoke encouragingly: "I had no notion . . . that I could help them to escape. I thought perhaps I could give them some little sense of historic background." What background? Anderson explained the Magna Carta and the French and American revolutions as "strikes."

Although he refused in February 1932 to accompany Theodore Dreiser on a crusade into the coalfields of Kentucky, Anderson was fully aware of the direction of his political concern. In May 1932, as he finished his labor novel, *Beyond Desire*, he confessed: "I'm becoming more and more a communist. I think it must be coming round—an inevitable thing. I guess this time is good for all of us." A proposed trip to Russia failed to work out, and Anderson's worry deepened. Fearing even worse economic times ahead, thinking that failing political action was requiring economic revolution, he was even willing, by June 1932, to abandon that most prized quality—individualism: "Men and the individuality, so much talked about, and expressed largely in the possession of money is, I am sure, at the bottom of our present mess. It makes half at least of the brutality and ugliness of life."

Sherwood Anderson's political action reached its height in the fall of 1932. First, President Herbert Hoover used federal troops to remove the ten thousand "Bonus Army" veterans from an illegal encampment in Washington, D. C. The group's demand for additional veterans' benefits surely seemed dubious to Anderson, but in a foiled attempt to confront Hoover personally in a defense of peaceful assembly and petition, the writer made his plea for universal freedom of speech. Second, in August of the same year, Anderson permitted his name to be used on the stationery of the National Committee for the Defense of Political Prisoners, a leftist group. And third, in an increasingly ecumenical concern, Anderson attended in Amsterdam the World's Congress Against War, which claimed to represent thirty million workers but which made almost no impression outside its meetings. As Anderson commented:

> The whole feeling of the meeting was for direct action against war by way of propaganda on the part of the writers and artists and by way of strikes on the part of the workers. I think it was the first time that the intellectuals and workers of many countries have actually got together in this way. There were thirty-five nations represented. Of course it was a shame that the capitalistic press all over the world remained almost absolutely silent about the meeting but that was to be expected.

Then the reaction began. The communist claim to superiority for a "classless society" caused Anderson to move, in October 1932, perceptibly back toward his belief in aesthetic, not political, art:

> Someone—some class—I'm pretty sure has, for a time, to dominate society.
> My own relation with the class at the bottom of society now is this—it will, in the end, produce more men of quality than any other class. This because poverty & hardship teaches.
> It will be, in the end, a question of the dictatorship of some dominant business man—representing that class, or this other.
> I'd rather trust the whole under class to produce out of hardship & experience. . . .
> As for us—the artists & intellectuals. . . . Let us not insist. Let us stand on our pride of class.
> I have a feeling that, in the end, if we are worth a damn—we'll survive.

Also, serious illness and an operation came to Eleanor, whom Anderson had been urging to marry him; and his love for her took him out of direct political involvement. On November 11, 1932, he modified his communist sympathy thus: "I am not so sure that simple stories of human beings, caught and held suspended in a civilization, are not better material for the ultimate revolution that must come here than anything else I can do." Anderson's immediate quarrel was evidently with leaders who expected him to write propaganda instead of art.

The following year Sherwood Anderson and Eleanor Copenhaver were married. The stability that Eleanor brought to her husband's previously disordered life was reflected in his more ordered political concerns. Achievement and fulfillment became again his goals, personally and socially:

> America is a land of builders. Our great glorious time has been the building age. We do not know leisure—do not want it.

Go among the down & outs now. Do they cry aloud for bread, clothes, shelter?

No. No.

"Give us work, work, work."

Trouble with talk of revolution is that we all see, in fancy, barricades in the street, people with their backs to the wall to be shot.

Who is being shot?

The capitalists.

But we are either all capitalists or we have dreamed of being. What is needed now is a new assurance. . . .

Work here for a thousand years.

The feet of the Marching Men should be the feet of the builders coming.

Let the revolution be incidental—the brushing aside of all who stand between men and the great work.

Anderson's own resolution of his optimistic concept of "work" was reenactment of his role as social observer. In 1934 he traveled widely over the United States, very carefully recording for *Today* magazine his impressions of miners, farmers, mill workers, job campers—how the people were accepting President Roosevelt's New Deal measures. What Anderson learned was that communism was not needed. For himself:

I think that perhaps, for a year or two, I did rather go over to something like a communist outlook. Now again I am rather uncertain about all that. This attempting to touch off the lives of human beings, in relation to the world about them, is much more healthy for me. I have no solution.

And for his nation:

Of this thing anyway I am pretty sure—the economists don't begin to get the half of it. I've an idea now that the big push toward some sort of revolution—if there ever was one—is over for the time. People in general don't want it—dread change of any kind.

What, I've a notion, we'll get is life going on, on a good deal lower plane, the masses of people settling down to cheaper living. They will stand for a lot and at bottom are not revolutionary minded. . . .

I've been about with the revolutionists a good deal and being with them always intensifies my own individualism.

Then I go with the rich and see how, generally, riches make life ugly.

IV

"Individualism" and "riches" are terms central to understanding Sherwood Anderson. His social and political comment in the early 1930's came when unregulated economic freedom had endangered the entire nation. Writers were needed then to inform both the citizenry and the government of hardship and of corrective measures. Anderson's observations, collected in *Puzzled America* (1935), reveal his proletarian sympathies and acute descriptive powers; whether Anderson's solutions were profound or not, he was, after all, a direct observer of the misery and poverty and despair he described.

Yet it was Anderson's respect for his own individualism that caused him to reject the glitter of communism for himself and for his nation. He respected his craft too much to cheapen it by writing propaganda on order, and he refused to become a Communist party member. And here "riches" enter. For, even with *Winesburg, Ohio,* Sherwood Anderson never in his writing career, from 1912 to 1941, made enough money to live at ease. (The money from *Dark Laughter* in 1925 went for building a country house that kept Anderson poorer than before.) But he never resorted to hack writing or commercialization of his talents after his break with advertising in 1923. As a poor man, Sherwood Anderson should have been tempted to accept complete communism, but as a writer, he remained independent. Anderson knew almost no leading politicians. He never publicly campaigned for any poltical party. His own life was singularly free of partisan politics and yet he followed the general course of the United States into social reform in the 1930's. Needed reforms made, he resumed his role as artist. At his death in 1941, Sherwood Anderson was writing from a full life when he called himself "a most fortunate man."

JOHN DOS PASSOS
(1896-1970)

by W. Gordon Milne

As THE ONE American novelist of the 1920–1960 period who in some degree touched upon most of the important social issues of the time—from industrial greed to Red scares to the role of the artist—John Dos Passos led his confreres in reproducing the intellectual currents of his age. This is quite in keeping with his view of the writer of fiction as an "architect of history,"[1] a sort of secondhand historian of the times in which he lives. Steadily reporting on the times, on the problems of militarism, economic inequity, class barriers, totalitarian systems, and the like, he examined these matters decisively and thoroughly, giving especially firm evidence of his political sympathies and interests. Using the past as a point of reference, particularly the Jeffersonian age, when democratic ideals truly flourished, he contrasted it with troubled twentieth-century America. Convinced that we are living, as he told F. Scott Fitzgerald, "in one of the damnedest tragic moments in history"[2] and that the United States went off the track at the time of World War I and had not regained its equilibrium, he castigated this "derailed" republic in novel after novel over a forty-year span. Yet in spite of his scorn and dismay, he remained hopeful—one is amazed at this—about the "promise of America" and of its "self-governing" system.

Dos Passos reached the height of his popularity with the publication of his original and very forceful trilogy *U.S.A.* (1938) at the end of the 1930's, but as everybody knows, he has not maintained his reputation. Of the various reasons assigned by the critics for his diminishing standing—the propaganda aspect of his work, its topical nature, the failure of recent readers to share the author's view that history has an ascertainable order,[3] the belief on the part of some that Dos Passos has reversed his political sentiments, or the unevenness evident in his technique—only the last possesses much validity. Weakly written novels like *Chosen Country* (1951), *Most Likely to Succeed* (1954), and *The Great Days* (1958) certainly have not helped their author's cause. However, his last book, *Mid-Century* (1961), marking, by virtue of its vigorously written narrative, biographical, and documentary passages and its creation of characters about whom the reader cares, a return to the form on display in *U.S.A.*, has brought renewed interest in Dos Passos. Joining the critics who championed him in the 1930's, Edmund Wilson, Percy Boynton, Harlan Hatcher, and Joseph Warren Beach, the present-day "assessors" like Alfred Kazin, Thomas West, and John Wrenn, aided by the paperback publishers, have launched what may become a boom—at least, a justifiable refurbishing of his reputation.

What all the Dos Passos critics, then and now, have properly emphasized is the presence from the beginning of his career of a concern for artistry as well as for propaganda. Never forgetting his initial indoctrination in aesthetics at Harvard—in the midst of that Eliot-Cummings-Hillyer coterie—Dos Passos has striven to advance his theses with artfulness as well as indignation. As a consequence, his works demonstrate technical inventiveness and a freshness of style which, along with their "message," give them life—indeed, enable them to contribute to the maturing of twentieth-century American fiction. Although not sacrificing his primary aim of influencing the reader ("the importance of a writer . . . depends on his ability to influence thought," *Occasions and Protests*, p. 9), Dos Passos has seldom allowed the "bias of social theory" to "distort his art"[4] and has maintained precise artistic standards while exercising his moral judgment upon the social tendencies of his time.

In functioning as an "architect of history" and attempting by means of the work of art to mold the course of social history, Dos Passos turned his fiction into a series of critical documents on the age, confronting contemporary problems from the time of his attack upon war in *Three Soldiers* (1921) to that of his assault upon labor in *Mid-Century*. His "documents" have been based upon a firm set of principles, sustained from first to last. Contrary to popular opinion, which has labeled him a political apostate, a liberal-become-conservative, his values have remained constant. Simply put, they comprise a hatred of "collectivisms," with their concomitant of centralized power,[5] an admiration for the "proletarian soul," and a persistent desire to protect this "soul" from the aggregates of power.

If Dos Passos were willing to accept any label for himself, it might be that of an "independent seeker," a nebulous term, to be sure, but one that suggests his perpetual focus both on individualism and on searching, with its implications of change. The various stereotypes that have been attached to him—the lost-generation aesthete, the fellow traveler, the ex-radical—have fitted only for a time. Underlying the "phases," however, has been an unflagging credo, a faith in the individual sturdiness of the plain people. "Individuality is freedom lived" (*Occasions and Protests*, p. 52).

To support this central concept, Dos Passos has sought, over the years, for a truly democratic, self-governing society, one which permits full scope for the individual. Initially very much disturbed by World War I, a brutal, oppressive force, epitomized for him in the machine image which dominates his *Three Soldiers*, he regarded it as enslaving the individual—particularly the soldier, of course, but also the greedy industrialist, the country's ruling elite, and especially the general public, whom the "elite," with its stream of rudimentary propaganda, constantly deceived.

Coming home from his wartime ambulance-driving and Red Cross stint "with the horrors" and determined to "blame somebody" (*The Theme Is Freedom*, p. 2), Dos Passos sought alternatives to America's badly functioning industrial democracy, which seem to jeopardize individual freedom. With a spirit of radicalism simmering as he felt called upon to test existing institutions, he was attracted by a variety of leftist movements: socialism ("We protested night and day. . . . Suddenly I believed I was a socialist. Even then I marveled a little at the suddenness with which passionate convictions develop in the youthful mind," *The Best Times*, p. 46); anarchism ("They were fanatics of course but there was humanity in their fanaticism. I never found among them that Marxist stirring up of envy, hatred and malice that corrodes the character of men and women," *The Theme Is Freedom*, p. 11); trade unionism—movements concerned, one observes, with the worker, the underdog, the downtrodden. His support of the Communist party in the 1920's and early 1930's—as the successor to the I.W.W. and as the archenemy of privilege—earned him, in the public eye, the Marxist label, but he did not then or later join the party. If admiring its nuisance value in exposing weaknesses in the capitalistic system, he soon became suspicious of its ruthless tactics, particularly its "using" the working class. He could never accept its doctrinaire attitude either ("I never could keep the world properly divided into gods and demons for very long," *The Best Times*, p. 71; "Maybe I'm not sure enough that I'm on the right side. Evil is so various," *The Theme Is Freedom*, p. 7). Clearly, Dos Passos was always the independent ("never much of a hand to work with organizations," *The Best Times*, p. 165), a crusader in his own way for freedom of speech, an even-handed judicial system, the rights of the miners, farmers' cooperatives, and so on.

Once Dos Passos had progressed from attacks upon corporation presidents and Marxist leaders[6] to government and labor officials, it became perfectly apparent that his continuing series of dissents was based on an objection to oppressive power in any form. Indeed, this objection has served as the *idée fixe* of his career. Early in the 1930's, he veered away from the Earl Browder–William Foster contingent because they made pawns out of the Kentucky miners. Then he soured on Franklin D. Roosevelt because the stifling bureaucracy of the New Deal militated against the average man. In the 1950's he chastised the labor leaders because they ignored the needs of the rank and file of union members. In *U.S.A.* he indicted America's "machine" civilization (the metaphor continued to be central in his writing) because it threatened individual liberty—for example, the creative instinct becoming subordinate to the pursuit of "success." These men and their organizations, he said, "fastened on society the dead hand of bureaucratic routine or the suckers of sterile vested interests" (*The Theme Is Freedom*, p. 238) instead of encouraging individual growth and personal freedom.

Again and again Dos Passos inveighed against this baneful thrust of power: Capitalism was cursed with a "too great concentration of power" (*The Theme Is Freedom*, p. 245); "the federal government became a storehouse of power that dwarfed the fabled House of Morgan" (*The Theme Is Freedom*, p. 162); the Communist party proved "a greater danger to individual liberty than all the old power-mad bankers and industrialists" (*The Theme Is Freedom*, p. 236); the labor movement turned into an "exploitation of the working man by a ruling oligarchy" (*Occasions and Protests*, p. 255). The conclusion is inescapable: Such power structures must be decentralized. A moral revolution must take place.

It is surprising indeed that despite all the evidence to the contrary, Dos Passos doggedly clings to his faith in this possibility, conceives that American society might be "born again" in this "interesting time to be alive" (*Occasions and Protests*, p. 290), believes that politics might become, as he would have it, "simply the art of inducing people to behave in groups with a minimum of force and bloodshed" (*The Theme Is Freedom*, p. 155). It is surprising that he continues to cherish, in short, "a Walt Whitman–narodnik optimism about people I've never quite lived down" (*The Best Times*, p. 87).

As Dos Passos's several novels reproduce the course of twentieth-century American history—the protest decades prior to World War I, the restless twenties, the darkly complexioned thirties, and the still uneasy forties and fifties—they become a kind of "litmus paper that gives you the mood of a society" (*The Theme Is Freedom*, p. 60). The author's very first work, *One Man's Initiation* (1920), sounds the keynote, the individual battling against society, trying to be "individually as decent as you can" in the face of economic and other wars. The struggle is intensified in *Three Soldiers*, where the gas and mud and vermin of the trenches (as well as the army bureaucracy) oppress man so horribly. Notwithstanding a decided shift of scene in his next novel, *Streets of Night* (1923), to Cambridge and Boston and aesthetic circles, the themes vary only slightly. Loneliness and a failure to adjust to the world characterize the three young people who play the leading roles.

The powerful urban novel *Manhattan Transfer* (1925), which marked his coming of age as a novelist, continues the pattern, with its corrosive picture of life in the big city, its inhabitants shuttling endlessly and progressing nowhere, victimized by materialism, racial prejudice, snobbery, and political corruption. The novel, in form, content, and mood, anticipates the trilogy to follow (*The 42nd Parallel*, 1930; *1919*, 1932; *The Big Money*, 1936). In its driving, adjectival style, precise capturing of an environment, and severe indictment of urban society, it—along with *U.S.A.*—constitutes the quintessential Dos Passos.

The trilogy succeeding these works, *District of Columbia* (1952), maintains the social commentary format, while at the same time stressing a sharper political orientation than the fiction which had preceded it. *Adventures of a Young Man* (1938) presents as its protagonist the idealist Glenn Spotswood, who, guided by worthy if not altogether farseeing motives, embraces the Communist party as the defender of the cause of the workers, the pecan shellers in Mexico, the miners in Harlan County, Kentucky. When he comes to realize that the Marxist leaders are opportunistically using the workers to obtain publicity and power for themselves, he shakes off the party line, is excommunicated, and is subsequently murdered. Dos Passos thus firmly rejects Marxism, though only after a reasonably deliberate weighing of the merits and demerits of its tenets and practice.

Number One (1943) concentrates upon another ideology, fascism, as embodied in the would-be dictator Chuck Crawford, a political figure deliberately built on the Huey Long model. Crawford possesses the virtues of energy, ambition, and some sense of the needs of the people, but in furthering his career he freely indulges in wire-pulling, slander, and shady business deals and, Dos Passos implies, far more closely resembles a Mussolini than the Lincoln with whom he likes to be compared. His "taintedness" rubs off, too, on those surrounding him, notably, in this case, the book's protagonist Tyler Spotswood, a sensitive intellectual gone sour.

The Grand Design (1949) provides a third variety of political experience, centralized bureaucracy, as represented by the New Deal. Its aim of a more equable society pleases Dos Passos, yet he questions its achievements and the genuineness of its "liberalism." The New Dealers, men with "flexible" standards, steer the nation uncertainly, some succumbing to influence-peddlers, some fooled by the left-wingers who seek to infiltrate the government. Dos Passos also implies that Mr. Big (F.D.R.)[7] grows more autocratic as World War II approaches, and that the New Deal principles—for example, a decent wage level and collective bargaining—tend to be forgotten in the Washington hurly-burly of gossip, backbiting, and "wheeling and dealing." Concluding that the Good American is victimized by the forces of corruption in society, as symbolized by the politics of the nation's capital, Dos Passos encourages a return to Jeffersonian agrarian democracy, which was based on a genuine concern for the welfare of the common man.

Dos Passos's novels of the 1950's have been called disappointing by most critics and readers, in spite of the presence in them of valuable social insights. Certainly the three to follow *District of Columbia*— *Chosen Country, Most Likely to Succeed,* and *The Great Days*—offer undistinguished stories and a good deal of clumsy writing. On the other hand, they do contain some penetrating comments— for example, in *Chosen Country,* on "radicalism." Dos Passos, one sees, remains disillusioned about the Marxist millennium, sharply satirizing "pseudo" party types like Hedda Gelber and Anne Comfort Welsh. *Most Likely to Succeed* extends the unattractive picture of the left, with its account of the Little Theater group,[8] the singularly unproductive "cell" meetings, the faddish communism of affluent Californians (the "Hollywood Reds"), and the misguided liberalism of those who blithely accepted the Russians as trustworthy allies after the Wehrmacht attack upon them in World War II. Dos Passos is still worried, if the "liberals" are not, about the suppression of individual liberties by the Marxist-oriented.[9] *The Great Days* looks backward to earlier themes, too, especially as it underscores its author's central thesis, a protest against naked power wherever found. Dos Passos unfolds his story against a post–World War II background, emphasizing the international jockeying for world leadership at the time, the uncertain ethics underlying the Nuremberg trials, and the continued presence of chicanery in business and government.

In the author's next novel (and, as it proved, his last), *Mid-Century,* the targets have not changed very much either, though Big Business has more or less been replaced by Big Labor. The idealism represented in such workers' movements as the I.W.W. has become tarnished ("It was," says the worker prototype in *Mid-Century,* Blacky Bowman, "the degradation of the wobblies that was tearing me down"), the newer labor leaders like Dave Beck, Dan Tobin, and Jimmy Hoffa are corrupt, and the communist invasion of the labor movement has proved most harmful. The McClellan Committee investigations repeatedly stress the powerlessness of the laboring man in the face of racketeer-infested unions. Misuse of union funds, sabotage tactics, the kickback, shakedown, and "protection" devices—all the indications of corruption oppress Dos Passos and enhance his disgust with America at midcentury. If man is to "strangle the still small private voice that is God's spark in [him]," to "drown in his own scum," as the novel's final words declare, the "narod- nik optimism" might seem misplaced. Dos Passos discomforts us, discom- forts himself, but still will not forsake his affirming humanism. After all, there is the example of General William Dean.

It is in *U.S.A.* that Dos Passos is seen to greatest advantage, both as an "architect of history" and as a skillful novelist. The trilogy, covering the years from 1899 to 1929, develops the theme of power throughout, illus- trating how the corporation (for example, the United Fruit Company) thwarts the individual and produces economic injustice, how war is a moral cheat and a waste, how "socialism" fails to benefit the common man. The woes of the country are summed up for Dos Passos in the Sac- co-Vanzetti case, the clearest violation, he felt, of America's fundamental principle of individual liberty.[10] If there is any hope of rejuvenation, it lies with the inventors, artists, and statesmen of moral courage and integ- rity whom he "profiles" (not, one notices, with the aimless, futilely drift- ing fictional characters), especially with the I.W.W. leader Eugene V. Debs, his symbol of the untamed spirit.

The 42nd Parallel establishes the subject and the format: the inter- woven "biographies," beginning with that of "Mac" (Fainy McCreary), the working man, and including public-relations counsel J. Ward Moorehouse and interior decorator Eleanor Stoddard, both involved in synthetic "rackets," white-collar worker Janey Williams, and mechanic- inventor Charley Anderson, whose talents are lost when he sells out to the "interests." Intermingled with the biographies one finds Dos Passos's other technical innovations: the newsreel, establishing the period and its atmosphere; the Camera Eye, impressionistic, largely autobiographical sections; and the profiles of the heroes and villains who have influenced their age—Eugene V. Debs, Luther Burbank, William Jennings Bryan, Big Bill Haywood, Minor Keith, of the United Fruit Company, Andrew Carnegie, Thomas Alva Edison, Charles Steinmetz, and Robert La Follette. Through the entire novel runs a list of the afflictions of twentieth- century American civilization: the military spirit, the profit system, the oppression of labor, the collectivist failures.

Dos Passos quickly introduces his solution for the afflictions, a Debsian socialism—the workers' cooperative commonwealth. The character "Mac" joins the I.W.W. and endorses its principles ("I want to rise with the ranks, not from the ranks"). Unfortunately, though, he does not suc- cessfully embody its spirit, his own career representing a lack of direction (simply a penchant for being "where the action is") and not suggesting a thorough dedication to the "cause." Moreover, the "wobbly agitation" meets with very little success, the Debs-Haywood influence quickly waning, the progressive La Follettes counterbalanced by the Keiths and Carnegies, the strikes and rallies achieving little, the individuals still held in check by the "organization" (as Steinmetz by his employer, the General Electric Company). The only success belongs to such as Ward Moorehouse and Eleanor Stoddard, who adapt to the times and make the "big money" through their calculating pursuit of their spurious professions.

The second part of the trilogy, *1919*, only heightens the gloom. A dark mood is established with the book's initial newsreel: the headlines of armies clashing at Verdun, the power of the stock exchange, a waiters' strike, the "shoal water" confronting the war veteran on his return home, and a mocking of Old Glory. The Camera Eye sections tend to display an equally sardonic tone (for example, the death motif in the first one), and the profiles as well (Jack Reed was "a likely youngster, he wasn't a Jew or a socialist and he didn't come from Roxbury"). Nor are the interpolated biographies any more cheery. The sailor Joe Williams is first observed in a grubby bar in South America, having deserted from his ship. Then follows a grim account of his voyage aboard a merchant ship to Liverpool, his imprisonment, for lack of proper papers, and gestapolike treatment, and his subsequent unhappy career, downhill all the way. Richard Savage fares considerably better, to be sure, being, like the Moorehouse-Stoddard duo, "adaptable," able to surrender his youthful idealism (the belief in a "new freedom" and "industrial harmony") in favor of not giving "a damn about anything any more." Surviving the war, taking on a job at the Peace Conference because it "will be a circus, and any chance to travel around Europe suits me," forgoing love and embracing dissipation (up to a point), then joining Moorehouse's firm, he becomes a notably successful "operator" in the capitalistic world. The girl he leaves behind him, Anne Elizabeth Trent, is victimized, however, caught up in the postwar whirl with nothing to support her and ending her life in a spectacular plane crash. Eveline Hutchins, the fourth "biographee," seems to be managing well in wartime Paris, mixing her Red Cross duties with a social round, yet there is ample evidence of her loneliness and lack of purpose, and, indeed, in *The Big Money*, we discover that she commits suicide. The final "story," that of Ben Compton, the revolutionary, has no happier solution. Beset by violence and treachery, he achieves little good and is, in fact, eventually expelled by the "party." Most of the characters arrive at similar dead ends, and the "cooperative commonwealth" about which the I.W.W. and Dos Passos dreamed seems impossible to establish in a world that is "no fun anymore, only machine-gun fire and arson . . . starvation, lice, bedbugs."

The power structure acts as Dos Passos's target again: the bureaucracy of the war machine ("getting the identity cards took another day's waiting around"), monopolism ("United Fruit . . . United Thieves Company"), reactionary government ("Lynch the goddam red . . . put the reds on the skids"). In the face of such forces, the reign of social justice must be postponed. Dos Passos is discouraged, too, by the lack of unity within the working class and by the fact that those touched with the revolutionary spirit often turn out to be traitorous like G. H. Barrow, selfish like Don Stevens, or, finally, disinterested like Jerry Burnham.

The book's profiles further indicate how far in the future the "new socialist civilization" remains. Status quoers Roosevelt, Woodrow Wilson, and J. P. Morgan run the country, the concerned individualists like John Reed and Paxton Hibben are pushed aside, and Wobbly leader Wesley Everest is castrated and lynched by a mob of businessmen. We are left with the chilling final profile of collective man, the Body of an American or the Unknown Soldier—a symbolic corpse.

The Big Money completes the somber survey. In describing the postwar world, Dos Passos aims his guns primarily, as the book's title suggests, at the capitalistic system. Money corrupts three of the four leading characters, Charley Anderson, Margo Dowling, and Dick Savage, as well as many who appear in their lives (for example, Sam Margolies, to whom the Mona Lisa means simply five million dollars). Only Mary French, the "Bolshevik," is unaffected—firmly devoted, to the end, to the workers' cause. Significantly, her "comrades" do not measure up to her standards. Don Stevens has already been exposed in *1919* as self-interested and ruthless, and Ben Compton has also been drawn unflatteringly, as an ineffectual and petty person. Such they continue to be,[11] and they are joined in fruitless wrangling by other left-wingers and "old-line socialists and laborleaders." The revolutionary movements make very little headway against the "big money" complex in a society gone mad with greed. If, in the novel's collection of "profiles," some superindividualists like Thorstein Veblen and Frank Lloyd Wright defy the pattern, the far more influential technocrat Frederick Taylor and the superbusinessman Henry Ford epitomize it. And again we are left with a disturbing final profile of collective man, the "Vag," Dos Passos's favorite symbol of the homeless wanderer, the alienated, little "lost man."

The trilogy, growing stronger and more fierce as it progresses, steadily develops the author's thesis that the world is a gray horror, filled with oppression, inequity, and false values. War and war profiteering, the bludgeoning of strikers, the abrupt dispatching of undesirable aliens, are the norm. At the center lies the Ward Moorehouse success story, the Fords and Samuel Insulls in the forefront, the Randolph Bournes and Joe Hills in the rear, the working people disregarded. Benjamin Disraeli's "two nations" have come to roost in America.

Though Dos Passos does not register his opinion about all this directly in *U.S.A.*, preferring to preserve the documentary approach and the objective narrative pattern, still, the reader can detect his tone and must define it as disillusioned, and decidedly so. His savage dislike of "industrial society" becomes at times, as Edmund Wilson said, "a distaste for all the beings who compose it."[12] So very few endearing characters populate the pages of the trilogy—not William Howard Taft, the "great buttertub," not William Randolph Hearst and his "hired gang," not Ward Moorehouse, the "goddam megaphone," and certainly not Woodrow Wilson, about whom Dos Passos is almost hysterically vindictive—that one does feel a sense of imbalance.

We are reminded that the work falls within the tradition of polemical writing, demonstrating both the virtues and the vices of the genre, a clarity, gusto, and force on the one hand, an excessive degree of denunciation and one-sidedness on the other. If impressed by the moving account of the Sacco-Vanzetti trial, one is at the same time distressed by the unfair portrait of Wilson as a hypocritical politician. If appreciative of the brilliant vigor of the Body of an American profile, one is at the same time bothered by the occasional didactic statement ("And you ask why the prestige of our nation has sunk so low in the world") or oversimplification (for example, Franklin Roosevelt as a power-hungry Caesar). Happily, Dos Passos avoids, for the most part, the shortcomings of "exposure literature," refusing to employ its rhetoric, character manipulation, and too simple structure and relying instead upon an original and lively technique.

His concern for technique is repeatedly demonstrated in *U.S.A.*, reflected, for one thing, in his utilization of a carefully thought out form. He sets up an elaborate structural pattern for the work, a scheme of enormous scope and containing multiple elements, most notably his four pioneering devices, the newsreels, Camera Eyes, profiles, and intertwined "life histories." All these function as separate entities yet at the same time fuse to enforce the leading ideas, lift and enliven the narrative, and produce a strong sense of mood. Above all, they bring into focus what is finally the book's protagonist—or antagonist—twentieth-century American civilization.

The newsreel sections, consisting of headlines, songs, slogans, and advertisements, serve to establish chronology and to create mood. Mixing the trite with the crucial, showing the inconsistencies in the American public image ("Army casualties soar," "peace dove in jewels given Mrs.

Wilson"), they generally convey a sense of the shoddy, restless wartime and postwar boom period.

Perhaps more interesting because less mechanically ironic and more specific are the Camera Eye passages. Written in a semi-stream-of-consciousness style, they are primarily devoted to an impressionistic rendering of the author's autobiography, yet they, too, establish time and atmosphere, giving some sense of how the private life is of a piece with the culture complex. The satirical mood often predominates, with reflections on the horrors of war as felt by a participant and on the absolute futility of his postwar military activity of piling scrap. Most charged with emotion, indeed a prose poem, is the Sacco-Vanzetti section in *The Big Money*, expressing intense unhappiness about the injustices cropping up in the American "way of life." As a rule, however, the Camera Eye confines itself to reflecting the character of the author, partly the sensitive artist but partly, too, the "protestant," questioning the assumptions of the genteel bourgeois class to which he belonged.

The hard-hitting and economically managed profiles seem the most effective device of all, in part because so thoroughly relevant and in part because so forcefully written. The "brief biographies" convey a pronounced sense of historical currents: the sketches of radical labor leaders like Joe Hill, of defeated politicians like William Jennings Bryan, of efficiency experts like Frederick Taylor introducing the principle of scientific management, of the entrepreneurial Henry Ford introducing the production line, of experimenters like Burbank and Edison, of rugged individualists like Veblen and the brothers Wright—all of the people who have affected their age. Presented in a kaleidoscopic, fragmented manner, sometimes akin to the method of the Camera Eye, the profiles foster a vivid impression of the "personality" and his significance; they are, one might say, Dos Passos's "representative men." Distorted they are by the author's bias—we like the Debses and La Follettes, hate the Hearsts and Insulls, just as Dos Passos would have us do—yet they prove to be reasonably accurate, and certainly stimulating, capsule histories.

The substance of the novels stems, of course, from the fourth device, the series of fictional biographies, twelve in all, which crisscross through the trilogy. Almost invariably recording a drifting, meaningless existence, the sketches attach to the individual destiny a strong sense of futility. The twelve principals are backed up by a very large cast of characters, also intermittently appearing throughout the trilogy, and also exemplifying not very purposeful lives. Individuals are driven by sexual desire, an urge for power (for example, labor leader Barrow or Senator Planet), and above all, by a wish for money and all the "conspicuous consumption" that it can buy. Since the material success often proves empty and the idols (for example, Rudolph Valentino) shallow, since no sustaining values support the restless, rootless characters, their happiness is minimal, and the nation's spirit seems thereby deflated.

Dos Passos offers, in the the course of his narrative, a national spectrum: working-class types like Mac and Joe Williams, radicals like Ben Compton and Mary French, social aesthetes like Eleanor Stoddard and Eveline Hutchins, businessmen like E. R. Bingham, lawyers, politicians, generals, even a handful of aristocrats. If extension rather than depth is underlined in the "lives," a stronger sense of milieu than of person, perhaps Dos Passos makes his point about the absence of individuality all the more strikingly thereby. The characters—the nation—caught up in a spluttering pinwheel of futility, suggest a blurred pattern of erosion.

The panoramic format of U.S.A., with the special devices for the most part deftly inserted and with a swift and flexible narrative sustained throughout, works well for Dos Passos. The structure has the fragmented chaotic quality needed to accentuate the fractured lives and fractured values. The tumbled-together headlines of the newsreels, sensory ramblings of the Camera Eyes, rushed phrasing of the profiles—all accentuate a headlong pace, one which crystallizes the concept of going nowhere, of lives involved in a weary treadmill.

In keeping with the mood of the work, the style and language employed by the author are almost uniformly flat. Perhaps the method might be called documentary-graphic or the deadpan voice. Enlivening this, however, is a staccatolike rhythm, achieved through the Dos Passos reliance on short paragraphs, sentence fragments, and a general lack of formal syntax and punctuation, and producing an impressively harsh, spasmodic effect. The controlling principle of the style appears to be directness, the nuances and shadings eschewed. Whether setting forth a character description, an action sequence, or a propaganda speech, Dos Passos uses simple language, often resorting to colloquialisms and profanity and rather seldom introducing an image or a figure of speech. When the latter do appear, they are unadorned and specific ("the trees and the brown stagnant river stewed in late afternoon murk like meat and vegetables in a pot"). If he complicates the style somewhat by the insertion of the big word ("ogival") or by a series of word coinages and combinations ("harveststiff hogcaller boyscout champeen cornshucker") or even by a lyrical prose poem (the Sacco-Vanzetti Camera Eye), the clipped, pulsating effect is generally retained. A case in point might be the often excerpted passage from the Henry Ford profile, "reachunder adjustwasher, screwdown bolt, reachunderadjustscrewdownreachunderadjust until ...," by means of which the conveyor-belt clatter of the assembly line is so well reproduced. Conceivably, the flatness causes a certain sense of monotony over the long span of the trilogy, but it usually succeeds in accentuating the vapidity and aimlessness and in heightening the irony (for example, the final lines of the Unknown Soldier profile—"Woodrow Wilson brought a bouquet of poppies"). The flatness is relieved, too, by the strong epithet ("toadfaced young man"), the chantlike repetitions, and the usually suitable talk of the characters (the vaporous phrasing of the "laborfaker" Barrow, the polished drawl of Judge Cassidy). The jargon and popular rhythms of the newsreel, the brisk fragments of the profiles, and the more image-strewn Camera Eye passages, filled with sounds and colors, contribute to the variety as well. Dos Passos's survey of the restless, simmering urban American environment is effected in wiry, terse, appropriately restless prose.

The "survey" contained in *U.S.A.*—and in his other novels as well—does, in sum, offer a challenging commentary on the quality of the American twentieth-century experience. The sometime "Greenwich Village radical" and always "warmhearted liberal" protested throughout his fictional career: against the tactics and goals of capitalistic enterprise, the "monstrous excesses" of communism, the stultifying bureaucratic machinery of big government, the extortionate activity of the labor bosses. In every case, he was motivated by a desire to protect the rights of the "common man," to obtain a better deal for the shipyard worker, the farmer, the miner, the migrant laborer, all those who had been mistreated by capitalists or "socialists" or bureaucrats or labor leaders. If quite clearly recognizing that the "little man" is by no means perfect, that one must allow for his self-seeking, shortsightedness, timidity, "abominable apathy and only intermittent public spirit" (*Occasions and Protests*, p. 61), yet Dos Passos retains his faith in that little man, in his capacity for self-government, in his possessing "enough goodness ... to ennoble his life on earth instead of degrading it" (*Occasions and Protests*, p. 4).

As a corollary to this, Dos Passos retains his faith in the American democratic process, persuaded that, its marked imperfections notwithstanding, it most readily safeguards individual freedom and the possibility of "selfgovernment." "Our system," he declares, "has never been perfect, but during 168 years the ordinary run of men have had a better chance to develop and live lives as they wanted to than during any other period we know anywhere else in the world" (*State of the Nation*, p. 2).

What draws him to the democratic system, also, is its permitting change and growth. As he said some years ago, "Selfgoverning democracy [is] not an established creed, but a program for growth" (*Occasions and Protests*, p. 4), and Americans must not cease to be dedicated to what Lincoln called "that something more than common," must not content themselves with the "sour postulate that American democracy is rotten.... If the first builders succeeded against great odds, why should we who have their foundations to build on necessarily fail?" (*The Ground We Stand On*, pp. 7, 12).

The "theme is freedom" still. The "American way" allows for that stubborn individualism manifested in the integrity of a Debs, the honesty of a Veblen, the independence of a Wright, as well as any political system. Despite the concentration of power seemingly inherent in industrial democracy, the average American should not forsake his "frontiersman" role, should, in the face of all obstacles, grit his teeth and hang on—and perhaps someday a "decent ordering of human affairs" will come about. In any event, America is Dos Passos's "chosen country" still, the best hope for an "old-fashioned believer in liberty, equality, and fraternity."[13]

NOTES

1. "A writer who writes straight," he said, "is an architect of history" (*Occasions and Protests*, p. 8). Throughout his career he has given evidence, in both his fiction and his nonfiction, of the pronounced "taste for history" (*The Best Times*, p. 14) that he had acquired as a very young man.

2. F. Scott Fitzgerald, *The Crack-Up*, Edmund Wilson, ed. (New York, 1956), p. 311.

3. Alfred Kazin has suggested this explanation for the author's "isolation" (see Alfred Kazin, "John Dos Passos: Inventor in Isolation," *Saturday Review*, March 15, 1969, pp. 16–19, 44–45).

4. Joseph Warren Beach, *The Twentieth Century Novel* (New York, 1932), p. 445.

5. One notes the view of Thomas West: "His present conservatism appears to reflect a sane and genial trust in the less centralized political organisms of the American past and a conviction that the shift of power toward Washington and the unions, however necessary in its beginnings, may become a threat equal to that which it once countered" (Thomas R. West, *Flesh of Steel* [Nashville, Tennessee, 1967], p. 55).

6. "Their strength was that they had a definite set of convictions they held to with religious fervor. . . . Their weakness was that they had no way of appealing to the desire for personal independence and to the basic creed that there should be fair play for all, which, thank God, is just as strong among American working people as it is in the rest of the population" (*The Theme Is Freedom*, p. 40).

7. Dos Passos's initial appreciation of Roosevelt was severely modified. "The political act I have most regretted," he remarked, "was voting for Franklin D. Roosevelt for a third term. . . . Had he retired at the end of his second term . . . he would have been one of the greatest presidents" (*The Theme Is Freedom*, p. 161).

8. The author is here, as so often, drawing upon his own experience, his association, in the early twenties, with the leftist theater. It was a disillusioning

contact: "the constant insidious underlying conflict with the hardshelled communists who were determined that any theatre that had anything to do with working people should serve the party" (*The Theme Is Freedom*, p. 42).
9. *Cf.* his statement in 1950: "If what we wanted from socialism was the growth of self-government and an increase in individual liberty and a wider distribution of goods among the masses of men, it's pretty obvious by now that the Soviet Union is not the place to look for any of these benefits" (*The Prospect Before Us*, p. 131).
10. He "seceded privately" from the United States government, Dos Passos later remarked, on "the night Sacco and Vanzetti were executed. It was not that I had joined the communists. . . . I had seceded into my private conscience like Thoreau in Concord jail. A man needs to do that from time to time in his life" (*The Theme Is Freedom*, p. 103).
11. Ben Compton, so proud of his oratorical ability, refusing to show friendship toward his fellow revolutionary Steve Warner because of the latter's Ivy League aura, strikes me as thoroughly childish, and I fail to agree with the critics who have singled him out as one of the positive characters in the trilogy.
12. Quoted in Daniel Aaron, *Writers on the Left* (New York, 1961), p. 349.
13. Quoted in Carl Van Doren, *The American Novel* (New York, 1949), p. 337.

WILLIAM FAULKNER
(1897-1962)

by Lewis A. Lawson

IN THE DECADE from 1918 to 1928 William Faulkner spent much of his time away from his hometown of Oxford, Mississippi. During this period he served briefly as a cadet in the Royal Flying Corps, worked at various jobs in New Haven, New York, New Orleans, and elsewhere, and attempted to establish himself as a writer, first as a poet, then as a novelist. He seems to have been a rather ordinary young man responding in a rather ordinary way to the immediacy of his existence. Probably he did not stay in any one place long enough to reflect upon contemporary events as outgrowths of the past. Certainly in neither of his first two novels, *Soldiers' Pay* (1926) and *Mosquitoes* (1927), does he show any interest in the historical factors which created the period of aftermath in which he was living.

Yet when he returned to Oxford to live, he could not have escaped observing the radical transformation in the culture from which he derived. As his subsequent fiction reveals, Faulkner very clearly saw that these cultural changes were in response to both internal and external causes. Inside his culture, there was a vacuum of leadership as the old patrician class lapsed into impotence; outside his culture, there were new social, economic, and political pressures as an alien class grew strong and aggressive. For the first time Faulkner realized a world of cultural density as he worked on two manuscripts, quite different in subject matter but alike in being essentially historical, in that they looked to the past for an explanation of the present. In one, "Flags in the Dust," he attempted to account for the decline of the patrician class, representa-

tives of which he called the Sartorises; in the other, "Father Abraham,"
he attempted to account for the rise of that threatening group that he
called the Snopeses.[1]

He himself would have served as a prime example of the final phase in
the deterioration of a patrician family. He was the eldest son of Murry,
who was the son of John Wesley Thompson, who was the only son of the
family patriarch, Colonel William Clark, to marry and sire children. But
despite his responsibility to uphold and enhance the name of his family,
Faulkner was in almost every way a failure, lacking even a high-school
education. To his fellow townsmen he was a conspicuous, even laugh-
able, spectacle, whom they called Count No'count.[2]

He would have had no difficulty, either, in discovering modes for the
invading class, the Snopeses, for they were now becoming dominant in
all Oxford's activities. These white people were part of a general migra-
tion and consequent cultural upheaval in northern Mississippi around the
time of World War I. Leonard W. Doob, studying the castes and classes
of Indianola, a little town not far from Oxford, concludes:

> Up until the World War ... the class system was almost identi-
> cal with the caste system: the upper and middle classes con-
> sisted of whites and the lower class was composed of the Negro
> caste. The supply of Negro sharecroppers was sufficient to cover
> the expanding and contracting demands of the white planters. A
> white man, then, was either a capitalist or a direct employee of
> a capitalist, or else he was a tradesman or a member of the
> so-called professional class. All of the white inhabitants, includ-
> ing the poor whites themselves, claim that during the first
> decade and a half of this century there were practically no white
> people who were compelled to belong to the lower economic
> class.

From the war on, though, many area Negroes migrated North to enjoy
greater economic and social opportunity, and poor whites from other
areas rushed in to fill the vacuum:

> As a result of this flow of immigrants, the social structure of the
> country around Southerntown [Indianola] was profoundly al-
> tered. No longer did class lines correspond to caste lines. For the
> addition of this group of people meant that the lower economic
> class thereafter contained white men and women whose caste
> affiliation was the same as that of the upper and middle classes.
> Economically, in a word, poor whites were on a level with the
> Negroes; but socially they belonged to their employers' group.[3]

Professor Doob's description of the result is convincing as to its sociological accuracy. But it does not convey the emotions of anger, disdain, and fear felt by the established white class as it viewed this invasion. This response, the kind that Faulkner made,[4] is better revealed by the patrician William Alexander Percy, an inhabitant of nearby Greenville:

> Our town of about ten thousand population was no better or worse, I imagine, than other little Southern towns. My townsfolk had got along pretty well together—we knew each other so well and had suffered so much together. . . . Unbeknownst, strangers had drifted in since the war—from the hills, from the North, from all sorts of odd places where they hadn't succeeded or hadn't been wanted.[5]

In small Mississippi towns such as Greenville, Indianola, and Oxford, the newcomers immediately became social threats, for they constituted an unassimilated, unfathomed part of the ruling white caste. They soon became an economic threat, for they were intelligent and ambitious. And when they attained even a minimal prosperity, they became a threat to the old politics operative in the community since 1890. From 1865 to 1890 many Negroes, despite illegal efforts to block them, had exercised their right to vote; in that year, though, a new constitution was adopted which established literacy and a poll tax as prerequisites to voting. Both obstacles were purported to be directed against the Negro, and certainly few white men were ever disqualified because of the literacy clause, but the poll tax effectively blocked unreliable poor whites as well as all Negroes from voting.[6] Thus the courthouse people and the banker and the merchants in the surrounding square could easily dominate the politics of such small towns. But when the country men moved into towns and began to earn a cash income, they could then pay their poll tax and participate in the "revolt of the rednecks," a populistic rebellion of small farmers and unskilled workers led by such men as James K. Vardaman and Theodore Bilbo.

As Faulkner worked on "Flags in the Dust" and "Father Abraham," he was forced to explore history for meaning, since his characters were now enveloped by an ethos that his earlier novels had lacked. And his search for the past and discovery of its complexity was the beginning of his political maturity. For in recognizing that man is the animal with a history, he was also accepting the converse, that man is the animal with a memory, a memory which will not allow itself to be ignored. Since he has a memory, man is freed of the necessity of endlessly repeating the behavior of the past; but having memory, he is obligated to learn from the behavior of the past in order to decide whether to perpetuate or repudiate it. Upon his reading of the past, then, rests man's effort to develop a teleology that will inform the present and thus determine his personal and public behavior. The alternatives to a strenuous sifting of history are equally disastrous, both to private and to public well-being. A slavish, unquestioning acceptance of the caste behavior of the past leads to a mechanical, unexamined performance in the present, in which adherence to the received code outweighs all other considerations. One who practiced such an acceptance would be, in David Riesman's terminology, a "tradition-directed man"[7] who employs what Anatol Rapoport calls an "ethics of retribution."[8] A slavish, unquestioning acceptance of the present, in ignorance or defiance of the past, leads to an equally mechanical, unexamined performance in the present, in which the attainment of an immediate goal outweighs all other considerations. One who practiced this kind of acceptance would be, again in Riesman's terminology, an "inner-directed man"[9] who employs what Rapoport calls an "ethics of activism."[10]

Faulkner seems to have been unprepared to confront head-on the reality of the inner-directed, activist Snopeses, to synthesize his various anecdotes about them into a pattern of action that would admit their rising position. Instead he concentrated upon "Flags in the Dust," which was published in a shortened version as *Sartoris* in 1929. In this first of his Yoknapatawpha novels, set in Jefferson (as Faulkner was to call his Oxford-like town) in 1919–1920, he offers a strange mixture of traditional and radical attitudes about the South. The depiction of institutions is as traditional as in any novel of the previous generation of southern literature. But the portrayals of Aunt Jenny DuPre, the aged voice of tradition, and Bayard Sartoris, the young veteran, indicate a radical departure from the caste attitude toward a uniquely individual view. Perhaps the tonal inconsistencies of the novel result from the fact that Phil Stone, Faulkner's friend and adviser, contributed ideas and incidents that were used.[11] Or it may simply be that Faulkner had not yet developed a fully coherent view of the world that he was to create. Whatever the reason, *Sartoris* frustrates the attempt to reconcile its various statements.[12]

In his delineation of the social hierarchy Faulkner speaks with the voice of an upper-caste member of his society. His characterization of the Negroes in the novel indicates an adherence to the stereotypes of Negro behavior shared by his fellow whites. Negroes are given the opportunity to appear as serious human beings—as when Bayard Sartoris spends Christmas morning with the Negro sharecropper and his family or when the Negro farmer and his son save Bayard from drowning—only if they pay proper deference to the white man. Otherwise, they are ridiculed, as when Caspey is beaten by the elder Bayard for his insolence. The Negro retainers of the Sartoris family, Simon and his grandson Isom, are viewed as humorous violations of the white standard in mentality and morality. Faulkner also speaks with the voice of an upper-class member of the upper caste. He describes in great detail the arrival and dispersion of the newcomers, the Snopeses, though he does not employ here the imagery that he elsewhere uses to imply their animalistic character. But while he does not intrude directly to indicate his antagonism toward them, Faulkner very carefully establishes the kind of activity in which a Snopes engages. The only member of this historyless, hence standardless, clan dealt with in any detail is Byron, who has the gall to aspire to the hand of Narcissa Benbow, daughter of an upper-class family, and who finally burglarizes both her home and the bank where he has been employed by old Bayard Sartoris.

There are some acceptable lower-class whites, to be sure. Old man Will Falls, who comes into town periodically from the county poor-farm to receive a dole of hard candy and chewing tobacco from old Bayard, is obviously acceptable because of his adulation of his dead leader, Colonel John Sartoris. There is also V. K. Suratt, later in Faulkner's saga to be transmuted into the admired V. K. Ratliff, who wears the caste marks of the redneck but who nevertheless achieves his acceptability because of his obsequiousness to the quality. And the MacCallums are described as a stalwart family of southern yeomen, ruggedly observant of traditional ways, who have remained in the country, thus acting in accordance with the Jeffersonian ideal of rural independence that Faulkner praised even in his last interview.[13]

At first it appears that Aunt Jenny is a strange new breed of southern womanhood, an iconoclast. She is constant in her ridicule of the evidences of foolhardiness offered to the world by the Sartoris men, establishing the Bayard who was an A.D.C. to Jeb Stuart as the archetypal figure of rash gallantry and then comparing every Sartoris male since with the original. Thus at first glance it appears that Faulkner has posited her as a norm character who by her attitudes suggests the response he wishes his readers to make.

But then in time Aunt Jenny's real role emerges; by her constant comment, even though it is ostensibly disparaging, she manages to preserve, even foster, the glamorous legend of Sartoris heroism as the essential formative influence upon the behavior of the living Sartoris men. In this fashion she has created a young John who values the heroic gesture more than life itself and willingly pays with his life in World War I for the opportunity to match his act against that of the family archetype. In this fashion she has created a young Bayard who returns from service overcome with shame for having survived and for having felt fear and who must, in an attempt to achieve expiation, obsessively escalate his gambling with death until he succeeds in losing, by crashing an obviously unsafe experimental aircraft. In this fashion she even incites old Bayard to gamble with his life and lose, he who had known the reality of the Civil War and thus had developed an immunity to foolish heroism that lasted over fifty years. Nor does she ever cease her attempts to perpetuate the tradition: Her desire to name young Bayard's son John, the name worn in the past by the rashest Sartorises, signifies to Narcissa, the boy's mother, Aunt Jenny's intention to create yet another cycle in the legend. Only, then, when Aunt Jenny is seen as the transmitter of a tradition that glorifies gallantry, preferably a dying gallantry, at the expense of those qualities necessary for the leading of a healthy, productive life, does it become apparent that Faulkner is really radical in depicting the apotheosis of traditional southern culture, aged womanhood, as the force responsible for the failure of modern southern manhood to shake off the burden of the past and live successfully and usefully in the present.

Faulkner is also revolutionary in his characterization of young Bayard Sartoris. Bayard seems at first to be simply a flat character, a wooden figure whose erratic actions are not authenticated through a rendering of his psychology. But seen against the background of his culture, Bayard begins to appear as a victim of the compulsion to live up to the expectations of his traditional aunt; thus it is appropriate that he, as an instrument totally dominated by exterior forces, have no vital, living, adjusting intellect; all he has is an anxiety that he will not be able to live up to the code and master its gestures. That he is expected to be a creature of gesture is implied by his given name; he is to conduct himself like the historical Seigneur Pierre Terrail de Bayard; he must live up to the concept of the cavalier that had energized southern culture at least since William Gilmore Simms's *The Yemassee* (1835). So compelled to live according to a predetermined scheme, so unquestioning of the real historical circumstances is he, that he dies because he cannot bear to live.

In *The Sound and the Fury* (also published in 1929, but written well after *Sartoris*) Faulkner continues to dissociate himself from the political philosophy that he had inherited. This time there is no deception about the nature of the tradition which provided the mythic substructure of the southern way of life. The chief adornment of the old order, southern womanhood, is revealed in the figure of Caroline Bascomb Compson as the whining, self-pitying parody of genuine motherhood that warps and enfeebles her children's ability to lead rich, authentic existences. Attended by her absurd brother Maury, the very caricature of southern chivalry, she early drives her husband to seek a state of continuous drunken detachment. Conditioned to idleness by the tradition that glorifies her kind as some sort of divine object, she takes to her bed after the birth of her children, to moan genteelly and lament upon her misfortunes. Lying there an ineffectual, self-deluded, and self-pampered old woman in the dilapidated house on the dwindling acreage, she serves as an eloquent metaphor of the decline of the South in the early twentieth century.

Her eldest son, Quentin, is another of Faulkner's cavaliers *manqués*. Deprived of his mother's love because of her preoccupation with the outrages that have befallen her, he grows into adolescence with a sensibility that seems to grow ever more detached from reality. Attempting to meet the ideals of his caste, he settles upon the protection of his sister's chastity as his knightly feat. Here he fails completely, finally suffering the indignity of being easily disarmed by one of her lovers, Dalton Ames. Once she has been married off by her mother to the cheat Herbert Head, Caddy is beyond salvation in Quentin's eyes. Despite his destruction of his watch and his careful avoidance of all indicators of time, he cannot stop time's passage, cannot return to the days of knighthood or unmake the mistakes he has made; thus his only option is to die a noble death, and he drowns himself.

Candace, Caroline's only daughter, attempts as a child to be the warm, comforting mother that her brothers need. She accepts the humanity of her idiot brother Benjy and gives him the only expression of love that he can recognize. She is tolerant of her brother Jason, who is already becoming, because of his mother's petting, a selfish and mercenary monster. She loves Quentin, even though he has already begun his attempts to invade her privacy and deprive her of freedom by his possessiveness. But, in adolescence, when her own maturity prompts her to establish her own individuality, she is so contemptuous of the prized ideal of cold, virginal femininity, of which her mother is so degenerate a version, that she becomes promiscuous, rebelling in the most flagrant and appropriate way available to her, and eventually she is expelled forever from her home.

To indicate just how base and worthless the old establishment has become, Faulkner transcends his own caste and class lines to perform, for the traditional Southerner, the unthinkable act. Unlike *Sartoris*, *The Sound and the Fury* contains no condescension toward the Negro. On the contrary, Dilsey Gibson, the black cook of the Compson family, is depicted with such sympathy and understanding that she emerges as Faulkner's sanest and most admired character. She is everything that Mrs. Compson is not, and the implication is that the tradition from which she derives is equally superior to the tradition from which Mrs. Compson derives. Unhampered by the artificialities of the white caste, she is free to rely upon the ancient Christian tradition, and with that faith she can endure.

Although not one of his most artistically successful novels, *Sanctuary* (1931) is a rich commentary upon Faulkner's outlook in perhaps his darkest period. In *Sartoris*, speaking of the Sartorises, Horace Benbow had observed: "They've just gone through with an experience that pretty well shook the verities and the humanities, and whether they know it or not, they've got another one ahead of 'em that'll pretty well finish the business." Horace seems to be thinking of World War I as the past experience and the approaching anomie as the experience to "finish the business." It is Horace Benbow, appropriately enough, who serves to unite the several threads of theme and action in *Sanctuary*, which has much the same setting and many of the same characters as *Sartoris*, though the time is 1929, ten years after that of the former novel. Horace alone has ties in the patrician world of Narcissa Benbow Sartoris, Aunt Jenny DuPre, Temple Drake, and her father, Judge Drake, in the uncouth world of Clarence and Virgil Snopes and Miss Reba, and in the criminal world of Popeye Vitelli, Lee Goodwin, and Ruby Lamar. More importantly, he alone cares that things are falling apart and tries to preserve any part of the heritage of justice and decency.

From the first confrontation, when Horace, the man with the book, faces Popeye, the man with the pistol, the line is drawn between the traditional and the rootless.[14] But the novel is not a battlefield with distinct fronts and easily identified opponents—the Sartorises and the Snopeses. Rather it resembles a guerrilla campaign where many different factions conduct their own independent operations for their own obscure reasons before uniting at the conclusion for the destruction of the "verities and the humanities." It was Horace Benbow who had foreseen their destruction ten years before; now it is he, ironically, who discovers the absolute and total corruption of the world in which he lives—both the Snopes portion *and* the Sartoris portion.

Almost every institution conceivable is depicted as evil and/or impotent. The "Christian" ladies of Jefferson force the hotelkeeper to turn out Lee Goodwin's common-law wife and her infant; a physician, proudly displaying his Masonic ring, is an employee of Miss Reba's bordello; the highest officials of the law in Memphis sport at Miss Reba's. But primary among institutions dealt with in *Sanctuary* is the judicial process. When the moonshiner Lee Goodwin is charged with murder, Horace Benbow volunteers to serve as his defense attorney, avowing rather foolishly that he "cannot stand idly by and see injustice—" before he is interrupted by the skeptical Aunt Jenny to be informed that he can never "catch up with injustice." What he counts on is a rational world in which there is still respect for universal order; what he views is an irrational world in which "there is a logical pattern to evil."

From the beginning the trial is a mockery. The drunken professional Virginian Gowan Stevens does not step forward as a witness to the events leading to the murder. Senator Clarence Snopes sells his information to anyone who will pay for it. Narcissa Benbow Sartoris, valuing her family's name above all else, betrays her brother's efforts to secure justice for Goodwin. Because he fears that the forces of justice cannot protect him from Popeye, the real culprit, Goodwin will not tell the truth in his own defense. Eustace Graham, the district attorney, ridicules the institution he serves by proclaiming in court: "This is no longer a matter for the hangman, but for a bonfire of gasoline." Temple Drake—whose prayer "My father's a judge" suggests that she thinks of him as a contravener, not dispenser, of justice—perjures herself, and Horace, probably out of some lingering romantic notion about the sanctity of southern womanhood, fails to cross-examine her and thus discredit her assertion of Goodwin's guilt. And, perhaps most indicative of the absoluteness of the corruption, her father, the respected jurist Judge Drake, of Jackson, makes no effort to see that justice is done.

With the mechanics of the judicial system thus travestied, it is no wonder that the jury deliberates only eight minutes before finding Goodwin guilty. When the absolute assurance of the jury about Goodwin's guilt is juxtaposed with the enormity of its mistake, the result is an example of the black humor that Faulkner employs several times in the course of the novel. It is clear that the humor is meant to emphasize the failure of the judicial system, when the Birmingham jury, also after only eight minutes, finds Popeye guilty of a murder which he did not commit. Even such justice as this is grotesquely mocked, though, when Goodwin is taken from jail by a mob and incinerated in the presence of Horace Benbow, whose eyes are burned clean of any illusions he may still have had about the value of traditional institutions.

Sartoris, The Sound and the Fury, and *As I Lay Dying* (1930) are all considerations of the family as a weakening institution. *Sanctuary* exposes a similar failure in various public institutions, especially the judicial process. In his next novel, *Light in August* (1932), Faulkner turns to a consideration of religion as a force capable of reinvesting meaning and dignity in modern anomic life—individual, family, and communal. His strategy is to portray a variety of individuals, each of whom has adopted a somewhat different mode of religious behavior.

One such individual is the Reverend Gail Hightower. The colligation of his names suggests the route that he will follow in life; "Gail," as the diminutive of "Gaylord," of the heroic past, will escape from the ugly present into a "high tower" of fantasy. He is not one of Faulkner's impotent cavaliers; he does not suffer from an inability to live up to the expectations of a chivalric tradition. On the contrary, he derives from a family in which the Civil War had been experienced in all its unheroic and useless destructiveness and in which disagreement about the moral rightness of the southern cause had existed. Indeed the immediate model for his behavior should have been his father, a Confederate chaplain of stubborn religious conviction as well as physical courage. It is Hightower himself who transmutes the sorry reality of his grandfather's death as a chicken thief into the vision of the legion of lancers charging down the dusk-filled street. And after he invokes the vision, he abdicates the opportunity and the challenge of responding to the present in order to live for its daily occurrence.

So compelling is his desire to celebrate the past that he sacrifices even his wife's existence to its glorification. So omnipresent is it in his mind that he cannot perform his public role as preacher to his community without rhapsodizing upon his true faith, which is the myth that he has created. And after he undergoes the ostracism that results from his violation of family and community responsibilities, he feels that he has earned the right to live unbothered in his fantasy. Although he does, with great reluctance, emerge from his isolation briefly, to attend the delivery of Lena Grove's baby, he remains furiously unwilling to involve himself with the pariah Joe Christmas until it is too late. Then there is a moment when it appears that Joe's death may shock him into an awareness of his guilt, but he is saved from that healthy despair by the return of his vision.

Another such individual is Joanna Burden. At first it would appear that, born of aged parents and reared virtually free of parental or cultural influences, she would be immune to the pressures of the past. But then it becomes evident that her family name signifies the effect that history will have upon her personality. Much has been made of Faulkner's apparent error in designating her forebears as Unitarians, rather than as strict Calvinists. But of more significance is the fact that her grandfather Calvin had disavowed Unitarianism, to embrace Catholicism for ten years, only to disavow it in turn to embrace his own creation of a faith of force motivated not by love but by hatred and fear. It is thus the family example of extreme vacillation of religious behavior—constant only in its extremism—that most determines Joanna Burden's conduct.

Her relationship with Joe Christmas is marked, therefore, by phases of behavior that are diametrically opposed to one another. Because of her preconditioning, Joanna can only view Joe as the personification of sin. In the first phase she sees him as a threat to her purity, achieved at the cost of isolated nonexistence. In the second phase she embraces her sin, loving not the person Joe with whom she copulates, but the image of sin which he vitalizes. And in the third phase she attempts to destroy the sin by transforming it into a docile symbol of her charity and reclaimed purity. It is at this point that she falls back upon the religion of force of her forebears, to plan her own redemption through the physical destruction of her obstinate sin-image. Since her religion has always required that Joe be the ritual Negro rapist, entering through windows and hunting her down

in darkened rooms, he, knowing only always to respond in kind, ritualisti-
cally slashes her throat with a razor.

Nor is Joanna the only person to view Joe Christmas as an object of
religious hatred. His grandfather Eupheus Hines, possessed of a fanatic
abhorrence of women and Negroes, is, in a cultural sense, Joe's father.
For it is he who, without any evidence, labels Joe's biological father a
Negro and then executes him for the crime of being a Negro rapist. Then
he allows Joe's mother to die in childbirth and, apparently thinking that
death would be a wasted punishment for an insentient baby, condemns
Joe to live—as a Negro. There is also Simon McEachern, who adopts Joe
only because he wishes to play God, whom he sees as a wrathful Father
wreaking punishment upon His children. The result is Joe's hatred of both
God and McEachern, his lifelong reliance upon force as the only mode of
interpersonal relationships, and his lifelong search for expiation for the sin
of being a black sexual being. This search ends at the hands of Percy
Grimm, who has become a self-ordained priest of militaristic racism,
when a peaceful, maybe even smiling Joe accepts his emasculation and
death.

Each of the people is so conditioned by a historical institution that he
views Joe Christmas as the objectivization of his own particular hatred
and fear. None of these people, therefore, can respond to Joe as a human
being; he remains for them simply an actor performing a certain social
role in their life drama. The community at large has the same view of
Joe, for once Lucas Burch has said that Joe is a Negro, the townspeople
continually expect Joe's actions to conform to their stereotype of Negro
behavior.

The only person to encounter Joe who does not deny his essential
humanity is the man from the hills, Byron Bunch. It is significant that
Byron's thoughts and behavior are never influenced by institutionalized
thinking. His only institutional affiliation is with a church whose denomi-
nation is not even specified, where he leads the choir. Beyond that role,
Byron is socially uncomplicated, a simple man who instinctively offers
help to those who need it, doing good not because it is good but because
it is needed. Like Dilsey Gibson, another Samaritan, he can bear things,
even as he complains that they are not only unfair but unbearable. For
his troubles he is rewarded with that personification of natural charm and
simplicity, Lena Grove.

In *Light in August* Faulkner had presented individuals who were victimized by history largely without knowing it. But in *Absalom, Absalom!*
(1936) he advances to a much more complex presentation of history.
Before, history had been treated as a static, simple, essentially known
quality which finally weighted down its unalert human vehicle. Now,
however, history becomes a dynamic, highly volatile quality that presents

first an aspect of startling clarity, then an aspect of shadowed obscurity, teasing and confusing the mind it penetrates while at the same time demanding that the mind subdue it.

Once again the medium through which the force of history passes is an aged woman, here Miss Rosa Coldfield. The recipient is Quentin Compson in the year before his death. When Miss Rosa commands Quentin's presence, to tell him the story of Thomas Sutpen, and then commands Quentin's company on her expedition to the dilapidated Sutpen mansion, it is as if history is demanding that Quentin confront it before his escape to Harvard. Thus it is the confrontation that is significant in the novel; neither the legend of Thomas Sutpen, which is really a capsule history of the South, nor the meager account of Quentin Compson hearing and then telling the story of Thomas Sutpen provides the final significance of the work; it is the rendering of the process of historical interaction between myth and recipient, a process now vivid and dramatic, now obscure and ambiguous, which causes many readers to regard the novel as Faulkner's best.

When Quentin is first summoned to Miss Rosa's house and told of her reason for selecting him as the recipient of the story that only she could tell, he seems politely bored. Her excuse for telling him, that he might in some future financial emergency write up her account and sell it, seems patently false. And, besides, the story at first appears to be only a recapitulation of a neighborhood legend which he has known all his life, that a local man, naturally a Confederate colonel, had once amassed a huge estate and built a magnificent mansion, the ruined shell of which still remained as a "haunted house."

It is the process by which the story is related to him that captivates his attention. First Miss Rosa and then his father, relying upon the account given by his father, General Compson, demonstrate for Quentin the human link between himself and the old legend that he had taken for granted. And then the very fact that both accounts are unsatisfactory, either because they reveal personal bias or contradict one another or leave gaps in the chronology, further engages Quentin's desire to sort the pieces and assemble the puzzle. At that point he seems to realize that the legend represents a microcosm of his cultural past, which he must accept and master if he is to perform satisfactorily and usefully in his own life. Thus he agrees to accompany Miss Rosa out to the house to discover whatever it is out there that so intrigues her and, in so doing, to come face to face with the historical reality of the legend that he had so easily accepted.

Even more than the first half, the second half of the novel is an illumination of a process. In these chapters Quentin and his Harvard roommate, Shreve McCannon, prompted by Mr. Compson's letter announcing the death of Miss Rosa, attempt to unravel the two disparate versions of the legend and then reweave them into a tapestry of historical probability. Between Miss Rosa's demonological version and Mr. Compson's tragic version of the actions of Thomas Sutpen there may emerge a composite version that Quentin and Shreve can accept as an approximation of the truth.

For Quentin the demythologizing process must be shattering indeed. In the received account of the southern past, all outstanding families derived from wealthy plantations in Virginia or Carolina at some indeterminate time in the past, provided models of domestic morality, social decorum, and public leadership before and during the war, and bore stoically the outrageous subjugation that occurred after their unjust and inexplicable defeat. Sutpen's reality, though, as far as it can be determined, departs radically from the mythic profile.

Rather than being the scion of an aristocratic house, Sutpen is born into a family of shiftless squatters. Rather than succeeding as an adult because of the superior training received from caste institutions, Sutpen is driven only by a desire for revenge. Rather than being the benign father to his family and servants, Sutpen is a monomaniac whose only concern is the unchallengeable fulfillment of his design. And, too, rather than being the noble monogamist of southern legend who idealized his wife, Sutpen has a succession of sexual partners, both inside and outside of marriage.

It may be in his role as sexual creature that Sutpen departs farthest from the mythic profile. Sex for Sutpen is not a method for the expression of love but rather the chief instrument for the fulfillment of personal policy. He thus rejects his firstborn, Charles Bon, because he suspects that Charles's mother may have a trace of Negro blood. He allows his second-born, Clytemnestra, to play the role of a slave Negress in her own father's house because her mother was a Negro slave. He seems to ignore his third-born, Judith, because although she has caste acceptability, she is a female and therefore has no dynastic value. He offers to couple with Rosa Coldfield and marry her if the issue of their coupling is a son. And he fatally rejects his fifth-born, Milly Jones's daughter, again because of the child's lack of dynastic value.

The biography of Thomas Sutpen, then, can really be stripped of all its aristocratic and military trappings and reduced to a recital of his perversion of the most admired human capacity, love. Apparently because of information provided by him, his only acceptable son, Henry, becomes the agent of his design and murders the unacceptable son, Charles, only to run away then and never sire a son, thus foiling the same design. The result is that only Charles Bon's Negro line is left to carry the blood of Sutpen, a line which reaches its nadir in the form of the feebleminded

Jim Bond, who wanders around the twentieth-century wreckage of Sutpen's once proud estate. Thus history in microcosm can suggest to Quentin Compson that the failure of the South to endure resulted fundamentally from its failure to recognize and cherish the basic human opportunity and obligation to love.

The revelations of Sutpen's legend seem to shatter Quentin. He cannot accept the fact that the dynamism of the old order was really provided in many instances by the very lower-class people he had been taught to scorn. Nor can he accept the fact that all the cherished values of the old order—nobility, gallantry, chivalry—resided finally upon such a basic evil as the denial of humanity, even the humanity of one's own children, through the institution of slavery. He protests too much, in response to Shreve's question, "Why do you hate the South?" for he could only hate the South that Sutpen's legend has revealed to him. But he cannot accept and master the new version of the past and pattern his own behavior upon a new awareness—behavior which would necessarily be in rejection of many of the previously held beliefs about his culture. Thus his suicide in a few months is a confession of the failure of will; he has seen the truth, but he cannot act upon it.

Employing technique as discovery, in Mark Schorer's phrase,[15] Faulkner had by 1941 evolved a code for himself:

> I have been writing all the time about honor, truth, pity, consideration, the capacity to endure well grief and misfortune and injustice and then endure again, in terms of individuals who observed and adhered to them not for reward but for virtue's own sake, not even merely because they are admirable in themselves, but in order to live with oneself and die peacefully with oneself when the time comes.[16]

At about the same time he conceived of a character who actually attained a realization of these verities.

Isaac McCaslin appears from the very start, in *Go Down, Moses* (1942), to have an excellent chance of succeeding in his attempt to discover truth from history. His immediate ancestors—his father, Buck, and his Uncle Buddy—from their actions in "Was," the first section of the novel, seem to have none of the aristocratic glamour that would have contributed to a family tradition which would strangle the tendency of any descendant toward liberalization. They seem to be astonished by the symptoms of the "Sir Walter Scott disease," to be perceived at "Warwick," home of Hubert and Sophonsiba Beauchamp. They never even finish the mansion begun by their father, preferring to live in a log cabin, to which they add rooms as needed. They seem embarrassed by the fact that they own slaves; they manumit some of their father's slaves just after his death and others later. Further, all of Isaac's aged relatives die when he is young, so that a different group constitutes his parental influence.

This group consists of the hunters whom he begins to accompany on the annual hunt when he is ten years old: McCaslin Edmonds, Walter Ewell, Major de Spain, and General Compson. The guide of the annual hunt is Sam Fathers, the part-Negro, part-Indian, who seems to realize that he must serve as priest for Isaac's participation in the rites of initiation. The procedure which Sam employs to lead Isaac through the rituals of separation, transition, and incorporation could serve as an example in Father Arnold Van Gennep's classic *Rites of Passage*.

Through his "novitiate to the true wilderness" Isaac undergoes the transformation into manhood that prepares him to read the waiting "scarred and cracked" commissary ledgers which compress the portion of history that directly affects him. At sixteen he is compelled by his achieved maturity to read them and thus learn of his heritage. Here is not a lay of chivalry; rather the very containers reveal the nature of their contents. Here are the recorded transactions in human chattel. And the transactions lend themselves to conclusions: that the human property could be so abused that it could be casually enjoyed, even if it was one's own daughter. The history of Isaac's grandfather Lucius Quintus Carothers McCaslin is the history in miniature of the white South's exploitation of both the red and the black races, is the history in miniature of the Garden and the Fall, is the history of sin.

In the woods Isaac penetrates to the truth, which his cousin Cass describes for him: "Truth is one. It doesn't change. It covers all things which touch the heart—honor and pride and pity and justice and courage and love." And with this insight Isaac is enabled to understand the truth that his father and uncle had only been able to "fumble-heed." But his acceptance of his guilt is only passive; the only method of expiation, he feels, is to relinquish the land which his family had gotten through an "edifice intricate and complex and founded upon injustice and erected by ruthless rapacity and carried on even yet with at times downright savagery not only to the human beings but the valuable animals too." Desiring only peace of mind, he formally relinquishes his inheritance, though what he really relinquishes is only responsibility, since he continues to receive a monthly sum of money from the estate which was his inheritance. Then he attempts to act in "emulation of the Nazarene," by becoming a humble carpenter. He will not accept Paul Tillich's contention that to be is to be guilty.

Isaac thus never secures from his introduction to Being any real being. The charge to him implied in the title *Go Down, Moses* is that he should work to set God's people free. But Isaac can only say, "Sam Fathers set me free." Isaac will not understand that with personal freedom comes personal reponsibility. He has succeeded in plumbing history in a quest for values—"honor and pride and pity and justice and courage and love"—but then he refuses to exercise the real power of politics that is derived from these values, "to create," in Albert William Levi's words, "harmony and integration in the chaos of life."[17]

As a character Isaac must have been the subject of Faulkner's experimentation to discover if penetrating to the verities necessarily insures that action to implement them will follow. The experiment demonstrated Isaac's political impotence, and Faulkner therefore judged him a failure as a responsible man:

> Well, there are some people in any time and age that cannot face and cope with the problems. There seem to be three stages: The first says, This is rotten, I'll have no part of it, I will take death first. The second says, This is rotten, I don't like it, I can't do anything about it, but at least I will not participate in it myself, I will go off into a cave or climb a pillar to sit on. The third says, This stinks and I'm going to do something about it. McCaslin is the second. He says, This is bad, and I will withdraw from it. What we need are people who will say, This is bad and I'm going to do something about it, I'm going to change it.[18]

Having seen that man cannot content himself merely to act in imitation of Jesus, Faulkner seems to have turned very quickly to the conception of man acting in imitation of Christ.[19] In the fall of 1943 he began what was to be published, after eleven years and much struggle in rewriting, as *A Fable*. A small, very incidental event near the beginning of that novel is perhaps symbolic of what Faulkner's political commitment because of the discovery of values will do to his artistry: General Gragnon remembers an aide who had discovered, in *Gil Blas*, "*the glory, the honor and the courage and the pride*," who hoped to write of these verities himself, but was destroyed when he left his rear assignment to go "inside the lines." *A Fable* has generally been regarded as much inferior to Faulkner's work of the thirties, precisely because he imposed abstract concepts upon his material rather than seeking living values within the material. The result is allegory, a forced fable in service of predetermined goals.

The irony is that Faulkner's supreme political achievement, the extraction of values from chaos, fatally destroyed what he must have hoped would be the crowning artistic and political statement of his career. Moreover, he expended so much of his energy in attempting to reverse the creative habits of an entire career that the other works written during the composition of *A Fable*, almost all of it concerned with tidy resolutions to problems raised in his early, questing fiction, are much inferior to those works in which he had no answers.

Still, in all, the end is not sad. Faulkner had written the fiction that would insure his fame as a writer. And through the writing he had developed his own code of values, so that he could not only see the three responses available to man but also understand that he himself must advance to the third stage. In a sense the most important character he created in the forties and fifties was his own. Thus he sacrificed the privacy that he had always cherished in order to step forward, "inside the lines," to testify. His testimony is given in the speeches, essays, and interviews of those last years; cumulatively they present a man professing. It is, of course, in his Nobel Prize speech, offered to millions who would never read his fiction, that he revealed most profoundly what he had discovered in the "truth so mazed":

> I believe that man will not merely endure: he will prevail. He is immortal, not because he alone among creatures has an inexhaustible voice, but because he has a soul, a spirit capable of compassion and sacrifice and endurance. The poet's, the writer's, duty is to write about these things. It is his privilege to help man endure by lifting his heart, by reminding him of the courage and honor and hope and pride and compassion and pity and sacrifice which have been the glory of his past. The poet's voice need not merely be the record of man, it can be one of the props, the pillars to help him endure and prevail.[20]

NOTES

1. There is as yet no full-length biography of Faulkner. The best available studies of Faulkner's manuscripts and revisions of proofs are James B. Meriwether, *The Literary Career of William Faulkner: A Bibliographical Study* (Princeton, New Jersey, 1961), and Michael Millgate, *The Achievement of William Faulkner* (New York, 1965).
2. Details of Faulkner's early life are to be found in, among other places, John B. Cullen, *Old Times in Faulkner Country* (Chapel Hill, North Carolina, 1961); Murry C. Falkner, *The Falkners of Mississippi* (Baton Rouge, Louisiana, 1967); John Faulkner, *My Brother Bill* (New York, 1963); and James W. Webb and A. Wigfall Green, *William Faulkner of Oxford* (Baton Rouge, Louisiana, 1965).

3. John Dollard, *Caste and Class in a Southern Town* (New Haven, Connecticut, 1937), pp. 452–453.

4. I have traced Faulkner's changing attitude toward Snopesism in "The Grotesque-Comic in the Snopes Trilogy," *Literature and Psychology*, XV (Spring 1965), 107–119.

5. William Alexander Percy, *Lanterns on the Levee* (New York, 1941), p. 230.

6. The best account of this era in Mississippi politics is Albert D. Kirwan, *Revolt of the Rednecks: Mississippi Politics, 1876–1925* (Magnolia, Massachusetts, 1964).

7. David Riesman, *The Lonely Crowd* (Garden City, New York, 1953), pp. 26–28.

8. Anatol Rapoport, *Operational Philosophy* (New York, 1953), pp. 106–109.

9. Riesman, pp. 29–32.

10. Rapoport, pp. 109–111.

11. Emily Whitehurst Stone, "Faulkner Gets Started," *Texas Quarterly*, VIII (Winter 1965), 142–148.

12. In *Faulkner in the University*, edited by Frederick L. Gwynn and Joseph L. Blotner (New York, 1965), p. 87, Faulkner describes his flash of creative insight about 1927 in language that strongly suggests an occurrence of what Arthur Koestler, in *The Act of Creation*, terms "the Eureka process." Faulkner seems to have envisioned much of what he was to spend his life relating, but he does not, so soon after the event, seem able to organize it.

13. See "Interview with Vida Marković" in James B. Meriwether and Michael Millgate, eds., *Lion in the Garden: Interviews with William Faulkner* (New York, 1968), p. 283.

14. This is the political confrontation that George Marion O'Donnell established, of course, in his pioneering study of Faulkner, "Faulkner's Mythology," *Kenyon Review*, I (Summer 1939), 285–299. I might acknowledge at this time, as well, my indebtedness to the Faulkner scholarship for my understanding of his works. I do not think, though, that I have relied heavily enough on any particular critic to necessitate individual citation.

15. See "Technique as Discovery" in James E. Miller, Jr., ed., *Myth and Method* (Lincoln, Nebraska, 1960), pp. 86–108.

16. Millgate, *The Achievement of William Faulkner*, p. 200.

17. Albert William Levi, *Humanism & Politics* (Bloomington, Illinois, 1969), p. 15.

18. Gwynn and Blotner, pp. 245–246.

19. Joseph Blotner, "Speaking of Books: Faulkner's 'A Fable,'" *The New York Times Book Review*, May 25, 1969.

20. "Address upon Receiving the Nobel Prize for Literature," *Essays, Speeches, and Public Letters by William Faulkner*, edited by James B. Meriwether (New York, 1965), p. 120.

JOHN STEINBECK
(1902-1968)

by Warren French

EXCEPT DURING Adlai Stevenson's campaigns for the Presidency, John Steinbeck was reluctant to commit himself to political positions, even though his reputation—what's left of it—rests principally upon his labors as a social tractarian.

The record of Steinbeck's overt political commitments may be gleaned from *The New York Times*. Following Eleanor Roosevelt's praise of *The Grapes of Wrath* in her syndicated "My Day" column in June 1939, Steinbeck paid his first visit to the White House as the guest of President Roosevelt in September 1940. However, Steinbeck apparently did not participate actively in a political campaign until after the completion of his mammoth novel, *East of Eden*, in 1952. Then he emerged in October as one of the leading writers in support of the Democratic nominee, and he provided the Introduction for a paperback collection of Stevenson's speeches.

He was not heard from during the 1956 campaign, but on June 22, 1957, in Copenhagen, he admitted to reporters that he helped prepare speeches for Stevenson, whom he regarded "as the most intelligent Presidential candidate we have had for a long time." He is quoted in *The New York Times* (June 23, 1957, p. 32) as saying that he worked on some of Stevenson's speeches "not only regarding their political aims, but also with a view to making them more understandable to the masses."

During 1960, Steinbeck served as chairman of Stevenson's advisory committee and led in the fight against intellectuals defecting to the Kennedy camp. After Kennedy secured the nomination, Steinbeck was not heard from. He came out actively in support of Lyndon Johnson, however, in October 1964, when he was one of thirty-three American Nobel laureates signing a statement declaring that the Democratic nominee had qualities of leadership his opponent did not possess. The same week Steinbeck was also announced as heading, along with Igor Stravinsky, a National Committee of the Arts, Letters, and Humanities for Johnson and Hubert Humphrey. Later, in April 1966, Johnson appointed the novelist to replace David Brinkley on the National Arts Council.

Steinbeck is entirely representative of an American type of great influence during the first two decades following World War II, the Stevenson Democrat. Steinbeck was indeed preeminent among the men of letters to whom this label could be applied; he was one of the many who, having lived through the frustrations of the Depression and the horrors of the war, hoped that the direction of the country might at last be entrusted to a quiet, introspective, cautiously idealistic man with roots in a characteristically American agrarian community.

The trouble with the Stevensonians during an age of affluence like the 1960's is that they were rarely able to convert their nebulous vision of a better society into meaningful specifics. They were driven into trying to see in the pacification of the Mekong Delta the restoration of Candide's garden. Steinbeck's most overtly partisan utterance, the Introduction that he contributed to the collection of Stevenson's speeches during the 1952 campaign, is a disappointingly bland statement of praise for Stevenson's style which avoids all but the most platitudinous comments on the issues of the election. Steinbeck's admission that he had favored Dwight D. Eisenhower until he was won over by Stevenson's rhetoric leaves the impression that the novelist felt that there was no fundamental ideological difference between the major American political parties. Steinbeck's allegiance was always to men rather than to parties.

Harland S. Nelson, in an article on Steinbeck's politics, says that the novelist "has no politics in the usual sense." He continues:

> Steinbeck the man doubtless votes Democratic as he says. But politics are accidental; in fact, as a remark in the *Travels* [*with Charley*] shows ("My family was Republican. I might still be one if I had stayed [home]"), they are determined by chance and environment. Steinbeck the novelist is a visionary, not a politician in either the organizational or ideological kind; he is too individualistic for the former, and not intellectual enough for the latter.[1]

The result is that Steinbeck's politics is "a set of attitudes (more felt than thought) about the state of man in his society and in the world."

Steinbeck's political ideas (or feelings) provide insight into American political behavior. He probably approximates more nearly the attitude of the average American than those writers who have adopted carefully contrived and clearly articulated political stances. Most Americans are not actually apolitical, but they are little interested in the machinery of politics and in formal statements of policy. They are suspicious of political thinkers and intellectual policy-makers. The American tendency has been to become stirred up over politics only during national elections or during local elections with strong emotional overtones or when particularly disturbing legislation is being debated; otherwise, politics has been left, by default, to the professional politicians—a breed generally looked upon with contempt and suspicion.

This situation has resulted from Americans' subscribing—for the most part—to their own interpretation of the doctrine that the best government is that which governs least, which is usually taken to mean that the government should exercise the smallest amount of control over the individual's behavior consistent with public safety and should make the smallest possible demands upon the time and thought of the average person. Steinbeck's political activity precisely exemplified this common tendency. He headed national committees and visited the White House (on dull days newspaper columnists can always make capital of the average American's desire to go to Washington to tell the President what to do), but it is doubtful that he ever participated in a partisan ward meeting or punched doorbells, soliciting votes.

Steinbeck's political behavior thus mirrored that of what can best be called the cautiously liberal segment of the American electorate. As Nelson points out, "the most enduring of Steinbeck's 'political' attitudes is an ineradicable distrust of civilization," with its concomitant political machinery. Steinbeck subscribed wistfully to the concept of "nature's nobleman" and saw some special nobility arising from an attachment to the soil. Although he was willing to travel along with the Okies to gather the material for *The Grapes of Wrath*, he shunned involvement in public political displays (in *Travels with Charley*, for example, he admitted avoiding the scenes of the civil-rights disturbances in New Orleans). As *The Winter of Our Discontent* makes manifestly clear, Steinbeck found something ignoble about the city and courthouse politics.

The strength of Steinbeck's feelings on the Vietnam question became known when the fervent young Russian poet Yevgeny Yevtushenko, whom Steinbeck had met in Moscow in 1965, wrote a verse "Letter to John Steinbeck" asking the novelist to speak out in protest against the bombing raids in North Vietnam. Steinbeck replied with an "open letter" to *Newsday*, a Garden City (Long Island) newspaper, in which he stated, "I am against this Chinese-inspired war," and continued, "If this were a disagreement between Vietnamese people, we surely would not be there, but it is not, and [as] I have never found you to be naive you must be aware it is not." The war, Steinbeck explained, "is the work of Chairman Mao, designed and generalled by him in absentia, advised by Peking, and cynically supplied with brutal weapons by foreigners who set it up."[2]

What is interesting about this statement is that, whatever may prove to be the truth about the Vietnamese conflict, if we substitute "Hitler" for "Chairman Mao," it fits exactly the situation during the Spanish Civil War. Steinbeck's political views became increasingly irrelevant, because—like many others of his liberal persuasion—he insisted on seeing the present in terms of the past. Steinbeck had frozen into a political position that in the 1930's enabled him to avoid fashionable error and made him the champion of common sense,[3] but that in the 1960's isolated him from the problems of affluence. (This judgment is grounded in the idea that in the 1930's the nation's problems were primarily those of underproduction and physical survival, but that in the 1960's—although there are still a sizable number of "disadvantaged" persons in the society—the problems were principally those of overproduction and spiritual disenchantment.)

What is most significant is how closely the thinking of the man who, regardless of critical demurrers, was one of the most distinguished twentieth-century American writers mirrored that of Lyndon Johnson, whose once awe-inspiring reputation as a political operator crumbled because of his inability to communicate with most people under forty. Johnson, like Steinbeck, insisted on responding to the problems of the 1960's as if they were those of the 1930's. The following passage from a fictional satire succeeds remarkably well in pinpointing Johnson's and Steinbeck's problem:

> President Pangloss asked Hari whether he had had an interesting journey. "Yes indeed," said Hari. "I escaped from a plane crash, was dragged through the mud by my feet like a dead man, beaten on the soles of my feet until I fainted, hung up by my thumbs, forced to invent a story that my father had murdered my mother to preserve my sanity, imprisoned for not having any papers, and finally condemned to die before a firing squad."
>
> "That reminds me of something that happened when I was a little boy," said President Pangloss. "We came of poor but honest folk and I used to have to walk ten miles to the little red schoolhouse over rough country to get my education. One day I noticed I was wearing a hole in my shoes, so to save my mammy and my pappy some expense I took them off and walked bare-

foot. I got a splinter in my foot but I didn't say a word to
nobody. I consider the Free Boots for Rural Schoolchildren Bill
one of the most important measures before the present session
of the Congress."

This remarkable reply led Hari to believe that President Pan-
gloss had so many problems on his mind that he did not really
hear what was said to him, and that he made conversation out
of politeness and was not really in search of information.[4]

Steinbeck seemed to show the same sensitivity to youth's account of its
experience as Leonard Wibberley's fictional president, who also confides
to his visitor, "I never do anything unless I'm right and I never say anything unless I am sure of it." Speculating on what might be learned
through a British investigation of the effect of violence on television upon
the behavior of youthful lawbreakers, Steinbeck confided in one of the
"Letters to Alicia" that he contributed to *Newsday*:

> In Sag Harbor we have a police chief, named John Harring-
> ton, who has a unique theory. When he has to pick up a juvenile
> for violent delinquency, he doesn't look for excuses to explain
> why the kid or the dame or the drunk did it. To our chief, vio-
> lence is bad, no matter what caused it. He makes his attitude
> very clear to the delinquents. The first time, you get another
> chance. The second time, you get spanked, and the third time,
> John throws the book at you.
>
> I know, Alicia, this is an old-fashioned and an outmoded atti-
> tude, but, do you know, we have less destructive delinquency in
> Sag Harbor than any place around. Even the kids know where
> they stand, and far from resenting it, they are kind of relieved.[5]

A few weeks earlier Steinbeck had explained in another letter from
London how these attitudes applied to the youthful protesters against the
Vietnam war:

> It seems to me that the protests against war are as nonsensical
> as the war itself. I have been fascinated with the burning of
> draft cards. The burners protest that they do it because they
> don't want to kill women and children. I wish I didn't have the
> little stinking suspicion that a part of the card burners' anxiety
> stems from the possibility that somebody might kill them. . . .
> The war in Vietnam has done one wonderful thing. It has
> created a positive passion for education in some American
> youths of draft age who had few scholarly enthusiasms before.[6]

In attributing a selfish, physical basis to what the protesters considered
purely symbolic acts based on an abstract moral vision, Steinbeck showed

that three decades later he still embraced the only explicit political ideology that he had ever spelled out. He describes the organization of a migrant camp in Chapter 17 of *The Grapes of Wrath*:

> The families learned, although no one told them, what rights are monstrous and must be destroyed: the right to intrude upon privacy, the right to be noisy while the camp slept, the right of seduction or rape, the right of adultery and theft and murder. These rights were crushed, because the little worlds could not exist for even a night with such rights alive.
>
> And as the worlds moved westward, rules became laws, although no one told the families. It is unlawful to foul near the camp; it is unlawful in any way to foul the drinking water; it is unlawful to eat good rich food near one who is hungry, unless he is asked to share.
>
> And with the laws, the punishments—and there were only two—a quick and murderous fight or ostracism. . . . The families moved westward, and the technique of building the worlds improved so that the people could be safe in their worlds.[7]

Two things are noteworthy here: The government arises only after the fact as an expedient to meet an immediate need, and the laws arise spontaneously from the naturally wholesome instincts of the people rather than from intellectual deliberations. Government to Steinbeck was not a thing but a process, ever evolving to meet the challenges of the moment and arising only in response to a physically present problem. That the same thinking still determined his concept of the Vietnamese situation is shown from the conclusion of his "Letter to Alicia" on draft-card burning:

> In all of the fury of patriotic and large-souled fribble-frabble the overlooked man is the President. I'm pretty sure he wants to get out of Viet-nam more than anyone else. But the lack of police protection at City Hall only proves what card burners haven't considered—you can't leave a yard with dogs snapping at your heels, and only a fool turns his back on a bull.

The great virtue of this dynamic, pragmatic concept of government is that it immunizes one against the seductions of dehumanized ideologies. A principal reason that Steinbeck and others were able to stand fast against the appeal of communism and other "isms" during the days of the American Depression, when many other writers became card-carrying members of the party or at least enthusiastic fellow travelers, is that they distrusted any "before the fact" system that claimed to have found a panacea for human ills. Steinbeck's reaction to communist claims was voiced by one of the most idealized figures in his fiction, Doc Burton, who in *In Dubious Battle* answers a radical organizer:

> Well, you say I don't believe in the cause. That's like not believing in the moon. There've been communes before, and there will be again. But you people have an idea that if you *establish* the thing, the job'll be done. Nothing stops, Mac. If you were able to put an idea into effect tomorrow, it would start changing right away. Establish a commune, and the same gradual flux will continue. . . . When group-man wants to move, he makes a standard. "God wills that we re-capture the Holy Land"; or he says, "We fight to make the world safe for democracy"; or he says, "We will wipe out social injustice with communism." But the group doesn't care about the Holy Land, or Democracy, or Communism. Maybe the group simply wants to move, to fight, and uses these words simply to reassure the brains of individual men.[8]

Lewis Gannett reports in "Steinbeck's Way of Writing' that "a New York editor in Pascal Covici's office read the manuscript of *In Dubious Battle* conscientiously and wrote a three-page single-space report indicating points at which Steinbeck's Communist organizer diverged from the orthodox party line as expressed by the ideologists of New York." Steinbeck was not concerned, however, with ideology but rather with the active behavior of a man whose quest for power could drive him to say, "We can't waste time liking people." Steinbeck felt that any political activity beyond the establishment of the basic, instinctive prohibitions described in *The Grapes of Wrath* was symptomatic of a personal lust for power that is perhaps best articulated by the old "leader of the people," in the story with that title that comprises the fourth segment of *The Red Pony*. The now frustrated old man who led the wagon trains across the plains explains to his grandson:

> It wasn't Indians that were important, nor adventures, nor even getting out here. It was a whole bunch of people made into one big crawling beast. And I was the head. It was westering and westering. Every man wanted something for himself, but the big beast that was all of them wanted only westering. I was the leader, but if I hadn't been there, someone else would have been the head. The thing had to have a head.

When the grandson suggests, however, that some day he, too, might be a "leader of the people," the old man smiles. "There's no place to go. There's the ocean to stop you. There's a line of old men along the shore hating the ocean because it stopped them."[9]

Fundamentally, there are two kinds of effective political leaders. Despite all the literature that has been written about political behavior, they have never been more clearly and concisely contrasted than in Alfred, Lord Tennyson's dramatic monologue "Ulysses":

> This is my son, mine own Telemachus,
> To whom I leave the scepter and the isle—
> Well-loved of me, discerning to fulfill
> This labor, by slow prudence to make mild
> A rugged people, and through soft degrees
> Subdue them to the useful and the good.
> Most blameless is he, centered in the sphere
> Of common duties, decent not to fail
> In offices of tenderness, and pay
> Meet adoration to my household gods,
> When I am gone. He works his work, I mine.

The young boy's father in *The Red Pony* is no pioneer, but a steady, stable farmer, who is attempting "by slow prudence to make mild a rugged people"; but neither the old man nor Steinbeck have any use for this Telemachus-type. Steinbeck insisted on equating growth and progress with "westering," as is apparent from this statement from his long essay "America and Americans":

> I have named the destroyers of nations: comfort, plenty, and security—out of which grow a bored and slothful cynicism, in which rebellion against the world as it is and myself as I am are submerged in listless self-satisfaction. A dying people tolerates the present, rejects the future, and finds its satisfactions in past greatness and half-remembered glory. A dying people arms itself with defensive weapons and with mercenaries against change. ... It is in the American negation of these symptoms of extinction that my hope and confidence lie. We are not satisfied. Our restlessness, perhaps inherited from the hungry immigrants of our ancestry, is still with us.[10]

This passage might suggest that Steinbeck was able to see the Vietnamese conflict not in ideological terms but as a necessary stimulant to American morale. He embraced—again like many of his countrymen—the puritanical notion that a nation can flourish only when it is fighting against physical odds—"westering." Certainly Police Chief John Harrington of Sag Harbor in his handling of delinquents, dames, or drunks is no Telemachus, subduing them, "through soft degrees ... to the useful and the good." The demands of creating a pleasant society in which everyone could share peaceably in the national affluence strikes people with such feelings as not just unlikely, but undesirable.

In effect, Steinbeck was arguing, we were using Vietnam simply to establish the continuing virility of our local brand of morality. In an interview after belatedly receiving the Nobel Prize, Steinbeck observed that it was more difficult in the 1960's than in the 1930's to determine who was an underdog, more difficult—to borrow the title of one of his most famous essays—to tell good guys from bad. The admission shows that Steinbeck's thinking had not become sophisticated enough to deal with the subtle problems of an age of affluence. Part of the trouble is that when values are principally physical—as in problems of survival—it is not difficult to perceive the differences between contenders; but when values are principally intellectual or spiritual—as in problems of adjustment—it may be very difficult to perceive differences. Furthermore, it is tacitly assumed that in any physical confrontation, one contender will be either destroyed or at least subjugated—so that "good" can be ascertained by "after the fact" observation. In intellectual confrontations, on the other hand, such "unconditional surrenders" are unlikely, so that an accommodation must be made so that the contenders can coexist without any monopoly on virtue (except in their own minds).

Steinbeck never felt that such accommodations could be achieved. Even though in *In Dubious Battle*, he has Doc Burton argue, "I don't want to put on the blinders of 'good' and 'bad,' and limit my vision," he also—in this blackest of his novels—has this man, capable of objectivity, simply disappear. There is also something appallingly naïve about Burton's further statement, "If I used the term 'good' on a thing I'd lose my license to inspect it, because there might be bad in it," because it suggests that one cannot work for a cause that one is not convinced is wholly good. Burton's observation suggests the true nature of Ethan Allen Hawley's otherwise incomprehensible mental anguish in *The Winter of Our Discontent*. Hawley feels acute anguish because he feels that he has used corrupt methods—as indeed he has—in securing title to a valuable piece of land. What he does not recognize is that he would have done something even more corrupt if he had allowed the land to fall into other hands in order to preserve his integrity unsullied. Steinbeck failed to recognize that one can no longer wrap himself in the flag of virtue and choose between "underdog" and "overlord."

In his great novels of the 1930's Steinbeck intentionally alerted the nation to the dangers that persistence in the stereotyped thinking fostered by the chimerical speculative abundance that a virgin continent once promised presented to a land that had failed to solve the problems of fairly distributing its resources. In the 1960's his novels unintentionally alert us to the dangers that persistence in the stereotyped thinking derived from the privations endured during the Depression and World War II present in coping with the problems of an age of affluence in which economic momentum can be maintained only by a program of controlled waste that is not destructive of human resources.

Steinbeck had trouble during the last two decades—as *The Winter of Our Discontent* especially suggests—because he still saw human problems in the currently irrelevant terms of clashes between exploiter and victim, the ignoble and the noble. He failed to grasp that in an age when a potential threat of atomic destruction hangs over the whole world—when man could annihilate himself—the question of who "wins" this or that particular physical engagement can hardly be a burning issue. Nobility is no longer even a possibility. The failure of Steinbeck's private politics was to reflect a general failure of American politics. There are many luxuries we can no longer afford. The political fastidiousness of the polite liberal—epitomized by Steinbeck—is surely one of them.

NOTES

1. Harland S. Nelson, "Steinbeck's Politics Then and Now," *Antioch Review*, XXVII (1967), 118–133.
2. *The New York Times*, July 11, 1966, p. 1. Although a copyrighted dispatch to *Newsday*, Steinbeck asked the publisher to make this "open letter" available freely to all communications media. Steinbeck subsequently visited Vietnam in January 1967 and sent a series of weekly dispatches back to *Newsday*, all supporting President Johnson's position.
3. In one of his rare public statements during the 1930's, Steinbeck did contribute to *Writers Take Sides*, Millen Brand, Dorothy Brewster, *et al.*, eds. (Concord, New Hampshire, 1938), in which American writers declared their support for the Spanish Republicans.
4. From Leonard Wibberley, *Adventures of an Elephant Boy* (New York, 1968), pp. 108–109. Wibberley is the author of the popular satire *The Mouse That Roared*. Modeled on Voltaire's *Candide*, *Adventures of an Elephant Boy* severely criticizes American policies in Vietnam.
5. February 19, 1966, p. 3W. "Alicia" is the dead wife of the publisher of *Newsday*. Steinbeck addressed her because he thought she might be especially sympathetic with his views. The ghoulishness of the series is in itself suggestive of the deadness of Steinbeck's politics. The "uniqueness" of Chief Harrington's theory is debatable.
6. December 24, 1965, p. 3W. (These letters appear in *Weekend*, a weekly supplement that accompanies the Friday issue of the daily *Newsday*.)

7. New York, 1939, pp. 265–266.
8. New York, 1936, pp. 143–145.
9. *The Portable Steinbeck*, rev. ed. (New York, 1946), p. 414. The grandson suggests that as a new leader he might go from the Pacific shore "in boats"—perhaps to Vietnam. Lewis Gannett's article appears as a preface to this volume.
10. New York, 1966, p. 143. It is interesting to observe that hardly anyone in the United States has thought Steinbeck's statements important enough to object to them; the protests against his views on the Vietnam war have all come from communist countries in Europe.

RALPH ELLISON and JAMES BALDWIN
(1914-   )   (1924-   )

by Donald B. Gibson

In 1968 THE *Negro Digest* conducted a poll of some forty black writers in order to determine (among other things) who was considered by them the most important black American writer of all time.[1] The writer who received far and away the most votes was Richard Wright. The result of that poll might come as a surprise to anyone who does not think of the relation between politics and literature, but anyone who does think about that relation and who knows something about black writers would not be surprised at all. Ralph Ellison and James Baldwin were among the first five writers chosen as most important (Baldwin third and Ellison fourth), but even so, I would suspect that the results of the poll would be surprising to many. Surely the same poll, if it had been conducted among writers generally or among general readers, would have turned out differently. Many readers consider Ellison not only the best black writer but the best novelist of the twentieth century. Many believe that no single American novel of our century stands up well against *Invisible Man*. Baldwin's reputation as a novelist is reasonably high, but many believe him to be the best essayist of this century. Yet both these writers ran behind Richard Wright. (Langston Hughes was second choice.)

The ultimate reason for the choice by the writers polled seems to me to lie in the area of politics. If this poll had been taken twenty or so years ago, I would suspect that some such writers as Phillis Wheatley, Paul Laurence Dunbar, or Countee Cullen might have been at least among the first five writers chosen. But the political conservatism of these writers, so clearly indicated by the form and content of their works, would not allow them to be considered today as important as Wright and others by the literate, sophisticated, and politically aware group of writers polled. Wright, on the other hand, far more so than Ellison and Baldwin, was a profoundly political man and as such was able to open up new territory for the black writer. Wright's radical perspective on politics and on literature (two inseparable perspectives) allowed him to write more openly, frankly, honestly, and unapologetically about the racial situation than any writer before him. Wright's *Uncle Tom's Children* and *Native Son* are the precursors of a great deal of literature by black writers subsequent to them. Such novels as John O. Killens's cataclysmic *And Then We Heard the Thunder* and John Williams's highly political *The Man Who Cried I Am* are novels which descend directly from Wright's work. It is the political perspective of Richard Wright, his radicalism (more so than the "art" of his work), which would cause him to be chosen by a large group of black writers as the most important black American writer of all time.

Ellison and Baldwin, on the contrary, are as intentionally nonpolitical in their writing as Wright is political.[2] Though their choice to be nonpolitical itself constitutes a political gesture, neither sees politics as central to the condition of life. Irving Howe, in discussing Stendhal, remarks that "in the whole modern era the nonpolitical temper implies political choice: and what is more, Stendhal, unlike many writers who follow him, knows this."[3] No doubt Howe would group Ellison and Baldwin among those modern writers who do not know this or who, if they know it, prefer not to go beyond the recognition of the fact. Their being nonpolitical is inseparable from their conception of the nature and function of literature as well as from their conception of themselves as writers. Both have made it abundantly clear that they consider literature primarily as art, that they see its end or function as aesthetic, that they are artists whose responsibility is to create, through mastery of craft, aesthetic objects.[4] Wright in comparison seems always to create with the idea in mind that he will influence social attitudes, that he will use his writing as a weapon to effect change. Even the autobiographical *Black Boy* has as its end to change society, and for that reason it is not simply, as its subtitle suggests, *A Record of Childhood and Youth*. This is not to say that it is not autobiography (despite the fact that there are disparities between the life revealed in the autobiography and the same events as revealed in "The Ethics of Living Jim Crow," the introductory essay to *Uncle Tom's Children*), but that it was written from a clearly conceived, socially oriented perspective.

Ellison's perspective, however, as revealed in *Invisible Man* and in his essays and interviews, is highly individualistic. His concerns seem finally to be far more personal and subjective than social. He is a strongly self-reliant individual who has gone to great lengths to protect and to prove his distinctiveness, his difference from any preconceived notions of his identity. He refuses to be defined in terms of his race. He admits his racial heritage proudly, but he will not allow assumptions about him as a Negro to define his reality. He resists being categorized in racial terms. This is understandable, for he knows very well that he is not personally the entity which is conjured up in the heads of the majority of Americans when they think of "Negro." However, in a paradoxical way, he denies his relation to the group of black people by insisting on his individuality, by going to great lengths to prove that he is not like *them*, but a unique individual who has escaped *their* limitations.

It is embarrassing to read that his horizons were broadened because he knew a white boy who was interested in electronics, because his mother brought home recordings of operas and copies of such magazines as *Vanity Fair*. It is embarrassing not because of the value it places on things "white," and not even because of its denial of the values implicit in black life and culture, but because it is not true. It is too simplistic and too obvious an attempt to assert his nonblackness. Ellison's desire to be recognized as an individual, understandably and sympathetically viewed as it may be, has political ramifications when that impulse is put forward in the American social context, for the most politically reactionary elements of the society say something of the same kind: Every American has the opportunity to succeed, and if he does not, it is because of some limitation in him and not because of inequities or other limitations within the system. More important, however, is the implication in Ellison's novels and in his other works that the resolution of complex social problems lies in the proper response of the individual.

This is finally the implication of *Invisible Man*. There is no way for black people to deal with the racial problem, the novel asserts, and the best that can be done is for us to withdraw into the inner recesses of our own psyches. Ellison may indeed not have *intended* to say this, but the political imperative of *Invisible Man* is clear enough: Given the complexities of the functioning of power, black people, and all others victimized by the system ("perhaps on the lower frequencies I speak for you"), should maintain Joycean "silence, exile, and cunning," though "cunning" may not be very meaningful when practiced "silently" and in "exile." There is no point in being, as the central character's grandfather was, "a spy in the enemy's territory" if the force one represents (spies for) is simply one's indignation.

Ellison's novel turns out finally to be the opposite of what it ostensibly is. It seems at first to suggest radicalism and then anarchy, but it ultimately denies both, for Ellison carefully and systematically closes off all avenues of action or retreat for the main character.[5] Every possibility for him to change his situation turns out to be a sham or otherwise not viable. The central character turns out to be a modern Hamlet who out-Hamlets Hamlet. "To be or not to be" is not a question he can ask, for he has answered all such questions and furthermore can make no decisions. (It is significant that he does not *decide* to go underground; he fortuitously falls into the manhole.) His whole sense of reality has been so altered that he has no touchstone, no frame of reference which will allow him to make distinctions and hence judgments.

The novel seems initially a radical novel because of the force with which it rejects in its opening chapter the status quo in regard to racial matters. Its attack on institutions, its negative assessment of the worth of institutions in regard to their value to the individual, is anarchistic. But in the end the political thrust of the novel is negated, for the central character's response after he has examined the institutions of his society, and after he has examined what is intended to represent all the viable alternatives for action, is to feel powerless to do anything, powerless to accept or to reject. His statement that he is coming out of his underground chamber—"I'm coming out. . . . And I suppose it's damn well time. Even hibernations can be overdone"—makes little sense. He can do nothing more than to stay where he is since there is no mode of action possible for him in the world. This is what he learns through the course of the action of the novel. The novel symbolically asks all the questions to be asked about the relation between men and social institutions and then explores in representative fashion the full range of possible response. On the one hand, there is for him the value of the order which institutions establish; on the other hand, there is his fear of the chaos which ensues when institutions do not exert their controlling influence. In the face of such an overwhelming dilemma the central character is completely paralyzed—the conflicts within him unresolvable:

> In going underground, I whipped it all except the mind, the *mind*. And the mind that has conceived a plan of living must never lose sight of the chaos against which that pattern was conceived. That goes for societies as well as for individuals. Thus, having tried to give pattern to the chaos which lives with the pattern of your certainties, I must come out, I must emerge. And there's still a conflict within me: With Louis Armstrong one half of me says "Open the window and let the foul air out," while the other says "It was good green corn before the harvest."

He has "whipped it all except the mind" in that he has survived his experiences and even put them in order through the telling, but when he understands all the alternatives, when the experience has been conceptualized, he cannot handle it—he can make no choices or judgments: The problem has been reduced to an opposition between order and chaos. Institutions are a means of creating order out of chaos, but the chaos, the narrator tells us, is always in the background. Half of him says, "Open the window and let the foul air out"—attack the institutions. The other half says something quite different—save the "good green corn," do not interfere with existing patterns of order, put off the harvest.

The opposition of and the tension between order and chaos prevail from beginning to end. Throughout the narrative the central character finds himself repressed by those forces ostensibly functioning as means to preserve order and repelled by chaos. He craves order, but the agents of orderliness seek to destroy him; the alternative, from his perspective, chaos, he cannot give himself over to, for chaos, too, threatens to destroy. The novel consists of a repeating series of encounters during which the central character confronts and deals with apparent order only to see it turn to chaos before his very eyes. Ultimately he cannot distinguish between the two. Institutions, organizations, individuals that are apparently attempting to order experience, serve only to mask chaos, a chaos which threatens unceasingly to prevail over all systems of organization. His abhorrence and fear of disorganization cause him to retreat into the ironic, nonlogical stance which we find expressed in the prologue. Logic fails and only the prelogical, the nonlogical associations which come to him from his culture, from his individual past, have meaning.

The paradox involved in the very conception of invisibility is relevant here. The black man, that highly visible entity in a predominantly white society, is said to be invisible. As a black man, he is not invisible. He is constantly identified as a black man, as the anecdote told by the central character at the beginning of the prologue indicates. He bumps into a man who calls him an insulting name—undoubtedly "nigger." Now, was he invisible to the man, or was he very, very visible? "Invisibility" means here that the man did not recognize the central character's particularity. He did not recognize that the narrator of the tale is a discrete individual who has characteristics which distinguish him from all others of his group. But what is also clear is that the narrator depends entirely upon external definitions to define not only reality but also his own existence. What the central character finds out finally is that he is nobody—and that he is in no better position at the end of the novel than he was at the beginning. He is nobody because by the end of the novel he has cut off any possibility of social identification, and unless identity is conceived as metaphysical in character, it cannot exist apart from a social context.

The central character says in the first paragraph of the first chapter that he eventually realizes that he is nobody but himself, but no person is himself—nobody exists simply in terms of his personal definition of himself. What he finds out finally is that he has no basis whatsoever for defining himself. He cannot *be* because he cannot *do*; he does not exist because he has negated every possible frame of reference which would allow him to identify himself. The novel is a series of revelations which shows the narrator disavowing all possibilities of identity. He refuses to commit himself to do anything, and since identity depends upon commitment, he can at best feel ambivalence. Feeling that commitment to existing arrangements of order is destructive and that commitment to altering these arrangements invites chaos and is also destructive, he finds himself in limbo.

The paradoxical nature of the situation of the central character is inherent in his evaluation of the meaning and the significance of his grandfather's deathbed statement of his philosophy of life, his technique of survival and offensive reaction:

> Son, after I'm gone I want you to keep up the good fight. I never told you, but our life is a war and I have been a traitor all my born days, a spy in the enemy's country ever since I give up my gun back in the Reconstruction. Live with your head in the lion's mouth. I want you to overcome 'em with yeses, undermine 'em with grins, agree 'em to death and destruction, let 'em swoller you till they vomit or bust wide open.

The meaning of the grandfather's statement lies in the tension between the poles of the antithesis it sets up: to overcome with assent, to undermine with grins, to agree to such an extent that illness or destruction will result. There is a certain logic in such an "attack," the logic of passive resistance, but such a response as the grandfather's is essentially moral and not political. The novel explores the ramifications of the grandfather's philosophy, and the central character would like to make it viable. But by its nature the grandfather's perspective cannot be viable in the situation in which the central character finds himself, for the success of passive resistance depends upon the opponent's knowing that he is being resisted. The grandfather lives underground, too, and his private feelings about what his grins and yeses mean are insignificant beyond his own private and personal experience.

Since "he had been the meekest of men," it is merely humorous that "the younger children were rushed from the room, the shades drawn and the flame of the lamp turned so low that it sputtered on the wick" when the old man makes his dying admonition. Order exists in the grandfather's life because he does not strike out, because his "subversion" never finds overt expression. Chaos threatens (and this is why the parents pull the shades and rush the children from the room) because of an attitude and not an action. The attitude is so real, despite the fact that it has no counterpart in action, that it threatens to bring down chaos on the family.

This is the psychological root of the central character's eventual inability to choose, to make a stand. From his perspective direct opposition to order, to authority, carries its own penalties. The grandfather deals indirectly with authority and the central character takes his cues from him. ("It was as though I was carrying out his advice in spite of myself.") "Live within the institutions," the grandfather says in effect, "but know that their power and influence are against you."

The "battle royal" exploits this tension. It is significant that the smoker during which it occurs is attended by "all of the town's big shots," for they are the leaders of the community, the keepers of the ark, the custodians of institutional values. Yet we see what happens there, the vulgarity, the blatant and basic inhumanity. The central character, however, because of his basic faith in institutions and in the men who represent them, does not see the deepest disparity between his role as a participant in the battle royal and his role as speaker and recipient of a scholarship. He feels some vague awareness, but he is not able to articulate it.

> I had some misgivings over the battle royal, by the way. Not from a distaste for fighting, but because I didn't care too much for the other fellows who were to take part. They were tough guys who seemed to have no grandfather's curse worrying their minds. . . . And besides, I suspected that fighting a battle royal might detract from the dignity of my speech.
> The harder we fought the more threatening the men became. And yet, I had begun to worry about my speech again. How would it go? Would they recognize my ability? What would they give me?

The deep irony of the scene results from the reader's awareness of the inappropriateness of the things that go on there, the distance between things as described there and things as they should be. It is noteworthy that the scholarship and briefcase are presented to him "in the name of the Board of Education" because it suggests that the function of the institution it represents is more negative than positive, more destructive than sustaining. "I was so moved that I could hardly express my thanks. A rope of bloody saliva forming a shape like an undiscovered continent drooled upon the leather and I wiped it quickly away." Here again apparent order masks chaos rather than contains it. The ironic ambivalence arising from the narrator's submerged awareness of the relation between order and chaos gives rise to countless images reflecting a duality of perspective:

> It was a beautiful college. The buildings were old and covered with vines and the roads gracefully winding, lined with

hedges and wild roses that dazzled the eyes in the summer sun. Honeysuckle and purple wisteria hung heavy from the trees and the white magnolias mixed with their scents in the bee humming air. ... Many times, here at night, I've closed my eyes and walked along the forbidden road that winds past the girls' dormitories ... on to where the road became a bridge over a dry riverbed ... on up the road ... to the sudden forking ... where the road turned off to the insane asylum.

Then in my mind's eye I see the bronze statue of the college Founder, the cold Father symbol, his hands outstretched in the breathtaking gesture of lifting a veil that flutters in hard, metallic folds above the face of a kneeling slave; and I am standing puzzled, unable to decide whether the veil is really being lifted, or lowered more firmly in place; whether I am witnessing a revelation or a more efficient blinding.

Why do I recall, instead of the odor of seed bursting in springtime, only the yellow contents of the cistern spread over the lawn's dead grass?

Each of the major episodes and events repeats the same complex, ironic attitude. Trueblood, in that episode with Norton, for example, represents chaos and disorder because he is "true to the claims of the blood" and not bound by traditional standards of conduct. Norton, the antithesis of Trueblood, at least ostensibly, turns out not to be as different as one would imagine. Norton has the same incestuous desires for his daughter as Trueblood has for his. Hence he is terribly shaken as he witnesses his inmost desires become real through Trueblood's narrative.

Bledsoe's position is revealed when he speaks frankly to the narrator about the acquisition and maintenance of power. Bledsoe presents a certain appearance both in his person and through the makeup of the college he heads. We must remember that the physical institution described at the beginning of Chapter 2 is the institution which he guides, and we are intended to see the relation between his character and the beautiful and orderly campus which has a road that "turned off to the insane asylum." He apparently represents orderliness, a bulwark against the darkness of chaos, but he turns out to be the devil himself, the archfiend, bent upon destruction when his personal ambition is thwarted. "I'll have every Negro in the country hanging on tree limbs by morning if it means staying where I am."

Similar analyses can be made of the Liberty Paint episode, the hospital scene, the Brotherhood, Ras the Destroyer, Rinehart, and finally of the whole novel. Such an analysis would reveal various individuals working to destroy or sustain social institutions. Institutions ostensibly have the function of serving individuals in a society, of shoring up human resources against the incursions of chaos. But institutions, because of their very nature, must in some sense stand against individuals, for they can neither recognize nor deal with individual claims against them. This is generally true. If one is a black individual (as the central character is, while at the same time emblematic of everyone) in a society whose people denigrate (the pun is intended) blackness, then the institutions, dedicated as they are to the preservation of the status quo, must of necessity be in large measure against him. What, then, does the black person do? Does he support that which thwarts the realization of his potential? Does he seek to destroy the institutions, the only protection from chaos? These are the questions which Ellison's novel poses and in its own way answers. There are no solutions to such questions. One can only withdraw, thus solving the problem privately. No action is possible, for there is no basis for action. This seems to be the implication of *Invisible Man.* He is as invisible at the end as he was at the beginning, and he is invisible because he *feels* he is. The conception of invisibility exists only as a response to a society which tells individuals they are invisible. There may be alternatives different from accepting as fact that one is invisible; at least many people think so, people who believe in the possibility of significant change.

It is in the area designated by the above considerations that *Invisible Man* makes a political statement. Insofar as it suggests that significant changes of a social nature are not possible and in many ways not even desirable, it is a vehicle for a particular political bias, for that sentiment happens to be held by large numbers of people who express it by means of political actions. Hence, despite Ellison's intentions, despite his professions about being an artist and that alone, he expresses ideas and attitudes which, once freed into the world, are likely to have political consequences.

James Baldwin is a political relative of Ellison, a relation revealed in their agreement about what literature is and does. On the surface Baldwin is nonpolitical in that his perspective is consistently moral rather than political, and he does not consciously or intentionally engage in political activity by virtue of writing. Ellison is more politically inclined in that he deals more directly with specifically political matters, even though he ultimately dismisses politics. As opposed to Ellison's, however, Baldwin's work suggests that there are means of solving basic conflicts between the individual and the society at large. Individuals within a given society need only be moral, need only conform to the imperatives dictated by traditional morality and by democratic idealism.[6] Baldwin is far more concerned than Ellison with themes supporting the necessity of love and responsibility. Ellison is therefore the more "modern," for moral bewilderment is much more in keeping with the temper of the times than the traditional moral certainty from which Baldwin proceeds. Ellison is less conservative than Baldwin and the very form of their fiction indicates that. Baldwin's plots, situations, and incidents are far more aligned with the traditional novel than are those of *Invisible Man*. This would seem to me not unrelated to his moralism.

Go Tell It on the Mountain is an intensely private and personal novel about a central character's progress through early adolescence. The novel, like Baldwin's second novel, *Giovanni's Room*, is written with no awareness on the part of the author of the political implications of its statement. It is clearly not a novel about "the emotional pressure exerted on the Negro's cultural forms by his exposure to white oppression."[7] If it were a novel about "white oppression" in any but the most indirect ways, it would thereby reflect more political concern and awareness on the part of the author than it clearly does. The problem of the novel from a political perspective is that it says nothing about oppression and very, very little about race as such. There are comments in the book about racial matters (as when John goes downtown to a movie and is conscious of his blackness), but they by no means relate to the essential meaning of the novel. The book strongly suggests that the individuals who appear in its world are as they are because of their individual and private personalities. There is no interest shown by the author in the effect of environment, of economics and politics, on the lives and destinies of the characters. This does not mean that the book need only be about such matters; surely all people have private experience which might be only in the most oblique way (if at all) related to politics and economics. It does mean, however, that an extremely important dimension has been left out, an error of the kind committed by the author who assumes that *only* that dimension is of significance and who neglects the diversity of experience.

Having largely omitted speaking critically in his novel of the larger social dimension, Baldwin makes, in an inverse way, an extremely important statement of a political character. It is a statement not unlike that made in Claude Brown's *Manchild in the Promised Land*, which announced to the world that Claude Brown, by dint of superior will, walked out of the Harlem ghetto, and that anyone else who wants to walk out need merely get up and start walking. Such an attitude belies the fact of the effects of years of oppression on black people. By omitting the political, economic, and social dimension, Baldwin suggests its relative unimportance. But clearly the character of the Grimes family and the relations among members of the family, to say nothing of the quality of their lives, are determined in large measure by those factors left out of Baldwin's picture. The nature of the problem may well be related to a statement made by Baldwin in a letter to his agent, Robert Mills, in February 1962:

> My whole attitude toward the fact of color undergoes several
> melancholy changes: I don't know where they will lead me, but
> I must buy the time to find out. There is a very grim secret
> hidden in the fact that so many of the people one hoped to
> rescue could not be rescued because the prison of color had
> become their hiding place. ... Life has the effect of forcing you
> to act on your premises ... and I have said for years that color
> does not matter. I am now beginning to feel that it does not
> matter *at all*, that it masks something else which *does* matter:
> but this suspicion changes, for me, the entire nature of reality.[8]

In his novel, color does not matter beyond the fact that the characters
move for the most part in a black world. Baldwin is primarily concerned
with the relation between John Grimes and his father, Gabriel, and from
the author's point of view the matter is private and unrelated to social
issues.

Another Country reveals far more social consciousness than either *Go
Tell It on the Mountain* or *Giovanni's Room* (which reveals none).
Nonetheless, Baldwin's stance is moral rather than political. He soundly
castigates a country that would cause Rufus's fate to be as it is, and
he blames America for being a loveless society, a society whose character is such that its inhabitants are incapable of loving either themselves
or each other. Baldwin chooses to see the central problem of the novel as
a problem of human relations. It is not a "race" novel; for that matter,
most of its characters are white. It would seem to be about race because
of its powerful opening chapter, but even there it is clear that Rufus's
essential problems are the results of hang-ups other than race, though
race plays a part. Rufus is a central symbol and his problems are simply
an extension of the problems of the other characters: their inability to
relate, to establish love relationships beyond the most tenuous. This
reflects again Baldwin's notion expressed in the letter quoted above:
"I have said for years that color does not matter." In the relationship
between Vivaldo (white) and Ida (black), for example, both have problems establishing relations with other people, but the problems are on a
par. Baldwin does not suggest that Ida's problems are any more or less
serious or significant than Vivaldo's, whose difficulties are from a different source and of a different character.

Baldwin is no more nor less sympathetic toward nor critical of the
black characters than the white. He is highly critical of Rufus and does
not attempt to mitigate his responsibility for Leona's fate. Rufus suffers
because he is a black man, but he suffers equally because of his character. In this respect *Another Country* is similar to *Go Tell It on the Mountain*. So much of the difficulty which the characters have is traced to such
vague and general sources that the thrust of the novel as a critique and

criticism of the society, which it intends to be, is lost. Baldwin is saying in effect in this novel that we Americans have failed to live up to our professed moral commitments and that the innocence and puritanism of the country are largely at fault. This novel is like the essays insofar as Baldwin's stance is moral indignation. He is simply furious that America possesses the character it has. But what about more pertinent issues such as jobs, housing, health, education, etc.? What of the issues beyond the personal and the private? Baldwin is not so much concerned about these as about the moral issues. Hence his novel is about love, and only a moralist who does not grant the role of politics in determining the quality of life could believe that love is so central. Solve the black man's economic problem, and then we can worry later about human relations. Baldwin would undoubtedly disagree:

> Freedom is hard to bear. It can be objected that I am speaking of political freedom in spiritual terms, but the political institutions of any nation are always menaced and are ultimately controlled by the spiritual state of that nation.

> Love takes off the masks that we fear we cannot live without and know we cannot live within. I use the word "love" here not merely in the personal sense but as a state of being, or a state of grace—not in the infantile American sense of being made happy but in the tough and universal sense of quest and daring and growth. And I submit that the racial tensions that menace Americans today have little to do with real antipathy—on the contrary, indeed—and are involved only symbolically with color. These tensions are rooted in the very same depths as those from which love springs, or murder. The white man's unadmitted and apparently, to him, unspeakable private fears and longings are projected onto the Negro. The only way he can be released from the Negro's tyrannical power over him is to consent, in effect, to become black himself.[9]

These sentiments are the wellsprings of Baldwin's stance in *Another Country*.

The quotations above go a long way toward indicating Baldwin's politics. He clearly believes that there is some system of values antecedent to politics. Theoretically there is—there is the system of values rooted in traditional Christianity, but Baldwin should know that Christians have been evading those precepts for hundreds of years and it is somewhat futile to call upon Christians to be moral now. Furthermore, Baldwin's politics relate to a conception of the universe, of the very nature of things, implied in the above quotations. He seems to assume an orderly and meaningful universe (as Christianity assumes), and the phrases he chooses to couch his meaning in, "spiritual state" and "state of grace," imply a specifically religious (if not Christian) perspective. Ultimately this suggests that Baldwin is an institutionalist who believes that in order to solve our problems an erring society need only be called back to the moral imperatives inherent within its institutions. This further means that political matters are at best of secondary importance.

From this point of view it is not difficult to understand Baldwin's response when Robert Kennedy as Attorney General called together a group of black "leaders," largely entertainers and writers, for the sake of determining what steps might be taken to alleviate the racial situation.[10] The meeting was chaotic, for the invited participants began and ended the meeting with hysteria, invective, vituperation, moral indignation, and tears. Baldwin was among the active participants. This is not to say that the reaction of the participants is not understandable, but it is to say that Baldwin's response during the affair would have been quite different had he been more of a political person than he is. His most recent novel, *Tell Me How Long the Train's Been Gone*, reveals the same position. There Baldwin expresses sympathetic understanding of the political perspective, but clearly enough it is not his own.

Because of the interrelatedness of things, the writer cannot help, whether he wills or no, being political in what he writes, be his politics implicit or explicit. Richard Wright knew this very well—neither Baldwin nor Ellison believes it. Too frequently our current modes of thought about literature have called us away from the fact of the political in literature; too much of our theoretical discussion of literature has encouraged us to believe that involvement with literature, either writing it or teaching it or reading it, is an activity unrelated to life. Neither Ellison nor Baldwin believes himself in his fiction to be a polemicist. Yet by the nature of literature, each has presented in his work ideas and attitudes which support certain political positions and reject others. This means that in such cases it is the responsibility of the critic to point out where the writer stands politically, for the writer, if we are to believe what writers such as Baldwin and Ellison tell us about their writing, may not know. Or if he knows, the responsibility of the critic is to inform the reader, for the reader deserves to know. A writer may wish to write in such a way as to create objects which he may wish to think of as "aesthetic objects." By all means let him do so. But let him do so with the full knowledge of what he is about. A ghost lurks in those conceptions of literature which consider it to be separate from present realities, and that ghost is the specter of politics. If writers and critics are to be political reactionaries or revolutionaries, then so be it. But let us realize and admit what is being said; let us define where we stand.

NOTES

1. Vol. XVII (January 1968). *Negro Digest* has since become *Black World.*
2. This seems to me the crux of the argument between Ellison and Irving Howe. From my perspective Ellison won the argument, but Howe was right in his assumptions about what literature is and what it should do. Howe was wrong, however, in seeing Ellison and Baldwin as "sons" of Richard Wright. Ellison's views of literature and his politics as well are far more closely aligned with Eliot's, Gertrude Stein's, Hemingway's, and Faulkner's (all writers whom he reports reading before coming to Wright) than with Wright's. Ellison's politics, and not his race, is the crucial element. The exchange between Ellison and Howe began in the autumn issue of *Dissent* in 1963 with Howe's article "Black Boys and Native Sons." Ellison's reply was printed as "The World and the Jug" in *The New Leader*, December 9, 1963. "A Reply to Ellison" by Howe and "A Rejoinder" by Ellison were printed in *The New Leader*, February 3, 1964. Howe's portion of the debate was reprinted in his *A World More Attractive* (New York, 1963) and Ellison's portion in *Shadow and Act* (New York, 1964).
3. *Politics and the Novel* (New York, 1957), p. 26.
4. Baldwin defines his position especially in "Everybody's Protest Novel," *Notes of a Native Son* (Boston, 1953). Ellison either implies or explicitly states this position in a number of essays and interviews. He is quite explicit in "The World and the Jug" (cited above), p. 20: "I can only ask that my fiction be judged as art; if it fails, it fails aesthetically, not because I did or did not fight some ideological battle."
5. Marcus Klein develops this point in "Ralph Ellison's *Invisible Man*" in S. Gross and J. Hardy, eds., *Images of the Negro in American Literature* (Chicago, 1966).
6. I exclude sexual morality here.
7. See Robert Bone's ingenious, wrongheaded "The Novels of James Baldwin" in *Images of the Negro*, p. 275.
8. "Letters from a Journey," *Harper's*, May 1963, p. 52.
9. *The Fire Next Time* (New York, 1964), pp. 120 and 128–129.
10. The psychologist Kenneth Clark was also present. The episode is reported in Arthur Schlesinger's *A Thousand Days* (Boston, 1963), pp. 962–963.

NORMAN MAILER
(1923-   )

by Robert Alter

> Politics as politics interests me less today than politics as a
> part of everything else in life.
>
> Norman Mailer, *Advertisements for Myself*

NORMAN MAILER IS the most stubbornly political of living American novelists, a fact that explains a certain element of tough strength in most of
his work as well as the increasingly problematic status of his fiction since
The Naked and the Dead. He is shrewdly realistic about political actualities yet doggedly hopeful about man's possibilities, and this peculiar mix
of wry knowledge and romantic faith has made it progressively more difficult for him to write in the fictional modes of conventional realism
about a play of political forces whose chief effects seem to him the
destruction of human meanings, the institutionalization of unreality, the
mass production of inobtrusive and bottomless despair.

The curve of Mailer's career traces out these difficulties with the clarity
of an almost formal symmetry. He begins in *The Naked and the Dead* by
trying to engage the political issues of the contemporary world with
fictional methods learned from the American documentary realists of the
1920's and 1930's. Moving on to a much more restricted fictional plan in
Barbary Shore, he confronts root questions of political theory in more
direct and analytic detail; the book as a result offers us moments of intellectual sharpness in a world that is novelistically flat. *The Deer Park*, the
culminating midpoint in Mailer's career till now, remain his most original
attempt to grasp the ultimate nature of our political condition by the

realistic representation of a contemporary milieu. Significantly, it was to have been the first section of an immense eight-part novel that would have followed its hero's tireless quest for experience on a course that could embrace the whole range of contemporary society. The scheme, as Mailer himself candidly admits, would have required the patience of a Zola and the imagination of a Joyce, neither of which he very obviously possessed. To be fair to him, one might add that such a concerted artistic attack on contemporary reality could be more easily launched from the political certainties of Zola's nineteenth-century socialist scientism or from the Olympian detachment of Joyce's apolitical, myth-minded cult of art, and, in all honesty, Mailer has found the comforts of such confident outlooks to be inadmissible luxuries in his own hard world.

A full decade passed from the publication of *The Deer Park* in 1955 until the appearance of Mailer's next novel, and during these years he devoted his best energies as a writer and thinker to direct reflection on American society rather than to the fictional re-creation of it—in the brilliant journalism and the sometimes zany but often penetrating social, political, and moral analysis of the occasional pieces collected in *Advertisements for Myself*, *The Presidential Papers*, and *Cannibals and Christians*. His two novels of the 1960's, *An American Dream* and *Why Are We in Vietnam?* could be viewed, somewhat uncharitably, as strategems for the rapid production of fiction by a writer no longer capable of writing fiction, but it might be fairer to conceive of them as venturesome attempts to reconstruct the political novel through parody, fantasy, and the magic of rhetoric when the nature of politics itself had eroded the bases of the traditional political novel. After these uncertain experiments, in *The Armies of the Night* Mailer has managed for once to bring together happily his gifts as novelist and journalist, reporting "history"—the grand assumptions of the term are his—as it happens while transforming it into the imaginatively rich stuff of novelistic reality with himself, an engagingly self-conscious comic hero, immersed in the action.

Mailer has the kind of imagination that delights in the nice observation of concrete particulars but at the same time is powerfully drawn to athletic, not to say fantastic, play with theory. The way he has variously resolved the pull between these two aspects of his imagination has in fact determined the formal disposition of his novels. The most impressive achievement of *The Naked and the Dead* is in the painstaking accumulation of acute observation: Mailer skillfully catches every line of ethnic feature, each elided nuance of regional accent, the tone and touch and look of particular American lives lived in particular American milieux, and the novel he builds from such observation has a massive solidity unlike anything he would write afterward. It was of course by choice that he never returned to this kind of detailed realism he could do so well, partly, one may assume, out of a sense that the techniques he had learned from James Farrell, Dos Passos, and Steinbeck were no longer appropriate to encompass American realities of the 1950's and 1960's but also because he must have realized that exhaustive realism deflected him from the aims that he, as a political novelist of a boldly theoretical bent, was trying to achieve.

For I would contend that there is a disparity in *The Naked and the Dead* between the impressive panoramic view of American society through the portrayal of the individual soldiers, and the expository dialogues between General Cummings and Lieutenant Hearn that constitute the core of the novel's political argument. Cummings, we recall, is the self-made ideologue of a homegrown American fascism, who lectures to Hearn, the proverbial well-meaning, self-deceived liberal, about the prerogatives of power, the "fear ladder" that the army establishes to reduce men to mere instruments, and about the future world order of godlike domination by the strong, for which the army itself serves as a vivid preview. The force of Cumming's theory of human nature and the dynamics of leadership is strikingly illustrated in the culminating action of the novel—the struggle for control of the platoon between Hearn and Sergeant Croft, that true wielder of power in the Cummings way, and Croft's mad drive to conquer Mount Anaka. Of all the long retrospective portraits in the book, however, only those of Croft, Cummings, and Hearn have real relevance to the political argument of the novel. America is wonderfully present in the detailed characterizations and family backgrounds of the other soldiers, from southern redneck and Mexican-American to Boston Irish and New York Jew, but in all this affectionate and faithful reproduction of an intimately familiar America it is hard to see where precisely in American life lie the roots of that native fascism which Cummings predicts and Croft embodies.

As Mailer in the 1950's made clear for himself the distinctive meaning of his enormous ambition as a writer, he came to recognize that the chief role to which he aspired was not descriptive but, in the proper biblical sense, prophetic: The "sour truth" he admits to at the very beginning of *Advertisements for Myself* is that he is "imprisoned with a perception which will settle for nothing less than making a revolution in the consciousness of our time." The uncompromising clarity of prophetic vision he sought in order to reveal the inner nature of the spiritual condition from which all our political ills issued could easily be clouded or thrown out of focus by excessive attention to surface detail, and this in essence is what happens through many pages—even brilliantly written pages—of *The Naked and the Dead.*

It may have been the awareness of just this difficulty that led Mailer in his next novel to hold all characters, events, and situations so tightly within the framework of a single theoretical question—the politics of rev-olution in a world of cold wars threatening to turn hot. *Barbary Shore* has almost the look of a philosophical dialogue on revolutionary politics with narrative bridges for counterpoint and illustration. The action is neatly isolated from the complications of any larger social scene by being set in a rooming house. The only significant characters all play clearly defined roles in the novel's political scheme: a former Stalinist revolu-tionary, a deranged Trotskyist girl, an F.B.I. agent, and the narrator, who has, perhaps too significantly, lost his identity in the last war and whose political education is the real subject of the novel. The sole apolitical character is Guinevere, the bizarre landlady, and she, too, fits into the scheme as the figure who binds Mcleod, the revolutionary, to the banali-ties of domesticity, the messy ambiguities and undeniable responsibilities of personal affection.

Whatever Mailer has done has been done above all with verve, but *Barbary Shore* is peculiar in its bleakness, what almost looks like a lack of energy. This is in part attributable to the expository quality of the dia-logue, which at points is only minimally dramatic, but it can be more directly connected with Lovett, the amnesiac narrator, who, working painfully to fill in the *tabula rasa* of his own mind and memory, has none of the imaginative zest or the stylistic flair of Mailer's other first-person narrators. One senses a kind of emotional and intellectual fatigue in Lov-ett—and this makes *Barbary Shore* most peculiar as a novel of edu-cation—which perfectly echoes the mood of radical politics in America during the McCarthy era and the first ominous stage of the cold war. "Out of all the futilities with which man attempts to express himself," Lovett tells Mcleod, "I find politics among the most pathetic." It is a sour irony that this prematurely defeated figure is the only one in the novel available as heir to Mcleod's vision of a truly human socialism. As Lovett himself says, setting out at the end of the book on his destiny of flight from the world's ubiquitous secret police, he is a "poor hope" to be the bearer of such a noble heritage. This general sense of dead air and grop-ing uncertainty in character and action is allied to the desperate irresolu-tion of the novel's political imagination. Lovett is convinced that the prospect of history without some hope like Mcleod's is insupportable, but all he can see on the historical horizon is endless war flowing from "the unyielding contradictions of labor stolen from men." The novel con-cludes, appropriately, in ominous irresolution, with an image of rudder-less drift and lack of vision and response in a world of darkly impending forces: "The storm approaches its thunderhead, and it is apparent that the boat drifts ever closer to the shore. So the blind will lead the blind, and the deaf shout warnings to one another until their voices are lost."

What is most important in the political argument of *Barbary Shore* for

Mailer's later development is the emphasis given to the idea of a modern society that radically perverts the natural human relation to life and death. Mcleod sums up for Hollingsworth, his F.B.I. antagonist, the nature of that brave new world which Hollingsworth and the powers he represents are bringing about: "For the first time in history, the intent of society will be to produce wholly for death, and men will be kept alive merely to further that aim." Mailer's first spokesman for this new order of death was General Cummings, who saw men as machines, and the machines of death themselves as objects of sexual beauty and potency. The same ultimate confusion occurs at a strategic point in Lovett's fragmentary memories of his war past. He recalls lying with a peasant girl while on guard duty, his fingers feeling the chill of the trigger handle, his eyes scanning a field under the shadow of his machine-gun barrel, while his body impersonally thrust within her. Later that same night, he dreamed of sex with artillery shells and polished steel; it was in the action after that, he sometimes thinks, that he received his memory-crippling wound.

Lovett's lived and dreamed nightmares of love submerged in death suggest what would become, for better or for worse, the principal dramatic focus of political and spiritual life in Mailer's subsequent fiction. Mailer was finding himself more and more oppressively confronted with a society that madly and absurdly controverted the most basic intuitions of the real and the imaginary, life and death, offering the critically realistic novelist about as much purchase as an Alice-in-Wonderland world conceived by the Marquis de Sade. In such an ambience of insidious absurdities, the sexual act could serve as the most concretely imaginable and humanly constant situation in which to measure and to represent the power of a man—or a culture—to affirm life or to convert the biological act of affirmation itself into its own opposite.

Characteristically, the realm of debauchery to which the epigraph of *The Deer Park* would seem to introduce us turns out to be represented with what amounts to an austerity of pained moral consciousness, the novelist's vivid sense of sweet promiscuous flesh darkened by his awareness of all the emptiness and fear and inward dying that converge in these carnal hungers. The novel is set in a Southern California resort town called Desert D'Or, a splendid never-never land restlessly populated by directors, producers, actors, Hollywood hangers-on, retired millionaires, ingenious procurers, and call girls of every kind, for every inclination. The only explicit political background that intrudes on the supercharged opulence of this vacation world is the communist witchhunt of a congressional investigating committee, which has resulted in the blacklisting of one of the principal characters, the director Charles Eitel. It is in this novel, however, that Mailer begins to deal with politics "as a part of everything else in life," and Desert D'Or, precisely because it is such a spectacular and isolated extreme of American life, is finally a pellucid image of American society at large, revealing what our collective lives covertly aspire to, where the moral roots lie that blossom into the rich flowers of evil of our social order and our political institutions.

Sergius O'Shaughnessy, the first-person narrator, has fled from the trauma of his experience as a bomber pilot in Asia to Desert D'Or for the very reason that it is the ultimate realized dream of an unreal world which is nothing but play. His reiterated distinction between real and imaginary worlds is absolutely crucial to this novel and, I would suggest, to all of Mailer's subsequent work:

> I had the idea that there were two worlds. There was a real world as I called it, a world of wars and boxing clubs and children's homes on back streets, and this real world was a world where orphans burned orphans. It was better not even to think of this. I liked the other world in which almost everybody lived. The imaginary world.

It may sound a little inane to say that the subject of any literary work is reality, since that is obviously true in some sense of all serious literature, but that otherwise vapid truism has a peculiar and informative applicability to all Mailer's fiction from *The Deer Park* on. What he confronts centrally for the first time in *The Deer Park* is the special power of American society to mask, sham, evade, forget reality, to seduce its individual members into giving up on engagement in the real world; and the ultimately political nature of his moral imagination is reflected in his effort here to show how this American style of cotton-candy insulation from reality allows a society to perpetrate horror and obscenity at home and abroad with hardly a twinge of conscience. It is perfectly right, then, for the large moral and political purposes of the novel that all the principal characters should be connected with the Hollywood movie world, the great American industry that builds empires of wealth and power out of the mass manufacture of cynically contrived daydreams. Charles Eitel engages our attention as a protagonist precisely because he is a successful inhabitant of the imaginary world who still knows what the real world is all about, still feels an aching tug of allegiance to it. A man of serious imagination, both moral and aesthetic, he began his career by trying to articulate an honest vision in his films—which is to say, by trying to engage reality through a genuine art—but ended up capitulating professionally and personally to Hollywood's viciously imaginary world, turning out enormously marketable films slickly pasted together with imaginary things. Eitel's refusal to name names for the House investigating committee is his last outward gesture of loyalty to the real world he had wanted to respond to as a younger man, but the logic of his intricate involvement in the dreams and pleasures of Hollywood existence brings him eventually to surrender this final vestige, too, of his earlier integrity.

The role of sex in these real and imaginary worlds is profoundly and suggestively ambiguous. The novel draws us at first into seeing certain neat oppositions, then reveals complexity and paradox within the apparent simplicity of assertion. The epigraph from *La Vie privée de Louis XV* immediately speaks of "depravity" and "vice" over against "innocence" and "virtue," and it is clear that the hyperconscious sexuality of the Desert D'Or people expresses the moral poverty, even the depravity, of their lives. There is abundant evidence in the book of an association between sex and the pleasure principle in opposition to the reality principle. Sex, in fake-romantic, glossy blowup, is after all the essential content of the celluloid dreams that Hollywood purveys. Sergius is impotent at the beginning of the novel precisely because he has been through the hellfires of the real world; when his body reaches for the caressing touch of a woman's naked flesh, his mind swarms with images of other flesh—burned, bloody, butchered, rotting—and he is unmanned. It is appropriate in his flight from this real world that the woman with whom he regains his virility is Lulu Meyers, a film star—every man's dream of a bedmate, Sergius muses—who combines a primly adolescent exterior with a kind of confused, fatigued worldliness. Using the familiar technique of the film industry itself, she subjects him on their first time together to the most tantalizing sexual teasing, again and again coyly denying what she seems to offer, until at last she gives herself to him, in gentle acquiescence, not with shared passion.

The ultimate role of sex, in fact, for most people in this quintessentially American world is the living out of pornographic fantasies. (One recalls the pathetic concluding scene in Mailer's story "The Man Who Studied Yoga," where the middle-class protagonist and his wife conscientiously make love before the home screen on which they are rerunning a pornographic film.) Sexual experience, then, is usually very lonely and sometimes can be quite cruel as well. Sex is both act and emblem, the endlessly alluring, endlessly disappointing activity of a society that enables and encourages its most powerful members to treat all others as the tools of their pleasure, a society where a pervasive psychology of power working to protect economic interests through political means perpetuates the burning of orphans by orphans with perfect equanimity. Marion Faye, the tormented pimp, has the courage of consciousness others lack in this world to see the damned nature of his moral condition in full clarity: The pleasure his mistress's body gives him also fills him with loathing, and he reaches the searing recognition that the logical fulfillment of his sexual relation with her is for him to drive her to suicide.

Faye's demonism—"Make me cold, Devil, and I will run the world in your name"—in fact lays bare the ultimate principle of action for most people and institutions in the novel: Subjugate others to your will, deny them their humanity, even, if you choose, their right to exist at all. The hierarchy of power at Supreme Pictures makes it a model of American institutional life, and the unnatural sexual proclivities of its president, greedily taking pleasure without the possibility of giving pleasure in return, offer a harshly satiric image of the utter instrumentalization of human relations.

But if sex among the inhabitants of the imaginary world is a mode of domination, a way of reinforcing isolation, it can also be the means of discovering reality, which involves, to begin with, the physical, psychic, and moral reality of another human being. This is what Eitel painfully, uncertainly learns from his liaison with Elena—that in direct opposition to the ethic of egoistic irresponsibility of the imaginary world, the sexual bond, if it is to remain human, must above all confer responsibility. "One cannot look for a good time, Sergius," the narrator imagines Eitel enjoining him at the end of the novel, "for pleasure must end as love or cruelty—or obligation." Love, to be sure, also implies obligation, but even without love there must be obligation, as Eitel learns with Elena, or there will be cruelty. The sexual connection, then, is always rich with possibility and fraught with consequences. It is ultimately *dangerous* in the sense in which Mailer uses that word when he speaks in his essays of existential experiences: Through it a man can make himself more human, realize the unknown possibilities of his own life implicated in the lives of others, or he can fulfill hidden potentials of destructiveness, adding to the sum of dread and deathliness that haunts human existence.

Something of this sort is meant, I would suppose, by the cryptic aphorism with which *The Deer Park* concludes: "Think of Sex as Time, and Time as the connection of new circuits." The hopefulness of the statement suggests both the strength and the weakness of Mailer as a political novelist from this point on in his career. Because he is able to see sex as rich in human possibilities in a world that on a larger scale seems to work steadily toward the elimination of such possibilities, the sexual act becomes the medium for a renewed expression of authentic heroism. It is difficult, however, for Mailer to maintain a persuasive connection between the small arena of erotic encounter and the large arena of society or, as he often wants, with the still vaster arena of the cosmos. Symptomatically, his story "The Time of Her Time," which follows Sergius O'Shaughnessy's between-sheets conquest of a resistant female will almost stroke by stroke, gives the appearance of being about something profound without convincing us of the profundity or showing us what it consists of. If one does not happen to view sex in the sectarian terms of a Reichian believer, just what are those "new circuits" for which Sergius has become a master electrician? In *The Deer Park* itself sex is a sharply effective instrument for a satiric exposure that is political "in the Aristotelian sense," as Saul Bellow's Herzog puts it, but in regard to the final affirmative statement of the novel, one wishes it were possible to see more particularly how Sergius's "existential" attitude toward sex can lead to an actual politics that will keep orphans from burning orphans.

These problems of connection become more pronounced in *An American Dream* as Mailer gives freer play to the religious musings that had preoccupied him from the mid-1950's on into the early 1960's. The miscellaneous pieces in *The Presidential Papers* are an invaluable guide to this novel, just as those in *Advertisements for Myself* are to *The Deer Park*. The idea of the hero that appears repeatedly in *The Presidential Papers* is the key to what Mailer describes as "existential politics"—a politics of adventure in which the results of decisions boldly taken remain forever unpredictable. Steve Rojack, the protagonist of *An American Dream*, former war hero and congressman, high-powered intellectual, television personality, heiress's husband, sexual virtuoso, is the existential hero Mailer tried to hope Jack Kennedy could be in his memorable essay "Superman Comes to the Supermarket." Mailer has since aptly described himself as a "Left conservative," and his conservatism is nowhere more evident than in his fascination, both political and aesthetic, with the idea of the hero as a saving power in the world. It is obvious enough that a main direction of the novel since Cervantes has been to show the tragic or absurd impossibility, the foolishness, the painful inappropriateness, of traditional notions of heroism in the modern world. In the face of this, the logic of Mailer's development as a writer and political thinker brings him to attempt in *An American Dream* nothing less than an imaginative reconstruction of the traditional hero.

Of course, he cannot really do this with a straight face, and so the novel is, as some of its more sympathetic critics have argued, a conscious literary put-on with a serious point, a freewheeling fantasy ultimately concerned with real things, part fairy tale, part comic strip, part melodramatic farce, part parody, at times perhaps an exercise in novelistic Pop Art, yet anchored in the social and moral actualities with which we live. I don't think such explanations are excessively ingenious in Mailer's defense because they do help make sense of our immediate experience in reading the book. On the one hand, one does feel that the novel seriously addresses itself to questions of the utmost spiritual urgency; it is literally and symbolically about matters of life and death. "Let me be not all dead," Rojack cries to himself, trying to resist the blandishments of the moon out beyond the balcony railing, and his words echo the desperate desire to find some liberation from the spreading blight of deathliness in modern life that has troubled Mailer since *The Naked and the Dead*. On the other hand, Rojack's adventures are splendidly, incredibly adventurous, and as such they are fun—sometimes high-spirited or arch fun, sometimes fun of a rather scary sort—for the reader to follow. One watches in bemused fascination as the tireless Rojack, Superman with a chair of existential psychology, edges along a ledge in a buffeting wind thirty stories up, braves it out with police and Mafia, thrashes his girl's Harlem lover, performs sexual acrobatics, and, of course, ecstatically consummates his desire to destroy the evil impinging on him by murdering his beautiful wife.

These flamboyant heroics are meant to constitute not an imaginary world but an imaginative one, which of course is virtually the opposite—a way of taking us, as Sergius aspired to do at the end of *The Deer Park*, to the heart of those realities which make possible, among other things, the incineration of human beings by other perfectly reasonable human beings. The final inadequacy of *An American Dream* is not in its lack of conventional realism but in the ultimate vagueness of its political and spiritual argument. Here I think that Mailer's preoccupation with his own private theology works against him as a novelist. Rojack, a true mythic hero, is repeatedly confronted with the antithetical alternatives of God and the Devil in different guises—Cherry and Oswald Kelly, the vision of the "jewelled city" and the dark abyss below the balcony, procreation and murder, Ruta's orifices, fore and aft. The trouble is that such large contrasts of ultimate good and evil are so schematically theological that they tell us very little about the complexities of motive and moral choice in the world we all have to live in. (The contrast here with *The Deer Park* is instructive.) To put this another way, it is very difficult, beyond a certain level of mythic abstraction, to know what *An American Dream* is really about, why certain episodes or actions are elaborated in the way they are or given the weight they are given. Ultimately, the dream of an instinctual, sensual, anarchic heroism that Mailer first articulated in "The White Negro" is apolitical because it is finally irresponsible, and he strains to intimate political implications for it in this novel.

The intriguing emphasis Rojack places on the sense of smell in his narrative is symptomatic of this final vagueness behind the striking concreteness of the novel. Of the senses, it is the one that seems the most animal-like, the least translatable into rational exposition, the closest to hunch and intuition. Rojack magically *senses*, for instance, in the whiff coming off Oswald Kelly an intricate compound of power, wealth, corruption, carnality, and demonic will. Such perceptions are both mysterious and mystifying but unfortunately shade into others that are merely unclear. Too many of Rojack's experiences finally reduce to the haziness of how they make him feel, whether intuitively they seem "right" or not. With his stress on feeling good, his repeated use of the impersonal "it" for this crucial intuition of feeling, he sounds a little like a Hemingway bull-fighter measuring his inner readiness for an engagement with the Devil himself, but the regrettable result is that Rojack usually fails to tell us very much in particular about his actual experience of good and evil: "Something was wrong, very wrong. It had been right for a little while, for an hour with Cherry in the room it had been almost right, and now it was bad again—some air of hurricane lay over my head." At what should be crucial moments of revelation, Rojack's language does not take us from the someness to the substance of what is going on.

Since Mailer conceives of giving oneself to the unknown as the essence of adventure, it is clear why intuition becomes so important for him, and it is also understandable that he should long for a politics of adventure in a world of blankly inhuman social and political "planning." In *An American Dream*, however, not only the consequences of actions remain unknown but also, too often, their essential meaning even after they have occurred. The book is finally a brilliant phantasmagoria insufficiently linked to particular meaningful referents, a kind of Byronic dramatic poem that expresses a state of spiritual longing more than it responds novelistically to man in society.

There is an element of militant genius in Mailer that makes most of what he has written interesting, original, in some way worthy of respect, but the soft underside of his genius is his tendency to self-indulgence, and that has been abundantly evident in his last two novels. One suspects that it has shaped too many of the pleasurable fantasies of *An American Dream*; in *Why Are We in Vietnam?* it exerts an almost constant pressure on the rhetoric of the novel. It may be that Mailer tries to do too many things at once here. There are patches of free-associating, science-fiction fantasy attacks on American reality in the manner of William Burroughs, but they are never sustained with Burroughs's manic intensity. There are brief theoretical analyses of the psychosexual ills at the root of corporation-run U.S.A., but these never achieve the subtlety or specificity of articulation of Mailer's own essays on similar matters in *Cannibals and Christians* and elsewhere. Above all, there is the serious parody—written, I fear, with an eye to Leslie Fiedler's *Love and Death in the American Novel*—of the archetypal American tale of the wilderness hunt for some absolute, primal beast. As in Faulkner's *The Bear*, the hunt is a rite of initiation into manhood, the son in this case setting out with his own father. As in Fiedler's reading of the American classics, a suggestion of homosexual love is introduced into the hunt, white man (D.J., the narrator) archetypally joined with red man (his "blood brother," Tex, who is part Indian).

Mailer's parodistic reconstruction of the American wilderness quest does succeed wonderfully through intermittently sustained moments. In the first kill of the hunt, in the primitive ceremony of drinking wolf's blood, in the naked confrontation with the great grizzly, he communicates a powerful sense of being "up tight with the essential animal insanity of things" and makes palpable truth out of the truisms about American fixations on mechanistic violence, American dread of lost or failed manhood—all of which may in fact tell us something important about the national sickness that drives us to bludgeon, bomb, and burn Asian peasants in an insane and self-defeating war. The major problem with this novel, however, is that the narrative and symbolic track of the hunt is constantly crisscrossed, interrupted, sometimes almost obliterated, by the gyrating pyrotechnics of D.J.'s self-delighting rhetoric. No characters are really allowed to exist—not even the narrator himself, who is a performance, not a character—and both plot and situation repeatedly get lost in D.J.'s verbal razzle-dazzle.

Mailer's narrator, to be sure, tries to justify the peculiar form his story takes. The main action, he reminds us, occurs "two years . . . before the period of D.J.'s consciousness running through his head, hence form is more narrative, memory being always more narrative than the tohu-bohu of the present, which is Old Testament Hebrew, cock-sucker, for chaos and void." The narrator's wildly free-associating manner, then, is in general an attempt to simulate the tohu-bohu of present consciousness, and the barrage of obscenities he uses is intended to break down protective posturings and pretense, to crack through the sterile, pastel plastic surfaces with which corporate America covers its failure of nerve and moral imagination. ("She don't talk that way, she just thinks that way," D.J. says of an obscene speech he has attributed to his mother.)

Obscenities, however, are also for Mailer a form of American folk eloquence, and that is perhaps the chief danger in his own use of them. Back in 1955 in a column for the *Village Voice*, he had written feelingly of obscenities that they were "our poor debased gutturals for the magical parts of the human body, and so they are basic communication, for they awake, no matter how uneasily, many of the questions, riddles, aches, and pleasures which surround the enigma of life." D.J., the disc jockey with the raucous bleeps, is trying to achieve an act of "basic communication" through his obscenity, but he, or his inventor, is too aware of the "magical" quality of obscene words, and as a result his narrative, especially when its language is most pervasively indecent, has too much self-conscious fine writing, in the old, ironic eighteenth-century sense of that phrase. The verbal raids on the real world, that is, are often dissipated in play with purely verbal effects. Nevertheless, there are moments of grace when the metaphorical acrobatics suddenly dive to some root of the American condition. Thus, D.J. at one point sees in his father's eyes a glimmer of a hidden mastermind with "a plastic asshole installed in his

brain" who is the incarnate spirit of American corporation life in all its
bureaucratized, dehumanized emptiness:

> I mean that's what you get when you look into Rusty's eyes. You
> get voids, man, and gleams of yellow fire—the woods is burning
> somewhere in his gray matter—and then there's marble aisles,
> better believe it, fifty thousand fucking miles of marble floor
> down those eyes, and you got to walk over that to get to The
> Man.

Both in *An American Dream* and in *Why Are We in Vietnam?* Mailer
strains to imagine "politics as a part of everything else in life" by representing it in acts—sex, murder, hunting—that become ritual and symbolic
as the tests of true or bogus heroism. *The Armies of the Night* reverses
this procedure, describing an overtly political event with an electric
awareness of the "everything else" that is implicated in it and that expli-
cates it. In this case the heroism which for Mailer is essential to any genuinely human politics is ironically focused in the comic heroic figure of
the novelist himself. His shrewd understanding of what he is doing, how
he as an observed character fits into the success of his account, is conspicuous throughout the narrative, is in fact one of the means through
which he persuades us of the authority of what he says. When history,
Mailer argues, becomes the kind of madhouse in which deadly serious,
utterly quixotic armies of protesters gather to "wound symbolically" the
central military headquarters of the world's mightiest superpower, a
peculiar perspective like his own may be uniquely valuable: "It is fitting
that any ambiguous comic hero of such a history should be not only off
very much to the side of the history, but that he should be an egotist of
the most startling misproportions, outrageously and often unhappily
self-assertive, yet in command of a detachment classic in severity." The
egotism is, I would suggest, a hold on sanity in an insane historical situation. Where collective moral sensibility translates itself into blank-walled
Pentagons, into flailing truncheons at home and flamethrowers in distant
places, a self-critical but irrepressible egotism is a way of asserting that
individual will and character still count for something, that it is still
imaginable, possible, perhaps even useful, to try to affirm one's own
humanity through action. The self-consciousness of the egotism is also a
matter of rhetorical effectiveness: What Mailer has to say about the
march on Washington and the social-political forces involved in it seems
even more persuasive because he is so convincingly perceptive throughout in his self-analysis.

The presence of Mailer as protagonist gives his report of the march on
the Pentagon something of the dramatic definition of a novel, and this
helps create an appropriate context for the novelistic imagination of

observed figures and scenes. Details are seen, that is, as they are in many of the older realistic novels, at once poetically and analytically, caught in a network of connected meanings, moral, social, and political. A banal fact like the unhappy effect of fluorescent lighting on faces becomes suddenly interesting, "symbolic," through the novelist's combination of precise observation and metaphorical imagination: "Like everything else in technology-land the fluorescence, being reductive, revealed nothing but negative truth." The novelist's eye for the nuances of difference in personal styles, his ear for the reverberations of implication in representative social types, enable him at least partly to achieve here through reportage what, in *Advertisements for Myself*, he had said he wanted to do in a novel—to discover "the psychic anatomy of our republic." When, for example, he describes an angry six-foot marshal about to silence prisoners, that real world where orphans burn orphans is made palpable through an act of imagination as it scarcely is anywhere in his fiction:

> He was full of American rectitude and was fearless, and savage, savage as the exhaust left in the wake of a motorcycle club, gasoline and cheap perfume were one end of his spectrum, yeah, this Marshal loved action, but he was also in that no-man's-land between the old frontier and the new ranch home—as they, yes *they*—the enemies of the Marshal—tried to pass bills to limit the purchase of hunting rifles, so did *they* try to kill America, inch by inch, all the forces of evil, disorder, mess, and chaos in the world, and *cowardice!* and city ways, and slick shit, and despoliation of national resources, all the subtle invisible creeping paralyses of Communism which were changing America from a land where blood was red to a land where water was foul.

The Armies of the Night is probably Mailer's most fully achieved book and certainly his most successful engagement of politics through a narrative form. The implications of this achievement, to be sure, for the future of the political novel are at best ambiguous. When horror, absurdity, bizarre incongruity, conscious and unconscious madness, come to dominate the institutions and public acts of political life, and political protest as well, fictional invention may pale by contrast or overstrain itself in the effort of competition with reality. Perhaps in such a predicament one valuable service a novelist can perform is to try to come to grips directly with actual events. It may well be that at this point in history we all need the aid of the novelist's imagination simply to help us imagine what seems to be more and more unimaginable—the real world in which we have to live, make decisions individually and collectively, and still struggle to shape a livable political future.

WILLIAM STYRON
(1925-   )

by Melvin J. Friedman

> I think that the best of my generation—those in their late
> thirties or early forties—have reversed the customary rules of the
> game and have grown more radical as they have gotten older—
> a disconcerting but healthy sign.
>
> William Styron, "My Generation," *Esquire*, October 1968

> One cannot lose more than the slave loses, he loses all inner
> life. He only retrieves a little if there should arise an opportu-
> nity to change his destiny. Such is the empire of might; it extends
> as far as the empire of nature.
>
> Simone Weil, "The 'Iliad,' Poem of Might"

WILLIAM STYRON ONCE called himself a "Southerner of good will who
lives in the North." He made this statement in the course of reviewing a
reissue of Lewis H. Blair's 1889 study *A Southern Prophecy* for *The New
York Review of Books* (April 2, 1964). Later in the same review Styron
touched on a familiar bias which was later to come back to haunt him
after the publication of *The Confessions of Nat Turner* in 1967:

> White Southern writers, because they are white and Southern,
> cannot be expected to write about Negroes without conde-
> scension, or with understanding or fidelity or love. Unfortu-
> nately, this is a point of view which, by an extension of logic,
> tends to regard all white Southerners as bigots, and it is an atti-
> tude which one might find even more ugly than it is were it

prompted by malice rather than ignorant self-righteousness, or a suffocating and provincial innocence [p. 3].

In 1964 this was all academic. Racial integration and civil rights were the rallying cry rather than black power, and Styron was emphatically an integrationist and pro–civil rights. The language of American *négritude* was not yet firmly a part of our national rhetoric, and Styron's " 'white' language" (Mike Thelwell's expression) was listened to attentively. He had already made clear, perhaps more convincingly than any other white American writer, that he stood for all the right things and was willing periodically to put aside his current novel in progress in order to take an uncompromising stand in print. Thus he came out dramatically against capital punishment in two articles in *Esquire* (February and November 1962) and helped save the life of a "subliterate" Negro, Benjamin Reid. He came out against the abuses of television in a piece he did for the April 6, 1959, *New Republic*. He was ostensibly complaining about the distortions the old *Playhouse 90* imposed upon his novella *The Long March*, but he was actually pointing to a larger failure: "In the end the real culprit in television is not *just* sponsor approval or official censorship, but an ignorant fear of the truth which permeates all other aspects of our society too, and which poisons art at its roots. It is almost as ignoble a censorship as censorship itself." William Styron has also been a confirmed Stevenson–Kennedy–Eugene McCarthy Democrat and even attended the 1968 Democratic convention in Chicago as a "delegate challenger" from Connecticut committed to McCarthy.

This, curiously enough, is the novelist and occasional journalist whom the black intellectuals were outraged at after the publication of *The Confessions of Nat Turner*. One has to be surprised that a writer with these undeniably liberal credentials could be accused of having a "vile racist imagination."[1] An earlier generation was willing to forgive Pound, Eliot, Wyndham Lewis, and Yeats their "reactionary" politics mainly because, as Stephen Spender remarked, "often their politics only shows that they care less for politics than for literature." The black writers of our time (we should be careful to exclude Ralph Ellison and James Baldwin) have proved unforgiving of the politics of William Styron. The following is typical of the kind of treatment he has received since the publication of *The Confessions of Nat Turner*: "If anything, the writing of Styron's book was a political gesture, albeit a muddled one; and on that point alone the author invited the kind of attack he received. At any rate, one can be fairly certain that the next white writer will think twice before presuming to interpret the Black Experience."[2] Styron has become the first literary martyr to the cause of black power—which too willingly forgets the liberal credentials of its white victims.

Styron, born in 1925 in Newport News, Virginia (not far from the events of the Nat Turner insurrection), served his apprenticeship in the creative-writing workshop of William Blackburn at Duke University. Two of his Duke stories appeared in a volume edited by Blackburn, *One and Twenty: Duke Narrative and Verse, 1924–1945*. One of these, "Autumn," is a rather trivial account of a fossilized prep-school English teacher who has the usual painful moment of self-recognition, but the other, "The Long Dark Road," seems now to be crucially important to his later development: It is the story of a Negro lynching. Styron tests the reaction of the event on a young boy, Dewey Lassiter, who offers a response somewhat similar to that of Nick Adams in Hemingway's "Indian Camp." As in the Hemingway story, we are confronted with a boy's amazement at the cruelty and harsh reality of the adult world—but this time the element of racial imbalance emphatically comes into focus. The setting of the story is Nat Turner country, both geographically and morally.

Styron worked on his first novel while registered in Hiram Haydn's creative-writing course at the New School for Social Research in New York City. *Lie Down in Darkness* (1951) fortunately does not reveal the effects of too much time spent in the classroom; Malcolm Cowley and others rather found it to be an agreeable product of time spent profitably in the workshop of William Faulkner. We see again, as in "The Long Dark Road," Styron's concern with the Negro and the liberal white Southerner's uncomfortable heritage of slavery. A line like the following is the kind of "gentle" reminder we find so often in Styron: "The ground is bloody and full of guilt where you were born and you must tread a long narrow path toward your destiny."[3] In *Lie Down in Darkness* we watch the decay of still another fictional southern family with the standard ingredients of the father who drowns his sorrows in drink and extramarital sex; the pampered, religiously neurotic, neurasthenic mother; the crippled, retarded daughter; and the daughter who ends by taking her own life. There are a variety of Negro characters who move in and out of the narrative focus, most of whom are viewed at a sympathetic distance. Styron has heeded the caution of William Faulkner by removing himself from the consciousness of the blacks in his first novel; he has explained this admirably in an article which he wrote many years later for *Harper's*:

Certainly one feels the presence of this gulf even in the work of a writer as supremely knowledgeable about the South as William Faulkner, who confessed a hesitancy about attempting to "think Negro," and whose Negro characters, as marvelously portrayed as most of them are, seem nevertheless to be meticu-

lously *observed* rather than *lived.* Thus in *The Sound and the
Fury,* Faulkner's magnificent Dilsey comes richly alive, yet in
retrospect one feels this is a result of countless mornings, hours,
days Faulkner had spent watching and listening to old Negro
servants, and not because Dilsey herself is a being created from
a sense of withinness: at the last moment Faulkner draws back,
and it is no mere happenstance that Dilsey, alone among the
four central figures from whose points of view the story is told,
is seen from the outside rather than from that intensely "inner"
vantage point, the interior monologue.[4]

Styron wrote this article at a time when he was about midway through
his own *The Confessions of Nat Turner.* He was probably looking more
ahead to this novel than back to *Lie Down in Darkness.* We seem to be
told here that *Lie Down in Darkness,* in which he refused to "think
Negro," in which he drew back "at the last moment" as Faulkner did in
The Sound and the Fury, was clearly a part of Styron's undaring literary
past. *The Confessions of Nat Turner,* published two years after the
Harper's article, is written "from that intensely 'inner' vantage point,"
from the first person of a Meursault (*The Stranger*) or of a Marcel
(*Remembrance of Things Past*),[5] but qualified by Styron's version of the
language of *négritude,* or what black Americans are fond of calling
"soul."

In the sixteen years separating *Lie Down in Darkness* from *The Confessions of Nat Turner,* Styron wrote the novella *The Long March*
(1953), the novel *Set This House on Fire* (1960), and a variety of critical reviews and essays. A Negro voice is heard at the end of *The Long
March,* but it has the same "Sambo" inflections as the ones heard at the
end of *Lie Down in Darkness* and *The Sound and the Fury;* now it is the
background voice of a Negro maid: "Do it hurt? ... Oh, I bet it does.
Deed it does."[6]

The Long March concerns a forced march in the Marine Corps, involving mainly reserve personnel called back because of the Korean conflict.
Maxwell Geismar was quite accurate in labeling it "a propaganda tale,
embodying that 'individual' protest which William Styron believes to be
so hopeless today."[7] Styron was himself a victim of Korea—he was called
back to active duty in the Marine Corps in 1950—and he seems in *The
Long March* to be berating the politics of the military; this was, in a
sense, his first political gesture as a man of letters. He came out against
war and the unfeeling rigors of the Marine Corps at a time when it was
unfashionable to do so. Three years after the first publication of *The
Long March* the famous Parris Island Marine incident, involving the
cruel excesses of Sergeant Matthew C. McKeon, brought to the attention
of the public many of the abuses Styron had already metaphorically sug-

gested. When Styron speaks in *The Long March* of being "astray at mid-century in the never-endingness of war" (pp. 117–118), he could as easily be speaking of Vietnam as of Korea. Styron, in a way, was already expressing the sentiments of the pro-McCarthy, anti-Vietnam song "Where Have All the Young Men Gone?" (heard so often at the 1968 Democratic convention) as early as *The Long March* and Korea.

Styron's next novel, *Set This House on Fire*, is his least *engagé*, his least "political." Yet Styron has never been able to find any kind of refuge in an ivory tower, and we should probably take seriously these words of Paul Valéry when speaking of anything written by Styron: "Besides, there are many degrees between a purely literary occupation and political activity. Let us say of the former that it consists *in writing to make people think or imagine*, and of the latter that it comes down to *writing (or speaking) to make people act*, and we shall then observe that the two motives cannot be clearly distinguished nor their results clearly separated."[8] The statement would seem to have special relevance to *The Long March*, but I can imagine it also being applied to *Set This House on Fire*. The hymn which Cass Kinsolving—the hero of the novel who makes the Sartrean choice between being and nothingness—intones at the end of the novel seems to have a great deal to do with the American Dream, which has been celebrated in American literature from James Fenimore Cooper and Mark Twain through *The Great Gatsby*:

> "Then you know, something as I sat there—something about the dawn made me think of America and how the light would come up slowly over the eastern coast, miles and miles of it, the Atlantic, and the inlets and bays and slow tideland rivers with houses on the shore, all shuttered and sleeping, and this stealthy light coming up over it all, the fish stakes at low tide and the ducks winging through the dawn and a kind of apple-green glow over the swamplands and the white beaches and the bays."[9]

There is clearly something political (in Valéry's sense of making *"people act"*) about Styron-Kinsolving's choice of America over Europe. Just as Styron's prose echoes F. Scott Fitzgerald's in the above passage—think of the end of *The Great Gatsby*—so do his sentiments about the confrontation between the American and the European scenes.

Styron's occasional essays, book reviews, and interviews reveal him always as a "Southerner of good will who lives in the North." His early pronouncements were mainly literary and tended to uphold the novelist, especially the young novelist, in the face of constant and unfair pressure from the critics. This statement from his introduction to the *Best Short Stories from the Paris Review* is fairly typical: "For in point of fact neither the novel nor, by extension, prose fiction in general has *fallen* on bad days; that desolate fancy that assumes that they have has been entertained by too many people—by young writers, needlessly, in self-pity; by a few shallow critics, arrogantly, out of self-satisfaction, not to mention a kind of weird self-promotion." He maintained a somewhat similar position in a forum printed in the Autumn 1955 *American Scholar*, called, significantly, "What's Wrong with the American Novel?"; in an early essay, "Writers Under Twenty-five," which first appeared in the 1963 volume, edited by William Blackburn, *Under Twenty-five: Duke Narrative and Verse, 1945–1962*; in various interviews printed in *The New York Times Book Review, Paris Review, Nouveau Candide, Les Nouvelles littéraires, Le Figaro littéraire*, and *L'Express*.[10]

The shift away from the purely literary seems noticeable when Styron begins to express himself on his novel in progress, *The Confessions of Nat Turner*. In the July 1963 *Esquire* ("Two Writers Talk It Over") he made clear in an exchange with James Jones his position on slavery: "The plantation slave . . . was brutalized spiritually in a way that the only analogy is to the victims of the Nazi concentration camps who *never revolted*" (p. 58). He was similarly forceful in the essay "This Quiet Dust," which he wrote for the April 1965 *Harper's*. (Mike Thelwell, one of Styron's most articulate opponents following the publication of *The Confessions of Nat Turner*, spoke of "This Quiet Dust" as a "brilliant and candid essay" and suggested that Styron would have done well to have had his final say on Nat Turner in this nonfictional piece.[11])

When *The New York Review of Books* was launched at the time of the *New York Times* strike early in 1963, as a protest against the gutless reviewing habits of the established weeklies and monthlies, Styron was on hand with a review of Frank Tannenbaum's *Slave and Citizen*. Styron here uses the same comparison which he used in *Esquire*, this time referring "to the ante-bellum Black Laws of Virginia, which even now read like the code of regulations from an inconceivably vast and much longer enduring Nazi concentration camp" (*The New York Review of Books*, Special Issue, 1963, p. 43). In this review Styron takes a scholarly stand on the historiography of slavery, preferring the conclusions of Stanley M. Elkins and Frank Tannenbaum to the more extreme positions of Ulrich B. Phillips (apologist for slavery) and Kenneth Stampp (theorist of slavery as an uncompromisingly brutal way of life). It is not so much that Styron disagrees with the moral position which Stampp takes in his classic study *The Peculiar Institution*, as that he feels a distinct difference between "plantation slaves" and "small-farm slaves": The analogy with Nazi concentration camps and the mentality of Auschwitz applies only to the first group. Nat Turner was a small-farm slave and Styron's treatment of him acknowledges the possibilities of decent behavior even within a "closed system" like slavery. Styron has Nat Turner express a subtle paradox which is paraphrased from something said by the nineteenth-century escaped slave Frederick Douglass: "Yet I will say this, without which you cannot understand the central madness of nigger existence: beat a nigger, starve him, leave him wallowing in his own shit, and he will be yours for life. Awe him by some unforeseen hint of philanthropy, tickle him with the idea of hope, and he will want to slice your throat."[12] Two of Nat Turner's masters, Samuel Turner and Joseph Travis, in quite different ways, "tickle him with the idea of hope," which, Styron seems to tell us, explains the insurrection according to both the politics and the psychology of slavery.

Styron reviewed Herbert Aptheker's *American Negro Slave Revolts* in the September 26, 1963, *New York Review of Books*. He comes out strongly against Aptheker's theory of "the universality of slave rebelliousness," mentions the only three slave conspiracies which amounted to anything (Gabriel Prosser in 1800, Denmark Vesey in 1822, and Nat Turner in 1831), and calls upon Stanley Elkins's "Sambo" thesis as a corrective to the "extremist" position of *American Negro Slave Revolts*. Again Styron disparages what he calls the "extremist revisionism" of historians who are too eager to offset apologists for slavery like Ulrich B. Phillips by assuming untenable theories in the opposite direction. He ends with the prophetic diagnosis which seems even more to the point some years later than it was in 1963: "The real revolt, of course, is now, beyond the dark wood of slavery, by people reclaiming their birthright and their direct, unassailable humanity" (p. 19).

Styron's reviewing habits for *The New York Review of Books* were eclectic enough to allow not only for Tannenbaum's and Aptheker's books on slavery and Lewis H. Blair's related *A Southern Prophecy* but also for Douglas MacArthur's *Reminiscences*, *The Consumers Union Report on Smoking and the Public Interest*, Andrew Turnbull's edition of *The Letters of F. Scott Fitzgerald*, and Terry Southern and Mason Hoffenberg's *Candy*—all between 1963 and 1964. His mood changes from cynicism (when confronted with such outrages as the memoirs of an autocratic, self-righteous general or the "mortally corrupting addiction" to cigarettes) to fascination (when confronted with the correspondence of a writer whom he truly admires) to geniality (when confronted with a novel which he can only take seriously as "a droll little sugarplum of a tale and a spoof on pornography itself"). The abiding qualities in these reviews are intense sincerity and "high seriousness" (in Matthew Arnold's sense). Styron refuses to take lightly even a casual reviewing assignment, which is another way—he must feel—of morally and aesthetically committing himself. His two later reviews in *Harper's* (February and April 1968) do much the same thing as the *New York Review of Books* pieces—but at greater length. The long review-essay on Andrew Turnbull's biography of Thomas Wolfe in the April *Harper's*, for example, has much the same fond elegiac quality as the review of Fitzgerald's letters.

Although Styron allowed himself these *divertissements* during the years when he was thinking through and writing *The Confessions of Nat Turner*, it is clear that most of his energies were directed toward analyzing the burdens of slavery and their implications for the black man living in the 1960's. Styron has always felt with Allen Tate and others of the original group of Agrarians who gathered at Vanderbilt "the peculiar historical consciousness of the Southern writer."[13] He has also known all along, as he remarked to James Jones in the July 1963 *Esquire*, that "the coming conflict's going to be one of color . . ." (p. 59). Given this prescience and this sense of "historical consciousness," it should not surprise anyone that Styron should finally turn his talents to the subject of the Nat Turner insurrection of 1831—and call this novel, in his author's note, "a meditation on history." This is an obvious way out for the southern literary sensibility when confronted with the sense of urgency Styron had been feeling more and more acutely since the days of Korea. Two other southern writers, Allen Tate and Robert Penn Warren (C. Vann Woodward has reminded us), began their careers by writing biographies of Stonewall Jackson and John Brown respectively. Styron claims to have been interested in Nat Turner for a very long time, as he remarked in that provocative exchange with James Jones in *Esquire*: "And I suppose I got interested in it many years ago when I was just a *boy*. The slave rebellion, you know, is known as Nat Turner's Rebellion: it took place not far from where I was born. So it was always somewhat in my background" (p. 58). Tate and Warren paid their debts to "the peculiar historical consciousness of the Southern writer" as the first gestures of their careers, whereas Styron held back, heeding the caution of his then editor at Random House, Hiram Haydn, until he felt the necessary ripening of his talent. Many of the black critics felt that he did not wait long enough.

The circumstances of the publication of *The Confessions of Nat Turner* are now quite familiar. Styron finished his manuscript early in 1967. Parts were serialized in *Partisan Review*, *Paris Review*, *Harper's*, and *Life* before Random House brought out the book in October 1967. The early reviews, except for the one by Herbert Aptheker (who no doubt remembered Styron's piece in *The New York Review of Books* on his *American Negro Slave Revolts*) in the October 16, 1967, *The Nation*, were generally favorable. The wisest of these were by C. Vann Woodward in *The New Republic* (October 7), Philip Rahv in *The New York Review of Books* (October 26), George Steiner in *The New Yorker* (November 25), and Louis D. Rubin, Jr., in *The Hollins Critic* (December). This is quite an array of talent to have mustered in one's support, and so Styron was clearly off to an auspicious start. Some of these reviewers brilliantly anticipated objections which were to be raised later—mainly by the black intellectual community. Thus George Steiner remarked: "He [Styron] has every artistic right to make of his Nat Turner less an anatomy of the Negro mind than a fiction of complex relationship, of the relationship between a present-day white man of deep Southern roots and the Negro in today's whirlwind. The essential imaginative need in this beautiful, honest book arises from a white sensibility exploring its own social, racial future by dramatizing, necessarily in its own terms, the Negro past" (p. 242). Louis D. Rubin, Jr., speaks the appealing language of "integration" and "civil rights" (which seems now especially distasteful to advocates of black power): "A Negro as seen by William Styron is in no important or essential way different from a white man. Social conditions, not heredity and biology, set him apart. The walls of separateness are man-made" (p. 6).

As long as reviewers stuck to purely aesthetic concerns, *The Confessions of Nat Turner* seemed to fare very well. Even the responsible historians who looked at it, like C. Vann Woodward and Martin Duberman, found it—especially historically—very much to their liking. But a suspicion began to creep in which echoed the famous equation that good prose equals bad history. Aptheker, for example, leaned heavily on the bad history part of the equation, although he said nothing about the good prose, in his review in *The Nation*. Still, in general, Styron had little to fear from either the literary-critical or the historical approach; it was politics which finally invaded his privacies as a novelist and seemed to deny his rights to both the "truth of fiction" and the "historical truth."

Styron was violating a "territorial imperative" and inviting the riposte he finally got in the form of *William Styron's Nat Turner: Ten Black Writers Respond*, according to Stephen Henderson in *The Militant Black Writer in Africa and the United States*. When Eldridge Cleaver rhapsodized about "the womb that nurtured Toussaint L'Ouverture, that warmed Nat Turner, and Gabriel Prosser, and Denmark Vesey, the black womb that surrendered up in tears that nameless and endless chain of Africa's Cream, the Black Cream of the Earth,"[14] he was speaking for the proud legacy of black power. If one is to accept the definition of black power offered in a symposium on the subject in *Partisan Review* (Spring 1968), that it "is a step in establishing a framework which rejects once and for all the white community defining what the black community should and should not do about its problems" (p. 199), one can see how Styron was crossing the invisible line which separates Afro-American or black history from white history. Nat Turner, the feeling is, belongs exclusively to the former and is the private domain of the black historian and black novelist.

Styron was to hear a good deal about his intrusion on sacred property in the early months of 1968. The establishment weeklies and monthlies had already had their affirmative say in the late months of 1967, and now it was the turn of the more "deprived" periodicals to express dissatisfaction. The blacks were marshaling their forces and engaged in a kind of group therapy—*The Confessions of Nat Turner* was presumably the source of the collective illness—with the publication of *William Styron's Nat Turner: Ten Black Writers Respond* on July 4, 1968. This volume was intended, from all indications, as a kind of declaration of independence from the likes of William Styron, who had betrayed and distorted black history by making Nat Turner into a less heroic and masculine figure than he was supposed to be historically. The ten writers who combined to offer this polemical judgment expressed themselves with much the same urgency and conviction—and with some of the same rhetoric—as the students in American universities who have been asking for autonomous black-studies centers and courses "relevant" to their needs. Styron comes out of this encounter as having written at the least an irrelevant book and at the most a potentially dangerous book.

John Henrik Clarke, the editor of the collection, sounds a characteristic note in the second paragraph of his Introduction: "The Nat Turner created by William Styron has little resemblance to the Virginia slave insurrectionist who is a hero to his people. This being so, then why did William Styron create *his* Nat Turner and ignore the most important historical facts relating to the real Nat Turner?" The implication of the entire volume, expressed in so many words by Mike Thelwell in the final essay, is that the "real history" of Nat Turner has yet to be written and it is the black man's special assignment to write it.[15]

Despite certain convincing literary judgments expressed in the essays by Mike Thelwell, Vincent Harding, and Ernest Kaiser, *Ten Black Writers Respond* is in the main an attempt to treat a novel as a symptom of a certain "diseased" mentality, as almost a social or historical document. Styron is never granted his *données* as a novelist. In a letter to *The New York Review of Books* (November 7, 1968) on this subject, the historian Eugene Genovese put the case admirably: "A novelist has room for an imaginative reconstruction. Many of Styron's critics refuse to recognize that a novel is a novel—even a historical novel is. The demand for historical exactness, if yielded to, would reduce every novel about historical figures to political hack work, which is invariably bad politics as well as bad art" (p. 34).

It is the political and social, ironically enough, which have been catching up with Styron. The charge of "social reaction" which C. P. Snow directed at T. E. Hulme, Joyce, and Pound begins to haunt the author of *The Confessions of Nat Turner*. The *ad hominem* attacks suggest that there is something of the racist, of the unreconstructed Southerner, in

Styron which finally got released with the writing of his most recent novel: This is the very thing that Styron referred to, in his review of *A Southern Prophecy*, as the tendency "to regard all white Southerners as bigots."

We should be more specific about the kinds of things which upset the black intellectual community. First of all, Styron used the first-person of an antebellum Negro for the telling of his novel. It was maintained that he could not possibly reproduce the texture of this language but instead had to rely on what Mike Thelwell calls "a 'white' language and a white consciousness."

Styron's contention that he was writing "a meditation on history" forced every variety of quibbling about his sources and his expertise as a historian. One of the sorest points was Styron's failure to mention Nat's wife and family but instead to have him practice masturbation and lust after white women. The evidence offered against Styron was principally the remark made by Thomas Wentworth Higginson in his article "Nat Turner's Insurrection," which originally appeared in the August 1861 *Atlantic*: "Thus, for instance, we know that Nat Turner's young wife was a slave; we know that she belonged to a different master from himself . . ." (p. 174). Particularly irksome to the blacks, apparently, is the way Styron tends almost to emasculate the leader of the 1831 insurrection and turn him into an effeminate *poète maudit*, a man of many words and few actions.

Another sign of the indifferent historian, we are told, is Styron's failure to acknowledge the rebelliousness of the slave and the slave's firm and inflexible commitment to overthrowing the system. *The Confessions of Nat Turner* depends too heavily on Stanley Elkins's "Sambo" thesis, which has been frequently criticized by black intellectuals. Styron's double standard for slavery, which accounts for the unlike dispositions of the "plantation slave" and the "small-farm slave" (see the *Esquire* exchange with James Jones), allows for nuances which have consistently offended the antagonists of *The Confessions of Nat Turner*—especially when Styron's Nat himself was a small-farm slave and tended toward docility and away from violence.

The historical documentation on Nat Turner has, in fact, never been reliable. Styron has indicated on several occasions that he depended on the original (1831) "Confessions of Nat Turner" as reported by Thomas R. Gray and on W. S. Drewry's *The Southampton Insurrection* (1900); both are apologies for slavery. He has also read widely in the literature of slave insurrections, covering the extremes of Kenneth Stampp and Herbert Aptheker on the one hand and Ulrich B. Phillips on the other, yet not neglecting the more moderate approaches of Stanley Elkins and Frank Tannenbaum. He has clearly done his homework—especially for a novelist bent more on "imaginative reconstruction" than on fact. Given, then, the scantiness of reliable historiography on his subject and the various licenses permitted a novelist, the claims of historical inaccuracy are patently unfair, foolish, and irrelevant. Every definition available on the nature and permissiveness of the historical novel, including the famous one of Georg Lukács in *The Historical Novel*, exempts the author from "being tied to particular historical facts" for he "must be at liberty to treat these as he likes."[16] We keep coming back to the fact of Styron's having trespassed on "restricted" territory and the fact, according to Robert Coles in the Summer 1968 *Partisan Review*, that certain black intellectuals have been "using William Styron as their scapegoat" (p. 413).

If we examine Styron's Nat Turner we cannot help being impressed by the amount of sympathetic care lavished upon him. He is a superbly "rounded" character (in E. M. Forster's sense) and with his occasional human failings goes a sense of endurance (one of Styron's favorite words, as it also was Faulkner's), commitment, and historical awareness. He is a more convincing figure than any described up to now by contemporary observers, historians, or fiction writers. The literature on Nat Turner has been vast but of a remarkably uneven quality and temper.[17] The 1831 "Confessions of Nat Turner" is a very undistinguished bit of prose which offered Styron an outline, and very little more, for his novel. Typical of the point of view expressed is this remark made by Thomas R. Gray in his prefatory note "to the public": "Many a mother as she presses her infant darling to her bosom, will shudder at the recollection of Nat Turner, and his band of ferocious miscreants." Thomas Wentworth Higginson, in his August 1861 *Atlantic* article, described a Nat who was in every way exceptional and a fit leader of his people—but the final portrait seems more a part of myth than of reality. W. S. Drewry's *The Southampton Insurrection* tries too hard to explain the benign aspects of slavery to care much about a believable image of Nat Turner.[18]

Nat appears frequently in slave novels of the nineteenth century, like G. P. R. James's *The Old Dominion*, Harriet Beecher Stowe's *Dred*, and William Wells Brown's *Clotel*. These portraits differ significantly. Thus he is described toward the end of Volume I of *The Old Dominion* as possessing traits "of almost all the peculiar weaknesses of the African race." The account goes on to suggest "a certain degree of ruthless cruelty and fierce passion within, though now concealed, if not subdued, by the command he had acquired over himself. . . . Nat Turner, though he had evidently a good command of language, and could express himself with great fluency and propriety, had that sort of thick and jerking utterance which characterises the African race."[19] The description in *Clotel*, on the contrary, is of "a preacher amongst the negroes, and distinguished for his eloquence, respected by the whites, and loved and venerated by the negroes."[20]

Historians, novelists, playwrights, and poets in the twentieth century have also tried to define his elusive qualities. Frank Lawrence Owsley, in his contribution to the Agrarian volume of 1930, *I'll Take My Stand*, handles the whole matter of the 1831 insurrection in one sentence: "In the South this abolition war begot Nat Turner's rebellion, in which negro slaves in Virginia under the leadership of Nat Turner, a freedman, massacred their masters, including women and children."[21] (Nat Turner was emphatically not a freedman and the sentence is an embarrassing bit of historical oversimplification!) Kenneth Stampp's *The Peculiar Institution* (1956) has a few excellent pages on Nat Turner; the discussion begins with this fine sentence: "No ante-bellum Southerner could ever forget Nat Turner." Herbert Aptheker has done more than any historian to flesh out the details of the insurrection and explain, affirmatively, Nat's contribution to it in both his *American Negro Slave Revolts* (1943) and in his *Nat Turner's Slave Rebellion* (1966). Yet he has clearly sacrificed the human side of Nat to an aggressive insistence on historical accuracy.

The three-act play of Paul Peters's *Nat Turner* (1944) is a sympathetic dramatization. The play moves slowly until the compelling final scene of the third act. The peddler, who is a kind of chorus-figure, makes this moving testimonial: "Nat Turner was a slave, but he opened their eyes. And when he dies, they'll say: 'Nat Turner was right. What he said was true. What he done was brave. In the name of Nat Turner, slavery must go. In the name of Nat Turner, his people must be free.' "[22] Robert Hayden's "The Ballad of Nat Turner" (contained in his 1966 *Selected Poems*) is a quite remarkable poem, although I cannot agree with Vincent Harding's statement in *Ten Black Writers Respond* that there is nothing in Styron's novel "in any way equal to the terse power found in Robert Hayden's poem" (p. 29).

A novel by Daniel Panger, *Ol' Prophet Nat*, appeared the same year as *The Confessions of Nat Turner*. Panger uses a simulated documentary form which involves two first-persons, that of the general narrator, who uncovers the Bible that contains Nat's marginalia, and that of Nat Turner himself, whose "confessions" fill most of the book. The unnamed narrator opens and closes the novel and occasionally breaks in on Nat's story with "helpful" remarks like "There was a gap in the writing at that point"[23] or "The writing on the four sides of the pages was faded beyond the point my eyes, even with the help of a powerful magnifying glass, could make sense from it" (pp. 40–41). The typography is different: The general narrator's passages are printed in a small, bold type which slants somewhat, while Nat's use the kind of roman type we are familiar with. *Ol' Prophet Nat* is probably faithful to the "letter" of history; it allows

Nat a wife, for example: "I find it a torment to tell of the woman who became my wife. I have had knowledge of and cared for only one woman in all my years and this woman was my wife" (p. 61). But as a novel it is markedly inferior to Styron's. Panger's Nat is a cardboard figure whose language is filled with clichés and romantic pieties. The pseudodocumentary approach of *Ol' Prophet Nat* seems somehow misplaced in a contemporary novel; it would have gone better with journalism or with popular history.

This brief survey of Nat Turner in history and literature is intended to establish two crucial points about Styron's novel: that the previous handling of the 1831 insurrection was erratic and capricious enough to allow Styron almost any liberty he might choose to take; that his own treatment of Nat Turner was far and away more realized and convincing than any before it. We can dismiss the charge of Styron's having a "vile racist imagination" by quoting just one passage from *The Confessions of Nat Turner* (p. 159). This is Samuel Turner's view of slavery (and indeed we have every reason to believe that it is also Styron's view):

> I have long and do still steadfastly believe that slavery is the great cause of all the chief evils of our land. It is a cancer eating at our bowels, the source of all our misery, individual, political, and economic. It is the greatest curse a supposedly free and enlightened society has been saddled with in modern times, or any other time.

Styron has had to live with the aftermath of *The Confessions of Nat Turner* perhaps more than any writer before him had to live with the aftermath of a published literary work.[24] The reviews of his novel seem finally to have stopped, but the reviews of *Ten Black Writers Respond* are still coming in, at this writing. Styron has graciously submitted to a large number of interviews in the years since *The Confessions of Nat Turner* was published. Among the most stimulating was the one in the November 1967 *Yale Alumni Magazine* (Styron is not a Yale alumnus, but he is an associate fellow of Silliman College, Yale University), with C. Vann Woodward and R. W. B. Lewis as questioners. Styron has suddenly became very newsworthy: Another interview, in the October 28–November 3, 1968, *Le Figaro littéraire,* caught Styron on his way home from a Russian congress *"des écrivains afro-asiatiques"*; he was the only American represented at the congress.

Styron's name has appeared on a variety of petitions in the past few years. He signed "An Open Letter" in the Spring 1968 *Partisan Review* protesting "recent attacks on the integrity and freedom of the academic community at the State University of New York at Stonybrook." He signed a group letter in the January 2, 1969, *New York Review of Books,* protesting the Russian invasion of Czechoslovakia, which includes this reveal-ing paragraph: "Loyal to our principles, we are total opponents of the American aggression in Vietnam and of imperialism everywhere. The Soviet invasion of Czechoslovakia is a severe setback for world socialism. It gravely impedes the antimperialist struggle. It is, therefore, our duty to demand an end to these acts which dishonour the Soviet Union." If there remains any question about the extent and direction of Styron's political commitment these days, it should be answered here, or if not in this group letter, certainly in his blistering write-up of the Chicago con-vention in the September 26, 1968, *New York Review of Books*: Called "In the Jungle," it is political journalism at its finest.

This essay has had as much to do with what Irving Howe referred to as "the literary problem of what happens to the novel when it is sub-jected to the pressures of politics and political ideology" as it has to do with Styron's own politics. Styron's career thus far has disproved the commonly held assumption that only Europeans know how to mix litera-ure and politics.

NOTES

1. See Ernest Kaiser, "The Failure of William Styron," in John Henrik Clarke, ed., *William Styron's Nat Turner: Ten Black Writers Respond* (Boston, 1968), p. 57. All subsequent references will be to this edition.
2. Stephen E. Henderson, " 'Survival Motion': A Study of the Black Writer and the Black Revolution in America," in Mercer Cook and Stephen E. Hen-derson, *The Militant Black Writer in Africa and the United States* (Madison, Milwaukee, and London, 1969), p. 74.
3. *Lie Down in Darkness* (New York, 1960), p. 69.
4. William Styron, "This Quiet Dust," *Harper's*, April 1965, p. 137.
5. See Styron's interview with George Plimpton in *The New York Times Book Review*, October 8, 1967; see also my *"The Confessions of Nat Turner*: The Convergence of 'Nonfiction Novel' and 'Meditation on History,' " *Journal of Popular Culture*, Fall 1967, pp. 166–175.
6. *The Long March* (New York, 1956), p. 119. All subsequent references will be to this edition.
7. *American Moderns* (New York, 1958), pp. 249–250.
8. Paul Valéry, *History and Politics*, trans. by Denise Folliot and Jackson Mathews (London, 1963), p. 274.

9. *Set This House on Fire* (New York, 1960), p. 499. For a detailed discussion of the "American Adam" ingredients in Styron see Augustine J. Nigro, "William Styron and the Adamic Tradition," unpublished Ph.D. dissertation, University of Maryland, 1964.

10. The imposing presence of French periodicals on this list should indicate the seriousness with which Styron is taken in France. See my "William Styron et le Nouveau Roman," in Melvin J. Friedman and Augustine J. Nigro, eds., *Configuration critique de William Styron* (Paris, 1967), pp. 85–109.

11. "The Turner Thesis," *Partisan Review*, Summer 1968, p. 404.

12. *The Confessions of Nat Turner* (New York, 1967), pp. 69–70. All subsequent references will be to this edition.

13. Quoted in C. Vann Woodward, *The Burden of Southern History* (New York, 1961), p. 24.

14. *Soul on Ice* (New York, 1968), p. 208.

15. Thelwell made this statement in a review of Harold Cruse's *The Crisis of the Negro Intellectual* in *Partisan Review*, Fall 1968: "It is the black intellectual's responsibility to rescue our black history from the deprecations of a self-justifying white guilt, to forge a new consciousness based on the truths of our history and culture, and begin to envision the form of our new community" (p. 622).

16. Quoted by William Styron from Lukács's *The Historical Novel* in an exchange with Herbert Aptheker, "Truth & Nat Turner: An Exchange," *The Nation*, April 22, 1968, p. 546.

17. An excellent bibliographical source for material on Nat Turner and slave insurrections in general is Ernest Kaiser's "The Failure of William Styron," *Ten Black Writers Respond*, pp. 50–65.

18. With qualification the same might be said about F. Roy Johnson's *The Nat Turner Slave Insurrection* (Murfreesboro, North Carolina), which happens to be dedicated to W. S. Drewry and was not published until 1966.

19. G. P. R. James, *The Old Dominion* (London, 1856), I, 290–292.

20. William Wells Brown, *Clotel* (New York, 1969; originally published in 1853), p. 212.

21. Frank Lawrence Owsley, "The Irrepressible Conflict," in *I'll Take My Stand: The South and the Agrarian Tradition* by Twelve Southerners (New York, 1951), p. 80.

22. Paul Peters, *Nat Turner*, in *Cross-Section: A Collection of New American Writing*, Edwin Seaver, ed. (New York, 1944), p. 280.

23. Daniel Panger, *Ol' Prophet Nat* (Greenwich, Connecticut, 1967), p. 16. All subsequent references will be to this edition.

24. One should see especially "The Uses of History in Fiction," *The Southern Literary Journal*, Spring 1969. This is a panel discussion involving C. Vann Woodward (as moderator), Ralph Ellison, Robert Penn Warren, and Styron. In the question period (faithfully reproduced here) Styron is the target of a variety of attacks from black questioners.

NOTES ON CONTRIBUTORS

JOHN W. ALDRIDGE was born on September 26, 1922, and educated at the University of Chattanooga, Breadloaf School of English, and the University of California at Berkeley. He began his teaching career at the University of Vermont, where for several years he held a special appointment as a lecturer in literary criticism and served as director of the School of Modern Critical Studies. In 1953–1954 he gave a series of the Christian Gauss Seminars in Criticism at Princeton. He has also held the Berg Professorship at New York University and has been a visiting professor at Queens College, Sarah Lawrence College, and the New School for Social Research. In 1958–1959 he was a Fulbright lecturer at the University of Munich, and in 1962–1963, at the University of Copenhagen. In 1964 he came to the University of Michigan, where he is professor of English. In 1951 he published his first book of literary criticism, *After the Lost Generation*. This was followed in 1952 by a critical anthology, *Critiques and Essays on Modern Fiction*. His other books include *In Search of Heresy*; a novel, *The Party at Cranton*; and *Time to Murder and Create*. In 1970 he published *In the Country of the Young*, his first work of social commentary, a study of the psychology and life-styles of the under-thirty generation. He is a regular book critic for the *Saturday Review* and writes frequently for *The New York Times Book Review*, *Harper's Magazine*, and the *Atlantic*.

ROBERT ALTER, born in New York in 1935, holds degrees from Columbia College and Harvard University and has also studied at the Hebrew University in Jerusalem. From 1962 to 1966 he taught in the English Department at Columbia University; in 1966–1967 he was a Guggenheim Fellow. Since then he has been at the University of California at Berkeley, where he is now professor of Hebrew and comparative literature. He is the author of *Rogue's Progress: Studies in the Picaresque Novel*; *Fielding and the Nature of the Novel*; and *After the Tradition*. A regular contributor to *Commentary*, he has also published essays in *The American Scholar, Daedalus, Midstream, Novel, Tri-Quarterly*, and other periodicals. In 1965 he was awarded the English Institute Essay Prize.

MONTGOMERY BELGION was born in Paris in 1892, a British subject by birth. He lived in New York for five years. In 1928 he was with the publishers Harcourt, Brace, when he arranged for André Malraux's novel *Les Conquérants* to be translated into English. Subsequently Malraux arranged for Belgion's book *Our Present Philosophy of Life* to be translated into French by Gallimard. The translation appeared in 1934, entitled *Notre foi contemporaine*. Other books by Belgion are *The Human Parrot, News of the French, Reading for Profit, Victors' Justice*, and two British Book Council pamphlets, *H. G. Wells* and *David Hume*. His latest book is *The Worship of Quantity: A Study of Megalopolitics*. Belgion volunteered in both world wars, and altogether has been a soldier for nine years of his life. From 1941 to 1944 he was a prisoner of war in Germany. He is married and since 1961 has lived in the English village of Titchmarsh, twenty-five miles from the city of Northampton.

BERNARD BERGONZI was born in South London in 1929. He left school shortly before his sixteenth birthday, and after working in office jobs for several years, spent a year studying under the late Edwin Muir at an adult college in Scotland. In 1955 he entered Wadham College, Oxford, and received the B.A. degree and subsequently the B.Litt. In 1959 he was appointed to the English Department of the University of Manchester and taught there until 1966, spending a year in the United States during 1964–1965 as a visiting lecturer at Brandeis University and a Beckman summer lecturer at Berkeley. In 1966 he moved to the new University of Warwick as a senior lecturer in English. His publications, covering many aspects of late-nineteenth- and twentieth-century literature, include the books *Descartes and the Animals, The Early H. G. Wells, Heroes' Twilight: A Study of the Literature of the Great War*, and *The Situation of the Novel*. He is also the editor of *Innovations, Four Quartets: A Casebook, Great Short Works of Aldous Huxley*, and *The Twentieth Century*.

PETER BIEN was educated at Haverford College and Columbia University. Professor of English at Dartmouth College, he has written a critical study of the British novelist L. P. Hartley, a monograph on Constantine Cavafy, and has translated three books by Nikos Kazantzakis: *The Last Temptation of Christ, Saint Francis*, and *Report to Greco*. He is presently working on a study of Kazantzakis's life and works in relation to Greek and European politics. Together with his wife, Chrysanthi Bien, and Professor John Rassias, of Dartmouth, he has written a textbook for the instruction of demotic Greek by the oral/aural method. In 1968 he received the Danforth Foundation Harbison Award for Distinguished Teaching. He is a member of the Modern Language Association, the Society for Religion in Higher Education, and is on the Executive Committee of the Modern Greek Studies Association.

MILTON BIRNBAUM is now chairman of the Department of English at American International College, Springfield, Massachusetts. He holds an M.A. and Ph.D. from New York University. In addition to giving courses in twentieth-century British and American fiction and in contemporary European drama, he lectures frequently on literature and philosophy before literary and religious groups. His articles have appeared in *Comparative Literature Studies, The Personalist, The Hibbert Journal, Texas Studies in Literature and Language, Xavier University Studies, The Journal of Popular Culture, ETC.: A Review of General Semantics*, and *The College English Association Critic*. A recognized authority on Aldous Huxley, he contributed the essay on Huxley's religious attitudes to *Mansions of the Spirit: Essays in Literature and Religion*. His full-length critical study of Huxley's writings and thought is being published by the University of Tennessee Press. In addition, he has served as editorial conultant for the *Publications of the Modern Language Association*.

G[EORGE] S[UTHERLAND] FRASER was born in Glasgow and brought up in Aberdeen. In the 1930's, while he was still a teen-ager, he began to publish poems and articles about literature. He served in World War II, visited South America and Japan on postwar cultural missions, and then worked for many years in London, broadcasting, reviewing, translating, and editing anthologies of modern poetry. Since 1958 he has taught English literature at Leicester University, spending one year as a visiting professor at the University of Rochester in New York. Perhaps best known in America for his incisive study *The Modern Writer and His World*, he has written critical books on Ezra Pound and Lawrence Durrell, edited the poetry anthologies *Springtime* and *Poetry Now*, published several collections of his own poems, and contributed the British Book Council pamphlets on Dylan Thomas, W.B. Yeats, and Lawrence Durrell.

WARREN FRENCH received his B.A. from the University of Pennsylvania and in 1954 his Ph.D. from the University of Texas. He taught at several universities in the South before moving to Kansas State University in 1962 and then, in 1965, to the University of Missouri–Kansas City. In 1970 he became chairman of the English Department at Indiana University–Purdue University at Indianapolis. Besides *The Social Novel at the End of an Era*, he has written three books for the Twayne United

States Authors Series: *John Steinbeck, Frank Norris,* and *J. D. Salinger.* He has also edited *A Companion to The Grapes of Wrath* and, with Walter Kidd, *American Winners of the Nobel Literary Prize.* During the past several years, he has been editing collections of original essays on American literature of recent decades: *The Thirties, The Forties,* and *The Fifties.*

MELVIN J. FRIEDMAN was born in Brooklyn, New York, in 1928 and was educated at Bard College, Columbia University, and Yale University. He has taught at the University of Maryland and the University of Wisconsin and is presently professor of comparative literature at the University of Wisconsin at Milwaukee. He has held fellowships from Yale University and the American Council of Learned Societies and was a Fulbright predoctoral fellow in Lyons, France, in 1950–1951. His published writings—in English, French, German, and Italian—are mainly concerned with twentieth-century fiction and drama, and he has contributed numerous essays and reviews to various scholarly journals. He has written and edited books on the twentieth-century experimental novel, Samuel Beckett, Flannery O'Connor, and William Styron. Recently, he edited *Samuel Beckett Now* and *The Shaken Realist,* and he has contributed essays in the past few years to books such as *Promise of Greatness: The War of 1914–1918.* An editor or an associate editor of three learned journals, he has also served as secretary and chairman of the Franco-American group of the Modern Language Association of America.

W[ILBUR] M[ERRILL] FROHOCK was born in South Thomaston, Maine, in 1908. He received the Ph.B., M.A., and Ph.D. degrees from Brown University and has taught at Brown University, Columbia University, Wesleyan University, and Harvard University, as well as at the Universities of Lille and Munich. From April to July 1970 he was a visiting *Dozent* at Heidelberg. He is the author of *The Novel of Violence in America, André Malraux and the Tragic Imagination, Strangers to This Ground, Rimbaud's Poetic Practice, Style and Temper,* and *Image and Theme: Studies in Modern French Fiction.*

DONALD B. GIBSON was born in Kansas City, Missouri, on July 2, 1933. He attended the University of Kansas City (B.A., 1955; M.A., 1957) and Brown University (Ph.D., 1962). He has taught at Brown University, Wayne State University, and the University of Connecticut, where he is now professor of American literature. A Fulbright Lecturer in American literature at Jagiellonian University, Krakow, Poland, from 1964 to 1966, he also lectured on nineteenth-century American literature at the American Studies Seminar in Falkenstein, Germany, in the summer of 1965. The author of *The Fiction of Stephen Crane*, he has edited *Five Black Writers: Essays on Wright, Ellison, Baldwin, Hughes, and Leroi Jones* and has published articles in *The Yale Review, Texas Studies in Literature and Language, The English Journal, The American Quarterly, Criterion,* and other journals. Currently, he is engaged in completing a book on the fiction of Richard Wright and establishing a theoretical basis for the study of literature as a social and political entity.

SHELDON NORMAN GREBSTEIN is professor of English and director of Graduate English Studies at the State University of New York at Binghamton, where he has taught since 1963. Earlier, he taught at the University of Kentucky and the University of South Florida. In 1968–1969 he was Fulbright-Hays Lecturer in American literature at the University of Rouen. During that year he also gave guest lectures at the University of Caen, and in England at the Universities of Hull, Edinburgh, and Strathclyde. Professor Grebstein took his degrees at the University of Southern California, Columbia University, and Michigan State University. His publications include a casebook, *Monkey Trial*, on the Scopes evolution trial; books on Sinclair Lewis and John O'Hara for the Twayne United States Authors Series; and, most recently, *Perspectives in Contemporary Criticism*, an anthology illustrating types of current critical practice. He has also contributed articles on modern American literature, including two previous essays on Dreiser, to a wide variety of periodicals and collections. His next book, *Hemingway's Craft*, will be published by the Southern Illinois University Press.

J. K. JOHNSTONE was born on February 12, 1923, at Ferintosh, Alberta, Canada, where he lived on a farm until 1945. From 1945 to 1950 he attended the University of Alberta, receiving his B.A. in 1948 and an M.A. in English literature in 1950. He then studied at the University of Leeds, England, where he received the degree of Ph.D. in English literature in 1952. His book *The Bloomsbury Group: A Study of E. M. Forster, Lytton Strachey, Virginia Woolf, and Their Circle* was published in London and New York in 1954. He was elected a Fellow of the Royal Society of Literature, London, in 1955. Mr. Johnstone has taught at Mirfield Grammar School, Yorkshire; the College of General Education, Boston University; and the University of New Brunswick. At present, he is chairman of the Department of English at the University of Saskatchewan, Saskatoon. He is married and has three children. He and his wife led a Boston University summer course in Europe in 1955 and a Nasson College semester abroad in Vienna in 1965. He has held a Nuffield Foundation grant in 1966 and Canada Council fellowships in 1966 and 1970 for study of the twentieth-century English novel.

Lewis A. Lawson received his doctorate from the University of Wisconsin in 1964. A native of Bristol, Tennessee, he is married and the father of a daughter and son. Since 1963 he has been on the faculty of the University of Maryland, where he is associate professor of English. He enjoys teaching both undergraduate and graduate courses in American and Southern literature. Mr. Lawson's publications have been in several different areas. With an interest in the application of psychological insights to literary criticism, he has published essays in *American Imago* and *Literature and Psychology*. His essays on aspects of the grotesque in Southern literature have appeared in *Renascence, Mississippi Quarterly, Poe Newsletter,* and *Patterns of Commitment in American Literature,* edited by Marston LaFrance. His essays on contemporary American literature have appeared in *College English* and *Texas Quarterly*. Currently, he is completing an anthology of articles on Sören Kierkegaard's influence on recent American culture and a study of Kierkegaard's utilization by recent American novelists, chapters of which have appeared in *Wisconsin Studies in Contemporary Literature* and *Texas Studies in Literature and Language*.

Sergei Levitzky, associate professor of Russian literature at Georgetown University, Washington, D.C., was born in Libau, Latvia, in 1910 of Russian parents. In 1938 he was awarded a Ph.D. degree from Charles University in Prague, Czechoslovakia. In 1949 he came to the United States; from 1955 to 1965 he worked for the Voice of America. He joined the Russian Department of Georgetown University in 1965. In addition to many articles on philosophy and literature, he is the author of *The Foundation of the Organic World Concept* (1948), *The Tragedy of Freedom* (1958), and *A Popular History of Russian Philosophy,* Volume I (1968), with the second volume now in preparation. The famous Russian thinker N. O. Lossky singles out Levitzky as a continuator of the philosophical thought of Father Sergius Bulgakov, Nicolas Berdyaev, and S. L. Frank.

Marie-Béatrice Mesnet was born in Paris on November 13, 1927. The daughter of a senior officer in the French Army, she started traveling in early childhood. In World War II she went to Tunis during the military operations in North Africa and later to a bombed Paris, under the German occupation. After the war, she spent two years in Canada, where she studied at McGill University, Montreal, receiving her B.A. with honors in English in 1947. In 1948 she was graduated from the Sorbonne, Paris, as a *licenciée ès lettres,* and in 1953 she was awarded a *Diplôme d'études supérieures d'anglais,* with the highest mark for the year. Her *mémoire* was published as a book in 1954 under the title *Graham Greene and the Heart of the Matter*. She has always maintained a special interest in Greene's work, and she later wrote an essay on *The Potting-Shed* which appeared in the monthly periodical *Etudes*, Paris, in September 1958. Her main literary activity, translation, has taken her to most parts of the world, starting with a complete tour of the United States under the Marshall plan in 1950. From 1953 to 1955 she worked in London with NATO and also contributed a few dramatized biographies of English poets to the French Programme of B.B.C. She has worked as a free-lance translator for most United Nations agencies, not only in the capitals of western Europe and in the Near East but also in places like Delhi, Tehran, Addis Ababa, Nairobi, and Capetown. She has visited many countries and knows many figures of the international, political, diplomatic, and literary worlds.

W. GORDON MILNE was born in Haverhill, Massachusetts, in 1921. He received a B.A. from Brown University in 1941, an M.A. from Brown in 1947, and a Ph.D. from Harvard in 1951. He was a Fulbright Guest Professor at the University of Wurtzburg, Germany, from 1958 to 1959. A member of Phi Beta Kappa, the Modern Language Association, and the American Association of University Professors, he is currently professor of English and chairman of the department at Lake Forest College, Illinois. He is the author of *George William Curtis and the Genteel Tradition*, *The American Political Novel*, and numerous articles in the field of American literature.

GEORGE A. PANICHAS is professor of English at the University of Maryland, College Park. He was born in Springfield, Massachusetts, on May 21, 1930. His teaching, research, and writing are in the area of the modern novel and the British novel between the two world wars. He also has strong interests in the area of comparative literature, especially in the interdisciplinary relations between literature (British, American, and continental) and politics, history, philosophy, and religion. His principal books include *Adventure in Consciousness: The Meaning of D. H. Lawrence's Religious Quest* and *Epicurus;* he also edited *Mansions of the Spirit: Essays in Literature and Religion* and *Promise of Greatness: The War of 1914–1918*. In addition, he has contributed to books, anthologies, and journals published in the United States and Europe.

VIVIAN DE SOLA PINTO was born in Hampstead, England, in 1895 and was educated at University College School, London, and Christ Church, Oxford. In World War I he served as an officer in the Royal Welch Fusiliers in Gallipoli, Egypt, France, and Belgium, and was wounded twice on the western front. In the summer of 1918 he was second-in-command to Captain Siegfried Sassoon, the late poet, in the 25th Royal Welch. In

1921 he was graduated with first-class honors from Oxford University and in 1926 was awarded the degree of D.Phil. He was professor of English at University College, Southampton, from 1926 till 1938 and at the University of Nottingham from 1938 till 1961. He was elected a Fellow of the Royal Society of Literature in 1929. He lectured in Belgium, Holland, India, Italy, the United States, and Yugoslavia, and he spent the academic year 1965–1966 as visiting professor at the University of California, Davis. His publications include *Sir Charles Sedley*; *Peter Sterry, Puritan and Platonist*; *The English Renaissance*; *Crisis in English Poetry*; *Restoration Carnival*; *Enthusiast in Wit*; *The Restoration Court Poets*; *William Blake*; and two volumes of verse, *The Invisible Sun* and *This Is My England*. He has also edited *The Poetical and Dramatic Works of Sir Charles Sedley*; *The Poems of John Wilmot, Earl of Rochester*; and (with Warren Roberts) *The Complete Poems of D. H. Lawrence*. Professor Pinto died on July 27, 1969.

Sir Richard Rees was editing *The Adelphi*, in association with John Middleton Murry, when he first met George Orwell, who was then about twenty-seven and had just returned from Paris, where he had been working as a dishwasher in restaurants. *The Adelphi* subsequently published many poems, reviews, and sketches by Orwell, including part of his first book. Orwell and Rees had been at Eton together but had not known each other, since Orwell was three years junior to the future editor of *The Adelphi*. Being a member of the Independent Labour party in the 1930's, Rees was able to introduce Orwell to trade-union officials and unemployed miners in Lancashire, who provided much of the material for *The Road to Wigan Pier*. The two writers saw little of each other during World War II, but after it, when Orwell went to live on the island of Jura, Rees spent many months there, during Orwell's last illness, when he was writing *1984*. In 1961 Rees published *George Orwell, Fugitive from the Camp of Victory*; he has also written on Simone Weil and D. H. Lawrence, has translated and edited four volumes of Weil's writings, and was the editor of two collections of Middleton Murry's criticism. He died unexpectedly on July 24, 1970.

Philip Thody, born in Lincoln, England, on March 21, 1928, was educated at Lincoln School and King's College, London. Since 1965 he has been professor of French literature at the University of Leeds and since October 1968, chairman of the Department of French. He has also held teaching appointments at the Universities of Paris, Belfast, and Birmingham and was a visiting professor at the University of Western Ontario, London, Ontario, at the University of California at Berkeley, and at Harvard University. His main publications include *Albert Camus: A Study of His Work, Albert Camus: 1913-1960, Jean-Paul Sartre: A Literary and Political Study, Jean Genet: A Study of His Novels and Plays, Jean Anouilh, and Laclos: "Les Liaisons dangereuses."*

GEOFFREY WAGNER is professor of English at the City College of New York. His numerous books include translations of Charles Baudelaire and Gérard de Nerval, a study of popular culture called *Parade of Pleasure,* and a work on Wyndham Lewis. His latest nonfiction, *On the Wisdom of Words,* examines the problems of language in a contemporary technology, while his most recent novel, *The Sands of Valor,* is a story of British tank troops in the Western Desert in World War II.

RAY LEWIS WHITE, a native of southwest Virginia, came naturally to the study of Sherwood Anderson, who spent the fourteen years before his death in the Virginia mountains. Mr. White was graduated from Emory and Henry College in 1962 and attended the University of Arkansas from 1962 to 1965. A member of Phi Beta Kappa and a Woodrow Wilson and N.D.E.A. Fellow, he has taught English at the University of Arkansas, North Carolina State University, and Illinois State University, where he is currently associate professor of American literature. Primarily interested in textual studies based on manuscripts, Mr. White has published critical editions of Sherwood Anderson's three autobiographies: *A Story Teller's Story, Tar: A Midwest Childhood,* and *Sherwood Anderson's Memoirs.* His other works on Anderson include *The Achievement of Sherwood Anderson, Return to Winesburg,* and *Checklist of Sherwood Anderson.*

NORRIS W. YATES, a native of Oregon, received degrees from the universities of Oregon and Wisconsin before being awarded the Ph.D. by New York University in 1953. For several years he has been professor of English at Iowa State University. He was a Fulbright lecturer in American literature at the University of Hamburg, West Germany (1964–1965) and at the University of Helsinki, Finland (1968–1969). From 1967 to 1968, he was President of the Midcontinent Chapter of the American Studies Association. His publications include *William T. Porter . . . A Study in the "Big Bear" School of Humor; The American Humorist; Robert Benchley;* and *Günter Grass.*

INDEX